Budapest Guide

Penguin Books

PENGUIN BOOKS

Published by the Penguin Group
Penguin Books Ltd, 27 Wrights Lane, London W8 5TZ, England
Penguin Books USA Inc., 375 Hudson Street, New York, New York 10014, USA
Penguin Books Australia Ltd, Ringwood, Victoria, Australia
Penguin Books Canada Ltd, 10 Alcorn Avenue, Toronto, Ontario, Canada M4V 3B2
Penguin Books (NZ) Ltd, 182–190 Wairau Road, Auckland 10, New Zealand

Penguin Books Ltd, Registered Offices: Harmondsworth, Middlesex, England

First published 1996
10 9 8 7 6 5 4 3 2 1

Colour reprographics by Precise Litho, 34–35 Great Sutton Street, London EC1
Mono reprographics, printed and bound by William Clowes Ltd, Beccles, Suffolk NR34 9QE

Edited and designed by

Time Out Magazine Limited
Universal House
251 Tottenham Court Road
London W1P 0AB
Tel: 0171 813 3000
Fax: 0171 813 6001

Editorial

Managing Editor Peter Fiennes
Editor Dave Rimmer
Deputy Editor Nicholas Royle
Consultant Editor Peterjon Cresswell
Researcher Grant Anderton
Indexer Jackie Brind

Design

Art Director Warren Beeby
Art Editor John Oakey
Designers Paul Tansley, James Pretty
Picture Editor Catherine Hardcastle

Advertising

Group Advertisement Director Lesley Gill
Sales Director Mark Phillips
Advertisement Sales (Budapest) Creative Partners

Administration

Publisher Tony Elliott
Managing Director Mike Hardwick
Financial Director Kevin Ellis
Marketing Director Gillian Auld
Production Manager Mark Lamond

Features in this Guide were written and researched by:

Introduction Bob Cohen. **Essential Information** Grant Anderton, Steve Carlson, Dave Rimmer. **Getting Around** Grant Anderton, Dave Rimmer. **Language** Bob Cohen, Ildiko Lazar. **Accommodation** Christina Crowder. **Budapest By Season** Peterjon Cresswell. **Sightseeing** Bob Cohen, Peterjon Cresswell, Adam LeBor, Carolyn Smith, Helen Teitelbaum. **History** Bob Cohen. **Budapest Today** Martin Iain. **Architecture** Carolyn Smith. **Budapest by Area** Dave Rimmer. **Restaurants** Bob Cohen, Peterjon Cresswell, Tim Randall, Dave Rimmer. **Cafés & Bars** Peterjon Cresswell, Dave Rimmer. **Shopping & Services** Christina Crowder. **Art Galleries** Melinda Frigyesi. **Museums** Helen Teitelbaum. **Media** Gábor Vajda. **Baths** Adam LeBor. **Film** John Nadler, Peter Palátsik. **Folklore** Bob Cohen. **Music: Classical & Opera** Stephen Loy. **Music: Rock, Folk & Jazz** Peterjon Cresswell. **Nightlife** Peterjon Cresswell, Dave Rimmer. **Sport & Fitness** Peterjon Cresswell. **Theatre & Dance** Christian Heppinstall. **Business** Tim Smart. **Children** Ildikó Lázár. **Gay & Lesbian** Christian Heppinstall. **Students** Gábor Vajda. **Women's Budapest** Lucy Hooker. **Trips Out of Town** Peterjon Cresswell, Dave Rimmer. **Survival** Grant Anderton. **Further Reading** Peterjon Cresswell, Dave Rimmer.

The editor must thank the following for an assortment of good reasons:
Lori Anderson, Peterjon Cresswell, Kevin Ebbutt, László Horváth, Ildikó Lázár, Tim Randall, Neil Tennant. Special thanks to Steve Carlson for stating the obvious.

Photography by Hadley Kincade except for:
pages 35, 36, 37 **Hungarian Tourist Board, United Kingdom Representation**; pages 62, 67, 70, 71, 72, 75, 80 **Hulton Deutsch**; page 249 **Austrian National Tourist Office**.

Thanks to **Danny Chau Photolabs**

Contents

About the Guide

This is the first edition of the *Time Out Budapest Guide*, one in a series of ten city guides that includes London, Berlin, New York, Madrid, Rome, San Francisco, Amsterdam, Prague and Paris. It gives a complete picture of post-1989 Budapest, from the major monuments and museums to the cornucopia of new clubs, bars, restaurants and shops that have sprung up in the 1990s. Far more than just a simple guide for weekend visitors, this book aims to point you towards the obscure, essential and eccentric, and ward you off the naff. We advise you what to see and what to avoid. Written and researched by people who live in the city, this guide offers an informed, insiders' view: Budapest as Budapesters know it.

Checked & Correct

All information was thoroughly checked and correct at press time, but please bear in mind that, particularly in a city such as Budapest, making a painful transition to a free market economy, things are liable to sudden and unpredictable change. Clubs and bars open and close with frequent regularity.

The 1,100th anniversary of the Magyar conquest falls in 1996, and the celebrations may cause some of the city's main roads to close temporarily or go under repair, so certain tram, bus and trolleybus routes are liable to unexpected alterations. Although this state of flux keeps the city exciting, it's wise to check opening times, dates of exhibitions, admission prices and other key details.

Addresses

Budapest is divided into 23 districts, *kerület*. These are indicated by a Roman numeral before the street name. District V is the town centre. Postcodes are written in four figures, the middle two indicating the district: 1051 is District V. The postman will recognise both forms but deliver a four digit-coded letter more quickly. We've used the Roman numeral form because it's easier for finding your way around town.

Although we have spelled out the words for 'road' (*út*) and 'street' (*utca*), on street signs and in other publications you may see 'utca' abbreviated to '*u.*'. As some streets in different districts may have the same name, it's always best to pay attention to which one you're heading for on the map. Other terms and abbreviations include: *híd* bridge; *rakpart* embankment; *tér* square; *köz* mews; *körút* ring road; *sétány* walk; *piac* market.

Prices

The prices listed should be used as guidelines. Because of inflation and fluctuating exchange rates, prices in shops and restaurants change rapidly. Most are quoted in forints, but some services which cater particularly to foreigners – upmarket hotels, say – give their rates in Deutschmarks. If prices and services vary wildly from those quoted, ask if there's a good reason. If there's not, take your custom elsewhere and then, please, let us know. We have endeavoured to give the best and most up-to-date advice, so we always want to hear if you have been ripped off or given the runaround.

Credit Cards

Compared to the UK or US, credit cards are not widely used in Budapest, although this is slowly changing. The following abbreviations have been used for credit cards: AmEx – American Express; DC – Diners Club; EC – Eurocard; JCB – Japanese credit cards; MC – Mastercard/Access; V – Visa.

Telephones

The telephone system in Budapest, like much else, is in a state of transition. Getting through to a particular shop, restaurant or venue – if it has a phone at all – can be difficult and the chances are that the person on the other end won't speak English. Particularly when booking a table at a Hungarian restaurant, it's often easier to go in person.

Right to Reply

The information we give is impartial. No organisation or enterprise has been included in this guide because its owner or manager has advertised in our publications. Impartiality is the reason our guides are so successful and well respected. We trust you will enjoy the *Time Out Budapest Guide* and that it helps you make the most of your stay. But if you disagree with any of our assessments, let us know; your comments on places you have visited are always welcome. You'll find a reader's reply card at the back of this book.

> There's an on-line version of this guide, as well as weekly events listings for Budapest and other international cities, at: http//:www.time out.co.uk.

Introduction

Budapest can at times seem like a trip to the 1930s. Old-time neon signs, arcane telephone systems, bone-shaking trams, ancient coat-check rules, toyshops in which wooden trains outnumber Nintendo games – it all seems to pop out of an old movie in which you are invited to play a bit part. You can play the role of tourist to the hilt, or you can step out of the script and improvise, experience the life of the city in a way you can't in many European capitals.

Budapest is, without question, one of the most magnificently situated cities in the world. But beyond its physical beauty, Budapest is a city with soul. History with a big H has always rolled up here and parked its car in Budapest's lot without permission. No empire could resist the temptation of burning it down and trying to reconstruct it in a new image. The living history of Central Europe is written in the scarred stones that are constantly recycled to rebuild Budapest anew from its periodic ashes.

Budapest's citizens take their history very personally, and more often than not feel personally slighted by it. The Turkish invasion, the Habsburg epoch, World War II and the 1956 rebellion fall from a Hungarian's lips as if these events occurred last week. Today, the fall of Communism in the late 1980s hangs in a psychic limbo somewhere between current events and history. The political changes brought economic uncertainty, with a large part of the population struggling harder than ever to make ends meet. Budapest, as ever, is undergoing a period of drastic change. And as always, Hungarians are putting their particular, and often peculiar, imprint on the flux of history and the face of their capital city.

Hungarians are a paradoxical lot – a European people speaking a maddeningly difficult Asiatic language, existing somewhere between the southernmost reaches of Germanic culture and the most northerly marches of Balkan influence. (Hungarians will invariably assent to the first observation and loudly decry any hint of the second.) This has stamped Hungarians with a unique personality – effervescently creative, often melancholic and fatalistic, firmly individualist, always opinionated – that provides a refreshing tonic to the growing homogenisation of Euro-culture. Hungarians love to talk, and absolutely adore being listened to. Every third greengrocer is a poet, every other blue-haired old lady once the proud mistress of a Minister of Education in a bygone regime.

Budapest is one of the few cities in Europe where it pays to let people know you are a tourist. No need to be ashamed. People want to meet you. While Budapest can now boast all the expected amenities, it still manages to offer startling value to travellers. After a pricey trek through Europe it is a relief to arrive in a city where a great meal can be had on even a backpacker's budget, where there's no need to cheat on the metro, and where the price of a mug of beer is worth writing home about, and even costs less than the postage.

The experience of reality, however, has its price. Hungarians treat visitors kindly, but many workers in the tourist sector such as cab drivers or waiters often regard them as walking wallets, so keep a close eye on the bill. Hungarian service can be infuriatingly slow, and sullen shop staff are the norm. Crime exists, but is rarely of the violent type and can be forgotten about after taking the most basic precautions. Cholesterol poisoning is a clearer threat, followed by overdosing on pastries.

The biggest danger, however, is that you will not want to leave at all. Over 40,000 foreigners now make Budapest their home – those stalwart expats who came, saw and fell in love with the city's bittersweet charm. When I came ten years ago, I thought my trip would last a month. I'm still here, still fascinated by the Hungarian's peculiar genius for survival, that remarkable capability for rebirth that is the soul of Budapest itself. *Bob Cohen*

Essential Information

If you learn nothing else in Hungarian, know at least that hello and goodbye mean the opposite of what you expect and if you say thank you as you hand over a banknote, you won't get any change.

Visas

Citizens of the United States, Canada and all European countries apart from Turkey and Albania can stay in Hungary for up to 90 days without a visa; only a passport is required. South Africans can stay up to 30 days. Citizens of Australia and New Zealand still need visas, which are valid for up to 30 days. Visas can be obtained from Hungarian consulates, on the border if arriving by car, although not by train, and at the airport. The simplest way to get a new stamp in your passport or renew a visa is to take a day trip to Vienna (*see chapter* **Trips Out of Town**) or take the train to Komárom (from Keleti or Déli) and walk over the bridge to Komarno in Slovakia. (To meet Slovakian currency requirements, you'll need to have a credit card or the hard currency equivalent of $15 in your pocket.) Do this too often, though, and you might start getting trouble from border officials.

Visas can also be renewed in Budapest at your local police station if you have exchange receipts to prove that you have been keeping yourself. In theory, all foreigners are required to show that they have access to the equivalent of Ft1,000 per day. In practice, such proof is rarely requested. If you do get asked, the production of a credit card will usually suffice.

If you want to obtain a work permit, however, things get somewhat stickier. You should expect a nightmare tussle with Hungarian bureaucracy. (*See also chapter* **Survival**.)

Customs

Coming into Hungary, any items of clothing or objects which could be deemed to be for personal use are exempt from duties. Individuals over 16 years old are also allowed to bring in 500 cigarettes, 100 cigars or 500 grams of tobacco, also five litres of wine, one litre of spirits and five litres of beer. Merchandise up to a value of Ft8,000 is allowed duty-free after which a 15 per cent duty

and 2 per cent customs tax are payable in addition to 25 per cent ÁFA (VAT). In practice, foreigners are rarely checked; these duties are designed more to stop Hungarians taking large sums of money out of the country. There is no limit to the amount of foreign currency that you can bring in. A limit of Ft10,000 applies, however, and only in notes of Ft1,000 or less.

It is forbidden to bring in drugs or arms.

On exit the following limits apply:
- wine – unlimited;
- spirits – 2 litres;
- 400 cigarettes or 20 cigars or 200g of tobacco;
- Ft20,000 of gifts. For more you need permission.

It is forbidden to take more than Ft10,000 out of the country. If you have more, hide it somewhere.

Insurance

Britain, Norway, Finland, Sweden and the former Warsaw Pact countries have reciprocal agreements guaranteeing free emergency treatment to their citizens. Non-emergency treatment is not covered though, and it is probably best to take out travel insurance if only to avoid the long queues at the state hospitals. This will also cover you for lost or stolen valuables.

Money

The Hungarian unit of currency is the forint, usually abbreviated as HUF or Ft – the convention we have used in this guide. The forint is divided into 100 fillér. There are coins for 10, 20 and 50 fillér (*see page 7* **What's a Filler For?**). Forint coins come in denominations of Ft1, Ft2, Ft5, Ft10, Ft20, Ft50, Ft100 and Ft200. All pre-1990 coins were withdrawn from circulation in summer 1995, so if you get a Ft10 piece with a star on it, keep it as a souvenir; it won't be useful for anything else.

Notes come in denominations of Ft50, Ft100, Ft500, Ft1,000 and Ft5,000. The Ft50 note is brown. The dark red Ft100 has a picture of Lajos

Banks

The usual opening times for banks are: 8.15am-6pm Mon; 8.15am-4pm Tue-Thur; 8.15am-1pm Fri. Apart from cash and traveller's cheques, most banks will also advance money on a credit card, but Postabank and Ibusz accept only Visa.

Bureaux de Change

These are now all over the main tourist areas and usually open from 9am-10pm daily. Rates are often poor but try:

Exklusiv
V. Váci utca 12 (117 2596). M1, M2, M3 Deák tér/tram 47, 49. **Open** 9am-10pm daily. **No credit cards.**

IBB/Intergold
VI. Teréz körút 62 (131 8361). M3 Nyugati/tram 4, 6. **Open** 10am-5.30pm Mon-Fri; 9am-12.30pm Sat. **No credit cards.**

24-hour Exchange Facilities

Cash machines are now popping up all over town. Apart from Visa and EC machines, which allow you to draw on a foreign bank account or credit card, there are also exchange machines. You slip in a foreign banknote, they spew forth forints. American Express has a 24-hour machine and both Nyugati and Keleti stations have round-the-clock change facilities.

Ibusz Bank
V. Petőfi tér 3 (118 5707). M3 Ferenciek tere. **Open** 24 hours daily.
Will change cash and traveller's cheques or else advance money on Visa, Diner's and JCB cards.

Cash Machines

These are increasingly common. Here is a centrally located selection.

Budapest Bank
VI. Király utca 16 (269 6300). M1, M2, M3 Deák tér/tram 47, 49. **Cards accepted** EC, MC.

Postabank
Nyugati station underpass. M3 Nyugati. **Cards accepted** V.

OTP
V. Deák Ferenc utca 7-9 (266 5255). M1, M2, M3 Deák tér/tram 47, 49. **Cards accepted** EC, MC.

Külkereskedelmi Bank
V. Szent István tér (269 0922). M3 Arany János utca. **Cards accepted** V.
VI. Andrássy út 17 (342 9547). M1 Opera. **Cards accepted** EC, MC, V.

Exchange Machines

K&H
V. Andrássy út 49 (268 0783). M1 Oktogon.
V. Károly körút 20 (118 1877). M2 Astoria.

Bureaux de change *usually open 9am-10pm.*

Kossuth, the nineteenth-century revolutionary. The blue Ft500 features poet Endre Ady. Béla Bartók's profile graces the green Ft1,000. And the orange Ft5,000 depicts István Széchenyi, the nineteenth-century moderniser of Hungary.

Banks & Foreign Exchange

Banks invariably give better rates than change kiosks, but it is worth shopping around as rates do vary. Traveller's cheques are exchangable at both banks and change kiosks, although sometimes at a worse rate than cash.

Black market trading is no longer really worth the bother unless you have Hungarian friends who need foreign currency. Don't be tempted to change on the street with various dubious characters. They are usually part of some organised mafia and will try to leave you with useless Yugoslav dinars or lighten your wallet by some similar con.

Forints can be changed back into hard currency at any bank (including the Ibusz desk at the airport) on production of exchange receipts which should have your passport number stamped on them. Half the total of the receipts can be exchanged up to a limit of $300.

All this will change when the forint goes convertible. There had been talk of this happening in 1996, but at press time no firm date was set.

OTP

V. Deák Ferenc utca 7-9 (266 5255). M1, M2, M3 Deák tér/tram 47, 49.

American Express

V. Deák Ferenc utca 10 (credit card 267 2313/traveller's cheques 266 8679). M1, M2, M3 Deák tér/tram 47, 49. **Open** 9am-6.30pm Mon-Fri; 9am-2pm Sat.

Currency exchange, Moneygrams, mail and fax delivery for card and traveller's cheque holders, hotel reservations, airline tickets and cash advances in hard currencies, all for various fees.

Credit Cards

Credit cards are becoming more widely accepted and American Express, Visa and Mastercard are accepted in several thousand outlets. This usually indicates that these establishments are tourist-orientated and therefore more expensive than the norm. For cash advances see previous section.

Tourist Information

Undoubtedly the best place for information is **Tourinform**. The other national tourist agencies can also help you, though not necessarily with a smile – the attitude seems to be that they are doing you a favour just by being there. Services are often duplicated. **Ibusz** is the best agency for accommodation. **Express** is essentially (though not exclusively) a student travel agency. Some sort of English will be spoken in most of these places. The easiest way to find out what's going on in Budapest are the weekly English-language newspapers *Budapest Week* and *Budapest Sun* available from some newsstands, and in hotels and at certain bars and restaurants. The more linguistically adventurous could try the free weekly listings publication *Pesti Est*, available at cinemas and bars, or *Pesti Műsor* from newsagents for Ft49.

Tourinform

V. Sütő utca 2 (117 9800). M1, M2, M3 Deák tér/tram 47, 49. **Open** *2 Mar-14 Nov* 8am-8pm daily; *15 Nov-1 Mar* 8am-3pm Sat, Sun.

The staff are very friendly, helpful, multilingual and have all the information you'll need for travel, sightseeing and entertainment.

Ibusz

V. Petőfi tér 3 (118 5707). M3 Ferenciek tere. **Open** 24 hours daily. **Credit** V.

The national tourist agency has branches all over Hungary and can book accommodation, organise tours and provide information as well as all the other normal travel agency services (flights, trains, holidays). The Petőfi tér branch will change money at all hours. There are branches at all main railway stations.

Budapest Tourist

VIII. Baross tér 3 (133 6587). **Open** 9am-5pm Mon-Fri. **No credit cards**.

Nyugati Station (132 6565). **Open** 9am-5.30pm Mon-Fri; 9am-12.30pm Sat. **No credit cards**.

Déli Station (155 7167). **Open** 9am-5pm Mon-Fri. **No credit cards**.

Money exchange, information, tours, holidays, flights.

Cooptourist

Nyugati Station (112 3621). **Open** 9am-4.30pm Mon-Fri. **No credit cards**.

Money exchange, information, tours, holidays, flights.

Express

V. Zoltán utca 10 (111 9898). M2 Kossuth tér. **Open** 8am-4pm Mon-Fri. **Credit** AmEx.

Friendly staff, currency exchange, some information, flights, student cards, youth hostel cards.

Maps

Unlike in Communist days, there is now a wide selection of Budapest maps available. Ironically, though, the old one is still the best: Cartographia's *Budapest Atlas* at Ft650. In handy book form, it contains all public transport lines, house numbers, a full street index and is sturdy enough to stand some battering about. For lovers of origami there is also a wide range of fold-out maps. Free maps of central Budapest can be picked up at **Tourinform** (*see above*) and should be enough to see you through a short stay.

Maps are available at most bookshops and travel agents, at Tourinform and at some newsstands. A good specialist map shop is Térképbolt (*see chapter* **Shopping**).

Street Names

Hungarian varieties of street can be confusing. The most common is utca, often abbreviated as 'u.', meaning simply 'street'. This should not be mixed up with an út, which is (usually) a big, wide, straight street or avenue – unless it's a körút, which means a ring road.

A tér is a square, a körtér is a circle or circus. Other varieties of Hungarian thoroughfare include: köz (lane), fasor (alley), sétány (parade), udvar (passage or arcade) and rakpart (embankment).

Public Holidays

New Year's Day (Új Év); 15 March, National Holiday; Easter Monday; 1 May, Labour Day; Whit Monday; 20 August, St Stephen's Day; 23 October, Remembrance Day; 25, 26 December.

There is usually something open on most holidays apart from the evening of 24 December when Budapest becomes a ghost town and even the non-stops stop. New Year's Eve is very lively, as is St Stephen's Day on 20 August, with fireworks on the Danube by Gellért Hill.

Time & the Seasons

Hungary is on Central European Time, which means it is one hour ahead of British time except for two brief periods at the beginning and at the end of summer.

Although Budapest can get very cold in winter and damn hot in summer, the climate is basically agreeable. However, the weather has proved unpredictable in recent years.

Spring *Average temperatures 2-10 degrees C in March; 11-22 degrees C in May.* May is probably the pleasantest month. Winter attire gets discarded though rain can sometimes dampen spirits.

Summer *Average temperatures 16-32 degrees C.* Most Hungarians leave Budapest whenever possible for the Balaton or the weekend house. It can get very hot, especially in July, but is otherwise fairly pleasant, especially when there's a breeze coming down the Danube. When there isn't, expect a pall of pollution.

Autumn *Average temperatures 7-23 degrees C.* The weather is lovely in September but does start to get cold in October when everything moves inside and the heating gets turned on.

Winter *Average temperatures minus 4-4 degrees C.* Winters are cold and quite long but not unbearably so: the air is very dry and the central heating is good. Snow usually falls a few times a year giving Budapest a completely different light. Smog can descend if there is no breeze to blow away the fumes from the coal used for heating.

Street Crime

Budapest is one of the safest cities you could visit. Although crime has risen considerably since the fall of Communism, even a woman alone can walk about almost anywhere day or night in relative safety. But as in any major city, a little common sense goes a long way. Watch out for pickpockets and purse-snatchers around Váci utca, the Castle District, Heroes' Square and at stations. Don't exchange money on the street. Be careful on trams 2, 4 and 6 where gangs sometimes operate. The prostitutes on Rákóczi tér are also reportedly adept at lifting items from pockets. It is probably a good idea not to walk alone at night around outlying areas of town or District VIII around Rákóczi tér.

If you are black, Asian or Middle Eastern in appearance, be careful of the growing number of racist, skinhead gangs. They hang around in outlying areas and metro stations, so consider taking a taxi if alone or in a dodgy-looking neighbourhood. The police tend not to be of much assistance.

You are obliged by law to carry identification on you at all times and the police can make spot checks. In practice you are unlikely to be checked.

For details of what to do if you are a victim of crime or lose your passport, *see chapter* **Survival**.

Weights & Measurements

Hungary has its own unique system for measuring out solids and liquids. A *deka* is ten grams; a *deci* is ten centilitres. In a bar, for example, you might be asked whether you want *két deci* or *három deci* (0.2 or 0.3 litres) of whatever liquid it was you just ordered. Wine in bars (but not restaurants) is usually priced by the *deci*. At a fruit stall, if you want 300 grams of apples, you would ask for 30 *dekas – harminc deka alma*.

What's a Fillér For?

Dig into your coin purse and rummage around. If you've been in Hungary longer than 24 hours, the odds are you'll find a few: fillér.

These appropriately named coins are tiny, tinny things representing divisions of the Hungarian forint. One hundred fillér make a forint; and they come in 10s, 20s and 50s. The very cheapest thing you'll find anywhere these days is a box of matches at Ft5. Fillér are almost completely useless – even streetcorner beggars refuse to accept them.

The Hungarian government phased out the old Communist forint coins in the summer of 1995. In their place Hungarians now have smartly styled forints that clink just like real money and say 'Hungarian Republic' instead of the old 'People's Republic'.

But they kept the fillér. Apparently the existence of this lowly currency unit is guaranteed by the Hungarian constitution. On the streets, however, the fillér is all but gone. Private shops and business all round up their prices to the nearest forint.

The fillér is one last vestige of the Socialist economy, tinkling in the tills of university and factory cafeterias, old-style markets and the corner newsagent.

So what do you do with them? Hungarian youths like rolling fillér down the long metro escalators. Fillér make handy tokens for an exceedingly cheapskate game of poker. And they look lovely laid out in glass jars along your mantelpiece.

Perhaps you might collect a few simply for their novelty value. At the autumn 1995 rate of exchange, a 10 fillér coin was worth £0.0005, surely one of the most worthless monetary tokens in the world.

Electricity

The current used in Hungary is 220v which works fine with the British 240v. If you have US 110v appliances you will need a current transformer. Plugs have two round pins so bring an adaptor for any other plug.

Opening Times

Hours vary according to the type of shop. Most shops open from 9am-5pm Monday-Friday, and 9am-1pm on Saturdays. Department stores usually open from 10am. Supermarkets, greengrocers and bakeries usually open at 6.30am or 7am and close around 8pm Monday-Friday, switching to 1-3pm on Saturdays. There are many non-stops, small 24-hour corner shops, where you can buy basic groceries, tobacco and booze. Most restaurants close by 11pm or midnight.

Smoking

Smoking is banned on public transport, in theatres and in cinemas but allowed everywhere else. Hungarians are among the heaviest smokers in Europe. It is quite normal for people to ask strangers for a cigarette or a light on the street and cigarettes are still often sold singly at kiosks and non-stops.

Telephones

The antiquated phone system is slowly being modernised and phoning home is no problem, although remember there are no cheap hours for international calls. Coin phone boxes take Ft5, Ft10 and Ft20 coins but your best bet is to use phonecards available at Ft500 and Ft1,100 from newsagents, post offices or men who stand around at stations with trays like cinema ice-cream sellers.

To make an international call, first dial 00, wait for a purring dial tone and then follow with the country code and the rest of the number. If you are phoning Hungary outside Budapest or calling a mobile phone, dial 06 first.

*The **phones** are being modernised – slowly.*

Tipping

There are no fixed rules about tipping in Hungary but it is customary to round up the bill or leave about 10 per cent for waiters in restaurants or bars (this is very often their only wage).

As you pay, tell the waiter how much change you would like. Saying *köszönöm* (thank you) as you hand over a note means you want them to keep the change. The same applies to taxis. You usually have to pay toilet attendants Ft20.

It's also customary to tip hairdressers, cloak-room attendants, repairmen, changing room attendants at baths and swimming pools, even doctors and dentists.

Water

The water is clean and safe to drink. In some old houses there are still lead pipes so run the tap for a few minutes before drinking.

Information Essential

When in doubt, do it backwards – that's the rule of thumb in these parts. Hungarians put their family names first and their first names last. Addresses begin with the postcode, are followed by the city, then the street name and finally the house, floor and flat numbers.

All the stuff that would go in the top right hand corner of a British or American letter (address, date etc) in Hungary, of course, is placed in the bottom left hand corner. And don't forget that dates are written like this: year/month/day.

Perhaps this follows from the Magyar tongue, which sort of works backwards as well. It's what linguists call an agglutinative language, in which all the defining bits of a word – the work that in English is done by prepositions and prefixes – get stacked up at the end of it. This is so different from English that it makes the process of learning Hungarian a little like having to rewire your brain. (*See chapter* **Language**.)

Also, remember that when going into a restaurant or bar, Hungarian men always enter before the woman. The final, surreal, touch is that Hungarians say 'Szia!' (pronounced 'seeya') where we would say 'helló' and say 'helló' where we might say 'see you'.
Helló!

Getting Around

With only three metro lines and a good network of buses, trolleybuses and trams – in addition to the chair-lift, cog-wheel railway and ferries on the Danube – Budapest is easy, and fun, to get around.

Budapest is easy to explore on foot. Most of the places you might want to go to fall within a relatively small central area, the rest of the urban sprawl consisting mostly of uninspiring tower blocks. If your feet get tired, use the comprehensive metro, tram, bus and trolleybus network. This is efficient and cheap and will get you within a few hundred yards of any destination. Taxis are fairly cheap if you stick to recommended companies.

Budapest is constructed around a series of concentric ring roads, with other main roads radiating from the centre. Traffic has increased in recent years as everyone acquires Western cars. Although congestion has not yet reached Western levels, the lack of parking means it is not advisable to use a car during daytime.

Arrival in Budapest

By Air

Ferihegy airport (157 9123) is 20km (15 miles) to the south-east of Budapest on the E60 road. There are two terminals, 5km apart.

Ferihegy 2
(arrivals 157 8000/departures 157 7000).
A modern terminal that deals with all Malév, Lufthansa, Alitalia and Air France flights.

Ferihegy 1
(157 2122).
Closer by 5km. Older than Ferihegy 2, it handles other flights.

Airport Minibus Shuttle
(157 8555). **Open** 5am-10pm or until the last flight.
The best way into town: for Ft800 they will take you to any Budapest address. Buy a ticket at the counter in the arrival hall, tell them where you're going, then wait for a driver to call your destination when they know how many others are going your way. It also works the other way round: call them to be picked up from anywhere in the city and taken back to either terminal. Accessible to wheelchair users.

Public transport
A Mercedes minibus with Centrum-Airport on the side runs from outside the terminal to Erszébet tér bus station. Tickets, Ft300, are bought on the bus, which leaves every half-hour from 6am-10pm. You can also take the 93 bus to Kőbánya-Kispest metro station and the blue M3 metro from there for the cost of one public transport (BKV) ticket for each (Ft35 from the airport newsagent). Last buses are at 10.40pm from Ferihegy 2 and 11.34pm from Ferihegy 1. Last metro leaves at 11.10pm, or there's the 182E night bus from the station.

Taxis from the airport
The taxis outside both terminal buildings are controlled by a mafia who fix prices at several times the norm. A taxi from the centre with a reputable company should cost Ft1,500.

Car hire
All the major car hire firms have stands at the airport (*see below* **Car Hire**).

Airlines

Air France
V. Kristóf tér 6 (118 0411/airport 1571 163). M1, M2, M3 Deák tér. **Open** 8am 4pm Mon-Fri. **Credit** AmEx, DC, MC, V.

Austrian Airlines
V. Régiposta utca 5 (117 1550/airport 157 6182). M1, M2, M3 Deák tér. **Open** 8.30am-12.30pm, 1.30-4.30pm, Mon-Fri. **Credit** AmEx, DC, MC, V.

British Airways
VIII. Rákóczi út 1/3 (118 3299/266 7770/airport 157 6970). M2 Astoria. **Open** 8am-5pm Mon-Fri. **Credit** AmEx, DC, MC, V.

Use one of the reliable cab companies.

Continental Europe's first underground.

Delta Air Lines

V. Apáczai Csere János utca 4 (266 1400/266 6420/airport 157 8860). M1, M2, M3 Deák tér. **Open** 8.30am-5pm Mon-Fri. **Credit** AmEx, DC, MC, V.

KLM

VIII. Rákóczi út 1/3 (266 5183/266 6279/266 1467/airport 157 0290). M2 Astoria. **Open** 8.30am-4.30pm Mon-Fri. **Credit** AmEx, DC, MC, V.

Lufthansa

V. Váci utca 19/21 (266 4511/airport 157 0290). M1, M2, M3 Deák tér/tram 47, 49. **Open** 8.30am-5pm Mon-Fri. **Credit** AmEx, DC, MC, V.

Malév

V. Dorottya utca 2 (266 5616). M1 Vörösmarty tér.
V. Ferenciek tere 2 (266 5913) M3 Ferenciek tere.
Both: **Open** 9am-4.30pm. **Credit** AmEx, DC, MC, V.
Malév's 24-hour information service for both terminals is on 157 9123. In addition, they have an office at each terminal: Ferihegy 1 (157 7554); Ferihegy 2 (157 7179).

Swissair

V. Kristóf tér 7/8 (267 2500/airport 157 4370). M1, M2, M3 Deák tér/tram 47, 49. **Open** 8.30am-4.30pm Mon-Fri. **Credit** AmEx, DC, MC, V.

By Bus

If arriving by bus you will be dropped at the bus terminal on Erzsébet tér (117 2562, 6am-6pm Mon-Fri; 6.30am-4pm Sat, Sun). There are exchange and left luggage facilities here (*see chapter* **Survival**).

By Train

Budapest has three main stations: Déli (south), Keleti (east) and Nyugati (west), all of which have metro stops of the same name. The Hungarian for station is *pályaudvar*, often abbreviated (in writing but not in speech) to *pu*. Keleti is the main station serving most trains to Vienna, Bucharest, Warsaw, Bulgaria, Turkey and north-western Hungary. Déli also serves Vienna and Austria as well as Croatia, Slovenia and south-eastern Hungary. The magnificent Nyugati is the main point of departure for Transylvania and Bratislava. Always check the station.

On arrival you will be bombarded with offers of taxis and accommodation. The latter are worth checking out. Avoid taxi touts and stick to the recommended companies in the ranks outside stations. All three stations have exchange facilities and tourist information but only Keleti and Nyugati have 24-hour left-luggage facilities.

MÁV Information

VI. Andrássy út 35 (322 8275/national enquiries 322 7860/international enquiries 342 9150). M1 Opera. **Open** 9am-6pm daily. **No credit cards.**
Often the easiest place to buy tickets in advance. Phone lines are manned until 8pm. After that, phone one of the stations listed below.

Keleti pályaudvar

VIII. Baross tér (113 6835). M2 Keleti/tram 44, 67, 23, 24, 36. **Lines open** 8pm-6am.

Nyugati pályaudvar

VI. Nyugati tér (149 0115). M3 Nyugati/tram 4, 6. **Lines open** 8pm-6am.

Déli pályaudvar

I. Alkotás út (113 6835). M2 Déli/tram 18, 59, 61. **Lines open** 8pm-6am.

Public Transport

The Budapest transport company (BKV) is cheap, efficient, and gets you to within about a hundred yards of any destination. Walking is not fashionable here. The network consists of three metro lines, trams, buses, trolleybuses and local trains. In summer there are also BKV Danube ferries. Maps of the system can be bought at main metro stations for Ft70. Street atlases (Cartographia's at Ft650 is the handiest) also mark the routes.

Public transport starts around 4.30am and finishes around 11pm although there is a limited night bus network along major routes. Tickets can be purchased at all metro stations, also at some tram stops and newsstands. A ticket is valid for one journey on one piece of transport (except the ferries, which have a separate system), so if you change from metro to tram, or even from metro line to metro line, you have to punch a new ticket.

On trams, buses and trolleybuses the contraption for validating your ticket is not intuitively designed. Slide the business end of your ticket (the bit with the circled numbers) into the black slot at the top of the red box, then pull the slot-thing towards you hard until it clicks. Maybe it's best first to observe how locals do it.

Day, three-day, weekly, fortnightly and monthly tickets are also available from metro stations although you will need a photograph to obtain anything but a one-day or three-day pass. Take your photo to Deák tér metro to be issued with a photopass. For a ticket longer than one day you have to ask for: *egy napi bérlet* (one day), *egy heti bérlet* (one week), *két heti bérlet* (two weeks) or *egy havi bérlet* (one month). All these tickets run from the day of purchase apart from the monthly which is valid per calendar month. It is possible to

ride without a ticket, but plain-clothes inspectors (who put on a red armband before demanding your ticket) are common and can levy somewhat arbitrary on-the-spot fines, usually around Ft600. Playing the dumb foreigner doesn't usually work.

Prices

Single – Ft35
10 tickets – Ft315
Day – Ft280
3-day – Ft560
Week – Ft750, Ft630 (not buses)
2-week – Ft1,000, Ft840 (not buses)
Month – Ft1,500, Ft1,260 (not buses)

BKV Information

(117 5518/342 2335).

Metro

The Budapest metro is safe, clean, regular and simple. There are three lines: yellow M1, red M2 and blue M3. These connect the main stations and intersect at Déak tér. The recently renovated M1 line, originally constructed for the 1896 exhibition, was the first underground railway in continental Europe. The other lines, constructed post-war with Soviet assistance, still have Russian trains.

Trains run every two to three minutes (length of time since the last train is shown on a clock on the platform). Validate tickets in the machines at the top of the escalators and in Déak tér passageways when changing lines. The first trains run from 4.30am and the last ones leave around 11pm.

Buses & Trolleybuses

There is a comprehensive bus and trolleybus network, the main lines being the 1 from Kelenföld train station to the centre and then following the M1 metro line, and the 7 connecting Bosnyák tér, Keleti station, Blaha Lujza tér, Astoria, Ferenciek tere, Móricz Zsigmond körtér and Kelenföld station. The castle bus (Várbusz), goes from Moszkva tér round the castle area and back. Buses with red numbers are expresses that miss out certain stops. Most stops and buses have times and stops listed.

Trams

Like many central European cities, Budapest has retained and expanded its tram network. The most important routes are the 4 and 6 which follow the Nagykörút from Moszkva tér to Féhervári út and Móricz Zsigmond körtér respectively, the 2 which runs up the Pest side of the Danube, and the 47 and 49 which run from Deák tér to Móricz Zsigmond körtér and beyond into wildest Buda.

Local Trains (HÉV)

There are four HÉV lines. You will probably only need the one to Szentendre from Batthyány tér, price Ft89 although a normal BKV ticket is valid

as far as Békásmegyer. After that it's an extra Ft54. First and last trains from Batthyány tér are at 3.50am and 11.40pm, and from Szentendre 3.30am and 10.30pm. Other lines run between Örs vezér tere and Gödöllő, Vágóhíd and Ráckeve, and Boráros tér and Csepel.

Night Buses & Trams

A reduced but reliable service works at night following the main routes and is usually full of drunks on week nights and teenagers at the weekends. Handiest are the 6É following the Nagykörút, the 182É following the blue M3 metro line, and the 78É from Döbrentei tér on the Buda side of Erzsébet bridge to Örs Vezér tere following, from Astoria, more or less the M2 route. On these routes buses run every 15 minutes.

Danube Ferries

Undoubtedly the most civilised method of travelling within Budapest, the BKV Danube ferries also offer a river ride which is exceedingly cheap when compared with the various organised tours. The local service runs from May to the end of September between Pünkösdfürdő north of the city and Boráros tér at the Pest foot of Petőfi bridge, stopping at most of the bridges, Vigadó tér and either end of Margaret Island. Fares vary between Ft50-Ft200. Boats, however, only run once every couple of hours, with extra services at weekends. Timetables are posted at all stops. Boats to Szentendre, Visegrád and Esztergom on the Danube bend leave from Vigadó tér. (*See also chapters* **Trips Out of Town** *and* **Getting Started**.)

Ferry Information

Jászai Mari tér terminal (Margaret Bridge Pest side) (129 5844). Or try BKV information as listed above.

Taxis

Rates in Budapest vary from the cheap to the outrageous. Stick to cabs displaying a large company logo. Others often have tampered meters or will take you by the scenic route. Avoid expensive Western-model cars hanging around outside hotels and tourist spots. They are usually crooks. Not that drivers of small cars are necessarily above ripping you off too. The cheap and reliable **Fötaxi** have red-and-white checkered patterns on their doors and can be spotted from a distance by their oval-shaped lights. If you're calling for a cab, the people at City Taxi speak English. If you're always calling from the same address, **City Taxi** have a databank which records your address the first time, meaning you merely have to give your telephone number on subsequent occasions.

A receipt should be available on request. Say: *számlát kérek*. A small tip is usual but not compulsory. All legitimate taxis should have yellow number plates, but having yellow plates doesn't guarantee that they won't try to fleece you. Make sure the driver turns on the meter as you start your journey. If he refuses, it is sometimes possible to negotiate a fare but it's probably best to look for another cab. The most reliable companies are:

City Taxi *(211 1111)*.

Főtaxi *(222 2222)*.

Tele5 *(155 5555)*.

Volán Taxi *(166 6666)*.

Car Hire

Cars and rates vary from Ladas to limousines. A credit card is usually necessary for the deposit. Check that the price includes ÁFA (VAT). There's an insurance charge and varying rates of mileage from free, a fixed amount free and a per kilometre charge. Longer-term rates are available. The main companies have desks at both airport terminals.

Americana Rent-a-car *Pannónia Hotel Volga, XIII. Dózsa György út 65 (120 8287)*. M3 Dózsa György út . **Open** 8am-7pm Mon-Fri; 8am-noon Sat, Sun. **Credit** AmEx, DC, MC, V.

Avis *V. Szervita tér 8 (118 4685)*. M1, M2, M3 Deák tér. **Open** 8am-8pm Mon-Sat; 8am-noon Sun. **Credit** AmEx, DC, MC, V

Budget *I. Krisztina körút 41-43 (156 6333)*. M2 Déli pu. **Open** 8am-8pm Mon-Sat; 8am-6pm Sun. **Credit** AmEx, DC, MC, V.

COOP Car *IX. Ferenc körút 43 (215 1681)*. M3 Ferenc körút. **Open** 8am-6pm Mon-Fri; 8am-1pm Sat, Sun only at airport (147 7328). **Credit** AmEx, DC, MC, V.

Europcar *VIII. Üllői út 62 (113 1492)*. M3 Ferenc körút. **Open** 8am-7pm Mon-Fri; 8am-noon Sun. **Credit** AmEx, DC, MC, V.

Főtaxi *VII. Kertész utca 24-28 (322 1471)*. M2 Blaha Lujza tér. **Open** 7am-5.30pm daily. **Credit** AmEx, DC, MC, V.

Bicycles

Budapest is not bicycle-friendly. Pollution is high and drivers are not used to cyclists. Bike use is on the increase, though, and the city has installed some bicycle lanes, but these are still rare. Bikes and tandems can be hired on Margaret Island opposite the bus stops at both ends.

Maps

City centre maps and metro maps are included at the back of this guide. Free maps are also available from Tourinform. More comprehensive maps are available at bookshops, travel agents and newsstands. All metro stations have detailed street and transport maps placed near the entrance.

Tourinform

V. Sütő utca 2 (117 9800). M1, M2, M3 Deák tér/tram 47, 49. **Open** *2 Mar-14 Nov* 8am-8pm daily; *15 Nov-1 Mar* 8am-3pm Sat, Sun.

Transports of Delight

Budapest has an assortment of enjoyably eccentric conveyances. The cog-wheel railway takes you up Széchenyi-hegy. It runs from opposite the Budapest Hotel, two stops from Moszkva tér on tram 56 or 18. Last train down is at 11.30pm.

The narrow-gauge Children's Railway (*gyermekvasút*) wends through the wooded Buda hills to Hűvösvölgy. Formerly the Pioneer Railway run by the Communist youth organisation,

many of the jobs are done by children. Trains leave hourly between 9am-5pm, tickets cost Ft60, Ft30 children (Ft100/Ft50 return).

Another way up into the hills is the chair-lift (*libegő*) up to Jánoshegy – at 520m the highest point in Budapest. Take the 158 bus from Moszkva tér to Zugligeti út. It costs Ft100 (Ft60 children) and runs from 9am-5pm May-Sept, 9.30am-4pm Oct-Apr. There are cafés at the top, and you can walk to Erszébet lookout tower or the Jánoshegy stop on the children's railway.

The funicular (*sikló*) takes a minute to run up from Clark Ádám tér to the Castle District. It's a short, vertiginous ride but the view is good. This runs from 7.30am-10pm and a one-way ticket costs Ft100 adults, Ft60 children.

Tram 2, which runs up the Pest bank of the Danube from Vágóhíd to Margaret Bridge, passing Gellért Hill, Castle Hill, Parliament and all the bridges, must be the second most beautiful public transport ride in Europe. (First prize would have to go to a *vaporetto* down Venice's Grand Canal.)

Language

Istenem! Úgy iszol, mint egy kefekötő! Or 'God! You drink like a brushmaker!' This from a nation which believes that Shakespeare sounds less impressive in its original language than it does in Hungarian – a tongue for linguists who like a challenge.

Perhaps nowhere else in Europe will the traveller be confronted by as great a linguistic barrier as in Hungary. The Hungarian language is renowned the world over for its difficulty, which for most foreigners boils down to the fact that Hungarian bears absolutely no resemblance to any language they may have previously encountered. In other countries, picking up a bit of the local lingo can be an enjoyable pastime. A few words of Portuguese? *Não problema*. A bit of Plattdeutsch? *Kein Problem*. A smattering of any Slavic tongue? *Nema problema*. Hungarian? *Nincs semmi gond!*

Hungarian is a Finno-Ugric language, part of the greater family of Altaic-Uralic languages that includes Turkish, Finnish and Mongolian. Much is made of Hungarian's relationship to Finnish, but that kinship is distant indeed. As the main language of the Ugric stock, Hungarian is related most close-ly to two small languages in the Ural mountains of northwest Siberia, Vogul and Ostyak. When the Hungarians moved southward and adopted the equestrian and agricultural cultures of the southern steppes they adopted many terms from Turkic and Iranian languages, such as names for livestock and farm implements (the words for 'customs official' (*vám*) and 'bridge' (*híd*) are borrowed from the Alan language, spoken today in Ossetia).

After the Magyars established themselves in Europe their language became infused with many Slavic, Latin and, later, German terms. The first written document containing any Hungarian – a few score place names in a mostly Latin document – was the 1055 deed of foundation for Tihany Abbey, these days preserved at Pannonhalma Abbey near Győr. Hungarian has shown itself to be an extremely conservative language, and medieval

Hungarian is easily understood by a modern Magyar. There are various regional accents but relatively few dialects, although Budapest boasts a slangy style of rapid-fire speech peppered with foreign vocabulary, especially borrowings from Yiddish, Gypsy and German.

There are so few terms in Hungarian that are cognate with words from the Indo-European language family that every new word requires prodigious feats of learning. Then comes grammar. Beginners memorise a whole series of conjugations simply to begin mangling the idea of 'I have' (*nekem van* 'it is for/of/to me'). Prepositions come

after the noun as suffixes, and their use is usually quite different from English, so that you have to know that 'to go to' may be different if you're going to a place that is enclosed, geographical, or personal (*házba*, to the house; *Pestre*, to Pest; *hozzánk*, to our house). Furthermore, each Hungarian town has its own post-preposition to indicate that you are in that town. You can be 'in London' (*Londonban*) but you are in *Budapesten*, *Pécsett*, *Debrecenben*. Easy, simple, clear Hungarian.

Luckily, Hungarian has a few features that make things easier. There is no gender, not even a different pronoun for 'he' and 'she'. Past and future

Hungarian Vocabulary

Even on a short trip to Budapest, it is useful to learn a few Hungarian words and phrases. *Igen* (yes), *nem* (no) and *jó reggelt* (good morning), *jó napot* (good day) and *jó estét* (good evening) are all fairly easy, but you'll probably find *viszontlátásra* (goodbye) a mouthful. In shops and among friends you can use the informal short version, *viszlát*.

Meanwhile, *szervusz* is an all-purpose, informal greeting meaning either hello or goodbye, as is the even more informal *szia*. Older women still like to be greeted with *kezét csókolom* (literally, 'I kiss your hand'). Confusingly, but inevitably, Hungarians usually use the English 'hello' to mean 'goodbye'.

The word *kérem* serves a lot of purposes. Its first meaning is 'please', but it also means 'excuse me' when trying to attract the waiter's attention; it can be the answer to *köszönöm* (thank you), and if you pronounce it as a question, it means 'pardon?'. If you don't understand what you are being told, you can also say *Bocsánat, nem értem* (Sorry, I don't understand). And then *Nem beszélek magyarul* (I don't speak Hungarian), although that will probably have become obvious by this point.

Hol van? (where is it?) is useful. The answer will probably include a lot of *itt* (here), *ott* (there), *innen* (from here), *onnan* (from there), *jobbra* (to the right), *balra* (to the left) and *egyenesen* (straight ahead).

You may want to ask local people about where to eat or find cheap accommodation, since hotel receptionists tend to send tourists directly to the most expensive places. *Hol van egy jó/olcsó/nem túl drága/magyar étterem?* (where is a good/cheap/not too expensive/Hungarian restaurant?) is the question to ask, and have a *térkép* (map) ready to make life simpler.

Hungarian makes a noun plural by adding '-k' and sometimes a link vowel to a noun. *Busz* (bus) becomes *buszok*, *csirke* (chicken) becomes *csirkék*. Just so that things don't seem too easy, you don't form the plural if you state the number of things, such as *négy alma* (four apples) or *száz forint* (one hundred forints).

When shopping in Hungary remember that shop assistants usually don't speak anything other than Hungarian. *Mennyibe kerül?* (how much is it?), *ez* (this), *az* (that) and some adjectives such as *kicsi* (small), *nagy* (large), *régi* (old), *új* (new), *piros* (red), *fehér* (white) and *fekete* (black) should help.

When you would like to ask for something, be it in a store or a café, say *Kérek egy/kettő/három lemezt/kávét* (I want a/two/three records/coffees). Finally, if you are completely lost, try *Beszél itt valaki angolul?* (does anyone speak English here?).

Pronunciation

Accents denote a longer vowel, except for é (ay) and á (as in father). The stress is always on the first syllable. Double consonants are pronounced longer (*kettő*, *szebb*).

Add 't' to nouns when they are the object of the sentence: 'I would like a beer' is *Kérek egy sört* (sör + t).

a – like 'o' in hot
á – like 'a' in father
sz – like 's' in sat
cs – like 'ch' in such
zs – like the 's' in casual
gy – like the 'd' in dew
ly – like the 'y' in yellow
ny – like the 'n' in new
ty – like the 't' in tube
c – like 'ts' in roots
s – like 'sh' in wash
ö – like 'ur' in pleasure
ü – like 'u' in French tu
ő, ű – similar to ö and ü but longer

tenses are relatively easy and regular. And Hungarians are delighted to hear foreigners attempt their language. If you intend to stay for more than a few weeks, the best book to learn Hungarian is probably *Colloquial Hungarian* by Jerry Payne (Routledge Publishers, London). *See also chapter* **Further Reading**.

A good rule of thumb is that the younger the Hungarian, the more likely they will be to speak English. Under Communism, Hungarians were forced to study Russian in school, and it became a badge of pride to fail the eight-year course – not the best experience of foreign language acquisition. Standards for foreign language ability have stayed rather low as a glance at any English-language restaurant menu will confirm. Common errors include such appetising terms as 'paste covered with greaves' for noodles with bacon bits, and 'fried innard glands' for sweetbreads.

Another infuriating feature of Hungarian English is that translations attempt to use the most convoluted English constructions possible – a hangover from the dense Hungarian literary style and a mistrust of colloquialism in print. Hungarian uses the article before each noun, so translations abound in 'the' constructions, such as 'The

Useful Phrases

Yes *Igen*
No *Nem*
Maybe *Talán*
(I wish you) good day *Jó napot* (kivanok) (formal)
Hello *Szervusz* (informal); *Szia* (familiar).
Goodbye *Viszontlátásra* (formal)
'Bye *Viszlát*
How are you? *Hogy van?* (formal) *Hogy vagy?* (familiar)
I'm fine *Jól vagyok*
Please *Kérem*
Thank you *Köszönöm*
Excuse me *Bocsánat*
I would like *Kérek...* (an object)
I would like (to do something) *Szeretnék...* (add infinitive)
Where is...? *Hol van...?*
Where is the toilet? *Hol van a wc?* (wc vay tzay)
When? *Mikor?* Who? *Ki?* Why? *Miért?* How? *Hogyan?*
Is there...? *Van...?*
There is none *Nincs*
How much is it? *Mennyibe kerül?*
Open *Nyitva*
Closed *Zárva*
Entrance *Bejárat*
Exit *Kijárat*
Men's *Férfi;* women's *Női*
Good *Jó;* bad *Rossz*
I like it *Ez tetszik*
I don't like it *Ez nem tetszik*
I don't speak *Nem beszélek*
Hungarian *Magyarul*
Do you speak English? *Beszél angolul?*
What is your name? *Mi a neve?*
My name is... *A nevem...*
I am (English/American) *(angol/amerikai) vagyok*
Railway station *Pályaudvar*
Airport *Repülőtér*
Ticket office or cash desk *Pénztár*
I would like to go to Pécs *Pécsre szeretnék menni*
I would like two tickets *Két jegyet kérek*
When is the train to Vienna? *Mikor indul a bécsi vonat?*
(At) three o' clock *Három óra (kor)*
I feel ill *Rosszul vagyok*
Doctor *Orvos*
Pharmacy *Patika*
Hospital *Kórház*
Ambulance *Mentőautó*
Police *Rendőrség*

Numbers

zero *nulla*
one *egy*
two *kettő* (note the form 'két', used with an object: **két kávé** *two coffees*)
three *három*
four *négy*
five *öt*
six *hat*
seven *hét*
eight *nyolc*
nine *kilenc*
ten *tíz*
eleven *tizenegy*
twelve *tizenkettő*
thirteen *tizenhárom*
twenty *húsz;* **twenty-five** *húszonöt*
thirty *harminc*
thirty-four *harmincnégy*
forty *negyven*
forty-one *negyvenegy*
fifty *ötven*
sixty *hatvan*
seventy *hetven*
eighty *nyolcvan*
ninety *kilencven*
one hundred *száz*
one hundred and fifty *százötven*
two hundred *kettőszáz*
three hundred *háromszáz*
one thousand *ezer*
ten thousand *tízezer*

Crucial Phrases

Where is a good bar? *Hol van egy jó kocsma?*
Cheers! *Egészségedre* (Egg-aysh-ayg-ed-reh!)
Which football team do you support? *Melyik foci csapatnak drukkolsz?*
God! You drink like a brushmaker! *Istenem! Úgy iszol, mint egy kefekötő!*
I love you *Szeretlek*
It is hopeless *Reménytelen*
Could you call a cab for me? *Tudna nekem egy taxit hívni?*

Start studying now: you should be able to stumble through a few words in a year or five.

Students of the School of the Agriculture study the biology and the animals'.

All these linguistic difficulties are well worth the effort, however, since every Hungarian knows that Hungarian is the perfect language. This is a qualitative judgement that any Hungarian will be happy to explain to you. Shakespeare, you will be told, sounds better in Hungarian than in the original English. The same holds true for Woody Allen films, Winnie-the-Pooh, and Flintstones cartoons (which are dubbed in squeaky voices, in rhyme).

The verb for 'to explain' is *magyarázni*, which is to say, to 'Hungarianise'. This may sound absurd, but Hungarians are very proud of their unique ability to understand Hungarian.

Today Hungarians are acutely aware of the need to learn foreign languages. Private language schools do a booming business teaching English and German, and the influence of western films and MTV means you may meet young Hungarians with a perfect command of Gangsta-Rap English in the strangest places.

Welcome in Hungary

There may no longer be a 'Welcome in Hungary' sign at the Austrian border, but there is a new mall in downtown Pest called the 'Made In World Center'. And you can still order 'Veal Gordon Blue' (usually, in fact, pork) in an establishment proudly displaying a sign that declares 'Second-Class Restaurant' (a relic of the old state licensing system).

Much of the blame for such merry mistranslations must lie with one László Országh, who edited the standard post-War Hungarian-English dictionary. Országh was a less than spectacular linguist who was known to confiscate his students' copies of other English dictionaries and tear them up in front of his classes. His main experience with native English speakers came during his term as a prisoner of war in 1945. The

only available native speaker was an errant bachelor from Nottingham who was paid for his assistance in beer. Not surprisingly, some of the entries in Országh's Dictionary are quite bizarre.

Many of these Országhisms are stubbornly defended by Hungarians, including translating *vadspenót* (wild spinach) as 'English/false mercury, good King Henry', and *fesztelenít* (to unscrew) as 'to uncock the cock'. The dictionary includes strange idiomatic explanations such as 'to sit down under an insult' and 'in consequence of the lucky concurrence of circumstance' (we'll meet again). Országh even invented the word *bólongatni* (to cause someone to nod their head) so that the word bolshevik would not come next to the word *bolond* (fool) in the Hungarian-English edition.

Accommodation

Budapest's hotels may be characterised by a mixture of faded elegance, Communist kitsch and state-sponsored off-handedness, but there aren't that many capitals where you can enjoy a mud pack in a spa pool in the centre of town.

The **Grand Hotel Corvinus Kempinski** – *if the Stones are in town, this is where they stay.*

Finding a place to stay in Budapest can be frustrating. This isn't because there aren't plenty of rooms, rather that the tourist information infrastructure is a shambles and little comprehensive information is available. Booking in advance is advised, though IBUSZ (open 24 hours daily) is reliable for local accommodation in a hotel, *panzió* (pension) or private rooms. American Express books hotels, but requires a credit card and a $10 service fee. For booking yourself, Tourinform can provide you with a free brochure listing most hotels and *panziók* in and around Budapest.

Peak seasons are in the late spring and early autumn (April-June, August-October). At these times, it's best to make reservations at least two weeks ahead to be sure of something in your price range. Also, book at least a month and a half ahead if planning to arrive during the second weekend of August, when the Hungarian Grand Prix takes place (*see chapter* **Sport**).

With the exception of the Hilton in the Castle District and the Kempinski on Erzsébet tér, the major hotels line the east shore of the Danube in Pest. All of them were either built after 1990 or have been renovated since then. While they claim to be five-star hotels, and services are extensive, there's little feeling of luxury, except perhaps at the Kempinski. Phone sockets that will accept modems are a recent innovation in all but the Hilton. Less expensive hotels are scattered around the city offering either the convenience of central location, or the quiet of the Buda hills. Among these hotels, those built after 1990 or under private ownership tend to have better rooms, more facilities and friendlier staff.

Most of the Communist-era hotels haven't yet shed tacky interior decoration, average restaurants and a cavalier attitude towards service. On the bright side, *panziók* are a pleasant alternative offering many of the same services found in a hotel and more personal service at reasonable prices. A *panzió* will often give rate reductions for stays longer than a few days.

Private rooms (*fizetővendég szolgálat*) are the least expensive choice in the city (between Ft2,000-Ft3,000 for a double per night). IBUSZ books private rooms and Keleti station is the hunting ground for Hungarians with rooms to let. Ask to see where you'll be staying before accepting a room or agreeing to a price. Though many are very comfortable indeed, rooms and their owners receive only cursory inspection by the tourism board. Stories abound of travellers being stranded in cramped District XVI spaces with a landlady from hell imposing unreasonable strictures of quiet and curfew.

Finding a more permanent residence in Budapest is, if anything, harder than finding a hotel. Word of mouth is best, followed by the *Expressz* daily classifed ad paper (*see chapter* **Media**). Watch out, though; most apartments are listed by agencies that will charge Ft2,000 to give you a list of addresses which may or may not be out of date. Housing is still subsidised and most of the people you might sublet from are paying ridiculously low rents. Foreigners are expected to fork out, though. Expect to pay up to Ft35,000-Ft45,000 per month plus utilities for a two-room flat in the centre.

Prices in the tourist industry are pegged to the Deutschmark and hotels list their prices in this currency, although payments can be made in forints. We have therefore listed hotel prices in this guide in Deutschmarks. At the time of going to press, DM1 was buying around Ft90, though this will doubtless change.

Unless otherwise noted, breakfast is included in the price. In most cases, breakfast consists of a cold buffet of bread, cheeses and cold-cuts. Hotels in the expensive range and some *panziók* offer an 'American' breakfast which includes hot and cold buffet. Price categories are as follows: a double room in a De Luxe hotel costs DM325 or more; an Expensive hotel DM220 or more; a Moderate hotel DM125 or more; the rest are budget.

Booking

American Express

V. Deák Ferenc utca 10 (266 8680/fax 267 2028). M1, M2, M3 Deák tér. **Open** *Oct-May* 9am-5.30pm Mon-Fri; 9am-2pm Sat. *June-Sept* 9am-6.30pm Mon-Fri; 9am-2pm Sat. **Credit** AmEx.
Free information and hotel reservations for holders of any major credit card and a $10 dollar fee.

IBUSZ

V. Apáczai Csere János utca 1 (118 3925/118 5707/fax 117 9099). M1 Vörösmarty tér. **Open** 24 hours daily.
IBUSZ books for approximately 80 per cent of Budapest's hotels and *panziók*, arranges private sightseeing tours and airline tickets, and changes money. Any private room with

even the remotest chance of being inspected by anyone is registered with IBUSZ.

Tourinform

V. Sütő utca 2 (117 9800). M1, 2, 3 Deák tér. **Open** 8am-8pm daily; *winter* 8am-3pm Sat-Sun. **No credit cards.**
No hotel booking, but Tourinform answers questions and has hotel information booklets.

De Luxe

Budapest Hilton Hotel

I. Hess András tér 1-3 (175 1000/fax 156 0285). M2 Moszkva tér then Várbusz. **Rates** *single* DM315-DM478; *double* DM410-DM596; *suite* DM596-DM922; *extra bed* DM95-DM118; *breakfast* DM32. **Credit** AmEx, DC, EC, JCB, MC, V.
Spectacular views overlooking the Danube are the trade-off for a location away from central Pest. Designed around a seventeenth-century façade and the remains of a thirteenth-century Gothic church, non-view rooms are more spacious and a one-of-a-kind open-air concert hall sits between the two main wings. Service is reputed to be among the best in town, which is reflected in high occupancy rates – booking several weeks in advance is advised.
Hotel services *Air-conditioning. Babysitting. Bars (2). Business centre. Car park (DM29). Coffee shop. Conference facilities. Currency exchange. Disabled: access. Laundry. Lift. Non-smoking rooms (50). Restaurants (2). Safe.* **Room services** *Hair-dryer. Minibar. Radio. Room Service. Telephone. TV.*

Grand Hotel Corvinus Kempinski

V. Erzsébet tér 7-8 (266 1000/266 6888/fax 266 2000). M1, M2, M3 Deák tér. **Rates** *single* DM348-DM438; *double* DM410-DM528; *suite* DM708-DM3,206; *extra bed* DM90; *breakfast* DM27. **Credit** AmEx, DC, EC, JCB, MC, V.
Built in 1992, everything still feels new in what is perhaps the only hotel in Budapest which offers true luxury in both service and facilities. Designed specifically for the hotel, Art Deco furnishings are unusual in rooms and bathrooms bigger than average, with extras such as down duvets and slippers. Suites are bigger than most Budapest apartments. Staff are attentive to detail and courteous without stifling, though the Kempinski Grill isn't spectacular. If Michael Jackson or the Stones are in town, this is where they stay.
Hotel services *Air-conditioning. Babysitting. Bars (2). Beauty salon. Business centre. Car park (Ft1,500). Conference facilities. Currency exchange. Disabled: access. Fitness centre. Laundry. Lift. Non-smoking rooms (60). Restaurants (2) Sauna. Solarium. Swimming pool.* **Room services** *Hair-dryer. Minibar. Radio. Room service. Safe. Telephone. TV.*

Forum Hotel Budapest

V. Apáczai Csere János utca 12-14 (117 9111/fax 117 9808). M1 Vörösmarty tér. **Rates** *single* DM320-DM360; *double* DM380-DM420; *suite* DM500-DM700; *extra bed* DM80; *breakfast* DM15-DM25. **Credit** AmEx, DC, EC, JCB, MC, V.
Business is the order of the day here and the lobby hums with deals in the making. Rather cramped rooms with tacky décor are compensated for by Danube views, a well appointed dining room and outstanding pastries in the coffee shop.
Hotel services *Air-conditioning. Babysitting. Bar. Beauty salon. Business centre. Car park (Ft1,300). Conference facilities. Currency exchange. Disabled: access. Fitness centre. Laundry. Lift. Non-smoking rooms (50). Sauna. Solarium. Swimming pool.* **Room services** *Hair-dryer. Minibar. Radio. Room service. Safe. Telephone. TV.*

The art nouveau **Hotel Gellért** *earned its lasting reputation during Budapest's 'silver age'.*

Atrium Hyatt Budapest

V. Roosevelt tér 2 (266 1234/fax 266 9101). M1 Vörösmarty tér. **Rates** *single* DM304-DM450; *double* DM382-DM528; *suite* DM495-DM787; *extra bed* DM78; *breakfast* DM29. **Credit** AmEx, DC, EC, JCB, MC, V.
Standard rooms open off the central atrium from which the hotel takes its name. Centrally located with Danube views and catering to business travellers, the Atrium is rather cavernous and in need of a facelift. The Balloon Bar, however, is an excellent spot with an unequalled view of the river.
Hotel services *Air-conditioning. Babysitting. Bars (2). Beauty salon. Car park (Ft1,600). Conference facilities. Currency exchange. Business centre. Fitness centre. Laundry. Lift. Non-smoking rooms (45). Restaurants (3). Safe. Sauna. Solarium. Swimming pool.* **Room services** *Hair-dryer. Minibar. Radio. Room service. Telephone. TV.*

Budapest Marriott Hotel

V. Apáczai Csere János utca 4 (266 7000/fax 266 5000). M1 Vörösmarty tér. **Rates** *single* DM128-DM245; *double* DM250-DM338; *suite* DM450; *extra bed* DM80.
DM601-DM1,985; *breakfast* DM24-DM27. **Credit** AmEx, DC, EC, JCB, MC, V.
Every room has a Danube view and the staff get top marks for excellent service. One of the favourites with the local business community for conferences, the Marriott has a reputation for looking after its guests. Above-average rooms and interior furnishings; the business lounge on the top floor has one of the best views in the city, though it's restricted to guests in 'Concierge'-level rooms.
Hotel services *Air-conditioning. Babysitting. Bar. Beauty salon (phone in autumn). Business centre. Car park (Ft2,000 indoor, Ft1,000 outdoor). Conference facilities. Currency exchange. Disabled: access. Fitness centre. Laundry. Lift. Non-smoking rooms (180). Restaurant (3).* **Room services** *Hair-dryer. Minibar. Radio. Room service. Safe. Telephone. TV.*

Thermal Hotel Helia

XIII. Kárpát utca 62-64 (270 3277/fax 270 2262). Trolleybus 79 Dráva utca. **Rates** *single* DM200-DM300;

double DM250-DM350; *suite* DM450, DM700. **Credit** AmEx, DC, EC, JCB, MC, V.
The clean lines of Scandinavian design are reflected in all aspects of this modern spa hotel. Two-storey windows overlooking the Danube brighten the lobby, and the white-tiled pool areas also benefit from lots of natural light. Rooms are comfortably decorated in light pine furniture and pastels, and suites have their own sauna. Above-average breakfast and lunch buffet. Five rooms with exceptional facilities for wheelchairs.
Hotel services *Babysitting. Bar. Beauty salon. Business centre. Car park. Conference facilities. Currency exchange. Disabled: access. Fitness centre. Hair-dryers. Laundry. Restaurants (2). Safe. Sauna. Solarium. Steam bath. Swimming pool. Tennis.* **Room services** *Minibar. Radio. Room service. Telephone. TV.*

Hotel Gellért

XI. Szt Gellért tér 1 (185 2200/fax 166 6631). Tram 18, 19, 47, 49 Gellért tér. **Rates** *single* DM128-DM245; *double* DM250-DM338; *suite* DM450; *extra bed* DM80.
Credit AmEx, DC, EC, JCB, MC, V.
Once one of Budapest's most spectacular spa hotels, the art nouveau Gellért (built 1912-18) earned its reputation in the interwar period – Budapest's 'silver age'. Restaurateur Károly Gundel, who also then ran the Városliget restaurant which still bears his name, entertained visiting dignitaries with Hungarian delicacies. In 1927, when he took over the restaurant here, the swimming pool with artificial waves was also created out back. Built on the site of an old Turkish bathhouse, turn-of-the-century charm still radiates from the spa facilities (also worth visiting in their own right: *see chapter* **Baths**). The hotel has been undergoing a room-by-room renovation. The new rooms are attractive with spacious bathrooms, but each is different so it's worth looking at several. There's also an excellent coffee shop and a pleasant terrace that is somewhat spoiled by heavy traffic nearby.
Hotel services *Babysitting. Bar. Beauty salon. Business centre. Car park. Conference facilities. Currency exchange. Laundry. Lift. Restaurant. Safe. Sauna. Solarium.*

Béke Radisson Hotel – *comfortable rooms.*

Swimming pool. **Room services** *Hair-dryer. Minibar.
Radio. Room service. Telephone. TV.*

Béke Radisson Hotel

*VI. Teréz körút 43 (132 3300/fax 153 3380). M3
Nyugati.* **Rates** *single* DM230-DM290; *double* DM 290-
DM350; *suite* DM600; *extra bed* DM60. **Credit** AmEx,
DC, EC, JCB, MC, V.
Cordial service accompanies a stay at the Radisson. Rooms
are comfortable with handsome, tasteful furnishings. Full
buffet breakfast in the skylit Shakespeare room is pleasant
and the pastries in the albeit excessively pink Zsolnay Coffee
Shop are recommended.
Hotel Services *Air-conditioning. Babysitting. Bars (2).
Beauty salon. Car park (Ft1,530). Casino. Coffee shop.
Conference facilities. Currency exchange. Disabled: access.
Fax. Laundry. Lift. Massage. Non-smoking rooms (30).
Restaurant. Sauna. Solarium. Swimming pool.* **Room
services** *Hair-dryer. Minibar. Radio. Room service. Safe.
Telephone. TV.*

Expensive

Ramada Grand Hotel

*XIII. Margitsziget (111 1000/fax 153 3029). Bus 26
from Nyugati.* **Rates** *single* DM190-DM280; *double*
DM240-DM330; *apartment* DM380-DM560; *extra bed*
DM50. **Credit** AmEx, DC, EC, JCB, MC, V.
Sharing the same facilities as the Thermal Hotel Margitsziget
through an underground tunnel, the Ramada has a much
pleasanter atmosphere and bigger, cleaner rooms. Though
not air-conditioned, most rooms have a balcony and all
contain period furnishings that reflect the hotel's 100-year
history. The charming lobby and outside terraces serving

the restaurant, ice-cream shop and pizzeria foster a turn-of-
the century feel.
Hotel services *Babysitting. Bars (2). Beauty salon. Car
park (Ft1,000, free outside) Conference facilities.
Currency exchange. Disabled: access. Fax. Fitness centre.
Laundry. Lift. Non-smoking rooms (20). Safe. Sauna.
Solarium. Swimming pool.* **Room services** *Hair-dryer.
Minibar. Radio. Room service. Telephone. TV.*

Thermal Hotel Margitsziget

*XIII. Margitsziget (111 1000/fax 153 3029). Bus 26
from Nyugati.* **Rates** *single* DM220-DM270; *double*
DM270-DM320; *suite* DM440-DM540; *extra bed* DM50.
Credit AmEx, DC, EC, JCB, MC, V.
A bustling place in the summer, the rooms are small with
outdated furnishings reflecting the rather dated 1970s look
of the entire hotel. Air-conditioning is often inadequate and
in summer open windows lead to copious mosquito bites.
However, the spa facilities are extensive, the restaurant next
door at the Ramada is pleasant, and the park on the rest
of the island a nice retreat. Taxis waiting outside the hotel
are known to charge exorbitantly; ordering a cab from the
concierge is recommended.
Hotel services *Air-conditioning. Babysitting. Bars (2).
Beauty salon. Business centre. Car park (Ft1,000, free
outside). Conference facilities. Currency exchange.
Disabled: access. Hair-dryer. Laundry. Lift. Non-smoking
rooms (46). Safe. Sauna. Solarium. Swimming pool.*
Room services *Minibar. Radio. Room service.
Telephone. TV.*

Buda

Hotel Aquincum

*III. Árpád fejedelem útja 94 (250 3360/250 4114/fax
250 4672). HÉV Árpád hid.* **Rates** *single* DM197-
DM272; *double* DM242-DM315; *suite* DM430. **Credit**
AmEx, DC, EC, JCB, MC, V.
Actually one of the pleasantest hotels in Budapest, the
Aquincum now claims to give five-star service after upgrad-
ing services. Built as a spa hotel, it hasn't quite reached
luxury level yet, but rates are extremely reasonable for what
you get. Skip the restaurant.
Hotel services *Air-conditioning. Babysitting. Bars (3).
Beauty salon. Car park (Ft1,200, free outside).
Conference facilities. Currency exchange. Disabled: access.
Fax. Laundry. Lift. Non-smoking rooms (16). Restaurants
(2). Safe.* **Room services** *Hair-dryer. Minibar. Radio.
Room service. Telephone. TV.*

Novotel Budapest Centrum

*XII. Alkotás utca 63-67 (186 9588/fax 166 5636). Tram
61 from Moszkva tér.* **Rates** single DM140-DM195;
double DM150-DM220; *suite* DM260-DM285; *extra bed*
DM46. **Credit** AmEx, DC, EC, JCB, MC, V.
The Budapest Conference Centre next door and a convenient
location for motorists are the only outstanding features.
Almost solely catering to businessmen, average rooms go
with the 1982 building. Facilities include Budapest's first
bowling alley.
Hotel services *Air-conditioning. Babysitting. Bars (2).
Beauty salon. Business centre. Car park. Conference
facilities. Currency exchange. Hair-dryer. Laundry. Lift.
Non-smoking rooms (40). Restaurants (3).* **Room
services** *Minibar. Radio. Room service. Safe. Telephone.
TV.*

Hotel Flamenco

*XI. Tas vezér utca 7 (161 2250/166 9619/fax 165 8007).
Tram 61 Tas vezér utca.* **Rates** *single* DM150-DM200;
double DM180-DM250; *suite* DM210-DM450; *extra bed*
DM50-DM60. **Credit** AmEx, DC, EC, JCB, MC, V.
A standard Socialist monstrosity from the outside, the

HG

HUNGUEST HOTELS
— traditional hungarian hospitality —

IF YOU WISH TO SPEND YOUR WEEKEND IN PLEASANT SURROUNDINGS OR LONG FOR A REAL RECREATION IN HUNGARY WE ARE PLEASED TO BE AT YOUR REQUEST. OUR HOTELS ARE LOCATED AT THE MOST BEAUTIFUL AND POPULAR HOLIDAY RESORTS OF HUNGARY. TAKING THIS OPPORTUNITY WE WOULD LIKE TO OFFER YOU SOME HOTELS WHICH TRULY REPRESENT OUR SERVICES.

HOTEL FORRÁS – Szeged,	Tel.:	62/430-130
HOTEL FLÓRA – Eger,	Tel.:	36/320-211
HOTEL RÉPCE – Bükfürdő,	Tel.:	94/358-058
HOTEL KIKELET – Pécs,	Tel.:	72/310-777
HOTEL SZILVÁS – Szilvásvárad,	Tel.:	36/355-159
HOTEL ÓZON – Mátraháza,	Tel.:	37/374-004
HOTEL SZIESZTA – Sopron,	Tel.:	99/314-260
HOTEL POSTÁS – Hévíz,	Tel.:	84/342-956
HOTEL HELIOS – Hévíz,	Tel.:	83/342-895
HOTEL AZUR – Siófok,	Tel.:	84/312-419
HOTEL PARK – Balatonföldvár,	Tel.:	84/340-118
HOTEL ERKEL – Gyula,	Tel.:	66/463-555
HOTEL NAGYERDŐ – Debrecen,	Tel.:	52/410-588
HOTEL BÉKE – Hajdúszoboszló,	Tel.:	52/361-411
HOTEL NAGYSZÁLLÓ – Galyatető,	Tel.:	37/376-011
HOTEL PALOTA – Lillafüred,	Tel.:	46/311-411
HOTEL MARÓNI – Sopron,	Tel.:	99/312-549
HOTEL FREYA – Zalakaros,	Tel.:	93/340-125
HOTEL PANORÁMA – Hévíz,	Tel.:	84/341-074
HOTEL EZÜSTPART – Siófok,	Tel.:	84/350-622
HOTEL FORTUNA – Balatonfüred,	Tel.:	86/343-037
HOTEL GIUSEPPE – Balatonlelle,	Tel.:	85/350-433

Flamenco's interior is a pleasant surprise with comfortable furnishings and professional staff. The coffee shop atrium is especially nice, as is the outside terrace restaurant with its view of the adjacent park and supposedly bottomless lake. Promising cave-like nightclub in basement. Enormous suites and not too far from the central business district.
Hotel services *Air-conditioning. Babysitting. Bars (2). Beauty salon. Business centre. Car park (Ft11,000 underground, Ft300 on roof). Conference facilities. Currency exchange. Disabled: access. Laundry. Lift. Non-smoking rooms (30). Safe. Sauna. Solarium. Swimming pool. Restaurant (2).* **Room services** *Hair-dryer. Minibar. Radio. Room service. Telephone. TV.*

Pest

K+K Hotel Opera
VI. Révay utca 24 (269 0222/269 1100/fax 269 0230). M1 Opera. **Rates** *single* DM173-DM240; *double* DM228-DM295; *extra bed* DM50-DM65. **Credit** AmEx, DC, EC, MC, V.
The ultra-modern interior radiates Austrian efficiency. Quiet, immaculate rooms, attention to detail, and a big buffet breakfast make a pleasant stay almost inevitable.
Hotel services *Air-conditioning. Babysitting. Bar. Car park (DM13). Conference facilities. Currency exchange. Fax. Laundry. Lift. Snack bar.* **Room services** *Hair-dryer. Minibar. Radio. Room service. Safe. Telephone. TV.*

Grand Hotel Hungária
VII. Rákóczi út 90 (322 9050/322 9150/fax 268 1999). M2 Keleti. **Rates** *single* DM121 DM220; *double* DM146-DM270; *triple* DM203-DM370; *suite* DM 370; *extra bed* DM70-DM100. **Credit** AmEx, DC, EC, JCB, MC, V.
A jovial atmosphere pervades a lobby buzzing with tour groups. Budapest's largest hotel has extensive, though not exceptional, restaurant and conference facilities. Rooms generally comfortable, but varying greatly in size.
Hotel services *Air-conditioning. Babysitting. Bars (2). Beauty salon. Car park (Ft1,020). Conference facilities. Currency exchange. Fax. Fitness centre. Laundry. Lift. Restaurants (2). Safe. Sauna. Solarium. Tennis court.* **Room services** *Minibar. Radio. Room service. Telephone. TV.*

Hotel Astoria
V. Kossuth Lajos utca 19-21 (117 3411/fax 118 6798). M2 Astoria. **Rates** *single* DM141-DM184; *double* DM184-DM242; *extra bed* DM48. **Credit** AmEx, DC, EC, JCB, MC, V.
Built between 1912-14 and lending its name to the busy intersection on which it stands, the Astoria is reasonable, central and reeks of old Mitteleuropa. Sitting in the elegant panelled and chandeliered café, it's easy to imagine why this was the favorite hangout of Nazi officers during WWII – though its proximity to the District VII ghetto must also have been a factor. Managed by the state-owned HungarHotels, the service is somewhat offhand. The spacious rooms on the street side are noisy, the smaller rooms in back more peaceful. The bar, alas, was at press time about to be converted into a McDonald's, but the baroque dining room has to be one of the most spectacular places to breakfast in Budapest.
Hotel services *Babysitting. Cafe. Car park. Conference facilities. Currency exchange. Disabled: access. Fax. Hair-dryers. Laundry. Lift. Restaurant. Safe.* **Room services** *Minibar. Radio. Telephone. TV.*

Hotel Taverna
V. Váci utca 20 (138 4999/fax 118 7188). M3 Ferenciek tere. **Rates** *single* DM172-DM196; *double* DM222-DM251; *triple* DM276-DM311. **Credit** AmEx, DC, EC, JCB, MC, V.
A standard business hotel right in the middle of the pedestrian district on Váci utca with one of the most informative

The **Hotel Astoria** *– reeks of Mitteleuropa.*

tourist information centres in the city. Some of the rooms are rather cramped.
Hotel services *Air-conditioning (96 rooms). Babysitting. Bar. Beauty salon. Car park (DM22). Conference facilities. Currency exchange. Fax. Laundry. Lift. Non-smoking rooms (45). Sauna. Solarium. Restaurant.* **Room services** *Hair-dryer. Minibar. Radio. Room service. Safe. Telephone. TV.*

Moderate
Buda

Alba Hotel Budapest
I. Apor Péter utca 3 (175 9244/fax 175 9899). Bus 16 Clark Ádám tér. **Rates** *single* DM140-DM165; *double* DM180-DM200; *extra bed* DM50 (payment in hard currency only). **Credit** AmEx, DC, EC, JCB, MC, V.
Owned by a Swiss chain and positioned at the foot of Castle Hill, the top three floors are air-conditioned and give a pigeon's eye view of the Víziváros. Rooms are spartan but spacious enough with large, well-lit bathrooms, and the three-bedded room is almost big enough to be a suite. The lobby is also rather stark, with only a small bar, but there's a large breakfast buffet and a Greek restaurant next door.
Hotel services *Babysitting. Bar. Car park (DM22). Conference facilities. Currency exchange. Fax. Hair-dryer. Laundry. Lift. Safe.* **Room services** *Minibar. Room service. Telephone. TV.*

Petneházy Country Club Hotel
II. Feketefej utca 2-4 (176 5992/176 5982/fax 176 5738). Bus 56 (red) Adyliget. **Rates** *small bungalow (2-4 beds)* DM165-DM195; *large bungalow (4-6 people)* DM215-

DM245; *extra bed* DM 30. **Credit** AmEx, DC, EC, EnRt, JCB, MC, V.

Also a country club for the local bourgeoisie, the 'hotel' is actually 45 private bungalows – four of which have disabled access – with a central building housing the reception, pool, restaurant and other services. Location far from the centre is made up for by a peaceful setting and loads of facilities for sport lovers. Horseback riding next door, organised bus and boat excursions, and pig killings during winter months (*see chapter* **Budapest By Season**).
Hotel services *Babysitting. Bar. Bicycles. Car park. Conference facilities. Currency exchange. Disabled: access. Fax. Laundry. Restaurant. Sauna. Solarium. Swimming pool. Tennis court.* **Room services** *Kitchen. Minibar. Room service. Safe. Sauna. Telephone. TV.*

Hotel Victória

I. Bem rakpart 11 (201 8644/fax 201 5816). Bus 16 Clark Ádám tér. **Rates** *single* DM140-DM185; *double* DM150-DM195; *apartment* DM250-DM350; *extra bed* DM60-DM80. **Credit** AmEx, DC, EC, JCB, MC, V.

One of Budapest's first private *panziók* occupies a townhouse site below the castle facing the Danube within easy reach of the main sights. Rooms are big, commanding a view of the river and it's far less expensive than the hotels on the Pest side. No restaurant, but the friendly staff can recommend good choices in the neighbourhood. American breakfast.
Hotel services *Air-conditioning. Babysitting. Bar. Car park. Currency exchange. Fax. Laundry. Lift. Sauna.* **Room services** *Hair-dryer. Minibar. Radio. Room service (drinks). Safe. Telephone. TV.*

Orion Hotel

I. Döbrentei utca 13 (156 8583/fax 175 5418). Tram 18, 19/bus 78 Krisztina körút. **Rates** *single* DM95-DM145; *double* DM130-DM198; *extra bed* DM32. **Credit** AmEx, DC, EC, MC.

Frequented by academic guests of local universities, the Orion is small but convenient for the centre, and the restaurant serves inexpensive Hungarian food.
Hotel services *Air-conditioning. Bar. Car park. Currency exchange. Fax. Lift. Restaurant. Safe.* **Room services** *Hair-dryer. Radio. Refrigerator. Room service. Telephone. TV.*

SAS Club Hotel

XII. Törökbálinti út 51-53 (248 0419, 166 9899/fax 248 0419). Bus 8, 8A Oltvány utca. **Rates** *single* DM60-DM132; *double* DM80-DM170; *apartment* DM149-DM256; *extra bed* DM28-DM32. **Credit** AmEx, DC, EC, JCB, MC, V.

Rooms in the two latest additions to the complex are quite large and comfortable though the older ones (dating from 1988) are now showing their age. Service is outstanding from young, helpful staff. Sports facilities in private health club down the road.
Hotel services *Babysitting. Bar. Bowling alley. Car park. Conference facilities. Currency exchange. Fax. Fitness centre. Hair-dryer. Laundry. Restaurant. Safe. Sauna. Solarium. Swimming pool. Tennis.* **Room services** *Radio. Refrigerator. Telephone. TV.*

Hotel Dunapart

I. Szilágyi Dezső tér, Alsó rakpart (155 9001/155 9201/fax 155 3770). M2 Batthyány tér. **Rates** *single* DM80-DM150; *double* DM130-DM180; *suite* DM170-DM220. **Credit** AmEx, DC, EC, JCB, MC, V.

Tiny air-conditioned cabin rooms look out towards an unusual water-level view of Parliament from this floating hotel. The restaurant is rather expensive, but the fine view south from the terrace on the back deck is well worth it on summer evenings.
Hotel services *Air-conditioning. Bar. Currency*

exchange. Fax. Laundry. Restaurant. Safe. **Room services** *Radio. Room service. Telephone. TV.*

Walzer Hotel

XII. Németvölgyi út 110 (267 1300/fax 267 1297). Tram 59 Liptó utca. **Rates** *single* DM125; *double* DM160; *triple* DM215; *extra bed* DM30. **Credit** AmEx, DC, EC, JCB, MC, V.

A newly built 'château' in which rooms with reproduction Biedermeier furniture look out over the garden neighbourhood and nearby cemetery. Immaculate, spacious bathrooms, pleasant common areas and well-appointed dining room with adjoining garden.
Hotel services *Babysitting. Car park. Currency exchange. Fax. Hair-dryers. Fax. Laundry. Lift. Restaurant. Safe.* **Room services** *Minibar. Radio. Telephone. TV.*

Hotel Panorama

XII. Rege utca 21 (175 0522/fax 175 9727). Bus 21 (red), or cogwheel railway (Fogaskerekű vasút). **Rates** *single* DM65-DM115; *double* DM100-DM150; *bungalow* DM85-DM200. **Credit** AmEx, DC, EC, JCB, MC, V.

The pre-WWII building exudes a rustic charm, though private ownership and a 1989 facelift have brought services up to date. Steps away from the top end of the cogwheel railway on Szabadság Hill, all of the rooms offer stunning views of either the city or the wooded hills behind. Fifty-six wood-panelled bungalows nestled among tall fir trees cluster around a small swimming pool and sauna/solarium creating the impression of a mountain resort transplanted into the heart of the city.
Hotel services *Bars (3). Car park. Conference facilities. Currency exchange. Fax. Laundry. Lift. Restaurant. Safe. Sauna. Solarium. Swimming pool.* **Room services** *Minibar. Radio. Telephone. TV.*

Pest

Hotel Liget

VI. Dózsa György út 106 (269 5300/269 5318/fax 269 5329). M1 Hősök tere. **Rates** *single* DM120-DM175; *double* DM146-DM202; *triple* DM230-DM256; *extra bed* DM42. **Credit** AmEx, DC, EC, JCB, MC, V.

Though pleasantly situated next to the Városliget, the Liget has a rather stark modern feel. Recently built by an Austrian-Hungarian firm, the place targets people on the move. Common areas are minimal and the entrance is dominated by the ramp to the car park. However, the 139 rooms are clean, spacious and 55 of them have air-conditioning.
Hotel services *Bar. Car park (DM12). Conference facilities. Currency exchange. Fax. Laundry. Lift. Massage. Non-smoking rooms (24). Safe. Sauna. Solarium.* **Room services** *Minibar. Radio. Room service. Telephone. TV.*

Hotel Erzsébet

V. Károlyi Mihály utca 11-15 (138 2111/fax 118 9237). M3 Ferenciek tere. **Rates** *single* DM125-DM155; *double* DM155-DM195; *triple* DM200-DM257. **Credit** AmEx, DC, EC, V.

The dark wood and beige interior betrays Communist-era origins, but staff are friendly and rooms air-conditioned. The restaurant/bar downstairs is rather naff with rustic illustrations of the epic adventures of Hungarian hero János Vitéz and the upstairs restaurant is reminiscent of a cafeteria. But central location and conference facilities make it popular with business travellers who want to avoid the pricier downtown hotels.
Hotel services *Air-conditioning. Bar. Babysitting. Car park. Currency exchange. Fax. Laundry. Lift. Hair-dryers. Restaurants (2). Safe.* **Room services** *Minibar. Radio. Telephone. TV.*

Hotel Art

*V. Királyi Pál utca 12 (266 2166/fax 266 2170). M3
Kálvin tér* **Rates** *single* DM95, *double* DM150; *suite*
DM200; *extra bed* DM50. **Credit** AmEx, DC, EC, JCB,
MC, V.

Near the quiet end of the Váci utca, this new small hotel is con-
venient for the centre and there are several good bars in the
neighbourhood. The attempt at modern decor leaves the pub-
lic areas rather stark, though the rooms themselves are very
good for the price. American breakfast.
Hotel services *Air-conditioning. Bar. Car park
(Ft1,000 a day). Conference facilities. Currency exchange.
Disabled: access. Fax. Fitness centre. Hair-dryer. Laundry.
Lift. Safe. Sauna.* **Room services** *Minibar. Room
Service. Telephone. TV.*

Nemzeti Hotel

*VIII. József körút 4 (269 9310/fax 114 0019). M2
Blaha Lujza.* **Rates** *single* DM79-DM130; *double* DM99-
DM160; *extra bed* DM30-DM35. **Credit** AmEx, DC, EC,
JCB, MC, V.

Red velvet chairs in the time-worn lobby looking out over
busy Blaha Lujza tér, a grand staircase and friendly staff are
this 100-year-old hotel's best features. Refurbishment in 1987
didn't quite bring this grand establishment back to its former glory and the rooms are still rather dark.
Hotel services *Bar. Car park (Ft600 a day). Conference
facilities. Currency exchange. Fax. Hair-dryers. Laundry.
Lift. Non-smoking rooms (10). Restaurant. Safe.* **Room
services** *Minibar. Radio. Telephone. TV.*

Hotel Ibis

*XIII. Dózsa György út 65 (129 0200/140 8393/fax 140
8316). M3 Dózsa György út.* **Rates** *single* DM72-DM105;
double DM100-DM170; *extra bed* DM30. **Credit** AmEx,
DC, EC, MC, V.

Part of the Ibis chain and with two-star services it's an economical hotel choice. Even though remodelling will be completed by summer 1996, the new room furnishings aren't
much of an improvement on the old décor.
Hotel services *Bar. Car park. Conference facilities.
Currency exchange. Disco. Fax. Hair-dryers. Lift. Non-
smoking rooms (66). Restaurants (2). Safe.* **Room
services** *Minibar. Radio. Room service. Telephone. TV.*

Budget
Buda

Gizella Panzió

XII. Arató utca 42b (182 0324). Tram 59 Farkasréti tér.
Rates *single* DM90; *double* DM120; *apartment* DM140.
No credit cards.
Economical use of space was the key to cramming all the
extras into this comfy hillside *panzió.* Nice views from most
rooms and from pool-side sun terrace.
Hotel services *Bar. Currency exchange. Fax. Fitness
room. Hair-dryer. Laundry. Safe. Sauna. Solarium.
Swimming pool.* **Room services** *Minibar. Radio.
Telephone. TV.*

Beatrix Panzió

II. Széher út 3 (275 0550). Bus 56 Kelemen László.
Rates *single* DM70-DM90; *double* DM80-DM100; *triple*
DM90-DM120; *apartment* DM100-DM150. **No credit
cards.**
The 12 rooms here are comfortable, though nothing special.
The location is good on a quiet street not far from Moszkva
tér. Guided tours available of the city and other destinations
in Hungary and weekly barbecues in the summer in the pret-
ty garden at the rear. American breakfast.
Hotel services *Bar. Car park. Currency exchange.*

The **Thermal Hotel Helia** *– de luxe spa hotel.*

Disabled: access. Fax. Safe. Sauna. **Room services**
Telephone. TV.

Buda Center Hotel

*II. Csalogány utca 23 (201 6333/fax 201 7843). Bus 39
Fazekas utca.* **Rates** *single* DM65-DM100; *double* DM80-
DM120; *triple* DM100-DM140; *apartment* DM200. **Credit**
AmEx, DC, EC, JCB, MC, V.
Conference facilities are in the office space which takes up
the other half of the building; services are minimal. Never-
theless, rooms are clean with new furniture. The downstairs
bar has an impressive selection of beers (including Guinness)
and the restaurant is Chinese.
Hotel services *Air-conditioning (DM30). Babysitting.
Bar. Car park (DM10). Conference facilities. Currency
exchange. Fax. Hair-dryers. Laundry. Lift. Game room.
Non-smoking rooms (10). Restaurant. Safe.* **Room
services** *Minibar. Telephone. TV.*

Queen Mary Hotel

*XII. Béla Király út 47 (274 4000/274 4001/274
4002/fax 156 8377). Bus 28 Béla Király út.* **Rates** *single*
DM110; *double* DM120; *triple* DM140; *apartment* DM140-
DM165. **Credit** AmEx, DC, EC, JCB, MC, V.
Popular with families bringing their children to the Pető
Institute (for children suffering from cerebral palsy) nearby,
this quiet *panzió* high in the Buda Hills will gladly arrange
discounts for extended stays.
Hotel services *Bar. Car park. Currency exchange. Fax.
Laundry. Safe. Sauna. Solarium. Restaurant.* **Room
services** *Minibar. Telephone. TV.*

Molnár Panzió

*XII. Fodor utca 143 (209 2973/209 2974/fax 209
2973/209 2974). Bus 53 Rácz Aladár.utca.* **Rates** *single*

DM70-DM90; *double* DM90-DM110; *triple* DM110-DM130.
Credit AmEx, DC, EC, JCB, MC, V 1 5 per cent charge.
Each of the 15 rooms are unique, tastefully decorated and
homey, and the service is meticulous. Spacious, airy bathrooms in several rooms – complete with sunken tubs – and
two wood-panelled rooms under the domed roof with balconies overlooking southern Pest. Quaint A-frame cabin in
the beautiful back garden. Opt to share a bathroom and
shave a little off the price. The terrace restaurant downstairs
is an excellent spot for summertime meals and 18 more
rooms should be available by the summer of 1996.
Hotel services *Bar. Car park. Currency exchange. Fax.
Fitness room. Hair-dryers. Laundry. Restaurant. Safe.
Sauna.* **Room services** *Minibar. Telephone. TV.*

UHU Villa

*II. Keselyű utca 1 (175 3876/fax 275 1002). Tram 56
Vadaskerti utca.* **Rates** *single* DM50-DM90; *double* DM80-
DM110; *apartment* DM100-DM140. **No credit cards.**
Turn-of-the-century villa nestled among tall fir trees in a
quiet valley ten minutes from Moszkva tér. Small but cosy
rooms and beautiful garden. American breakfast.
Hotel services *Bar. Car park. Fax. Safe. Solarium.*
Room services *Minibar. Telephone. TV.*

Kulturinnov Hotel

*I. Szentháromság tér 6 (155 0122/fax 175 1886). M2
Moszkva tér then Várbusz.* **Rates** *single* DM65; *double*
DM90; *extra bed* DM37. **Credit** AmEx, DC, EC, JCB,
MC, V.
Location and price are the attractions here in a building that
also houses the Hungarian Cultural Foundation and some of
the National Archives. Upstairs and to the right from the
huge vaulted entry, the dormitory-type rooms have few lux-
uries, but the Mátyás Church and the Castle District are right
outside the door.
Hotel services *Bar. Conference facilities. Fax. Lift.
Safe. Telephone.*

Ábel Panzió

*XI. Ábel Jenő utca 9 (tel/fax 185 6426/209 2537/209
2538).* Tram 61 **Rates** *double* DM80-DM90. **No credit
cards.**
The most beautiful *panzió* in the city. An ivy-covered turn-
of-the-century house set on a quiet side street and fitted with
period furniture in common areas. Rooms are sunny and
clean with simple modern furniture. Breakfast around a common dining table overlooking a terrace and well-kept garden
recalls a mode of travelling long since past.
Hotel services *Bar. Car park. Fax. Hair-dryer. TV.*
Room services *Safe. Telephone.*

Diana Panzió Budapest

*II. Modori utca 14a (274 2110/274 2109/fax 274 2110).
Bus 56 Hársfa étterem.* **Rates** *single* DM50-DM65; *double*
DM60-DM70. **No credit cards.**
High in the Buda Hills, this elegant new three-storey building with a terraced rose garden and well-appointed common
rooms is a hidden treasure. Rooms and bathrooms are generally spacious and several have balconies. Friendly service,
kitchen facilities available on request and rate reductions for
longer stays. American breakfast.
Hotel services *Bar. Billiards. Car park. Computer
access. Fax. Kitchen. Laundry. Safe. Sauna. Weight room.*
Room services *Telephone. TV.*

Hotel Express

*XII. Beethoven utca 7-9 (tel/fax 175 3082). Tram 59
Királyhágó tér.* **Rates** *single* DM29; *double* DM48; *triple*
DM63; *quad* DM76. *No credit cards.*
One of the few remaining cheap hotels is frequented by
people with backpacks. Showers and toilets in the hall, but
rooms are clean if a bit worn.
Hotel services *Car park. Currency exchange. Fax. Safe.*

Spa Hotels

Budapest is the only European capital that
is also a major spa town. Consequently,
Budapest has long been a destination for
travellers seeking the benefits of the warm
mineral-laden waters.

The **Thermal Hotel Helia**, **Gellért**,
Thermal Hotel Aquincum, **Thermal
Hotel Margitsziget** and the adjacent **Ramada** all have spa facilities on the premises.
Besides swimming pools, saunas and thermal
pools of varying temperatures (use of which
is included in room price), they all provide a
range of medical and beauty services which
include massage, mud packs, hydrotherapy
and medical examinations. Most also cater
for special dietary requirements and have
special packages for different 'cures' lasting
from a weekend to several weeks.

Budai Sport Centrum

*XII. Jánoshegyi út (202 4397/275 4029/fax 156 7167).
Bus 21 (red).* **Rates** *single* Ft3,600; *double* 4,500; *triple*
Ft5,000. **No credit cards.**
High above the city on János Hill about 20 minutes from
Moszkva tér, this is the place for Budapest's most inexpen-
sive rooms with a view. Lots of sport and relaxation possi-
bilities in the acres and acres of parkland nearby.
Hotel services *Bar. Car park. Fax. Fitness room.
Jacuzzi. Laundry. Safe. Sauna. Solarium. Tennis.
Restaurant.* **Room services** *Radio. Refrigerator.
Telephone. TV.*

Pest

Benczúr Hotel

*VI. Benczúr utca 35 (342 7970/fax 342 1558). M1
Hősök tere.* **Rates** *single* DM47-DM125; *double* DM92-
DM146; *triple* DM103-DM177. **No credit cards.**
The main attractions of this rather stuffy hotel are reason-
able prices to go with a central location for adequate services.
Tacky décor survived an early 1990s renovation, as did
rather dark cramped rooms. The desk staff have difficulties
with anything other than basic English, though you can get
your teeth fixed by the in-house dentist.
Hotel services *Bars (2). Car park. Conference
facilities. Coffee shop. Currency exchange. Dentist.
Fax. Laundry. Lift. Restaurant. Souvenir shop. Thai
massage.* **Room services** *Minibar. Radio.
Telephone. TV.*

Lucky Hotel

*XIV. Vezér utca 180 (183 5300/fax 251 2179). Trolley
77, 82 Komócsy utca.* **Rates** *single* DM80-DM90; *double*
DM100-DM110; *apartment* DM140-DM160. **Credit**
AmEx, DC, EC, JCB, MC, V.
Rather far out in Zugló, this brand-new private *panzió* is nevertheless good value and will arrange discounts for longer
stays. Rooms dominated by too much yellow still manage to
be spacious, though the tiled shower stalls are reminiscent
of a gym locker room.
Hotel services *Air-conditioning (8 rooms). Bar. Car*

The **Backpack Guest House** *organises outings for cavers, water-skiers and bungee jumpers.*

park (Ft300 a day). Conference facilities. Currency exchange. Fax. Hair-dryer. Laundry. Restaurant. **Room services** *Minibar. Room service. Safe. Telephone. TV.*

Richter Panzió

XIV. Thököly út 111 (163 3956/163 5735/fax 163 3956). Bus 7 Amerikai út. **Rates** *single* DM70-DM90; *double* DM80-DM100. **No credit cards.**
On the inner edge of a Pest garden district, the Richter is in a pleasant neighbourhood less than ten minutes from the city centre. Staff are helpful, though services are minimal.
Hotel services *Bar. Car park. Fax. Jacuzzi. Laundry. Sauna. Safe.* **Room services** *Telephone. TV.*

Passzió Panzió

XIV. Zoborhegy utca 34B (184 2098). Trolleybus 77 Egressy út/Cinkótai út. **Rates** *single* DM80; *double* DM70 DM80; *triple* DM80-DM90. **No credit cards.**
For neither the faint of heart nor wobbly of feet, the narrow stairways leading to the rooms are perilous at best. Wood-panelled rooms are plain but comfortable. The restaurant and bar feign elegance, but eating out on the terrace recalls a country *csárda* with inexpensive, hearty Hungarian food.
Hotel services *Bar. Car park. Currency exchange. Fax. Laundry. Restaurant.* **Room services** *Radio. Telephone. TV.*

Hotel River Club

XIII. Népsziget út 18 (221 4167). M3 Gyöngyösi utca go down Meder utca and walk over the bridge on to the island. **Open** Mar-Oct. **Rates** *single, double* Ft1,600; *4/5 bed* Ft1,400. **No credit cards.**
A relaxed atmosphere, ample grounds, boating and tennis opportunities, and tasty fresh fish on the terrace at the bar across the street make up for sparsely furnished rooms. Formerly the weekend retreat for Budapest party functionaries, Népsziget or 'People's Island' is now truly open to the public. It's a shady quiet haven on the Danube about 20 minutes from the city centre. (*See also chapter* **Sport**).
Hotel services *Bar. Car park. Fax. Safe. Tennis.*

Youth Hostels

Between the beginning of July and the end of August, the most reliable place to find a hostel is Keleti station as regular tourist offices don't list youth hostels. Several new companies have sprung up to take over and book student dormitories vacant during the summer and all of them have aggressive roving representatives at Keleti to lure you to their hostel. They'll find you, sometimes even before you leave the train. Expect to pay between Ft700-Ft1,000 for dormitories and Ft1,400-Ft2,400 for singles and doubles. You don't have to have an ISIC or Youth Hostel card, but production of one will get you a discount. Services are what you'd expect, though most don't have a curfew. Breakfast is extra, but sheets and hot showers are usually provided. More Than Ways is the largest summer hostel organisation with 11 kollégiums and one year-round hotel.

Ananda Youth Hostel

XIV. Kőseg utca 21 (tel/fax 220 2413). M2 Örs Vezér tér. **Rates** *double* Ft950; *4 bed* Ft850; *dorm* Ft650; *breakfast* Ft80. **Credit** AmEx.
Quiet family-run hostel at end of metro line.
Laundry. Lockers. Kitchen. Safe. Sheets (Ft60).

Backpack Guest House

XIII. Takács Menyhért utca 33 (185 5089). Bus 7 Tétényi út. **Rates** *dorm* (5-7 bed) Ft700-Ft800. **No credit cards.**
The party hostel in Budapest is always packed with international youth looking to spend their travellers' cheques in a place where beer is affordable. Kitchen walls covered with pictures and postcards lend homey atmosphere to late-night

drinking sessions. Caving, water skiing and bungee jump-
ing excursions for the brave. Overflow dorm down the road.
Laundry (Ft400).

Citadella Hotel
XI. Citadella sétány (166 5794/fax 186 0505).
Bus 27 from Móricz Zsigmond körtér. **Rates** Ft800.
No credit cards.
Sleep in ten- to 14-bed dormitories inside the Citadella over-
looking the Danube. Standard hotel rooms also available.
One of the most popular cheap lodgings in town.
Bar. Currency exchange. Fax. Safe (Ft100).

Csillebérci Ifjúsági Központ
*XII. Konkoly Thege utca 21 (156 3533/275 4033/fax
175 9327). Bus 21 (red) Normafa.* **Rates** *double*
DM18-DM22; *triple* DM23-DM28; *bungalow* (2-4 bed)
DM45-DM60; *camping* DM9-DM14; *breakfast* DM4.5.
No credit cards.
Youth hostel with 200 beds in the former Pioneer camp
grounds. Extensive sport facilities.
*Bar. Sauna. Swimming pool. Telephone. Tennis court.
Restaurant.*

More Than Ways
*XIII. Dózsa György út 152 (140 8585/129 8644/fax 120
8425) M3 Dózsa György út.* **Rates** *single* Ft1,580; *double*
Ft1,280-1,560; *dorm* Ft1,080. **No credit cards.**
Hostel at this location open all year, 11 other collegiums in
summer, and an information booth at Keleti station.
Bar. Kitchen. Laundry. Lockers. Safe.

Camping

Numerous camping grounds surround Budapest,
though services and prices vary. A brochure,
Camping, is available free at Tourinform and lists
camping areas throughout the country. For group

camping, contact individual sites. Prices vary
depending on size of sites and facilities available.
Several are located on the Danube and offer open
water swimming, though considering the polluted
state of the river, this is not advised (nor is eating
anything you fish out of it). In general, expect to
pay Ft150-Ft650 for a tent site, Ft100-Ft900 for a
caravan site and Ft150-Ft450 per person plus
small tourism tax.

Csillebérci Autóscamping
*XII. Konkoly Thege utca 21 (156 3533/275 4033/fax
175 9327). Bus 21 (red) Normafa.*
*Bungalows for rent. Showers. Restaurant. Post office.
Swimming pool. Tennis.*

Hárs-Hegyi Camping
*II. Hárshegyi út 7 (115 1482/fax 176 1921). Bus 22
from Moszkva tér.*
Bungalows for rent. Showers. Restaurant.

Hawaii Camping
*XIII. Népsziget 26 (189 3347/fax 129 5682). M3
Gyöngyös utca.*
*Fishing. Food shop. Disabled: toilet. Music club. Showers.
Swimming and boating in open water.*

Római Camping
*III. Szentendrei út 189 (168 6260/fax 250 0426). HÉV
Rómaifürdő.*
*Bungalows for rent. Food shop. Medical office. Music
club. Restaurant. Propane. Swimming pool.*

Tündérhegyi 'Feeberg' Camping
*XII. Szilassy utca 8 (06 60 336 256). Bus 28 from
Moszkva tér.*
Bungalows for rent. Showers. Swimming pool.

The **Citadella Hotel** – *a youth hostel and one of the most popular cheap lodgings in town.*

Budapest by Season

From pig-slaying to chucking perfume at village women, Hungarians certainly know how to have a good time. Just make sure you do it in season.

Seasons change suddenly in Hungary but, come snow or sunstroke, Hungarians do things by tradition – many of which have managed to survive 40 years of Communism. Of the two main holidays, New Year's Eve (*Szilveszter*) is party time, but Christmas (*Karácsony*) is a stay-at-home affair when Budapest closes down.

Bear in mind that while birthdays are celebrated with family, 'name days' provide Hungarians with a regular excuse to have a drink with friends.

Information & Tickets

For regular information on events, read *Budapest Week* or the *Budapest Sun*, English-language weeklies available at most newsstands. Or try:

Tourinform
V. Sütő utca 2 (117 9800). M1, M2, M3 Deák tér. **Open** *Apr-Oct* 8am-8pm daily; *Nov-Mar* 8am-3pm Sat-Sun.

Nemzeti Filharmónia
V. Vörösmarty tér 1 (118 0441). M1 Vörösmarty tér. **Open** 10am-1.30pm, 2pm-6pm, Mon-Fri. **No credit cards.**

Central Theatre Booking Office
VI. Andrássy út 18 (112 0000). M1 Operaház. **Open** 9am-1pm, 1.45pm-6pm, Mon-Thur; 9am-4.45pm Fri. **No credit cards.**
Branch: *II. Moszkva tér 3 (212 5678). M2 Moszkva tér.*

Public Holidays

New Year's Day (1 Jan); **Revolution Day** (15 Mar); **Easter Monday; International Labour Day** (1 May); **Whit Monday; Saint Stephen's Day** (20 Aug); **Remembrance Day** (23 Oct); **Christmas Day, Boxing Day** (25, 26 Dec).

Spring

Fresh breezes blow in from the Buda Hills and the Budapest Spring Festival ushers in more modest counterparts in Debrecen, Kaposvár, Kecskemét, Sopron, Szentendre and Szombathely. Cash tills start ringing from the first signs of tourist buses in March.

March 15 Public Holiday
Revolution Day commemorates poet Sándor Petőfi reciting his *Nemzeti Dal* (national song) on the steps of the National Museum in 1848, the event commonly held to have launched the national revolution. Budapest gets decked out in red, white and green and there are gatherings at Petőfi's statue in Március 15 tér and outside the National Museum.

Budapest Spring Festival
Tickets and information: *Festival Ticket Service, V. Bárczy I. utca 1-3 (118 9570, 266 4051).* **Box office** *Feb-Apr* 10am-6pm Mon-Fri.
The biggest event in the arts calendar, so tickets sell out early. The accent is firmly on classical music, but dance and folk music are also featured. *See chapters* **Theatre & Dance** *and* **Music: Classical & Opera**.

Easter Monday Public Holiday
Among the traditional painted eggs and chocolates you may see the pagan rite of *locsolkodás* (the splashing), when males chase females and spray them with cheap perfume. This is less common in Budapest than it is in rural areas.

Labour Day
1 May (public holiday).
No longer a forced wave at medal-festooned leaders along Dósza György út, May Day still brings a few old Communists out of the woodwork and into the main parks to indulge in beer, sausages and a moan about today's prices. It's also becoming popular as a spring event for families with lots of music and events for children.

IFABO
Hungexpo, Budapest International Fair Centre, X. Albertirsai út 10 (263 6000). M2 Örs vezér tere then bus 100. **Open** 8am-3pm daily. **Information** *ECI Expoconcept Int GmbH, Stiftgaße 31, Vienna 1070 (43 1 523 7011).* **Date** May.
Hungary's largest computer fair, with more than a thousand companies showing off the latest communications and data processing technology.

Summer

Summer is long and sticky. Budapesters tend to leave the heat and traffic fumes to the tourists: the city empties at weekends and for most of August. In July, there are events all over Hungary: the open-air arts festival in Szeged, the Kaláka Folk Festival

On 20 August, **St Stephen's Day,** *Hungarians celebrate their founding father, Szent István.*

by Diósgyőr Castle in Miskolc, the international dance and folk festival at the National Theatre in Győr, the season of concerts at the National Theatre in Pécs or the Horse Fair in the Hortobágy. *See chapter* **Trips Out of Town.**

Book Week

Information *Mariann Csizmádi, Hungarian Publishers' Association, Tenth Floor, V. Vörösmarty tér 1 (118 4651).* M1 Vörösmarty tér. **Open** 9am-4pm Mon-Thur; 9am-2pm Fri. **Date** first weekend in June.

For more than 60 years Hungarian writers have gathered together, a chance for those living in Transylvania, Slovakia and Vojvodina to catch up on the latest news from the centre of Hungarian-language publishing. Expect a large open-air fair and short theatrical performances in Vörösmarty tér (M1 Vörösmarty tér) and readings at the **Petőfi Museum**, *V. Károlyi Mihály utca 16 (117 3611).* M3 Ferenciek tere. **Open** *Apr-Oct* 10am-6pm Tue-Sun; *Nov-Mar* 10am-4pm. **Admission** Ft 60; Ft20 concessions.

WOMUFE

XI. Budai Parkszínpad. Kosztolányi Dezső tér (166 9849) Tram 6/bus 1, 7, red 1, 27, 40, 127, 153 to Móricz Zsigmond körtér.
Information *Music Mix, V. Váci utca 33.(138 2237)* M3 Ferenciek tere. **Open** 10am-6pm Mon-Fri; 10am-2pm Sat. **No credit cards. Date** June.

Budapest's annual World Music Festival is staged near the supposedly bottomless lake in the park between Kosztolányi Dezső tér and Móricz Zsigmond körtér. Organiser Robert Mandel, one of the world's leading exponents of the cranklute, doesn't have much funding so the three-day programme tends to be a hot-potch of whoever's on tour at the time.

Criminal Expo

Budapest Kongresszusi Központ, XII. Jagelló út 1-3 (186 9588). Bus 8, 8A. **Open** 9am-4pm Mon-Fri.

Information *Compexpo, V. Kálvin tér 5 (117 1933).*
Open 9am-4pm Mon-Thur; 9am-2pm Fri. **Date** June.
Budapest, although much safer than most European cities of its size, is a crossroads for international crime. Since 1992, the Criminal Expo has brought traders together to ply the wares for businesses and individuals to protect themselves against the domestic version.

Budapesti Búcsú

Information *Hungarian Art Festival Federation, V. Vörösmarty tér 1 (117 6222).* **Open** 9am-4pm Mon-Thur; 9am-2pm Fri. **Date** last weekend in June.

The city celebrates the 1991 withdrawal of Soviet troops from Hungary. A weekend of music, dance and theatre in assorted parks and public spaces around town.

Open-air Theatre Summer Festival

Information *Szabad Tér Színház, XII. Városmajor (175 5922).* **Open** 8am-4.30pm daily. **Date** June-Aug.
Outdoor music, dance and theatre at three main venues: Margaret Island Open-air Theatre (111 2496), bus 26; Hilton Hotel Dominican Yard, I. Hess András tér 1-3 (175 1000), M2 Moszkva tér and Várbusz; and the Buda Park Stage, XI. Kosztolányi Dezső tér (166 9849), bus 7. Performances are mostly Hungarian only, but this need not matter for the children's puppet theatre in the afternoons.

BudaFest

Information *VIP-ARTS Management, II. Vöröstorony lejtő 3 (176 7264). Bus 11.* **Open** 10am-5pm Mon-Fri. **Date** mid-Aug.
A week of top-flight performances at the Opera House, VI. Andrássy út 22 (153 0170/131 2550), M1 Opera, open 11am-7pm Tue-Sat, 10am-1pm, 4pm-7pm, when there is a performance. BudaFest is the major arts festival in town over the summer, bringing foreign ballet and opera stars to entertain bewildered rich Americans. *See chapter* **Music: Classical & Opera.**

Hungaroring

Information *Formula 1 Kft, V. Apáczai Csere
János utca11(118 7610). M 1, M2, M3 Deák tér.* **Open**
8am-6pm one month before the event. **Date** second
weekend of Aug.

The major event of the Hungarian sporting year, the Grand
Prix is under continual threat of extinction. In 1995 only last-
minute backing from Parliament persuaded the Formula One
authorities to keep it in the calendar. Most Hungarians cannot afford the Ft 10,000-Ft 20,000 seat prices anyway. Certain
luxury hotels put on special events at the weekend. The
course itself is at Mogyoród, 24km east of Budapest on the
M3 motorway. (*See chapter* **Sport & Fitness**.)

Diáksziget

*Óbudai sziget. HÉV to Filatorigát and cross to the island
or 142 bus.* **Information** from the office rented by
Diáksziget Kft, advertised on posters around town. 1995
office: *IX. Lónyay utca 18B (215 5124). M3 to Kálvin tér.*
Open 10am-6pm. **Date** mid-Aug.

A marriage of celebrations from two ancient cultures, hippy
(Woodstock) and Communist (World Youth Festivals), Diáksziget (Student Island) is the brainchild of former dissident
musician turned media superstar Péter Müller. On an island
north of Budapest, Müller and his team put on seven days
of music, film, dance, theatre and cabaret, keeping admission and camping prices low. If you can't face camping out
for a week, get yourself a day ticket. (*See chapter* **Music:
Rock, Roots & Jazz**.)

St Stephen's Day

Public holiday. **Date** 20 Aug.

The day when Hungarians celebrate their founding father,
Szent István. At 9pm there is a fireworks display from Gellért
Hill, best viewed from the Pest side of Danube, where the
embankment fills with oohing and aahing crowds. The day
also marks the festival of the new bread and every town, village and hamlet stages minor events, the most notable being
the Flower Carnival in Debrecen.

Autumn

Horse chestnuts fall in Castle Hill and Budapesters
regain their city from the tourists, who leave in
droves before seeing the capital at its finest: the
Indian Summer of early autumn. Cultural life
starts with a series of festivals around town and
clubs start bringing bands back from lazing
around Lake Balaton.

Budapest International Wine Festival

Information *Interkoncert, V. Vörösmarty tér 1 (118
4542). M1 Vörösmarty tér.* **Open** 9am-4pm Mon-Thur;
9am-2pm Fri. **Date** Sept.

Grape harvesting (*szüret*) involves wine tasting, folk dancing and general merriment. In Budapest, under-funded wine
companies woo international buyers with chamber concerts
in the Castle District and wine tasting and folk dancing in
Vörösmarty tér. For a better feel of a real *szüret*, head out of
town to Székszard or Eger.

Cosmic Civilisations

Pataky Művelődési Ház, X. Szent László tér 7-14. Bus 9.
Information Sándor Pusztai (173 1334). **Date** Sept.

A day of lectures, films, videos and general discussion about
UFOs, alien abductions and whether God was or was not an
astronaut. Translators can be provided.

The Operaház or Opera House – one of the venues for the **Budapest Autumn Festival**.

Christmas lights along Váci utca.

Budapest International Fair (BNV)
Hungexpo, Budapest International Fair Centre, X.
Albertirsai út 10 (263 6000). M2 Örs vezér tere then bus
100. **Open** 8am-3pm daily. **Date** Sept.
The BNV is Hungary's biggest shop window and 1996 is the centenary as the BNV was launched to celebrate the millennium of the Magyar conquest. Nearly half a million visitors came to the 1994 show, which mainly focused on furniture.

Budapest Autumn Festival
Information *Szabad Tér Jegyiroda, XIII. Hollán Ernő utca 10 (111 4283). Tram 2, 4 or 6 Jászai Mari tér.*
Open *May-Sept* 10am-6pm daily; *Oct-April* noon-6pm daily (to 5pm Fri). **Date** late Sept-mid-Oct.
A contemporary arts festival with the accent on film, fine arts, dance and theatre.
Venues: *Nemzeti Színház, VII. Hevesi Sándor tér 4 (341 3845). Trolleybus 73, 76.* **Open** 1-7pm daily.
Petőfi Csarnok, Városliget, XIV. Zichy M. utca 14 (251 7266). M1 Széchenyi fürdő. **Open** 9am-10pm daily.
Várszínház, I. Színház utca 1-3 (175 8011). Bus 16, castle minibus. **Open** 1.30-6pm daily.
Ernst Museum, VI. Nagymező utca 8 (341 4355). M1 Operaház. **Open** 10am-6pm Tue-Sun.

Budapest Music Weeks
Information *Nemzeti Filharmónia, V. Vörösmarty tér 1 (118 0441). M1 Vörösmarty tér.* **Open** 10am-1.30pm, 2-6pm, Mon-Fri. **Date** 25 Sept-end Oct.
For the last 30 years this festival, which begins on the anniversary of Bartók's death, has opened the concert season. Classical concerts take place at either the Vigadó, V. Vigadó tér 5 (138 4721), M1 Vörösmarty tér, open 10am-6pm Mon-Fri, 10am-2pm Sat; or at the Zeneakadémia, VI. Liszt Ferenc tér 8 (342 0179), M1 Oktogon/tram 4, 6, open 10am-noon, 4-8pm, Mon-Fri; 1-8pm Sat, Sun when there is a concert. (*See chapter* **Music: Classical & Opera**.)

Music of Our Time
Information *Nemzeti Filharmónia, V. Vörösmarty tér 1 (118 0441). M1 Vörösmarty tér.* **Open** 10am-1.30pm, 2-6pm, Mon-Fri. **Date** late Sept.
A ten-day contemporary music festival featuring a select group of composers. The event has rather lost its impetus since the organisers, Nemzeti Filharmónia, formerly the state concert ticket agency, has lost most of its funding.

Remembrance Day
Date 23 Oct (public holiday).
The anniversary of the 1956 Uprising is a national day of mourning. When Soviet tanks put down the rebellion, 30,000 people died and 200,000 fled the country. Former leader Imre

Nagy was executed. He was secretly buried at Plot 301 in Újköztemető Cemetery, where wreath-laying ceremonies take place on this day every year. There is also a flag-raising ceremony in Kossuth tér, an event which right-wing nationalist groups have tried to take over in recent years. The date of 23 October also marked the declaration of the new republic in 1989.

Winter

Temperatures plummet abruptly in late October and from mid-November Budapest's stores prepare for the Christmas rush. In the countryside, the main event is the *disznóvágás*, pig killing, day-long slaughter parties in November or early December. Everyone is invited, especially the unfortunate porker, traditionally slain at dawn.

Mikulás
St Nicholas' Day. **Date** 6 Dec.
On the eve of 6 Dec, children put out their shoes on the window sills for Santa to fill with chocolates, fruit and little pressies. He is helped by *krampusz*, the bogey-man, who threatens to steal naughty children from their beds. In most cases his appearance is token: small *krampusz* puppets, hung on a gilded tree-branch, *virgács*, are also left by Santa.

Christmas
Date 25, 26 Dec (public holiday).
Trees and tacky presents line the Nagykörút from mid-December. The traditional meal is carp, happy to be out of the Danube mud and in the clear water of the Hungarian family's bathtub – until the evening of 24 December, when the festive meal and present-giving take place. Christmas is a family affair and apart from special events in major hotels, the city shuts up shop for two days from lunchtime on 24 December. Those staying in Budapest would be advised to accept any invitation going or curl up at home with a hefty novel. Life doesn't get back to normal until after New Year.

Szilveszter
New Year's Eve. **Date** 31 Dec.
This is when people take to the streets in style, down the Nagykörút and Blaha Lujza tér in particular. Most major places of entertainment will put on a special event. Buses and trams in Budapest run all night. The national anthem solemnly booms out of everyone's radios at midnight. Afterwards, it's Champers, kisses, handshakes and fireworks. Merriment goes into the next day, a public holiday, when *kocsonya*, a dish made from pork fat, wobbles its way into your hungover consciousness.

The Farsang Season
Date Feb.
Masked balls, *farsang*, test Hungarians' ingenuity to make the wildest fancy dress. The wildest ball of all is at Mohács, site of the Turkish victory over the Hungarians in 1526. The *busójárás*, the masked procession the last weekend before Lent on Carnival Sunday, is a re-enactment both of spring rites and of the battle. For more information, contact the Bartók Béla Művelődési Központ, Vörösmarty utca 3, Mohács 7700 (69 311 828).

Hungarian Film Festival
Date Feb.
Tickets and information: *Filmunió Hungary, VI. Városligeti fasor 38 (351 7760). Bus 33/trolleybus 33.*
Open 8am-4.30pm Mon-Thur; 8am-2pm Fri.
Since 1969 the Magyar Filmszemle has been trying to attract the film world to the cinemas of Budapest during a long weekend in early February. Translations are provided for the main features. (*See also chapter* **Film**.)

Sightseeing

Whether you want to burrow beneath Buda, have fun with the Funicular or roam round Roman ruins, Budapest has no shortage of exciting sights to see.

The area that is now Budapest has been settled since pre-Roman times. Wars, invasions, revolutions and occupations, from the Mongol horde who gatecrashed in 1241 through to the aerial bombardments and street battles of 1945, have wiped out much of what was here before the latter half of the nineteenth century. Even the Castle District is largely a reconstruction of a reconstruction.

Nevertheless, from the Ottoman period until the Communist days, each phase in Budapest's history has left its mark, and there are even some extant Roman ruins, though these are poorly cared for. In particular, the expansion of Pest and the invention of Hungarian national identity that took place in the late nineteenth century, when the country finally attained a measure of autonomy within the Austro-Hungarian Dual Monarchy, have left both a series of grandiose monuments and some extraordinary architecture. Much of this costs nothing to see. Such admission prices as there are will usually be negligible, although guided tours can be costly. Even the farthest flung sights – such as the ruins and museums of Óbuda, assorted cemeteries and architectural experiments on the outskirts of town – are easily accessible by public transport. Apart from in the most-visited places, however, English documentation will be thin on the ground.

Areas where sights are clustered together include the Castle District, Gellért Hill, the Város liget/Hősök tere and Lipótváros, the northern part of District V. (*See also chapters* **Budapest By Area**, **Museums** *and* **Architecture**.)

Fisherman's Bastion – *piscine vantage.*

detail – some restored, some unearthed by wartime bombing for the first time in centuries. Carvings and figureheads still sprout from painted walls. Fountains and statues litter the streets and squares. The best time to look around up here is early in the morning before the tourists all decant from their coaches. Go for a stroll and, if you imagine away the parked cars, Buda castle looks much as it did hundreds of years ago. (*See also chapters* **Budapest By Area** *and* **Museums**.)

Fisherman's Bastion

Halászbástya
I. Várhegy. Várbusz/bus 16. **Admission** Ft50. **Open** 24 hours daily. **No credit cards**.
There are several stories explaining why this vantage point has a piscine name. Some claim that the Fisherman's Guild defended this part of the Castle; others that there was a medieval fisherman's quarter down below. Certainly no one ever cast a line into the river from up here. Built between

Buda

The Castle District

We've picked out the most obvious items, but the whole Castle District, both beautiful seen from across the Danube and fascinating to explore close up, is one great big attraction – UNESCO has designated it a World Heritage Sight. Built, destroyed and rebuilt many times throughout the centuries, when the Red Army finally took Castle Hill in 1945 only four out of 200 buildings were still habitable. Painstaking postwar reconstruction has recreated much of the Buda of the Habsburgs. The original street pattern of the medieval city has been retained, together with much of the architectural

Look for THE **KODAK EXPRESS**
logo wherever **YOU** are,

you WILL *find* TOP **Kodak Quality.**
"1 hour photo development service"

TOP QUALITY KODAK EXPRESS SHOPS IN BUDAPEST:

Rapid Foto, 1157 Zsókavár u. 2. • Foto-Video-Hifi, 1161 Csömöri út 30. • Foto Point, 1191 Vak Bottyán u. 75. • MTI Foto, 1016 Krisztina krt. 24. • Kovács Foto, 1026 Szilágyi Erzsébet fasor, Budagyöngye • Tower Foto, 1201 Kossuth Lajos u. 30. • Prompt Foto, 1052 Arany János u.-i Metro • Ringfoto, 1097 Gyáli u. 3 • Color Foto Professional, 1065 Nagymező u. 37-39. • Sajtólabor, 1085 Gyulai Pál u. 12. • Color Quick Foto, 1039 Rákóczi u. 36.

A Kodak és a Kodak Express védett márkajegyek

*The wrought-iron gate (centre) of the **Royal Palace** was designed by Jungfer Gyula.*

Travel Service

American Express Hungary Ltd.
H-1052 Budapest, Deák Ferenc u. 10.
Telephone: (361) 266-8680

A worldwide network of over 1.700 Travel Service and
Representative Offices in more than 130 countries

- Foreign Exchange
- Travelers Cheque Refund
- Emergency Cheque Cashing
- MoneyGram
- Emergency Card Replacement
- Cardmember Remittance
- Automated Teller Machine
(24 hour Service)

- Airline Tickets
- Travel Planning Assistance
- Hotel Reservations
- Car Rental Bookings
- Sightseeing Tours
- Reconfirmation of Airline Tickets
- Inbound Service
- Client Mail Service

Assistance with problem solving – consider us your home away
from home

Office Hours:

June-September
Monday through Friday
☞ 9:00 a.m. to 18:30 p.m.
Saturday
☞ 9:00 a.m. to 14:00 p.m.

October-May
Monday through Friday
☞ 9:00 a.m. to 17:30 p.m.
Saturday
☞ 9:00 a.m. to 14:00 p.m.

1890-1905 by Frigyes Schulek and intended to harmonise with his romanticised reconstruction of the nearby **Mátyás templom**, there are seven turrets, one for each of the original Hungarian tribes. It's worth Ft50 for the view.

Mátyás templom

I. Szentháromság tér 2. Várbusz/bus 16. **Open** *7am-7pm.* **Admission** free.

This neo-Gothic extravaganza takes its name from the great Hungarian King Mátyás the Just (aka Good King Mátyás) who twice got married here. Parts date from the thirteenth century, but much was reconstructed in the nineteenth century and like most of the Castle District the church is a historical mish-mash. When Istanbul, rather than Vienna, ruled Buda, the church was converted into a mosque. The building suffered terribly during the 1686 siege of Buda and was mostly restored in the nineteenth century by Frigyes Schulek, who returned to the original thirteenth-century plan but also added his own decorative details, such as the gargoyle-bedecked stone spire. The interior is almost cloyingly detailed and includes the entrance to the Museum of Ecclesiastical Art in the crypt (*see chapter* **Museums**).

Royal Palace

I. Budavári palota. Várbusz/bus 16. **Open** times vary depending on museum.

The former Royal Palace has been destroyed and rebuilt many times. What you see today is a postwar reconstruction of an architectural hotch-potch from the eighteenth, nineteenth and twentieth centuries. The first royal residence here was constructed by King Béla IV after the 1241 Mongol invasion. It was probably under the reign of King Mátyás (1458-90) that the Royal Palace reached its apogee. Mátyás's Renaissance-style palace had hot and cold running water and fountains and gargoyles that sometimes spouted wine. This palace was badly damaged during the Turkish siege of 1541. The area was completely laid waste when captured from the Turks in 1686. Empress Maria Theresa caused a new 203-room palace to be built in the late eighteenth century. This was badly damaged in the 1848-49 War of Independence, then reconstructed and expanded once more, only to be trashed yet again at the end of World War II. That battering revealed Gothic and Renaissance foundations, which have been included in the post-war reconstruction. Visitors are thus greeted by a melange of architectural styles including Baroque and Gothic elements. The Palace now houses a complex of museums, including the **Budapest History Museum**, the **Hungarian National Gallery** and the **National Széchenyi Library**.

Turul Statue

I. Szent György tér. Várbusz/bus 16/Sikló.

Wings outstretched and with a sword grasped in fierce talons, Gyula Donáth's giant bronze eagle (1905), visible from across the Danube, shrieks at tourists getting off the nearby Sikló. The best view is from the steps leading down to the Palace where his pained expression smacks more of constipation than ferocity. This mythical protector of the Hungarian nation raped the grandmother of Árpád, legendary conqueror of the Carpathian Basin, and sired the first dynasty of Hungarian kings. Later he flew with the invading tribes, carrying the sword of Attila the Hun. In Siberian mythology the eagle is the creator of world, lord of the sun. By claiming ancestry from this creature, ancient Magyars believed they were descended from gods. In the nineteenth century romanticised eastern origins stressed a cultural and ethnic difference from the hated Austrians. Yet by 1896 Habsburg Emperor Franz Joseph was portrayed as the second Árpád, founder of the thousand-year Dual Monarchy. The Turul myth, co-opted to serve this new master, was positioned here by the Palace. The turul-eagle is a common motif on turn-of-the-century Budapest buildings. The main gates of the Parliament building have a row of fierce wrought-iron specimens and golden turuls guard the Szabadság híd.

Gellért Hill

Cave Church

Sziklatemplom

XI. Gellérthegy (185 1529). Just up from Szent Gellért tér, opposite the side of the Gellért Hotel. Tram 19, 47, 49/bus 7. **Open** *8am-9pm daily.* **Admission** free.

Although the caves were inhabited 4,000 years ago, the Cave Church was only dedicated in 1926. It feels much older. The church was popular enough to be expanded in 1931 by Count Gyula Zichy, archbishop of Kalocsa, who had helped re-establish the Hungarian Paulite order of monks. The monastery next door opened in 1934, and the white-robed monks resumed their work after an interval of 150 years – their order had been dissolved by Emperor Joseph II and sent into exile. The Communists jailed the monks in the 1950s and the cave was boarded up for decades, re-opening in August 1989.

Buda Caves

Budapest's caves are unique because they were formed by hot thermal waters underground, rather than by cold rainwater from above. This created unusual rock formations rather than gigantic dripstone columns or cave chambers. Szemlő-hegy and Pálvölgy were only discovered this century. Both provide a cheap, refreshing afternoon's entertainment. For the Catacombs of Buda Castle, *see chapter* **Museums**.

Szemlő-hegy

II. Pusztaszeri út 35 (115 8849). Bus 29. **Open** *9am-4pm, Mon, Wed-Sun.* **Admission** Ft120; Ft60 concs. **No credit cards.**

Szemlőhegyi Cave is one of rare beauty, formed by thermal waters. Its entrance was only discovered in 1930 and it was opened to the public 56 years later. Although the tour is short, some 2km covered in 25 minutes, the weird and bulbous mineral formations spark the imagination. The air is clear and clean; Szemlő-hegy is an underground therapy center for those suffering from respiratory illnesses. The hourly guided tours are in Hungarian or German, but an English tour can be booked in advance. At the entrance you'll find a café and a modest exhibition room.

Pálvölgy

II. Szépvölgyi út 162 (188 9537). Bus 65, 65A. **Open** *9am-4pm Tue-Sun.* **Admission** Ft120; Ft60 concs. **No credit cards.**

Just a ten-minute walk from Szemlő-hegy, Pálvölgy is the only Buda cave that evokes the sense of awe and curiosity that drove explorers underground in the early part of the twentieth century, when these caverns were discovered. A sign warns three groups against entering: children under four and the physically and alcoholically challenged, so don't visit the bar by the entrance until after you've negotiated the 600-odd steps, steep climbs and low-hanging rock formations. This is the longest, most impressive cave in the Buda Hills and potholers uncover new sections every year. Hourly guided tours last 30 minutes; English-speaking tours by appointment.

*Built in 1904, the 11-metre **Gellért Statue** dominates the Buda side of the Margaret Bridge.*

Citadella

XI. Gellérthegy. Bus 27.

After the failed Hungarian revolution of 1848, the Habsburgs built the Citadella in 1851 as an artillery redoubt. Its commanding view put the city within easy range should the Magyars choose to get uppity again. The Ausgleich of 1867 that gave Hungary a measure of autonomy under the Dual Monarchy meant that its guns were never fired in anger against the city. In fact the new administration planned to destroy it as a symbol of reconciliation, but that proved too costly. The site now houses a youth hostel, restaurant and disco as well as an exhibition of the area's history since its earliest settlement by the Celts. It's quiet up here and the views north and south along the Danube are splendid.

Gellért Statue

XI. Gellérthegy. Tram 18, 19/bus 7.

A short walk down the hill from the Citadella is the enormous statue of St Gellért. Built in 1904, this 11-metre sculpture of the bishop raising his cross dominates the Buda side of the Elizabeth Bridge. Below it is an artificial waterfall, which dates from the same time. Like so many Hungarian heroes Bishop Gellért (Gerard) met a tragic end – the bishop, originally an Italian missionary, was the country's first Christian martyr. Legend has it that in 1046 he was nailed into a barrel by pagans and summarily rolled down Gellért Hill into the Danube.

Liberation Monument

Felszabadulási emlékmű
XI. Gellérthegy. Bus 27.

Perched above the Citadella and visible from all over the city is the 14-metre Liberation Monument. It was originally commissioned as a memorial to the son of Admiral Horthy, Hungary's pre-war and wartime dictator. But his son was killed while test-piloting a plane during World War II and then in 1945 the Soviets arrived. A rapid switch of ideological allegiance proved simple for sculptor Zsigmond Kisfaludy-Stróbl. A palm branch was substituted for the propeller blade the statue was originally supposed to be

holding, and – hey presto! – the same design was commemorating the liberation of Budapest from the Horthyites by the Red Army. Local wits dubbed Stróbl 'Strébel' – which means to 'climb' or 'shift from side to side'. Political zig-zags aside, the sculpture is magnificent. The statues of Soviet soldiers which once stood below have been moved to the **Statue Park** (*see chapter* **Museums**).

Elsewhere in Buda

Church of St Anne

Szent Anna templom
I. Batthyány tér 8 (201 3404). M2 Batthyány tér. **Open** for services at following times: 6.45-9am, 4-7pm, daily; 7am-1pm Sun and public holidays. **Admission** free.

Visited at dusk, as weary shoppers pop in to say their prayers, St Anne's captivates all the senses. The whispering of catechisms echoes around its emptiness and there's a faint smell of incense in the air. Earthquakes, floods, metro construction and Stalinism couldn't destroy one of Hungary's finest Baroque monuments. If you only visit one church in Budapest, this should be it. Construction began in 1740, to the plans of the Jesuit Ignatius Pretelli. Máté Nepauer, one of the most prominent architects of the Hungarian Baroque, oversaw its final completion in 1805. The façade is crowned by the eye-in-the-triangle symbol of the Trinity, while Faith, Hope and Charity loiter around the front door. The theatricality of the interior is typical of the Baroque. Larger-than-life statues are frozen in performance on the High Altar, framed by black marble columns representing the Temple of Jerusalem. The Trinity above is held aloft by angels, cherubim strike poses around the supporting altars, and a heavenly orchestra perches atop the undulating line of the organ pipes. But despite all the melodrama St Anne's feels remarkably suburban. With the vases of flowers and framed oval paintings of saints and notables, it's easy to imagine that you're admiring the chintz in God's front room. Speckled turquoise-green walls and potted trees framing the altar of St Francis Xavier add to the cosy effect.

Clark Ádám tér

I. Clark Ádám tér. Tram 19/bus 16, 86, 105.

Adam Clark was the man responsible for building one of Budapest's most famous landmarks, the Lánchíd (Chain Bridge), the first permanent crossing of the Danube. William Tierney Clark (no relation) actually designed the thing but it is Scottish engineer Adam Clark who has been honoured with a small square at the foot of the bridge. Adam Clark, who settled in Hungary, is remembered for preventing the Austrians blowing up the nearly completed bridge in 1849. He also at one point had to talk the Hungarian General Dembinszky out of setting fire to it. Adam Clark later constructed the tunnel that cuts under Castle Hill, in a straight line opposite the bridge. The elongated doughnut-shaped thing nestling in the bushes by the Sikló is Budapest's kilometre zero – the point from which distances from the capital are measured – making Clark Ádám tér the official centre of town.

Funicular

Sikló
I. Clark Ádám tér. Tram 19/bus 16, 86, 105. **Open** 7.30am-10pm daily. Closed every other Monday. **Tickets** Ft100; Ft60 children.

The fastest way to get to the Castle district from the bottom of the Chain Bridge, the mini-funicular railway crawls slowly up the side of Castle Hill in a minute or two. The panorama of Pest unfolds as you ascend. Until it was hit by a shell in the Soviet bombardment of 1945, the sikló had functioned continually since it first climbed up the hill in 1870. It was restored and electrified (it was originally hauled by a steam engine) in 1986.

Tomb of Gul Baba

Gül Baba Türbéje
II. Mecset utca 14 (no phone). Tram 4, 6. **Open** 10am-4pm Tue-Sun. **Admission** Ft30; Ft10 concs. **No credit cards.**

Perched at the top of Buda's last surviving Turkish street is the northernmost Islamic place of pilgrimage in Europe. Gül Baba was a Turkish Dervish and member of the Bektashi order. His name means 'father of roses' and according to local folklore, he introduced the flower to Budapest, thus giving the name Rózsadomb (Rose Hill) to the area. Several beds of roses surround the small domed structure. Actually he died just after the capture of Budapest in 1541 and never had time to plant any roses. Inside the mausoleum there are verses inscribed by Turkish traveller Evliya Tselebi in 1663 as well as antiquities and furnishings donated by Hungarian Muslims. It's a peaceful spot, suffused with the air of tranquillity that always shrouds Islamic holy sites.

Pest

Basilica of St Stephen

Szent István Bazilika
V. Szent István tér 33 (117 2859). M3 Arany János utca. **Open** at mass times 7am-9am, 5.30-8pm, daily. *Treasury* 10am-5pm Mon-Sat, 1-5pm Sun. **Admission** Ft40, Ft20 concs.
Tower 10am-5pm daily. **Admission** Ft150; Ft100 concs
For evening concerts, tickets from VII. Erzsébet körút 29.

Designed in 1845 by József Hild, but only consecrated in 1905, the Basilica is Budapest's largest church. Construction

Station to Station

First and last experience of Hungary for many travellers, Budapest's main railway stations are its real frontiers.

Keleti announces the East. The giant neon Orion, mark of the socialist television company, presides over the platform frenzy. Armies of students hustling for youth hostels assault your train; tannoy voices are quiet incomprehensible to foreign ears.

This Beaux Arts palace, finished in 1884, has gone to seed like the society that aped Napoleonic style. Smoke-blackened paintings in the international ticket hall are by Mór Than and Károly Lotz, decorators of the Opera House and Parliament. Oeil-de-boeuf windows line the curving roof and the lacy ironwork on the main gates contrasts with the heaviness of stone. Yet the huge arching window is defaced by a blue neon clock.

Outside stands a statue of Gábor Baross, pioneer of the phenomenal Hungarian rail expansion that began in 1867 and was used by the Hungarians to keep its empire's minorities dependent: all railway lines had to go through Budapest. To this day there is still no direct line from Vienna to Zagreb.

With St Stephen's crown perched on its apex, Nyugati is Budapest's oldest station. Constructed by the Eiffel Company (1877), the symmetry of its main shed and the weightlessness of the thin cast iron supports calm the pressure of departure. The ironworked arching is more reminiscent of Parisian greenhouses than a hectic railway terminus and the outside world seems remote as yellow trams blur through the glass façade. Postmodernity has cheapened its refinement. With boilers of occasional 'nostalgia' trains snorting steam, it's still possible to imagine Nyugati's heyday. But the Beaux Arts restaurant is now a McDonald's with synthetic plants and bulbous white lights.

Déli, ruining the view from Castle Hill, is the newest of Budapest's stations. While its prewar terminus was the haunt of newlyweds off to honeymoon in Venice, modern Déli brings you back down to earth. The stench of urine hits as you leave the metro. Fly-posters peel and people sleep rough. This really is the last resort. Finished in 1977, György Kővári's design exemplifies Communist shoddiness and superficiality. Its metal cladding is buckling and the marble facing falling off in dirty great lumps.

was so disrupted by wars and the deaths of its two major architects that one wonders if God actually wanted it built at all. The original dome collapsed in an 1868 storm. An exasperated Miklós Ybl, its new architect, had the entire building demolished and rebuilt the original neo-classical edifice in the heavy neo-Renaissance style favoured by the Viennese court. In World War II the Basilica was devastated by Allied bombing. Restoration only began in 1980 and has yet to be finished. Many prominent artists contributed to the interior, best appreciated during the evening choral and organ concerts. Gyula Benczúr's painting of Szent István offering the Hungarian crown to the Virgin Mary rises above one of the altars, and Miksa Róth's stained glass windows depicting the Holy Kings decorate the Chapel of the Sacred Right. Here lies the main reason to visit. The mummified fist of Szent István lives in a Mátyás templom-shaped trinket box – a bit like Thing from the Addams Family. Ft20 in the slot lights up this gruesome relic.

Inner City Parish Church

Belvárosi Plébiánatemplom
V. Március 15 tér (no phone). M3 Ferenciek tere. **Open** 9am-12.30pm, 6-7pm, Mon-Sat; 6.30-7.30am, 6-7pm, Sun; *Latin Mass* 10am Sun.
Founded in 1046 as the burial site of the martyred St Gellért, this is Pest's oldest building, although little of its original structure remains. It's an extraordinary mixture of styles – Gothic, Islamic, Baroque and neo-classical – testifying to the city's turbulent history. The beauty of its interior is in the light and shadow of the Gothic vaulting. Several side chapels contain their own altars. Most of the older detail is in the sanctuary, around the altar. You will have to dodge unfriendly 'Stop tourists!' signs or visit on a Sunday after the Latin mass to see them. Behind the High Altar you'll find Gothic sedilias and a Turkish prayer alcove, surprisingly intact from when the church was used as a mosque. Outside, it's still possible to make out the Gothic stones. The remains of the Roman outpost Contra Aquincum lie north of the church.

Central Synagogue

Nagy Zsinagóga
VII. Dohány utca 2 (342 8949). M2 Astoria. **Open** *synagogue* 10am-3pm Mon-Fri, Sun. **Entrance** by donation. *Museum* 10am-3pm Mon-Fri; 10am-1pm Sun. **Admission** Ft100. Heroes' Temple prayer 6pm Fri, 9am Sat.
Designed by Lajos Förster and completed in 1859, this is the second-largest synagogue in the world after New York's Temple Emmanuel. Seating 3,000 and too big to heat, it has never been used in winter. The synagogue is a monument to the patriotism of the Hungarian Jewish bourgeoisie. Newly cleaned brickwork glows in blue, yellow and red, the heraldic colours of Budapest. Fresh gold leaf gleams on Moorish domes, their orientalism a reaction against Austrian rule. Interlaced eight-pointed stars in the brick detailing, continued in the stained glass and mosaic flooring inside, are a symbol of regeneration – appropriate once again with the nearly completed $10 million, ten-year facelift financed by the Hungarian government and Tony Curtis's Emmanuel Foundation. The divisions of its central space are based on the cabbalistic Tree of Life, giving it a similar floor plan to a Gothic cathedral. The dark wooden pews are numbered, some poignantly tagged with names of those long dead, and its freshly painted ceiling entwines Stars of David outlined in gold leaf. An inscription of Jaweh surrounded by a blaze of glory radiates above the Arc of the Covenant, lit from overhead by an opening in its covering dome. The synagogue's annex, the Heroes' Temple, designed by Ferenc Faragó and László Vágó in 1929-31, is a memorial to Hungarian Jews who died fighting in World War I. The simple concrete arching colonnade encloses the Garden of Remembrance, now a mass grave for Jews massacred by fellow Hungarians in 1945. Imre Varga's weeping willow memorial to those killed in concentration camps is visible from Wesselényi utca. Family names of the dead are inscribed on its leaves. Towards the end of World War II, 20,000 Jews were herded inside here, 7,000 of whom perished within.

The fastest way to get from the bottom of the Chain Bridge to the Castle district – the **Sikló.**

Danube Bridges

*Budapest's first modern crossing of the Danube was the Chain Bridge or **Lánchíd**.*

Budapest is the most Danubian of all the settlements on central Europe's main waterway. The river defines the city, separating the mentalities of Buda and Pest. On a national level the bridges join rural Hungary with cosmopolitan Europe – an economic necessity recognised by Count István Széchenyi who organised the construction of the Lánchíd (Chain Bridge), Budapest's first modern bridge.

But the Danube has been a psychological as well as a political frontier since it formed the *limes* of the Roman Empire, separating urban imperialism from the nomadic cultures of the unconquered plains beyond. The Romans built the first permanent crossing: a wooden construction which stood not far from today's Árpádhíd.

Projections of national and civic self-image characterise the design of today's bridges. The Lánchíd, guarded by stone lions and lit up at night, has a strength and grandeur despite its postcard picturesqueness. It opened in 1849 after the defeat of the Independence movement, yet crystallises the optimism of metropolitan expansion and national ambition. Conversely, the mythical turuls and the shields of 'Greater' Hungary on Szabadság híd (Freedom Bridge, 1896 – originally named Franz Joseph I Bridge) betray an ambivalence towards the future.

The views from the Elisabeth (Erzsébet) and Margaret (Margit) Bridges are more memorable than the structures themselves. But Margaret Bridge has a Parisian sophistication, mirroring the self-perception of Pest's emerging bourgeoisie.

While the bridges opened up new areas of Budapest for development, the older city suffered. Construction of Erzsébet híd (1903) destroyed Pest's medieval centre and the Tabán near Castle Hill. Hungary's first heritage campaign was formed to save the Inner City Parish Church and the road off the bridge obligingly swerves round it.

The Danube bridges have a strategic vulnerability, their destruction a blow to civic and national pride. The Austrians attempted to blow up the Lánchíd in 1848. The Nazis demolished them all in 1945. Memorials to a temporary bridge which carried public transport until 1956 can be found near the Parliament and on the opposite quay at Batthyány tér.

Jewish Budapest

Beyond the **Central Synagogue** lies Budapest's historic Jewish quarter, established in District VII in the eighteenth century and peaking in the second half of the nineteenth century, as the Jewish population of the city grew from 16 per cent in 1872 to 21.5 percent in 1900.

The block behind the Central Synagogue has the Jewish Museum; the Heroes' Synagogue (1931), named for Jewish soldiers killed in World War I; and the Károly Goldmark cultural hall. The headquarters of many Jewish organisations are located just around the corner at VII. Sip utca 12 (M2 Astoria).

Imre Varga, who sculpted the Holocaust memorial in the Central Synagogue's courtyard, also created a statue of Raoul Wallenberg, the Swedish diplomat who saved more than 20,000 Budapest Jews. Communist authorities insisted it be placed far from the city centre – so today it stands out in Buda on II. Szilágyi Erzsébet fasor (tram 56).

The Orthodox community complex is at the corner of Dob utca and Kazinczy utca – dominated by a 1910 synagogue whose façade gracefully follows the curve of Kazinczy utca. It is in use but needs restoration. The Rumbach Sebestyén utca Synagogue – a Moorish structure designed by Viennese architect Otto Wagner – can only be seen from the outside. Restoration has bogged down amid ownership disputes, and its future is unclear.

Nearby, the Gozsdu udvar, a series of interlocking courtyards which was once packed full of tradesmen's workshops, runs from Dob utca through to Király utca.

Though Király utca was 70 per cent Jewish a century ago, the only remaining religious building is a small 'hidden' synagogue just off it at Vasvári utca 5, currently used by Hasidic Jews. There are several such in Budapest; to get around the prohibition against Jewish land ownership, the community would rent all the flats in a building, enabling them legally to build a house of worship in the courtyard.

As some Jewish families grew wealthier, they left District VII and built the upper-class, elegant Bauhaus buildings in District XIII around Pozsonyi út and Szt István Park. Many would later serve as Wallenberg's safe houses, protecting Jewish families during the war.

The past ten years have seen some revitalisation within Budapest's Jewish community, estimated currently at over 80,000. Eastern Europe's only rabbinical centre is at VIII. József körút 27. There are four Jewish day schools and a newly opened community centre (VI. Révay utca 16). District VII, although it is no longer majority Jewish, remains the heart of the Jewish community.

Budapest's oldest synagogue, dating back to medieval times, is in the Castle District at I. Táncsis utca 26. András Landherr's 1821 Óbuda Synagogue, one of Budapest's earliest neo-classical buildings and now a TV studio closed to the public, is at III. Lajos utca 163 (HÉV Árpád híd/tram 1).

City Park

Városliget
VI. Dózsa György út. M1 Hősök tere.

The Városliget, laid out by the French designer Nebbion, is where Budapest comes to stroll. Towering over the greenery and the small artificial lake, used for boating in summer and ice-skating in winter, is the Vajdahunyad Castle, a Disneyfied version of the Hunyad clan's castle that still stands near Hunedora in Romania. Together with neighbouring buildings the castle embodies every architectural style in Hungary up to the nineteenth century. The Baroque part houses the **Agriculture Museum**. In the courtyard stands Miklós Ligeti's sculpture of the hooded Anonymus, chronicler to the court of Béla III. People take snaps of each other sitting his lap. There is also a statue of George Washington in the park, erected in 1906 in gratitude to America for providing a home for Hungarian immigrant communities, whose contributions paid for the statue. Apart from the **Transport Museum**, the **Széchenyi Baths** complex, the

*Designed in 1845 by József Hild,
the **Basilica of St Stephen** is
Budapest's largest church.*

State Circus, the restaurants **Robinson** and **Gundel**, and the **Petőfi Csarnok** concert hall outside of which is a week-end flea market (see chapter Shopping), the Városliget is also home to the city's **Zoo** and **Vidám Park**. **Hősök tere (Heroes' Square)** is essentially the park's main entrance.

Former Royal Post Office Savings Bank

Magyar Királyi Takarék Pénztar
V. Hold utca 4 (111 4432). M3 Arany János utca. **Open** *cashier's hall* 7.30am-1pm Mon-Fri. Rest of building closed to public.

Ödön Lechner's recently restored masterpiece (1901) is Budapest's most innovative building, worthy of a Gaudi or Jujol. The buildings all around allow tantalising glimpses of its flashing white ceramic or writhing gold serpents crowning green tiles. Lechner's finesse lies in the restraint of his folk-motif detailing combined with a meticulous attention to form. The exuberant colours and sinuous shapes put eclectic Budapest to shame. The bank was founded for peasants and other working people. The folk-art sources and playfulness of the decoration are part of the bank's accessibility. The lights flanking its entrance writhe like sea horses and Zsolnay bees march up to hives perched on top of the verticals. Floral motifs pattern its upper reaches, like the embroidery on those

FAMILIES' FAVORITE!

BUDAPEST ZOO

The **WILDEST PLACE** in town from 1866!

In Városliget (City Park), near Hösök tere (Heroes' Square)
(Metro line No. 1 - Station: Széchenyi fürdö)
(Trolley bus No. 72 - station: Állatkert (Zoo)

One of the most interesting monument zoos in the world!

2500 animals of 400 species, 2500 plant species,
a best park and resort area of the city.

OPENING TIME: FROM 9.00 AM TO SUNSET

BUDAPEST ZOO AND BOTANICAL GARDEN
Budapest, 1146, Állatkerti krt. 6-12.

white lace tablecloths sold around Váci utca. The cashier's hall is the only part accessible to the visitor. Lechner's irreverent style was abhorred by the establishment and banned from public buildings in 1902. This, alas, was his last major commission. Other Lechner buildings worth seeing include the **Museum of Applied Arts** and the Institute of Geology at XIV. Stefánia út 14.

Gozsdu udvar

VII. Dob utca 16/Király utca 15. M2 Astoria, M1, M2, M3 Deák tér/tram 47, 49.

Built at the turn of the century, Gozsdu udvar was once the heart of Budapest's working-class Jewish quarter, crammed with dozens of tiny shops and tradesmen. The seven courtyards, which stretch for 200 metres between Király utca and Dob utca, echoed to the sounds of German and Yiddish, Hungarian and Romanian as newcomers poured into Budapest to try to make new lives for themselves as restrictions on Jewish life were eased. Many of those families vanished in the Holocaust, but Gozsdu udvar retains its atmospheric feel, especially at night.

Gresham Palace

V. Roosevelt tér 6. Tram 2.

Beautifully situated, its iron peacock gates in line with the Lánchíd, the Gresham Palace is crumbling away. Designed by Zsigmond Quittner and built in 1906 for the Gresham Insurance Society (a gold-haloed relief of Charles Gresham, the company's founder, still surveys the Danube) it had all the latest gadgets in its prime, including the central vacuum system, a Hungarian invention. The glass-roofed arcade is a public right of way and it's possible to sneak up the stairs and find stained glass windows by Miksa Róth. The Gresham was in the frontline at the end of World War II and further damaged in 1956. Home to a raucous cabaret in the 1930s, the arcade now boasts a casino, hairdresser and Chinese restaurant. Residents have recently blocked the sale of the building to a hotel chain which would have restored the façade but left them homeless. The Gresham Palace will thus continue to crumble for some time to come.

Heroes' Square

Hősök tere

VI. Hősök tere. M3 Hősök tere.

As a symbol of confident nineteenth-century nationalism, Heroes' Square is unbeatable. Completed for the 1896 Magyar Millennium that celebrated the anniversary of Hungarian tribes arriving in the Carpathian basin, the grandiose use of space encapsulates the conviction that Hungary then was a nation going places. It's flanked by the **Műcsarnok** and the **Museum of Fine Arts** and centred on the Archangel Gabriel, perched on top of a 36-metre column and staring boldly down Andrássy út, Budapest's answer to the Champs-Elysées. Gabe gets pole position because, according to legend, Pope Sylvester II sent a crown to King Stephen after his personal intervention. Perched in the two colonnades are statues of assorted Hungarian kings and national heroes, from St Stephen to Lajos Kossuth. Now often crowded with skateboarders in reversed baseball caps, Heroes' Square has witnessed many key events of modern Hungarian history – most recently the ceremony to mark the reburial of Imre Nagy, leader of the 1956 revolution, the event that in June 1989 marked the the rebirth of democracy in Hungary. Nagy's remains are at **Újköztemető Cemetery.**

Great Market Hall

Nagy Vásárcsarnok

IX. Fővám tér (218 5322). Trams 2, 47, 49. **Open** 7am-6pm Mon-Fri; 7am-1pm Sat.

The three-storey Great Market Hall was opened in 1897. It was a spectacular shopping mall in its day, featuring barges gliding down an indoor canal, used to deliver the stallholders' goods, with a railway line that went up to the market's gates. Under Communism the building began to crumble and fall apart, but the city council decided to restore the site rather than demolish it and the market reopened in 1994 with a gleaming new Zsolnay tile roof. Even without the indoor canal, it is still pretty grand. About 30,000 shoppers a day pass through the hall, trawling the 180 stalls. It's liveliest on a Saturday morning.

Margaret Island

Neither Pest nor Buda, the Margaret Island (Margitsziget), which stretches from Margit híd to Árpád híd, a walk of about 20 minutes, is named after the thirteenth-century King Béla IV's ultra-pious daughter, St Margaret. The ruins of her Dominican nunnery still stand on the island's east side not far from the remains of a Franciscan church. Margaret Island is also known as 'Rabbit Island', a reference to ancient times when this island was wooded, difficult for humans to get to, and filled (presumably) with rabbits.

In summer the island is jammed with people heading to either the Hajós Alfréd swimming pool or the Palatinus strand to swim and splash about. The Hajós pool complex includes a diving pool, an open-air pool and a children's pool. At the Palatinus, as well as at the Thermal Hotel Margitsziget, there are thermal baths fed from springs on the island. (*See also chapters* **Sport & Fitness** *and* **Baths**.)

Several relics survive from the island's time as a religious centre. On the east side are the ruins of the Dominican church and convent, where there is a shrine to St Margit herself. Further north is the Premonstratensian Chapel, orginally built in the twelfth century on an older site and reconstructed in 1930-31. North of the Dominican ruins is an array of busts and sculptures of Hungarian artists and writers, near the Open-Air Theatre and the UNESCO-protected water tower.

In the summer it's possible to hire bicycles (bring ID to leave as a deposit) or strange pedal-powered and canopied two-seated contraptions. Lazier visitors ride in a horse-drawn buggy.

For all its central location Margaret Island feels pleasantly distant from the city. Private cars are banned and the island is the ideal place for an afternoon spent lazing about or strolling among the 10,000 trees.

Turkish Buda

Almost all of the physical evidence of the Turkish era can be found in and around Buda. The Pasha's residence, the 'serai', was located on today's Színház utca in the castle district, while the 'Red Hedgehog House' on I. Hess András tér housed members of the Janissary corps. Most buildings left by the Ottomans either fell into disuse in the eighteenth century, or were destroyed in 1945. A few Turkish gravestones, topped by turban-like carvings, can still be found in the bushes beneath the southern wall of Buda castle, above the abandoned Communist youth park on Attila út.

There are still the **Rudas** and **Király** baths, however (*see chapter* **Baths**), and the **Tomb of Gül Baba** on II. Mecset utca. This last resting place of the Bektashi dervish is the world's northernmost Islamic place of pilgrimage. The Buda hills were also home to Sufi dervish sects.

On the Anjou Bastion in Castle Hill, just west of the **Museum of Military History**, stands the grave of the last Pasha of Budapest, Vizir Abdurrahman Abdi Arnaut Pasha, with an inscription in Turkish and Hungarian advising future generations that the Pasha wasn't such a bad fellow, as Turkish pashas go. He was killed at the age of 70 near this spot in 1686, as Habsburg-led forces took the Castle. The **National Museum** in Pest also displays an Ottoman Pasha's tent, captured during the wars of the seventeenth century.

Perhaps the gentlest reminder of the Ottoman years are fig trees, the northernmost in the world, that still grow on Gellért Hill.

New York Kávéház

VII. Erzsébet körút 9/11 (322 3849). M2 Astoria. Tram 4, 6. **Open** *café* 9am-11pm; *restaurant* noon-4pm, 6.30pm-midnight. **Credit** AmEx, DC, EC, MC, V.

Don't visit for the mediocre restaurant or the overpriced *cappucino* (*see also chapter* **Cafés & Bars**) but do go look at the architecture. Built in 1894 by Alajos Hauszmann, the spectacular neo-Baroque interior with twisting columns, cheeky cherubs, lush velvets, marble and gold leaf caused a sensation at its opening and still draws crowds of tourists to what was once the main hangout of literary and artistic Budapest. Nymphs and satyrs cavort around the ceilings, and 'New Yorkia' brandishes a miniature Statue of Liberty near the expresso bar. Peering through the plastic plants you can also spot caricatures of the journalists of the 1950s and '60s who made it their haunt, a refuge from the newspaper offices that used to occupy the upper floors. Rammed by a tank in 1956, its façade still hasn't been renovated. Visit before it all falls down.

Opera House

Operaház

VI. Andrássy út 22 (153 0170). M1 Opera. **Open** *box office* 10am-7pm Tue-Sat; 10am-1pm, 4-7pm, Sun. Guided tours available in English 3pm, 4pm daily (further info 131 2550 ext 156). Doors for performances open 6pm.

Miklós Ybl's neo-Renaissance Opera House was the most culturally significant of the monuments built to commemorate the Millennium celebrations. Completed in 1884, it was also one of the few actually finished in time. Financial constraints forced Ybl to scale down his proposals, but the interior is still lavish. Seven kilograms of gold were used to gild the intimate auditorium and 260 bulbs light up the enormous chandelier. Its cultural importance has always been linked to Hungarian national identity. Ybl, who personally supervised every detail, subverted the implied colonialism of the Viennese-favoured neo-Renaissance style by incorporating masonic allusions, such as the smiling sphinxes and the alchemical iconography on the wrought-iron lampposts. Ferenc Erkel, the Opera's first director, composed the doleful Hungarian national anthem. Operas by Erkel, Liszt, Kodály and Bartók are still prominent on the programme. (*See also chapter* **Music: Classical & Opera**.)

Párizsi udvar

V. Ferenciek tere 10-11/Petőfi Sándor utca 2-8. M3 Ferenciek tere.

Henrik Schmahl's Párizsi udvar was completed in 1913 and still functions as a shopping arcade today. Gold leaf mosaics announce its presence to the street, neon signs glow enticingly from the cavernous oriental interior, and 50 nude ceramic figures solicit from portholes above the third storey. Outraged critics charged the arcade with 'lacking good taste and discretion' – not bad going considering the moral and aesthetic standards of the time. It began life as the Inner City Savings Bank, a function clear in its ornamentation. Bees, symbols of thrift, can be found throughout the building, while heavenly banking is presided over by the archangel Gabriel on the white pyrogranite reliefs below the gable. Classical-style mosaics with gorgons' heads and theatrical masks smother the porch, juxtaposed with Islamic geometric motifs. This curious eclecticism continues inside the arcade which is best viewed from the Piccoló Bar. Alcohol can only heighten the effect of the intricate detailing although you wouldn't want to be sitting there if any more panels fall out of Miksa Róth's arched glass ceiling. The mock grandeur of the arcade tails off into Kigyó udvar, 1970s strip lighting starkly filtered through metal lattice. Gone are the days when they made tack with flair.

Parliament

Országház

V. Kossuth Lajos tér. M2 Kossuth Lajos tér. Tours in English. When Parliament is sitting: 10am Wed-Sun. In recess: 10am, 2pm Mon-Fri, 10am, 12.30pm Sat; 10am Sun. **Tickets** Ft400; Ft100 concs from Door 10 to right of main entrance.

Centrepiece of the extraordinary invention of national history that transformed Budapest at the turn of the century, Imre Steindl's Országház was completed in 1902, six years too late for the Millennium celebrations it was intended to crown. The building is an exercise in establishment kitsch. The freshness of its '80s restoration denies it the authority

So that they wouldn't lose their homes, residents of the Gresham Palace recently blocked its sale to a hotel chain.

Szabadság tér – *site of the 'sacred flagstaff'.*

On the Tiles

If one feature makes Budapest's turn-of-the-century architecture distinctive, it's the ubiquitous Zsolnay roof tiles and ceramic moulding. In the 1880s Vilmos Zsolnay, at his family's Pécs factory, experimented with frost-resistant glazing. Architects such as Ödön Lechner and Miklós Ybl worked closely with the ceramicists to achieve new colours, glazes and effects on buildings such as the **Former Royal Post Office Savings Bank**, **Museum of Applied Arts, Operaház** and **Párizsi udvar**. The **Nagy Vásárcsarnok** is roofed with Zsolnay tiles, as is the reconstructed **Mátyás templom**. Under Communism the Zsolnay works was turned over to the manufacture of ceramic insulators for power lines. Now the factory is back to producing tiles and mouldings that have allowed eye-catchingly coloured roofs and intricate ceramic detailing to be restored all over town.

that age and decay might have lent. Bright lights and 88lbs of gold leaf bestow a glittering vulgarity. The spiky profile dominates the Pest embankment of the Danube. The incongruous neo-Renaissance dome is crowned by a neo-Gothic spire, making it look much like one of those pointy Prussian helmets. Ferocious turul birds guard its main entrance and shields of Hungarian nobilty line its façades – an equation of national citizenship with the aristocracy (at the time of its construction, only 5 per cent of Budapest's adult population had the vote). Angels support the coat of arms of pre-Trianon Hungary, the empire a gift from God. The dome is 96m high, an allusion to the Carpathian conquest of 896. Underneath, 16 Zsolnay Hungarian rulers perch on supporting columns. The guided tour will take you to the chamber of the former Upper House. Note the numbered cigar holders outside the door, where members left their havanas burning during debates, and the shield of Transylvanian prince János Hunyadi, vanquisher of the Turks, where a wolf bays at a crescent moon beside a gold star.

Serbian Orthodox Church

Szerb templom
V. Szerb utca 2-4 (137 4230). M3 Kálvin tér. **Open** *for High Mass only* 10.30am Sun. *Service* 60-90 minutes.
Announced at the corner of Veres Pálné utca by painted tiles of St George spiking the dragon, this secluded church was begun in 1698 following the Turkish defeat, and subsequently modified in the mid-eighteenth century. Constructed to serve the Serbian craftsmen and merchants who lived in this waterside district, it still has a congregation of their descendants, plus refugees from the current war. The church is only open for Mass on Sundays. It's an overpowering experience. With clouds of incense and votive candles flickering, the service is sung throughout by priests. Acoustics are superb. As the litany reverberates around the glowing ochre interior, the light picks out the gold leaf of the neo-Renaissance iconostasis which hides the gleaming altar. The congregation stands during mass. Carved wooden pews with high arms give you something to lean on as your head goes dizzy and the ethereal blue of the ceiling frescoes starts to spin. Visitors leave spellbound.

Szabadság tér

V. Szabadság tér. M2 Kossuth Lajos, M3 Arany János utca.
Constructed during Hungary's brief flirtation with imperialism and conceived as the hub of the fin-de-siècle economy, Liberty Square was intended to be an image of imperial prosperity, its air of permanance masking the volatility of economic expansion. It's still dominated by the Dual Monarchy's central bank (now the National Bank at number 9) and the Hungarian Stock Exchange (now headquarters of Magyar Televizió at number 17). Symbolism was paramount for the builders of Szabadság tér. Built on the site of the Új Épület, the Habsburg barracks where leaders of the nascent Hungarian nation had been imprisoned and executed in 1849, they attempted to defeat their former oppressors through the weight of architecture. Nationalism triumphed at the expense of good design. The former Stock and Commodity Exchange was completed in 1899. With distorted perspective and exaggerated scale, the mammoth proportions of its entrance and central vaulted hall are terrifying. In the 1920s Szabadság tér became the site of the 'sacred flagstaff', a Hungarian flag flown at half mast over a mound of soil from territory lost at Trianon. Following World War II, the Soviet army erected an obelisk commemorating its dead on top of the flagstaff, destroying the sacred mound. The obelisk still stands, with a star on top and reliefs of Soviet soldiers besieging Budapest on the base. One nationalist memorial remains. The 'eternal flame', a block away up Auflich utca on the corner of Báthory utca, commemorates Count Lajos Batthyány, prime minister of the 1848 provisional government, imprisoned in the Új Épület and executed by firing squad in October 1910. The American Embassy, meanwhile is housed at number 12.

Új Színház

VI. Paulay Ede utca 35 (269 6021). M1 Opera.
Open for performances. **Tickets** from box office
or Andrássy út 18. **Closed** mid-June-Sept. **No
credit cards.**
Originally built as the Parisiana nightclub (1910), Béla
Lajta's striking symmetrical geometric design peeps out
from behind the far grander Ballet School on Andrássy út.
It's well worth the short detour. Nine ceramic angels with
gold inlaid wings carry turquoise mosaiced plaques with the
letters of its name. The polished granite of its façade is punctuated by grey monkeys. Ziggurat motifs on the door, continued inside, hint at the possible Babylonian origins of his
inspiration. Meticulously restored inside, it now functions as
a children's theatre. Most productions are in Hungarian, but
it's worth the price of a ticket simply for the interior.

Vidám Park

*XIV. Állatkerti körút 14/16 (343 0996). M1 Széchenyi
fürdő.* **Open** *summer* 9.45am-8pm Tue-Sun; *winter*
9.45am-sunset Tue-Sun. **Admission** Ft50; Ft20 children.
No credit cards.
What this amusement park lacks in modern Western rides
it more than makes up for with a certain ramshackle charm.
Attractions include a beautiful old merry-go-round, an
assortment of old-fashioned test-your-weight machines,
'dodzsem' cars, laughably tame ghost trains, and an ancient
big dipper made of wood, part of which has to be replaced
each year as it wears out. There's also an amusement park
for toddlers right next door. (*See also chapter* **Children**.)

Zoo

Állatkert
*XIV. Állatkerti út 6-12 (268 1970). M1 Széchenyi
fürdő.* **Open** *summer* 9am-7pm Tue-Sun; *winter*
9am-4pm Tue-Sun. **Admission** Ft200, Ft100
children Sat, Sun; Ft150, Ft80 children Tue-Fri. **No
credit cards.**
Budapest's Zoo, completed in 1911, once had buildings which
placed every animal in an architectural surrounding supposedly characteristic of its place of origin. All that remains

of these are Neuschloss-Knüsli's extraordinary Elephant
House and Main Gate. There's also a Palm House built by
the Eiffel company. The Zoo is badly in need of renovation
and many of its cages and pens with their morose-looking
inhabitants would not pass muster in the west, particularly
those housing the big cats. Children can pet tame animals in
the Állatsimogató (stroking zoo), open in the summer. (*See
also chapter* **Children**.)

Farther Flung

Farkasréti Cemetery

Farkasréti temető
*XI. Németvölgyi út 99 (166 5833). Tram 59 from Moszkva
tér/bus 8, 8A, 53.* **Open** 7am-9pm Mon-Fri; 9am-5pm Sat,
Sun. **Admittance** free.
Tucked away in the hills of District XI, it's here you'll find
one of the most outstanding works of Imre Makovecz – the
mortuary chapel (1975). Giant wings of the souls of the dead
open to lead you inside the wooden-ribbed oesophagus of a
mythical beast. Be discreet on entering as the chapel is in
pretty much constant use. In the cemetery itself you'll find
the grave of Béla Bartók and lots of intriguing winged wood-
en grave markers. Look out for inscriptions in an ancient
runic Székely alphabet. Detailed maps of the cemetery's 'residents' can be picked up from the information building to the
left of the main gate.

Kerepesi Cemetery

Kerepesi temető
*VIII. Fiumei út 14 (133 9125). M2 Keleti/tram 23, 24,
28.* **Open** 7am-6pm daily. **Admission** free.
Declared a 'decorative' cemetery in 1885, Kerepesi is where
you'll find the names behind the streets. Politicians, poets,
novelists, singers and industrialists, chosen by governments
to represent the way they wanted their eras remembered.
Street names might change, but corpses are not disinterred,
giving you a comprehensive overview of the Hungarian
establishment of the last 100 years. Monumentally planned,
it's a popular place for a stroll. Wide leafy avenues direct

Heroes' Square or **Hősök tere** – *an unbeatable example of nineteenth-century nationalism.*

Roman Ruins

Although the Roman camp at Aquincum in what is today Óbuda was one of the most developed in Europe, there is little left of it today. Apart from **Aquincum Museum**, the carcasses of two amphitheatres are all that will really interest the lay visitor.

The Romans arrived here at the time of Christ. The province of Pannonia was a buffer zone protecting central Europe from unwashed heathens such as the Hungarians. Aquincum was its capital and they first set up a garrison around what is now III. Flórián tér. The military amphitheatre on the corner of III. Nagyszombat utca and III. Pacsirtamező utca is now in need of serious weeding. The gates are open should you wish to do some. In its heyday it seated some 14,000 spectators.

Further up Pacsirtamező utca, at number 63, are the ruins of the soldiers' baths, encased in glass but closed to visitors, and at Flórián tér a few columns stand defiantly under the Szentendrei út flyover. All these ruins are in serious need of care and attention.

The civilian town developed in 2 AD further north by the present HÉV stop Aquincum. This is also the site of Budapest's Hell's Angels chapter, who zoom past the bits of aqueduct still standing by the main road to Szentendre. This road now divides **Aquincum Museum** from the civilian amphitheatre opposite. This amphitheatre is more intimate and accessible, hence the litter and graffiti.

To protect the crossing point over the river in Pest, the Romans built Contra Acquincum. Its stubby remains are now part of the small park in Március 15 tér where owners let their dogs loose around the smelly stones.

By the fourth century, the Romans had left Aquincum to the Huns, the Hell's Angels, the Hungarians and their dogs.

---

you towards strategic mausoleums – romantic novelist Mór Jókai and arch-compromiser Ferenc Deák, bourgeois revolutionary Lajos Kossuth and that other nationalist favourite, Count Lajos Batthyány. Nearby, music hall chanteuse Lujza Blaha is tucked up in a four poster bed, serenaded by adoring cherubs. Toeing the party line in death as in life, the regimented black grantite gravestones of communist cadres carry identical gold stars, while the totalitarian proportioned Worker's Pantheon has its own special gate on to Fiumei út. Anarchist poet Attila József, thrown out of the 1930s Communist party but rehabilitated during the 1950s, was buried here more than 20 years after his suicide. Styles of burial have changed over the years. Thousands mourned the first prime minister of post-Communist democracy, József Antall, in a candle-lit vigil, yet his grave is marked by a simple cross.

Napraforgó utca experimental housing estate
Napraforgó utcai Mintatelep
II. Napraforgó utca 1-22. Tram 56/bus 5.
Built in 1931, the 22 houses on this fascinating street exemplify different styles of the modern movement. Modelled on the Deutsche Werkbund's Weißenhofsiedlung in Stuttgart and sponsored by Budapest's Municipal Council, it was intended to demonstrate the possibilities of combining industrial production methods with traditional craftsmanship. But Napraforgó's charm is that this is not presented as 'great' architecture. These are people's homes. Key movers of the estate were Lajos Kozma and KR Kertész. Kozma, who had worked with Béla Lajta on the Rózsavölgyi House, designed numbers 5, 6 and 8, complete with portholes and rounded balconies. Kertész's villas are the most didactic. While the brick detailing and ceramic icons of number 9 exude a folksy traditionalism, the smooth white planes of number 11 celebrate the machine aesthetic of the avant garde. József Fischer's deep orange number 20, everyone's favourite with its curving flat roofed gable echoing the wiry staircase that disappears around the corner to the top flat, is the epitomy of sophistication.

Újköztemető Cemetery
X. Kozma utca 8-10 (260 5549). Tram 28, 37. **Open** dawn-dusk, hours vary depending on season; always open *Aug-Apr* 7.30am-5pm, *May-July* 7am-8pm, daily.
It's surprisingly lively for a place of the dead. The main entrance bustles with old women selling flowers and the gravestones are packed in close. People visit to see the final resting place of Imre Nagy, the prime minister who defied the Soviets in 1956. You'll find him in Plot 301, with 260 others executed for their part in the Uprising, in the farthest corner of the big map to the right of the entrance. Empty coach parks, a traffic barrier and police guard let you know you've arrived. Transylvanian markers outline the mass grave behind a Székely gate proclaiming a 'National Pantheon'.

Wekerle Housing Estate
Wekerle lakótelep
XIX. Kispest. M3 Határ út/bus 48, 99.
Like a rustic Transylvanian version of an English garden suburb, the Wekerle (1910-14) started life as the Kispest Worker and Clerk Settlement and is still mainly working class. The architects, Fiatal Csoport (the 'Young Ones'), strove to improve the national standard of proletarian and peasant housing. A sense of unreality pervades the estate. Bicycling old ladies career down ash-lined lanes. Snack bars are run from garages, but there are few shops. The estate has its own kindergartens, schools and police station. Kós Károly tér, surrounded by apartment blocks, is the centrepiece. Pitched roofs tower over long thin windows and wooden balconies. The wooden arch over the junction of Hungária út and the square has recently been restored. There's a cinema and a bar, but the catholic church takes central place. The residents' association at number 10 has a noticeboard displaying the millions of forints you now need to buy a Wekerle flat. Architectural romanticism is fashionable again.

*Imre Steindl's magnificent **Parliament** dome is 96 metres high, an allusion to the Carpathian conquest of 896.*

History

Key Events

Early History

c1000 BC Celtic and Illyrian tribes inhabit Danube Basin.
c500 BC Proto-Hungarians begin south-west migration from Siberia.
35 BC Rome conquers Danube Basin, known as Pannonia.
6 AD Pannonians rebel against Romans.
430-452 Huns make Hungary base for European excursion.

The Hungarians Enter Europe

700-850 Hungarians serve as vassals of the Khazar Empire in southern Russia.
895 King Árpád leads Hungarians across Carpathians into the Danube Basin.
955 King Otto of Bavaria defeats Hungarians at Augsburg, ending period of Hungarian raids on western Europe.
972 King Géza, along with his son Vajk, converts to Western Christianity.
1000 Vajk enthroned as King István (Stephen) with a crown donated by Pope in Rome.
1006 Revolt of pagan Hungarian leaders.
1066 First written example of Hungarian (the Tihany Abbey Codex).
1222 'Golden Bull' signed by nobles at Rakós meadow, defining the Hungarian nation.
1241 Mongol Invasion.
1243 King Béla IV decrees the building of fortified towns. Buda gains in importance.
1301 King Otto dies heirless, ending the House of Árpád.
1310 Robert Charles of Anjou crowned King of Hungary.
1396 Hungarians defeated by Ottoman Turks at Nicopolis.
1456 János Hunyadi defeats Turks at Belgrade.
1458 Hunyadi's son, Mátyás, crowned King of Hungary. Budapest's first 'golden age'.
1490 King Mátyás dies, leading to chaos between nobles and peasants.
1514 Peasants revolt, unsuccessfully, under György Dózsa. Repressive Tripartum law enacted, reducing peasantry to unarmed serfdom.

The Turkish Era

1526 Turks, led by Suliman the Magnificent, defeat Hungarians at battle of Mohács. Turning northward, they burn Buda and retreat.
1541 Buda occupied by Turks as provincial capital.
1683 Turks defeated at Siege of Vienna.
1686 Habsburgs defeat Turks at Siege of Buda. Buda burned. Again.
1699 Turks relinquish claims to Hungary at Peace of Karlowitz.

The Habsburg Era

1703 Hungarians led by Ferenc Rákóczi rebel unsuccessfully against Austrians.
1723 Habsburgs claim right to rule under the Hungarian crown.
1740-80 Empress Maria Theresa institutes social reforms. Immigration encouraged.
1808 The Embellishment Act sets guidelines for the urban development of Buda and Pest.
1839-49 Construction of the Lanchíd (Chain Bridge) across the Danube.
1848 Hungarians rebel unsuccessfully against the Austrians. Again.
1867 The Ausgleich is signed, uniting Austria and Hungary as equals.

1870 Imperial railway system established with Pest as hub.
1873 Pest, Buda and Óbuda united as a single city, Budapest.
1896 Budapest hosts Hungarian Millennial Exhibition.
1901 Hungarian Parliament Building, the world's largest, opened.
1914 Austria-Hungary enters World War I.
1918 Austria-Hungary loses World War I.
1918 Hungary declares independence from Austria.
1919 Hungary declares a shortlived Soviet Republic under Béla Kun. Romanian Army temporarily occupies Budapest. Admiral Horthy returns to Budapest. 'White Terror' against leftists.
1920 Treaty of Trianon signed. Hungary loses two thirds of its territory to neighbouring states of the 'Little Entente'.
1938 Hungary, now allied with Nazi Germany, receives a part of Slovakia under the Second Vienna Awards.
1940 Hungary awarded most of Transylvania by Germany. Hungarian troops assist in Nazi invasion of Yugoslavia.
1943 Hungarian Army defeated by Russians at Battle of Stalingrad.
1944 Admiral Horthy kidnapped by Nazis, fascist Arrow Cross Party begins murders and mass deportations of Jews to concentration camps.
1945 Red Army captures Budapest.

Communist Hungary

1945 Communist Party given control of occupied Hungary.
1946 Hungarian monarchy abolished and a Hungarian People's Republic declared.
1948 Land ownership collectivised.
1949 Mátyás Rákosi, Communist Party chief, institutes a show trial against traditional Hungarian Communist Party leaders. All are executed.
1953 Stalin dies. Rákosi replaced temporarily with Imre Nagy, and then by Ernő Gerő. Hungary beats England 6-3 at Wembley.
1956 Hungarians revolt against Russian occupation. An independent Hungarian Socialist State is proclaimed under Imre Nagy, but falls to Russian tanks after two weeks. Budapest in ruins again. János Kádár placed in power by Russians.

The Kádár Era

1963 Kádár declares a partial amnesty for those jailed for their role in the 1956 revolt.
1968 Hungary aids Russia in crushing the Prague Spring in Czechoslovakia. Kádár institutes his 'New Economic Mechanism' allowing restricted private enterprise.
1978 The Crown of Saint Stephen is returned to Hungary by the United States.

The Change of Systems

1989 János Kádár dies. Mass demonstrations in streets of Budapest. 'Reform Communists' declare intention to allow democratic elections. East Germans flee to west via Hungary. The Communist Party declares itself defunct.
1990 Hungarian elections elect conservative government headed by the Hungarian Democratic Forum. With József Antall as Prime Minister and Árpád Göncz as President Hungary is declared a Republic.
1994 Socialist Party trounces Hungarian Democratic Forum in second democratic election. Gyula Horn named Prime Minister.

Early History

What with successive waves of Goths, Gepids, Alans and Vandals, Budapest didn't have an easy time during the days of the Roman Empire.

Budapest's strategic and majestic geographical location has long made it the key to the major events and trends in the history of the Danube basin. Perched on limestone hills which rise abruptly above the Danube, some 20 kilometres below the dramatic bend which sends the river flowing southward to the Black Sea, Buda's location offers a virtually impregnable defensive position and potential control of Central Europe's main waterway to all those who occupy it

The earliest history of the region, like so much of Europe at the time, was a decidedly lowbrow affair. Archaeologists have turned up evidence of human habitation as early as 500,000 BC. Agricultural communities sprang up around the River Tisza, where large neolithic sites have been discovered. During the first millennium BC, Illyrian populations shared the plains with groups of Celtic peoples, known as the Eravi. The recent excavation of a large Celtic site on Gellért Hill is the first Eravi settlement found in Budapest itself.

It isn't until the expansion of the Roman Empire under Julius Caesar that the Danube basin enters written history. The region was conquered without resistance in 35 BC, officially incorporated into the Roman Empire in 14 BC under the name Pannonia, then promptly revolted against Rome in 6 AD. This encouraged the Romans to build up their defences through military settlements. Several Hungarian towns begin their modern existence at this point, including Pécs, Szombathely and Buda.

Known to the Romans as Aquincum for the copious mineral waters that flow from the limestone rocks of the Buda hills, Roman Buda was a modest trading town on the very edge of the Roman Empire. Today, one can visit the ruins of classical Aquincum in the Óbuda district (*see chapters* **Sightseeing** *and* **Musuems**), which boasts the remains of an ancient amphitheatre. More Roman ruins (the aptly named 'Minor Aquincum') can be seen along the Danube in Pest, at Március 15 tér just north of the Erzsébet bridge.

THE ASIANS ARE COMING!

As the Roman Empire withered, political and cyclical climatic changes in Central Asia forced the first of a series of migrations of various Altaic peoples westward in what becomes known, depending on

to whom you are speaking, as either the 'Age of Barbarians' or the 'Age of Migrations'. The Romans, no longer able to maintain their overextended Empire against repeated waves of Goths, Gepids, Alans and Vandals, began to withdraw from Pannonia.

In 430, the Huns, a central Asian confederacy of Turkic-speaking nomads, burst into Europe. Under the leadership of Attila they defeated the armies of Romans and vassals alike until finally, in 453, the Pope came in person to beg mercy. Attila returned to Pannonia without sacking Rome, but died mysteriously on the very night of his wedding to the princess Ildikó.

With the death of their leader, the Huns returned to their central Asian homelands. Next out of Asia were the Avars in the seventh century. They, in turn, came under pressure from the Bulgar Empire, another Turkic-speaking confederacy from the Volga steppes. Meanwhile, Transdanubia in the west was being populated by more sedentary, agricultural Slavs, most closely related to today's Slovenians. Many place names bear witness to early Slav settlement, such as Pécs, Debrecen, Balaton and Visegrád.

Roman Buda was known as **Aquincum**.

The Hungarians Enter Europe

If you lived in Frankish Europe in the first century AD, the last face you wanted to see bearing down on you was a Hungarian one – rampaging hordes of Magyars prompted the following amendment to the Catholic mass: 'Lord save us from sin and the Hungarians'.

The origins of the Hungarian people is a topic hotly debated to this day, most loudly by Hungarians themselves (*see page 63* **Hungarian Origin Theories**). The Magyars are a branch of the Finno-Ugric language grouping, a subgroup of the Altaic language family which includes the Finns, Turks, Mongolians and a host of Siberian peoples. (*See also chapter* **Language**.) The earliest Hungarian homeland was in the dense forests between the Volga river and the Ural mountains. Hungarian's closest linguistic relatives today are Vogul (Mansi) and Ostyak (Hanti) spoken by 35,000 fur trappers and fishermen on the left bank of the Ob river in the northern Ural region of Siberia. You can still buy 'three fish' using Hungarian if you ever find yourself on the Ob in need of lunch.

These proto-Hungarians broke off from their northern relatives around 500 BC and moved south

*It is possible that early Magyars may have ridden with the fearsome **Attila, King of the Huns**.*

into the central Volga region. In the first centuries AD, the Hungarians came into contact with Turkic cultures pushing west; one group became known as the Huns. It is possible that some Magyars rode with Attila, but historically speaking, the Magyars first became known in the seventh and eighth centuries as vassals of the Turkic-speaking Khazar Empire between the Black and Caspian seas. The Khazars engaged nomadic tribes, such as the early Hungarians, to act as border guards.

In the ninth century, the Hungarians left their base in 'Levedia' (today's Ukraine) and settled in the land of 'Etelköz', meaning 'between the rivers', in today's Moldavia. From here they raided deep into Frankish Europe. St Cyril described the horde of Magyars he met in 860 as *luporum more ululantes*, 'howling in the manner of wolves'. Faced with a howling gang from Asia pillaging the Holy Roman Empire, western Christendom reacted by amending the Catholic mass with the words 'Lord save us from sin and the Hungarians'

While the main Magyar armies spent the spring of 895 raiding Europe, their villages in Etelköz were devastated by Bulgars and Petchenegs. The surviving tribes of Magyars, led by their king, Árpád, fled across the Verecke pass in the northern Carpathians and on to the Hungarian plain in 895. Meeting little resistance from the local Slavs, Goths and Avars, the Hungarians pushed their

competitors, the Bulgars, south of the Danube, and began raiding as far west as France, Germany and northern Spain. The Hungarians were defeated by King Otto I at the Battle of Augsburg in 955. Retiring to Pannonia, the Hungarians realised that alliance with a major power might be a good idea. This meant dealing with the Christian Church.

Hungary was sandwiched between the Holy Roman and Byzantine empires and King Géza, Árpád's grandson, requested missionaries be sent from Rome to convert the Magyars to the western Church, a fact still trumpeted by Hungarians as a decision to be 'linked with the west'. King Géza was baptised along with his son, Vajk, who took the name István (Stephen) upon his accession to the Hungarian throne on Christmas Day 1000.

King István didn't have an easy time convincing his countrymen. Tribes loyal to the older, shamanic religion led a revolt against István in 1006. One consequence was the death of Venetian missionary Saint Gellért (Gerard), who was put into a spiked barrel and rolled down Gellért Hill into the Danube by miffed Magyar traditionalists. King István crushed the revolt and set about destroying the power of the chieftains by appropriating their land and setting up a new class of nobles. He also began minting coins, forging alliances, building castles and all the other things that early medieval rulers did on the road to feudalism.

Hungarian Origin Theories

Ever since the Hungarians arrived in Europe, conjecture as to their origins has been rife. The Byzantines mislabelled them 'Turks' or 'Ungeri' after the 'Ten Arrows' confederation of Central Asian tribes. Medieval Hungarian chroniclers recorded that the Hungarians came from 'Magna Hungaria' somewhere in the east, and ever since King Béla IV sent the monk Julianus to the Volga to search for those lost Magyars, Hungarians have been diligently researching their origins.

For a long time, Hungarians were fascinated by the myth of Hun origins. Poet János Arany's epic poem about the Huns, written in the nineteenth century, influenced several generations of Hungarians into believing a literary device to be the explanation of their national origins. (Attila is still a common first name here.) In the 1840s explorer Sándor Körösi Csoma travelled to Tibet and China in search of lost Hungarians. He didn't find any, but he did remain convinced that the Uighur Turks were the ancient progenitors of modern Hungarians. This idea found eager adherents during the

pre-World War II epoch among right-wing 'Turanian' parties, who envisioned a Turko-Uralic master race including both the Hungarians and the Japanese. Strangely enough, the idea has recently been revived, and Hungarian archaeologists are again digging around in Uighur cemeteries.

Political prejudice has led some Hungarians to the idea that descent from the Uralic Voguls and Ostyaks, who live in what used to be the Soviet Union, was a commie plot to tie the Magyars to Mother Russia. A favourite alternative theory is that Hungarians are descendants of the Sumerians, and thus, by extension, are the founders of modern civilisation. This is supported by the fact that half a dozen Sumerian vocabulary items sound vaguely Hungarian.

Given the way the political wind blows, there is always room for another theory. Assorted Hungarian 'linguists' have published studies 'proving' that the Hungarians are related to the Incas, the Australian Aboriginals, the California Miwok Indians and the Tibetans.

Medieval Hungary

It took Ghenghis Khan's invading Mongols to galvanise King Béla IV into building defensive castles – one was erected at Buda, which soon dominated the Hungarian realm.

With St Stephen's conversion to Christianity, Hungary had made a religious and political commitment to the Holy Roman Empire. But the country was still in a state of cultural flux between east and west, as symbolised by the mixed Byzantine/Roman manufacture of St Stephen's crown (*see page 65* **Crown of St Stephen**). Budapest itself was, at this time, of little importance. The main centres of power were the King's palace in Székesfehervár, the Queen's residence in Veszprém and the seat of ecclesiastical power in Esztergom.

Stephen's son, Imre, died young, and the next 200 years saw a succession of weak kings and struggles for the throne of the House of Árpád. Turning mounted central Asian nomads into medieval European serfs did not prove easy and revolts among the tribal Magyar nobility were common until the late twelfth century.

The tensions between landowning nobility and the office of the King were finally settled by the signing of the 'Golden Bull' under King András in 1222. This document granted landed nobility exemption from taxation (among other privileges), recognised the 'Nation' as such, and laid the framework for an annual assembly of nobles, the Diet. This was held in Rákos meadow in Pest; the annual gathering of the nation's high and mighty provided a push that helped Pest grow into a central market town.

All was going well, in a medieval kind of way, when the next big gang from central Asia gatecrashed central Europe. The Mongol invasion of 1241 devastated Hungary as towns were sacked, crops were burned, and entire regions depopulated. The Mongols retreated a year later after the death of Ghenghis Khan, but the experience was sobering for King Béla IV, who caused a series of defensive castles to be built. Buda became the site of one such castle, and once built, it soon came to dominate the Hungarian realm.

In order to repopulate the devasted countryside, Béla IV invited foreign craftsmen, traders, clergy and peasants from the west, especially Germans,

Czechs and Italians. Central Asian Cumans and Jász who had fled the Mongol onslaught were granted land east of Pest as border guards.

Béla's son, King András III, died heirless, thus ending the House of Árpád. Robert Charles of Anjou was crowned King of Hungary in 1310. Under his son, Louis the Great, Hungary's frontiers were extended by alliance to include Dalmatia, the Banat of Serbia and part of Poland.

In 1396, Hungary's King Sigismund led an ill-fated attack on the Turks at Nicopolis, ending in a defeat that marked the beginning of the Turkish advance into Europe. Things went from bad to worse until a Transylvanian prince, János Hunyadi, stemmed the Turkish advance in Serbia and finally regained control of Belgrade in 1456. Church bells rang all over Europe. Hunyadi's death soon after led to the usual bloody struggle for the throne, and in 1458 one of Hunyadi's sons, Mátyás Corvinus, found himself king by default at the age of 16.

With Mátyás, Buda became the true focus of Hungarian life, a position it has never surrendered since. Revered as Hungary's 'Renaissance King', Mátyás undertook extensive building within **Buda Castle**. Among his achievements was the Royal library, one of the world's largest, intended to attract wandering scholars to Buda.

Mátyás also created one of the first standing armies in European history. Comprising professional soldiers, foreign and domestic, the 'Black Army' was able to keep both Turks and rebellious nobles at bay. Meanwhile, his second wife, Queen Beatrice, introduced courtly customs and fashions from her native Italy to the relatively backwoods court of Hungary.

Hungarian historians refer to these years as the 'Hungarian Renaissance' a term which should be taken with a few grains of salt. Still, as medieval courts go, Mátyás's showed a distinctly humanistic streak. Mátyás spent a lot of his time galloping around the countryside, disguised as a peasant and seeking out injustices in the feudal system, which, given the nature of medieval society, must have been quite an easy job. To this day, his name still symbolises justice and good governance. 'Mátyás is dead' goes the oft-spoken Hungarian saying, 'and justice died with him.'

Certainly, when Mátyás died heirless in 1490, the legacy of culture and order he had built more or less collapsed. It soon became business as usual for the unruly nobility, who chose a Bohemian, Ulászló, as king. Under Ulászló the nobles began appropriating common land and taxes, they sold off the Buda library and dismissed the standing army. In 1496 a pogrom against the Jews broke out in Buda, and the survivors then fled en masse to Bulgaria.

In 1514 the Pope ordered a new crusade against the Turks. Hungary's peasantry, under the leadership of György Dózsa, a Transylvanian Captain, rallied near Pest and turned against the nobles. As is usual with peasant revolts, the peasants were quickly and soundly defeated. Dózsa was executed in particularly artful fashion: he was enthroned as 'king of the peasants' on a red-hot iron dais.

With Dózsa's defeat the nobility voted in a new law which superseded the Golden Bull of 1222. The Tripartum law, which was effectively in force right up to 1848, reduced the peasantry to serfdom and forbade them to bear arms. The timing could not have been worse.

Crown of St Stephen

The greatest treasure of the Hungarian nation is, indisputably, the crown of St Stephen. Much more than a mere relic of a bygone king, to Hungarians it symbolises their independence and alone confers legitimacy on the governments of the nation.

Born Vajk, son of Grand Duke Géza who converted to Catholicism and great-great grandson of Árpád, St Stephen (Szent István in Hungarian) assumed the throne in 1000 AD. The upper part of the crown was a gift from Pope Sylvester II in Rome, and is decorated with gems and small images of eight of the apostles, while the lower part of the crown is of Byzantine manufacture and was added later by King Géza I. The two crowns were probably joined together during the reign of King Béla III (1172-96).

Stephen's acceptance of the crown acknowledged fealty to the Holy Roman Empire. It's just the sort of bauble a medieval Pope might give to a recently converted pagan chieftain he wasn't too sure about, but it's nevertheless an impressive bit of Byzantine-Gothic finery and, under constant armed guard, is exhibited in the **National Museum** along with St Stephen's golden orb and embroidered coronation cape.

The crown has had some interesting adventures. During the Mongol invasion in 1242 it was smuggled to safety in the back of a hay cart. Somewhere along the way it got dropped and the crown now has a sportingly bent look.

As the symbol of the legitimacy of Hungarian governments, the Habsburgs carried the thing off to Vienna for a while. Under the Dual Monarchy it was understood that the Habsburg emperors would rule Hungary in the name of St Stephen's crown, and would travel to Budapest for a special coronation ceremony.

At the end of World War II, the crown was again smuggled out of Hungary, this time by forces wishing to deny legitimacy to the Communists. It languished in Fort Knox until 1978 when President Jimmy Carter decided to return it to Hungary. Emigrant Hungarians in the US were outraged that Carter would thus legitimise a Communist government.

Turkish Rule

While the countryside was lashed by border warfare, Buda developed into a provincial Ottoman town – churches were converted into mosques and the thermal springs inspired the construction of Turkish baths.

The **Tomb of Gül Baba** – one of the few remaining Turkish structures in Budapest.

When the young Hungarian King Lajos II, with 10,000 armoured knights, met the Turkish cavalry on the swampy plains of Mohács on 29 August 1526, 80,000 Ottoman spahis routed the Hungarians in under two hours. King Lajos, thrown from his horse, drowned in a muddy stream, trapped in heavy armour. After Mohács, the Turks turned north, sacking and burning Buda. They retreated briefly, but returned in 1541 to occupy the castle. Thus Buda became the seat of power in Ottoman Hungary, rebuilt as a Turkish provincial capital.

Hungary was divided in three. A rump Hungary ruled by the Habsburgs existed in the west and north. The Turks controlled the heartland with Transylvania nominally independent as a principality under Turkish control. While the countryside became a theatre of border warfare on the marches of Ottoman Europe, Buda developed into a provincial Ottoman town. The **Mátyás templom** (Matthias Church) was converted into a

mosque, and the thermal springs inspired the construction of Turkish baths (*see chapter* **Baths**). An Ottoman chronicler recorded that Buda boasted four major mosques, 34 smaller mosques, three dervish monasteries, and ten schools.

Sephardic Jews, refugees from the Spanish Inquisition, settled along today's Táncsics Mihály utca. Muslim Gypsies, known as 'Copts' (that is Egyptians) settled around the Vienna Gate working as armourers. The bulk of Buda's Turkish residents lived below the Castle in today's Víziváros, behind Batthyány tér and around today's Bem tér. Bosnians and Serbs worked in the Ottoman gunpowder factories and conducted trade along the Danube. This neighbourhood, between the Castle and Gellért Hill became known as Tabán (from the Turkish *tabahane*, or armoury). The neighbourhood continued to be a centre for southern Slavs, and it was here that the modern Serbo-Croatian literary language was created during the nineteenth century. (Tabán became a centre for artists and peasantry night life until the quarter was torn down on the orders of Admiral Horthy in the 1930s: he felt it spoiled his view from the palace.)

Pest was a city mostly populated by Magyars. Few Hungarians resided in Buda, since there were no churches there. The upheaval of the Protestant Reformation made itself felt throughout the Hungarian region during the Turkish occupation. The rulers didn't care about the theological squabbles of their Christian subjects. Still, anti-clericalism and wariness of the Catholic Habsburgs among the petty nobles made an attractive recruiting ground for Protestant reform in Hungary, while the austere tenets of Calvinism found eager adherents in the Great Plain. The Turkish defeat at the siege of Vienna in 1683 signalled the end of the Turkish threat to Christian Europe. In 1686 the Habsburgs turned the tables on the Ottomans, attacking their stronghold at **Buda Castle** and defeating the Turks after a six-week siege. The victors looted and pillaged Buda and Pest, so that Buda was again reduced to a pile of post-war rubble, while Pest was virtually depopulated. After a further decade of war the Turks lost the rest of their Hungarian realm and relinquished their claims at the Peace of Karlowitz in 1699.

Habsburg Budapest

Buda, Óbuda and Pest, lurching from military defeat and depression to the boom of the golden years, finally merge to form a single city, the sixth largest in Europe by 1900.

At the beginning of the eighteenth century, Buda and Pest were ruins. As an Austrian principality, Hungary was ruled by Vienna, but governed as a province from Pozsony (today's Bratislava). The Habsburgs suspended the constitution and placed the country under military occupation. Counter-Reformation measures were undertaken to ensure nobles' loyalty to the Catholic Habsburg rulers, including the sale of 42 Protestant pastors as galley slaves in Naples. In the mean time, claims for land redistribution after 150 years of Turkish rule proved fertile ground for corruption.

In 1703 the Hungarians rebelled, led by the Transylvanian magnate Ferenc Rákóczi. Once again Hungary was shattered by a War of Independence. This one lasted eight years and ended with the signing of the Treaty of Szatmár. Rákóczi died in Turkish exile. To prevent further rebellion by the feisty Hungarians, the Austrians blew up every castle in the country and ordered that the walls be dismantled from each fortified town or church. Today, the visitor to Hungary can visit the ruins of many such castles, but if you want to see intact castles you will have to go north to Slovakia.

Buda's strategic and economic value was not lost on the industrious Austrians. Rebuilding would take time, but it is during this period that Buda and Pest began to acquire the central European character that makes this city at times seem even more *mitteleuropäisch* than its sister, Vienna.

The reign of the Empress Maria Theresa (1740-80) marks the beginnings of the real integration of Austria and Hungary. Hungary's nobility began to look more and more towards Vienna as the centre of power. While the upper crust built baroque palaces and commissioned ornate churches, the majority of the peasantry lived as impoverished serfs using medieval agricultural technology.

One of the Austrians' ambitious programmes was to repopulate Hungary with immigrants from throughout the Habsburg realms. Lands left fallow by centuries of war and rebellion were laid open for settlement. In the west and south, German settlers from Swabia, known as Svábs, were given land, while Slovaks, fleeing overpopulation in the Carpathian highlands, settled on the great plains. Buda was reborn as the German town of Ofen, while Pest developed into a commercial centre for the grain and livestock produced on the Hungarian plains and shipped along the Danube.

Evidence of the immigration policy is still evident in the makeup of Budapest's suburban villages. In the Buda hills, villages such as Budakeszi and Zsámbék boast bilingual Sváb communities. In the Pilis Hill villages to the north one finds Svábs mixed with Slovaks, Gypsies, and Serbian communities who fled here during Turkish times.

Meanwhile, Jews began moving back to the city from Bohemia and Galicia, settling in Pest, just

Empress Maria Theresa – *reigned 1740-80.*

beyond the the now dismantled city walls in what is today District VII. This neighbourhood became the centre of Hungarian Jewry, and is still the most complete Jewish quarter remaining in eastern Europe, known, since WWII, as the Ghetto. (*See chapters* **Budapest By Area** *and* **Sightseeing**.)

Apart from a few revolts (such as the Transylvanian Székely Rebellion in 1764), the eighteenth was a relatively quiet century, in which Hungary was seen as an agricultural backwater feeding an ever more industrialised Austria. Maria Theresa's successor, Joseph II (1780-90) began a reform programme of taxing noble estates, granting rights to serfs and constructing hospitals and schools. Ever the pragmatist, Joseph retracted these reforms on his deathbed, allowing his more conservative-minded successor, Leopold II (1790-92) to reinstate the wonderful world of feudalism.

Repercussions of the French Revolution were felt all across Europe; Hungary was no exception. A conspiracy of Hungarian Jacobins was nipped in the bud, although their ideas gained an audience through the Hungarian-language writings of Ferenc Kazinczy. As the nineteenth century dawned, Hungarians eagerly embraced the Magyar tongue as a revolutionary and literary language. After centuries of war, immigration, and official neglect, the Hungarian language was now spoken only by peasants, and only in the Calvinist east of the country did any of the nobles continue to speak Magyar. Loath to use German, the language of the occupying Austrians, many continued to use Latin between themselves, using Hungarian, or any other local languages, only when speaking to peasants. Hungarian now began to revive as a literary language, uniting people as 'Hungarian' instead of 'Habsburg'.

REFORM

The period of national revival in the early nineteenth century is known in Hungary as the Reform. Buda and Pest perked up under the Embellishment Act, an 1808 law which began to plan the city on more modern development ideas. After a particularly nasty year of Danube floods in 1838, first Vienna and then Pest were redesigned along a pattern of concentric ringed boulevards.

The personality who embodies the Hungarian national emergence in the early nineteenth century was Count István Széchenyi (1791-1860). A figure of amazing energy, Széchenyi – as a writer, entrepreneur, ardent capitalist and patron of the arts – set the trend among the nascent urban nobility by being an ardent Anglophile. Having visited England several times, he introduced such British inventions as flush toilets, steam shipping on the Danube and horse racing, as well as founding the Hungarian Academy of Sciences.

Among Széchenyi's English inspirations was the first bridge across the Danube. Hitherto traffic between Buda and Pest had been conducted by ferry or by a rather clumsy removeable pontoon bridge. Széchenyi imported the English designer William Tierney Clark and Scotsman Adam Clark as supervising engineer and the Széchenyi Lanchíd (Chain Bridge) was constructed between 1839-49. (*See chapter* **Sightseeing**.)

While Széchenyi championed the ideal of economic development within the Habsburg Empire, other members of the Hungarian Diet were less accommodating to the Austrians. Lajos Kossuth, one of the now landless gentry who were flocking to Pest, became an eloquent voice of nationalist and liberal sentiment against Austrian rule.

Pressure on Habsburg internal affairs elsewhere led to a lessening of repression in 1839, and a reform-orientated liberal Diet was convened, led by Ferenc Deák. Lajos Kossuth became the editor of the leading Hungarian newspaper, the *Pesti Hírlap*, and his editorials lambasted the Austrian administration. Kossuth stressed increased political independence from Vienna, and his uncompromising stand led to his becoming the bitter opponent of Count Széchenyi.

Against this background the Parisians rose and overthrew the French monarchy for the second time. Civil nationalist uprisings spread across Europe like wildfire, threatening the old monarchical order. On 3 March 1848, Kossuth delivered a parliamentary speech demanding an end to the feudal sysytem – tax privileges, serfdom, the whole lot. On 13 March, the revolutionary spirit reached the streets of Vienna.

THE REVOLT OF 1848

Two days later, on 15 March 1848, Kossuth met with the cream of Hungarian dissident liberals in the Pilvax coffeehouse in Pest to develop a revolutionary strategy. Among them was the poet Sándor Petőfi who, later that day, famously read his newly penned poem Nemzeti dal ('National Song') on the steps of the **National Museum** – an event still commemorated annually. A proposal for a liberalised constitution with Hungary given far-reaching autonomy was dispatched to Vienna that day and consented to by the Hungarian Diet and the frightened Imperial government. On 7 April the Emperor sanctioned a Hungarian Ministry headed by Lajos Batthyány, and including Kossuth, Széchenyi and Deák. Hungarian was made the language of state; freedom of the press, assembly and religion were granted; noble privileges were curtailed; and peasants were emancipated from serfdom.

This might have satisfied less demanding nationalist sentiments, but Kossuth, as Finance Minister, wanted a financial and military structure separate from the Imperial Austrians. The new Hungarian Diet went against the Emperor and voted in funding for the creation of a 200,000-man army. Kossuth's intentions were noble, but his tactic was shortsighted. Hungary's minorities comprised over 50 per cent of the population, and they essentially lost all rights under the new constitution. Vienna, occupied with its own security problems, organised a Croatian invasion of Hungary to induce a compromise and soon the entire region was at war. The Hungarians could not expect much aid from the ethnic minorities within the scope of Kossuth's rather narrow nationalism.

During the early, heady days of the rebellion, Pest was the scene of fervent pro-independence sentiment. But Buda and Pest fell early to the Austrian Army and the Hungarian government moved to Debrecen while fighting continued. By the spring of 1849, the Hungarian troops had the upper hand.

A newly enthroned Habsburg Emperor, Franz Joseph, appealed to the Tsar of Russia for help in defending the endangered European institution of absolute, incompetent and unresponsive monarchy. The Tsar, of course, agreed. With the help of Russian troops the rebellion was quickly, and brutally, crushed, and Kossuth, like his predecessor Rákóczi, fled to Turkey.

Petőfi was dead on a battlefield in Transylvania and Count Széchenyi suffered a nervous breakdown and spent the rest of his days in a sanatorium. The Hungarian generals who surrendered to the Russians at Arad were shamefully executed, and the anniversary of that day is still a national day of mourning.

TURNING DEFEAT INTO GOLDEN AGE

With the crushing of the 1849 rebellion, Hungary fell into one of its periodic post-defeat depressions. Thousands went into exile. Hungarian prisoners were made to construct a huge Austrian military blockhouse, the **Citadella**, atop Gellért Hill. Its guns were intended as a deterrent to any future Hungarian attempts to dislodge Habsburg power.

The Austrians' military defeat in Italy in 1859, however, made accommodation with the Magyars a political necessity. In Pest, the remnants of the Liberal Party coalesced around Ferenc Deák, who published a basis for reconciliation with the Austrians in 1865.

The Ausgleich, or Compromise, of 1867 made Hungary more of an equal partner in the Habsburg Empire. Austria-Hungary was to be a single nation with two governments and two parliaments, although ruled by Habsburg Royalty who would recognise the legitimacy of the unclaimed crown of St István. New tariff agreements made Hungarian products more competitive than before, and the agreement allowed for the establishment of a Hungarian army. In 1868, Transylvania, in violation of agreements, was incorporated into Hungary proper, while Croatia was unhappily suborned to the Hungarian Crown.

*The **Citadella** – built by Hungarian prisoners.*

THE RISE OF PEST

The 50 years between the signing of the Compromise and World War I are rightly remembered as the Golden Years of Budapest. The city boomed with new industry and building, and the population exploded from 280,000 in 1867 to almost a million on the eve of war. In 1867 Buda and Pest together were the seventeenth largest city in Europe; by 1900 Budapest was the sixth.

Part of the prosperity was due to the better trade position won by Hungary in the 1867 agreement. With trade tariffs reduced, Hungarian products quickly flooded the rest of the Austrian Empire and came into demand abroad. The Danube provided the main route for grain sold north to Germany and for manufactured goods shipped south towards the Balkans. An extensive rail system was introduced with Pest as its hub. In 1870 Pest appointed a Council of Public Works, modelled on the London Metropolitan Board of Works, to supervise the reconstruction of the city.

Buda, Óbuda and Pest were officially united as a single city, Budapest, in 1873. There were monumental urban development projects, including the construction of boulevards such as Andrássy út and the Nagykörút (*see chapter* **Budapest By Area**). Gentry and noble families competed to have palaces constructed in the garden suburbs that sprung up around the old city centre.

Hungarian culture was focused on the Pest side. Buda was primarily a German-speaking town of dour burghers and irrelevant nobility, but arts and politics were increasingly being conducted in

Hungarian on the Pest side. The booming growth of the Hungarian language went hand in hand with the Magyarisation policies of Prime Minister Kálmán Tisza (1875-90). Tisza suspected that the Austrians could endanger Hungary's newly strengthened position by leverage among the non-Hungarian minorities of the Empire just as it had in 1848. His response was an programme designed to assimiliate the assorted Croats, Slovaks and Romanians of the Hungarian realm.

Tisza declared that all schools would have to teach in Magyar, and attempts were made to have Magyar become the language of churches. The assimilation policy laid the groundwork for the minority unrest and resentment that festers to this day among Hungary's neighbours.

The corollary to the minority issue, however, was that adoption of Hungarian became the linguistic ticket to success in Budapest. A lively literary life began to grow in Hungarian, as artists, students, politicians and society figures met to congregate and socialise in Pest's many coffeehouses.

THE 1896 EXHIBITION

By the 1890s, Budapest was the fastest-growing metropolis in Europe. The Emperor Franz Joseph, on the twenty-fifth anniversary of the 1867 agreement, decreed that Budapest was a capital equal to that of Austria. Budapest became the focus of a new sense of Hungarian national confidence. In anticipation of the millennial anniversary of the Honfoglalás, the Hungarian invasion of the Danube Basin, a huge exposition was planned for 1895. The untimely death of the exhibition's designer caused a delay, but with typical Hungarian aplomb this was taken care of by an official declaration that the invasion occurred in 896, and since then history books have been amended to the new date.

The Millennium celebration in the **Városliget** (City Park) was an expression of national confidence. Continental Europe's first underground railway whisked visitors beneath Andrássy út to the fairground at today's **Hősök tere** (Heroes' Square), where they were met by the gargantuan memorial to King Árpád and his tribal Magyar chieftains. A miniature of Transylvania's Vajdahunyad Castle was constructed to house exhibits and today still houses the **Agriculture Museum**. Across the way, the Wampetics Gardens, home to celebrity chef Károly Gundel (now the **Gundel** restaurant), served up traditional Hungarian cuisine prepared with a French flair making Hungarian food the culinary fad of the new century.

TOWARDS THE TWILIGHT

In the wake of the Millennium celebration, Hungarian confidence in the bright future was at an all-time high. The turn of the century was the golden age of Hungarian literature and arts. Mór Jókai was one of the most widely translated novelists in

Béla Bartók – *took folk traditions as a base.*

the world. Endre Ady's volume of new poetry, *Új versek*, sparked a veritable literary explosion. Béla Bartók and Zoltán Kodály were creating the study of ethnomusicology and composing masterpieces of modern music based on Hungarian folk traditions. Budapest became the in-spot for the vacationing upper crust of Europe.

Amidst the heady confidence in culture, politics began to take an ominous turn. The city had largely been developed on credit, and the apparent opulence of Pest façades to this day contrasts with the poverty of the courtyards within. Working class unrest had first asserted itself on the first great May Day demonstration in 1890 and its influence grew over the next decade.

The new Hungarian **Parliament** building, opened in 1902, was the largest in the world, naively anticipating a long and prosperous rule. It was never a site for decorous politics, however, as representatives were not allowed to read speeches, leading to a tendency for rambling outbursts, nationalist *braggadacio* and occasional riots among the representatives, as in 1904. The ageing Deák wing Liberals were challenged by newer right-wing elements who introduced Austrian-influenced anti-Semitism, previously alien to Hungarian political and social life, into political dialogue.

THE LIGHTS GO OUT

National tensions within the Habsburg Empire came to a head in the years just before World War I. Hungary's Magyarcentric and high-handed administration of the majority of peoples within the realm had helped fuel resentment and nationalism.

When Gavrilo Princip, the leader of a minor Serb radical student group in Habsburg-occupied Sarajevo shot dead the Archduke Franz Ferdinand, war was declared against Serbia. What should have been a minor provincial police action rapidly turned into World War I.

Although Hungary could count itself lucky that the war was not fought on Hungarian land, by 1918 the Habsburgs, with Hungary beside them, faced defeat along with their German allies.

The Horthy Era

Admiral Miklós Horthy, hero of the Battle of Rijeka, enters Budapest mounted on a white horse at the head of 25,000 troops – so begins the 'White Terror' in which Communists, Social Democrats and Jews are hunted down and killed.

With the signing of the Armistice on 11 November 1918, World War I came to an end, and with it the Austro-Hungarian Empire. Hungary declared its independence as a republic on 16 November, with Mihály Károlyi as president. The country was faced by serious shortages, unresolved minority problems, and a ring of unsympathetic neighbours aligned with France. No clear demarcation line existed in the border regions, and Serbian troops occupied Pécs while the French camped in Szeged.

Hungarian diplomatic efforts at the Peace Conferences in Versailles went badly, and when the allies showed their determination to hand over two-thirds of Hungary's territory to the neighbouring states of the Little Entente, the Károlyi government resigned and handed power to the Social Democrats. They in turn made a coalition with the new Hungarian Communist Party.

On 21 March the Hungarian Soviet Republic was declared by Béla Kun, who went about forming a Red Army, nationalising banks and sending emissaries to the new Soviet Union. Kun hoped, as much as any Hungarian nationalist, to regain the territories lost in the war, but the Soviets did not heed his calls for aid. In response to the threat of expanding Bolshevism, Czech and Romanian armed forces entered Hungary. The Hungarians fought doggedly, but nevertheless the Romanian Army reached Budapest on 3 August 1919. Kun and his ministers fled to Vienna, most never to return (among them László Moholy-Nagy, the Bauhaus genius, and Béla Lugosi, under-Minister of Culture and future Dracula). The Romanian Army did little to endear themselves to the citizens of Budapest. They bivouacked in the middle of the posh Oktogon intersection and plundered the city at will, finally leaving Budapest in November 1919.

Hungary entered a new phase of history when Admiral Miklós Horthy, hero of the Battle of Rijeka, entered Budapest mounted on a white horse at the head of 25,000 Hungarian troops. The weeks that followed were known as the 'White Terror', as Communists, Social Democrats and Jews were hunted down and killed for collaboration with the Kun regime. On 25 January 1920, elections brought in a Christian-right coalition Parliament, with Admiral Horthy acting as regent in place of a claimant to the crown. Hungary was now a political incongruity – a monarchy without a king, led by an admiral without a navy.

On 4 June 1920, the Treaty of Trianon was signed in France (*see page 73* **The Trianon Obsession**). Traffic in Budapest came to a halt, shops closed, black flags flew from buildings. Overnight, Hungary lost two thirds of its territory and a third of its Hungarian population. Budapest was now the only major city in Hungary, a city of one million in a country of seven million. Refugees clogged the city, unemployment raged and the economy virtually came to a standstill.

THE 'SILVER AGE'

A new political coalition, led by the Christian National Party and the peasant-orientated Smallholders' Party, came to power under the leadership of Count Gábor Bethlen, a hard-nosed conservative. He kept left and right in check and worked abroad to gain international credit and sympathy.

In October 1921, Habsburg pretender Charles IV flew in from Switzerland to head a monarchist coup with the help of loyalist troops. Horthy crushed the coup at the airfield in Budaörs, assisted by a paramilitary militia led by radical right-wing leader Gyula Gömbös. Their relationship would have serious consequences, as Gömbös's increasingly anti-Semitic appeals to nationalism became more and more the accepted political tone.

Admiral Horthy – *entering Budapest.*

Raoul Wallenberg – *safe houses for Jews.*

The Horthy governments advocated economic growth of rural areas and referred to Budapest as a somehow 'un-Hungarian' den of iniquity. Yet Budapest continued to be the economic and social focus of the nation's growth. Financial stability returned in the late 1920s, but when world stock prices collapsed in 1929, labour discontent rose sharply. Count Bethlen resigned and Horthy appointed Gyula Gömbös as Prime Minister.

TOURIST CAPITAL OF EUROPE

Budapest in the 1920s and 1930s was not quite as dark as politics would suggest. Whereas the turn of the century was referred to as Budapest's Golden Age the inter-war period is remembered as the Silver Age, at least in art and society.

During the 1920s, Hungary's spas and casinos were the playgrounds of European high society. The Prince of Wales, the King of Italy, Evelyn Waugh and countless millionaires flocked to Budapest for the good life it promised, including the legalised brothels that offered both discretion and the *filles hongroises* who were well known for their beauty. When HL Mencken visited in 1930 he wrote to his wife: 'This town is really astounding. It is far the most beautiful that I have ever seen. I came expecting to find a dingy copy of Vienna but it makes Vienna look like a village.'

Culturally, Budapest was experiencing a renaissance. The coffeehouses still provided a home for an active literary output that was gobbled up by an adoring public. Avant-gardists grouped around Lajos Kassák and his Bauhaus-influenced journal *Ma* (*Today*), while liberal nationalists such as

Gyula Illyés created a distinctly Hungarian genre of literature known as the *népi írók* ('folky writers'), focusing on peasant themes and village histories.

THINGS GO ASTRAY

Nevertheless, the organic make-up of Budapest society was coming apart. The Jews of Hungary were the first to feel the changing winds when access to higher education and certain professions were curtailed under the Numerus Clausus law in 1928. Prime Minister Gömbös was attracted by dreams of a Fascist Hungarian-Italian-German 'axis' (Gömbös coined the term), and worked to bring Hungary closer to Nazi Germany. German investment gained the Fascists influential friends and Oktogon was even renamed Mussolini tér.

When Germany annexed Austria and invaded the Sudetenland in 1938, Hungarian hopes for regaining the lands lost in the Trianon treaty soared. The second Vienna Award in November 1938 returned a part of Slovakia to Hungary, and in 1940 Hungary was awarded most of Transylvania. When Germany declared war on the United States after Pearl Harbor in 1941, Hungary immediately followed suit.

Still, all was not entirely fine between the Hungarians and the Germans. Gömbös had died and the new Prime Minister, Count Pál Teleki, who mistrusted the Nazis, worked to keep Hungary out of combat and resisted German demands for increased deportations of Jews. Teleki, an anglophile noble of the old school, would not stand for Germany infringing on Hungarian sovereignty *vis-à-vis* its own citizens, even Jews. Hungary, however, invaded Yugoslavia alongside the Germans in 1940, and when Vojvodina was returned, Hungarian troops took part in massacres of Jews and Serbs. When Hungary joined Germany in the invasion of Russia, Count Teleki committed suicide.

Hungary's participation in the Russian invasion was disastrous. At Stalingrad in January 1943 the Russians captured the entire Hungarian second army. As the Soviets closed in on Budapest, American and British bombing sorties against Hungarian arms factories began to level parts of Angyalföld and Zugló in Pest. The Nazis tightened their internal control of Hungary with the arrival of German troops in March 1944. Hungarian officials continued to resist German demands for more Jewish deportations, but it became harder when Adolf Eichmann moved his SS headquarters to the Buda Hills. Jews were herded into the Ghetto in District VII, while the **Astoria Hotel** across the street served as Wehrmacht Headquarters.

In October 1944, Admiral Horthy saw that there was no hope in continuing the war and made a speech calling for an armistice. The SS responded by kidnapping Horthy and on the morning of 15 October 1944 German troops occupied the **Buda Castle Palace**. The Nazi puppet Ferenc Szálasi and his Fascist Arrow Cross Party took control of Hungary. Extra trains were put on to take Budapest's Jews to the gas chambers at Auschwitz. Arrow Cross thugs raided the ghettos, marched Jews to the Danube bank and shot them. With Russian tanks at the outskirts of Pest, Jews were marched to concentration camps in Austria.

Many of the Jews who survived owed their lives to Raoul Wallenberg, a Swedish diplomat posted in Budapest. Wallenberg had safe houses set up for Jews around Budapest, and issued many with fake Swedish passports. One moment Wallenberg would be charming in negotiations with German officers, and the next he would be personally pulling Jews off trains bound for Auschwitz. When the Russians surrounded Pest, Wallenberg drove off to meet them. He was never seen again. Soviet authorities claimed he died in 1947, but survivors of the Siberian prison camps reported that he may have been alive as recently as the 1970s. A memorial stands to him in Buda.

Just as Marshall Malinovski's tanks were about to enter Budapest in November 1944, Stalin gave a personal order for the Red Army to split and pursue German divisions in south Hungary. The Germans made a last-ditch stand in Budapest. The result was that Budapest and its citizens were

Access to education was denied to **Jews.**

caught in the crossfire of an artillery battle that lasted months, killing many more civilians than combatants. The Russians advanced west through Pest's neighbourhoods in bloody door-to-door fighting. By the time the Red Army took control of Pest, the Germans had entrenched themselves in Buda around Castle Hill. While Russian tanks could easily control Pest's boulevards, the fighting in Buda's twisting, medieval streets was hellish. By the time the Germans finally surrendered on 4 April 1945, the castle was in complete ruins, and not one bridge was left standing over the Danube.

The Trianon Obsession

Hungarian obsession with the Trianon Treaty reminds even the most casual visitor that in this part of the world the wounds of history have still to heal.

When the Treaty Conference in Versailles dealt with Hungarian territorial claims after World War I, Hungary sent its best diplomats but was in a terrible bargaining position – on the losing side and surrounded by states which had gained military control of Hungarian regions inhabited by disgruntled minorities. The Serbs, Czechoslovaks and Romanians who, aligned with France, were known as the Little Entente, all pressed claims for regions previously part of Hungary.

The treaty did contain some glaring injustices. Romania was granted not only Transylvania, but also the mostly Hungarian towns of Szatmár, Nagyvárad (Oradea), Arad and Temesvár (Timişoara) simply because the rail line which linked them seemed a strategic prize. Southern Slovakia contained large regions with a dense Hungarian minority simply because the Danube formed a neat frontier.

Throughout the 1920s and 1930s it seemed that there was no other political goal besides the

regaining of lands lost in the treaty. The slogan of 'Nem! Nem! Soha!' ('No! No! Never!') was chanted as speech after speech was made condemning the treaty. Ire about Trianon and an attempt to reclaim former territories was a direct factor in Hungary's decision to align with Nazi Germany.

In most cases, the treatment of the newly created Hungarian minorities in the lost Trianon regions was remarkably bad. Language rights were lost, schools were closed, and most of the talented Hungarians left for 'Small Hungary'.

Today, Hungarians remain outraged over Trianon and politicians regularly invoke the treaty. In 1990, when Hungary's Prime Minister József Antall claimed that he was the 'Prime Minister of 15 million Hungarians', neighbouring countries rounded on him to accuse him of 'Trianon Revisionism'.

Today, Hungarian minorities in former Yugoslavia, Romania and Slovakia feel that their rights to self-determination in simple things such as schooling and choice of names are under attack. The thousands of Transylvanian Hungarians who live and work illegally in Budapest are a reminder that flawed treaties never die – they just age gracelessly.

Communism

Life under János Kádár meant food in the shops, but it also meant banned books and 'psychological hospital' prisons for those who voiced dissent – could this really be workers' Utopia?

When Budapest residents finally climbed out of their basements and shelters, it was as if they had been transported to some desolate planet. One of Europe's most beautiful cities had been reduced to a heap of smoking rubble. Rebuilding Budapest would occupy its citizens for the next 30 years.

The task of restoring order fell to the Soviet military government, who placed loyal Hungarian Communists in all positions of power. Nevertheless, an election held in November 1945 was won by the Smallholders' Party, the only legitimate pre-war party still in existence. Even with extensive vote rigging, the Communists garnered a mere 17 per cent, but Soviet authorities insisted that they remain in power, and nobody was in a position to argue.

Soon, in February 1946, the Monarchy was abolished and a Hungarian Republic proclaimed. Two weeks later the Paris Peace treaty was signed, which compounded the loss of land under Trianon by granting a slice of east Hungary to the Soviet Union. Communist authorities controlling the Interior Ministry set up the special secret police force, known as the ÁVO and run by László Rajk, to root out dissent. Thousands of Hungarians were summarily picked up off the streets and sent to the Soviet Union for *malenkaya robota* ('a little work'). Many were never heard from again.

Changes in the social fabric of Budapest were also part of post-war city planning. Budapest neighbourhoods lost some of their unique social identity as the Communists attempted to homogenise areas in support of a classless society. Apartments went to whomever the local *tanács* (council – a new term translated from the Russian 'soviet') decided. The empty flats left by the annihilation of the Jews in the Budapest's Districts VII and VIII were given to migrant workers, many of them Gypsies. Other neighbourhoods, now anonymous block jungles such as Lágymányos or Angyalföld were envisaged as 'Workers' Utopias'.

The Communists went forward with the nationalisation of industry and education. In 1948 a plan was introduced to collectivise landholdings, effectively neutralising the Smallholders' Party. The Communist hold on Hungary was complete.

Tension arose between those Hungarian Communists who had spent the war in the Soviet Union and those who had lived underground in Budapest. In 1949, the scales of power tipped in favor of the Moscow loyalists, led by Mátyás Rákosi. Using the spectre of pro-Yugoslav 'Titoism' as a weapon, old-time party members – among them secret police chief László Rajk – were tried as foreign spies and executed.

By the early 1950s, Hungary was one of the dimmest lights trimming the Iron Curtain. Informers were everywhere, classic Hungarian works of literature were banned, church leaders were imprisoned and the middle class families who had once been the soul of Budapest were persecuted as class enemies. During his years in power Mátyás Rákosi pursued a cult of personality that even Stalin found embarrassing. Rákosi's face was seen on huge street murals, his picture hung in every office. Schoolchildren wrote poems about him while peasant women embroidered his ugly mug on pillows of red silk.

A brief respite came with Stalin's death in 1953. Rákosi was removed from office and replaced with Imre Nagy, a more humanistic Communist with a sense of sympathy for Hungarian national ideals. It didn't last long. Rákosi, backed by Moscow, accused Nagy of 'deviationism' and came back into power in 1955.

HUNGARIAN REVOLUTION OF 1956

By June 1956, well known Hungarian intellectuals and writers began openly to criticise the Rákosi regime, using the forum of the Petőfi Writers' Circle for unprecedented free debate. The Kremlin, now led by Krushchev, poured oil on the flames of discontent by replacing Rákosi with the equally despicable Stalinist, Ernő Gerő.

On 23 October 1956, Budapest students marched to the statue of the 1848 Polish hero General Bem to express solidarity with reform policies taking place in Poland. The demonstration continued across the river to Parliament, its ranks swelled by thousands of workers, then moved to the Hungarian Radio Headquarters on Bródy Sándor utca behind the National Museum. During the demonstration, sharpshooters from the ÁVH (as the ÁVO were now known) on the roof of the Radio building shot into the crowd. Police and members of the Hungarian Army who were in the area responded by attacking the ÁVH men, and street fighting

In November 1956 Russian tanks entered Budapest – Hungarians put up a dogged defence.

broke out. When Russian tanks showed up, they were met by determined fire from partisan freedom fighters who had been armed by rebel workers from the arms factories in 'Red Csepel', one of the staunchest Communist districts in Budapest.

By 23 October, all of Hungary was in revolt. The statue of Stalin which stood near Heroes' Square was sawn off at the ankles, pulled down and spat on by angry crowds. ÁVH men were pulled out of the Interior Ministry and executed on the street. Imre Nagy was reinstated as Prime Minister and General Pál Maléter pledged the loyalty of the Hungarian Army to the new government. Many political prisoners were freed.

After the first few days of fighting, Russian troops began a hasty retreat from Hungary on 29 October. For the next few days a dazed euphoria swept the nation. Hungarians believed that the West would come to their aid, as promised daily by Radio Free Europe. It was an unfortunate miscalculation, compounded by the Suez Canal Crisis, which distracted Western attention.

On 1 November, claiming Hungary had illegally seceded from the Warsaw Pact, Russian tanks re-invaded and on 4 November once again entered Budapest. As tanks rolled down the boulevards, Hungarians put up a dogged defence. Battles took place at the Kilián Army Barracks (corner of Üllői út and József körút) and the fortresslike **Corvin cinema** nearby. In Buda, armed workers fought to prevent the approaching tanks from entering Pest through Széna tér. At Móricz Zsigmond

körtér students stopped tanks by spreading oil on the cobbled streets and pulling grenades on strings underneath the stalled vehicles.

Soon, however, Hungarian resistance was crushed. Imre Nagy took refuge in the Yugoslav embassy, but was captured when he accepted an armistice agreement. He and most of the other members of the Hungarian Revolutionary council were executed in secret. Thousands of Hungarians were sent to prison and 200,000 fled the country.

THE KADAR YEARS

The post-rebellion stranglehold on Hungary lasted until the 1960s, when amnesties were granted and János Kádár began a policy of reconciliation. His was a balancing act between hard-line Communism and appeasing the population. While Hungary maintained a strong Cold War stance and toed the Moscow line on 'Western Imperialism', Hungarians enjoyed a higher standard of living than most of Soviet eastern Europe. Hungary was known as 'the happiest barracks in the bloc'.

Life under Kádár meant more food in the shops, but it also meant banned books and 'psychological hospital' prisons for those who voiced dissent. Unlike his predecessors, Kádár allowed limited celebration of certain national traditions. Petőfi and Kossuth were extolled as precursors of the proletarian revolution. During the 1960s, Hungary finally began to resemble its old self. The rubble from World War II and the 1956 revolution was cleared away, historic buildings were restored. Tourism

began to grow again, although Western visitors could still find themselves followed around by government spies after dinner.

Kádár's balancing act was well proven in 1968. When Czechoslovakia irked the Soviets with the reform atmosphere of the Prague Spring, Hungarian troops loyally participated in the invasion. At the same time, however, Kádár introduced his 'New Economic Mechanism', an economic reform that broke with hard-line Communist theory and laid the ground for entrepreneurship. Kádár came to represent 'Communism with a human face'.

During the 1980s, however, it became obvious that the 'New Economic Mechanism' was flawed. Hungary became ever more dependent on foreign trade, and inflation rose. The black market in Western goods belied the ability of a command economy to provide basic goods and services, and Hungary's relations with its Warsaw Pact neighbours began to show signs of strain.

A growing number of writers and other public figures started to test the limits of open criticism, and by the 1980s Hungary was the centre of cast ern Europe's boom in underground *samizdat* literature. Typically, the Hungarian government was not pleased, but instead of jailing dissidents outright, authorities played a cat-and-mouse game with *samizdat* publishers, prosecuting them not for what they had written but for distributing their literature without using the national postal service, an economic crime. Western support for open debate came in odd ways. Billionaire Hungarian financier George Soros made deals to supply basic materials for hospitals and educational institutions. Soros also provided scholarships for Hungary's dissidents to study democratic practice at Universities in the West, and made the production of *samizdat* literature commonplace by flooding the country with free photocopy machines.

As it became obvious that the aged Kádár was no longer fit to rule, younger party members began to take positions of power. Known as the 'Miskolc Mafia', after the city where they had begun their political careers, many, such as Prime Minister Károly Grósz and his successor Miklós Németh, openly tolerated debate, while opening more doors for 'market socialism' and freer expression.

GOODBYE, IRON CURTAIN

In 1989 the bubble burst. In June, people took to the streets to rebury the remains of Imre Nagy. It was a hero's funeral attended by thousands. Soon after, a huge demonstration was held at Heroes' Square to protest against Romania's treatment of its Hungarian minority. Allowing public protest was a major shift in government policy.

*The **Soviet Army Memorial** at Szabadság tér (Liberation Square), formerly the site of the 'Sacred Flagstaff'.*

*The **Liberation Monument** – minus its star.*

Two events in the early summer of 1989 signalled the end of Communism. One was the government declaration that political parties could form to discuss the possibility of free elections in the future. The second was the mass exodus of East Germans to the West through Hungarian territory. When Hungary ceremonially cut the barbed wire fence on its Austrian border, thousands of East Germans poured into Hungary on 'vacation'. Those declaring that they wished to go to the West were housed and fed by the Hungarian government. East Germany's faltering Communist government was incensed when trainloads of refugees were taken by the Hungarian government on 'tours' that dropped them conveniently next to the Austrian border.

Hardline Communists in Hungary were alarmed and some factions called out the old Communist Workers guard in August 1989. An armed militia of geriatric hardliners, the Workers' Guard, shot several East Germans before the more moderate Hungarian Army protested and put an end to the vigilantism. The failure of the Workers' Guard marked the end of Communist hegemony.

Soon the 'reform Communists' led by Imre Pozsgay announced that free elections would take place in 1990. The Communist party threw in the hat, changed its name to the Hungarian Socialist Party and declared that it was running in the elections.

Hungary had tipped over the first domino. The collapse of Communism followed throughout eastern Europe. Hungarians breathed a sigh of collective relief, and then got down to the very Hungarian business of politics.

Post-Communist Hungary

Anyone expecting a honeymoon in Budapest had a rude awakening as dreams of a boom turned into the reality of a bust – but, at the very least, motorists could trade in their Trabants for three years' free public transport.

Early 1990 was a period of intoxicating possibilities for Hungarians. Conversations were focused on the newfound freedom, democracy and market capitalism. It was a new era and many Hungarians were quick to position themselves in the emerging economic and social picture. Just as many, however, found themselves bystanders, watching the changes from afar, confused and frustrated by yet another upheaval in history. With elections set for March 1990, Hungarians set about forming political parties – lots of them. Eventually, of 150 or so parties about six became contenders. The old dissidents coalesced around the Free Democrats (SZDSZ), while a national student activist group formed the Young Democrats (FIDESZ). The Communists split into the Socialist Party (MSZP) and the hardcore Workers' Party (Munkáspárt). Christian Democrats and the reformed Smallholders' Party held broad appeal. The Hungarian Democratic Forum (MDF) represented a mishmash of conservative and nationalistic views.

The SZDSZ and the MDF ran neck and neck during the first democratic elections since World War II, with the MDF winning the first round of Parliamentary elections. During the run-offs, however, the MDF began to use nationalist, sometimes anti-Semitic rhetoric, which many interpreted as an attempt by the MDF to present themselves as *népi-nemzeti* ('folkish-national') conservatives. It was a rhetoric that would pigeonhole the MDF for the next five years, eventually weakening their voter base and leading to splits within the party.

With a conservative, MDF-led coalition in Parliament, medical historian József Antall became Prime Minister, while dissident writer Árpád Göncz assumed the largely ceremonial position of President. The 'change of systems' (*rendszerváltás*) brought more than just democratic government. The face of Budapest changed as new businesses opened and the bright windows of Western fast-food restaurants and brand-name clothing shops began to replace the classy old neon. Business centres sprouted all over the city. Street names were changed, so that Lenin Boulevards and Marx Squares are no longer, and their respective statues and monuments were sent to the **Statue Park**. The ubiquitous red stars were taken down, and a law was signed that made any public use of 'symbols of tyranny' (such as red stars, hammers and sickles, as well as swastikas) a criminal offence.

Budapest's new Mayor, Gábor Demszky, was one of the original underground *samizdat* publishing heroes of the 1970s. An ardent environmentalist, Demszky has led a crusade against the pollution caused by ageing Eastern Bloc vehicles in Budapest, particularly Trabants. Budapest residents can now trade in their tiny East German cars for three-year public transport passes or low cost loans to buy newer cars.

DISTURBING SIGNS

As economic changes took place, a new class arose in Budapest, the entrepreneur or *menedzser*. Many young Hungarians found new opportunities working in Western businesses. Many others, however, found the changes confusing and Hungarians have been overwhelmed by new regulations. Unemployment rose as state industries were privatised and closed down. The standard of living for many, particularly pensioners, dropped below Communist-era levels, when prices were fixed and services were all state-subsidised. Crime rose as the divide between rich and poor grew sharper, although rates remain laughably low compared to virtually any other world capital, and violent crime is rare.

Expectations were high that Hungary would lead the eastern European pack in foreign investments and development. Instead, because of Hungary's foreign debt, small internal market and botched privatisation process, the expected boom turned out, in the hands of the MDF, to be a bust.

Western brand-name clothing stores have replaced many of the classy, old neon shop signs throughout Budapest.

*Writer **Árpád Göncz** – became President when József Antall was made Prime Minister.*

Prime Minister Antall, whose illness had been an increasingly public secret, died in December 1993. Stiff and paternalistic, he appealed to Hungarians who found his aristocratic bearing attractively old-fashioned. Others were surprised by Antall's inability or lack of willingness to condemn right-wing radicals within his governing coalition.

In spite of the polarisation of rich and poor, and the tense tenor of political debate, Budapest remains a relatively easy-going city. Politics remain in the realm of the loudly abstract, while life goes on in its quietly normal and antic way. Hungarians view politics the way other people watch football – passionately, with strong partisan feelings, and from the safe distance of a seat in the stadium. While politics has become a national obsession, few are willing actively to take part.

Even so, the June 1994 national elections were tamer than expected. The Socialist Party, led by former Communist Foreign Minister Gyula Horn (the man who in 1989 had given the order to open the border), won by a landslide. Voter dissatisfaction with nationalist rhetoric, the protracted war between government and media over control of state TV (*see chapter* **Media**) and the slowness of privatisation under the MDF gave way to a naive nostalgia for the good old days of the mid-1980s.

The Socialists, however, with their SZDSZ coalition partners, have prescribed a no-nonsense policy of belt-tightening for Hungary, and this has meant forint devaluations, slashes in funding for welfare and education, rocketing energy prices and shock-therapy privatisation measures designed to get the Hungarian economy on track with Europe for eventual EU membership.

Yet regardless of the changes that sweep through Hungary every few decades, Budapest remains one of the world's most wondrous cities, managing to maintain its beauty and dignity without hiding the wrinkles and warts that provide it with such a sense of character. Budapest wears its age and the scars of its history for all to see.

Budapest Today

'It's my party and I'll cry if I want to.' Budapesters may enjoy shedding a tear or two and the old guard may mutter about the good old days, but progress rumbles on.

Take an early evening stroll through Lipótváros in late summer and you will see Budapest as the old city was designed and built to be seen: wide streets full of imposing *mitteleuropäisch* architecture, stone façades recently re-pointed and boasting a fresh coat of pastel paint. Among the massive blocks, light from the setting sun will illuminate the small parks and squares that dot the area. Here you'll find locals walking dogs, strolling with babies in prams or playing chess at concrete tables. When Hungarians talk fondly and proudly of their capital, chances are it is a scene like this they have in mind.

Now take a mid-afternoon stroll through Őrmező or Újpest on a cloudy early autumn day. You will see Budapest as residents prefer not to think of her, but very likely see her every day: large, grey

apartment blocks where the lift isn't working, where local colour means hip hop squiggles on the wall and the only public areas are asphalt football pitches surrounded by rusty mesh fences.

It's a contrast that has surprised many visitors, whose preconceptions seem to veer towards either one or the other. There is the elegant Budapest of old, with its impeccable coffee houses, grand millennium architecture and colourful gypsy musicians patrolling exquisite high-ceilinged restaurants. There again is dull, grey Budapest with its surly waiters, factories adorned with red stars and where scuffling on the stairs at midnight means one less neighbour to compete with in the morning bread queue.

Which is true, then? Well, neither, now; but they both were once and both have left something of themselves behind. Budapest and its citizens have been living and coming to terms with their legacies in public view since 1989.

With the Fall of the Wall, the countries within the former Warsaw Pact were thrown into the spotlight for the first time in decades. In Hungary's case, the country had not received such attention since 1956. And while in many countries the spotlight revealed a dark, repressive, corrupt shambles of a society – exactly what the West expected to see on a Cook's Tour behind the Iron Curtain – the beam that swept over Hungary illuminated something subtly different.

There was a socialist government, true, but one that had long before eschewed the word 'Communist'. There was poorly built mass housing, but also a surprising number of comfortable privately owned homes. There were mammoth state-owned enterprises, complete with bureaucrats speaking fluent officialese, but also hundreds of small private businesses and many East-West joint ventures. While the bureaucrats were clad in desperately unfashionable suits of polyester, the youth in Váci utca were dressed in brightly coloured fashion garments that would not look out of place in Austria or Switzerland.

A stroll down Váci would also reveal a high degree of familiarity in brand names: Marlboro, Nescafé, Coca Cola and a myriad other products that were quietly being manufactured under licence. Visitors were shocked to find what the inhabitants of Austria and Italy had known for some time but had never quite got around to advertising: Hungary was different, the 'Communist' country with the proverbial human face.

It was, in fact, something of a playground where the careful visitor could breathe in history, sunbathe, eat, drink and party in a European context for the by now largely mythical ten dollars a day. It was hardly surprising that the country had been playing host to ten million foreign visitors a year, a figure soon to increase to a staggering 15 million (one and a half times the population). It was hardly surprising also that Western businesses in search of new markets often turned to Hungary first.

More surprising was the author of this state of affairs – former First Secretary János Kádár, once known as the 'Butcher of Budapest' for his role in crushing the 1956 Uprising. Kádár realised, however, that oppressive societies were inherently unstable as well as unproductive, and slowly, so as not to alarm the Soviet Union, introduced a number of reforms aimed at increasing Hungary's productivity and standard of living. Journalists called this phase 'goulash communism', and predicted that, with the death of Kádár, it wouldn't last.

It didn't, but not for the reasons predicted. There was no hard-line crackdown when Károly Grósz succeeded, just the wide realisation that Hungary's boomtime had been bought with fool's gold. The country was to all intents and purposes bankrupt, saddled with enormous foreign debt. It was at that point when the demise of Communism in Hungary began to seem inevitable.

The euphoria surrounding the 'System Change' and the farewell to the last of the occupying Russian troops was all too brief. The first Prime Minister, József Antall, was dogged by ill-health and an increasingly strident hard-right element in his own party. A nationalist mood prevailed and squabbles about media independence clouded more pressing economic issues. The privatisation process stalled early and the many tax concessions offered to new businesses (often with foreign investment) were phased out, partly to dull the cries that the country was being sold by the kilo to foreigners, but mainly because the government desperately needed the tax income to service the enormous foreign debt.

Another source of income was the population itself, which was (and still is) subjected to a massive personal and indirect tax burden, and one with surprisingly little to show its victims as a result: unemployment was on the up and up, inflation also, only faster, yet services such as health, public works and schooling were decaying fast. Much was said to suggest the government was frittering away its income, either to keep ministers in employment passing ever more bewildering legislation, or to rid the country of its symbols of its Communist past (the drive to change street names and tear down statues of Communist heroes cost millions of dollars). It seemed lawyers, accountants and cartographers were the only thriving professions; everybody else had to become at least marginally adept at tax fraud to keep going.

Against this backdrop, the opinions of the people of Budapest were as divided as they ever have been. A patient listener in quiet corners where Hungarians drink together would frequently be told (often by the same person) that things were better under the Old System, that the ex-Communists should be imprisoned or shot or both, that the West should pay more to support Hungary, that the West should be excluded from all privatisations, that the Common Market and NATO meant salvation, that imports from the EU were killing the country. If, as it is said, the Hungarians enjoy themselves while crying, the population at this time was having a ball.

Antall's death in December 1993 was followed by the second general election, at which the new-look Socialist Party romped home in coalition with the Social Democrats. The current government has attempted to redress the last few years of indecision and lack of direction. Once again the target of extreme austerity measures has been the hapless man in the street, whose continuing survival is a testament to Hungarian tenacity.

The average Budapest resident is now rather tired and cynical, and readily believes things will get worse. He will probably admit that life was easier in the goulash communist days, but will say there have been many benefits gained over the last few years that are worth having. A place of his own to live will be the first priority, followed by a decent car, decent food and a holiday abroad – perhaps Corfu this year. And money? Very important, but thankfully hard work, business acumen and a bit of luck will ensure success these days, and your political record or beliefs are an irrelevance. True, connections still matter, but they are no substitute for hustle or maybe a well-timed bank note into the right hands.

If pressed, the Budapester may admit that the Czech Republic has overtaken Hungary on the way to the twenty-first century, but will hotly deny that Prague would be a better place to live. Budapest has more life, and the Hungarians are better qualified at enjoying themselves, he will tell you. Although very little of the necessary renovation work has been completed in the capital due to lack of funding, the Budapester will tell you that their home city is still one of the most attractive and vibrant in Europe, and you as a visitor will see little to contradict this. And although crime increases daily, and the police seem quite incapable of coping, he will deny reports spread by alarmist tour operators that Budapest is dangerous. Here again, he will be right, particularly in comparison with other west European capitals. When told of pick-pocketing or crooked taxi drivers, he will shrug and ask you to show him a town where such things don't occur.

Most citizens are disturbed by the increasing division of wealth, and concerned at the growing number of the poor and needy. True to cynical form, the average Hungarian will probably not expect the government to do much about it and will instead try to make sure his family and himself are covered. The social cloth is a much closer weave in Hungary than further west and families – even quite widely spread ones – do support each other in times of need.

Above all, the Budapest resident is now his own man at last. He can be counted on to look after his children, help his friends, probably pick up the tab at dinner (because he likes entertaining and is still very hospitable), but can no longer be expected to think what someone else wants him to think. If he seems intolerant of racial minorities in his city, devoid of courtesy in traffic or aggressively vocal on why the government are all fools or why the tax department should look elsewhere for their next few thousand and leave him the hell alone, then, in his view, fair enough: this is his city.

And the city is the citizen, writ large.

Architecture

Revolutions play havoc with a city's building styles as new regimes set about eradicating all signs of the old order, but Budapest retains elegant epochal echoes among crass creeping commercialisation.

In 1904, leading Budapest modern architect Béla Lajta complained about the international styles that dominated the city: 'The visitor from abroad should find houses here that speak Hungarian, and those houses should teach him to speak Hungarian himself.'

Attempts to create a distinctive sense of place have preoccupied Budapest's architects since the early nineteenth century. Successive waves of occupation have left the city's architecture polarised: between that of its occupiers and that of supporters of the national cause. Hungary's own imperial position during the Dual Monarchy has also left its mark. Class antagonisms, state ideology and commercial colonisation have put Budapest's buildings into the frontline.

Things are not always what they seem. Architectural style and form have been consciously used as propaganda. History has been reinvented time and time again. Yet this creative tension has only enhanced the beauty of Budapest.

Pre-World War I

Repeated sieges of Castle Hill destroyed the pre-Turkish city, yet Habsburg rebuilding after the seventeenth-century reconquest of Buda often incorporated medieval ruins. Reconstruction after World War II uncovered many more Gothic remains, which were then combined with the restoration. Baroque façades, particularly on I. Úri utca, often include Gothic windows and door frames. Reconstructed merchants' houses can be found on I. Tárnok utca 14 and 16 and distinctive sedilias, seats for servants in the gateways of mansions, can be seen at I. Országház utca 9, I. Szentháromság tér 5 and 7.

MIHRABS & BATHHOUSES

A century and a half of Turkish occupation has also left surpisingly little trace. Many churches were turned into mosques. The **Belváros Parish Church** still contains a *mihrab* (prayer niche) and the Alsó Viziváros Parish Church on I. Fő utca 32 has the distinctive ogee-shaped Turkish windows on its south wall. Minarets were destroyed once the Habsburgs recaptured the city in 1686 and mosques were turned back into churches. Even the tiny domed **tomb of Gül Baba** was consecrated as a chapel by the Jesuits.

The greatest Turkish contribution to Budapest were the bathhouses. The **Rudas**, **Rác**, **Király** and Czázsár (part of the **Lukács** complex) baths are still in use under their original copper domes.

CHURCHES & GARRISONS

The Habsburg reconquest found Budapest with a largely Protestant population. The Baroque style was critical to the counter-reformation, its curving sensuality and rich iconography a deliberately seductive contrast to Protestant austerity. The **Church of St Anne** on Batthyány tér is one of Hungary's most striking Baroque monuments.

Hungarian Catholic authorities revived the medieval cult of the holy kings. Frescoes and altar statues of István, László and Imre can be seen in the Krisztinaváros and Erzsébetváros Parish Churches (I. Krisztina tér and VII. Rózsák tere). Szent István's Holy Right Hand resides to this day in the **Basilica**.

The largest secular Baroque buildings are military. The Városház (City Hall) at V. Városház utca 9-11 was built as a hospital for veterans of the war against the Turks. The **Citadella** fortress on Gellérthegy was built to assert Habsburg control after the Hungarian defeat in 1849.

The aristocratic mansions and artisans' houses of the Castle District have been faithfully restored. The rich terracotta pinks and ochres, greens and blues of the façades are complemented by the elegant patterns of doors and window grilles. The former Erdődy Mansion (Táncsics Mihály utca 4), now the **Music History Museum**, and the tiny mid-eighteenth-century Baroque courtyard blocks all over the Castle District are particularly inviting. Houses in the *copfstil*, a Hungarian late Baroque style, can be found at Fő utca 20 and Batthyany tér 3. Their characteristic undulating tiled roofs have little eye-like windows peeking out.

SEVERITY & RATIONALITY

The Embellishment Committee, set up in 1808 to develop Pest, chose the neo-classical style for areas such as the Lipótváros, challenging the feudalism of aristocratic Buda. The cultivation of national identity and the aspiration to a modern industrial

*Ancient middle eastern symbolism is evident in Béla Lajta's motifs on the **Új Szinház**.*

economy is clear in the surviving neo-classical monuments. Pannonia, with the Hungarian coat of arms on her shield, sits in the tympanum of the **National Museum**. Mihály Pollack's Grecian design followed the idiom set by the British Museum and the Altes Museum in Berlin and was the fourth museum of its kind in the world. The 1830s also saw the construction of the Lánchíd, the first permanent crossing of the Danube.

BACK TO THE FUTURE

In the decades of the Dual Monarchy after 1867, Budapest expanded with astonishing speed. Preparation for the 1896 Millennial celebrations spurred the building of the capital's most important monuments. The **Opera House, Parliament,** the rebuilding of the **Mátyás templom**, expansion of the **Castle**, and the current layout of the **Városliget** all date from this time.

Monumental planning was designed to legitimise the city's new status as an imperial capital. Boulevards such as Andrássy út, Bajcsy-Zsilinszky út and the Nagykörút carved through the poorer areas of the city and facilitated the policing of growing unrest.

A selective reinvention of Hungarian history pervades these new monuments. Both the neo-Gothic style of the Mátyás Templom and the neo-Romanesque **Fisherman's Bastion** romanticised medieval Christian values. The **Turul statue** by the Palace and the intricate ironwork of the Parliament gates allude to the mythical pagan-divine ancestry of Árpád, legendary founder of the Hungarian nation.

The 1896 exhibition had a profound impact on design in the years that followed. But all that remains of the structures that filled the park is Vajdahunyad Castle, a Disney-like fantasy that now houses the **Agriculture Museum**.

TIME BANDITS

The extravagantly vulgar decoration that characterises the eclectic and neo-Renaissance styles reflected the ambition of the growing bourgeoisie. Buildings were designed from pattern books. Neo-Gothic and neo-Renaissance entrance halls clash with neo-Baroque ornamentation, but the eclectic extravagance of the now crumbling courtyard blocks of Districts V, VI, VII and VIII is superficial. Façades decked with cherubs, devils, and voluptuous caryatids hide courtyards with the sparsest of detail, and where entire families often lived in only one room.

Allusions to alchemy and freemasonry abound. The neo-Gothic entrance hall of V. Báthori utca 24, where sphinxes sit on Hermes' winged helmet, is particularly intriguing. The blatant masonic symbolism of leading nineteenth-century architect Miklós Ybl's Opera House is echoed in his Várkert Bazar (now the Várkert Casino at I. Ybl Miklós tér) and the Basilica.

Colossal debts incurred in the city's expansion are reflected in the opulence of financial institutions. The proportions of the former Stock and Commodity Exchange (now the headquarters of Magyar TV) on **Szabadság tér** were deliberately distorted to overawe with the power of money. The former headquarters of the Domestic Savings

Museum of Applied Arts – *an Oriental feel.*

Bank, now the British Embassy, at V. Harmincad utca 6, is one of the few accessible to the visitor. The magificent undulating glass ceiling of the former cashier's hall has survived virtually intact.

THIS MODERN AGE

The new construction techniques of the late nineteenth century were used to the full. The recently renovated **Nagy Vásárcsarnok,** and **Nyugati station,** built between 1874-77 by the Eiffel company, revel in palatial use of iron and glass.

Experimentation with new materials was one of the driving forces behind Art Nouveau. The villas and apartment blocks of Districts VI and VII beyond Oktogon are the best examples, particularly along VI. Városligeti fasor and VII. Munkácsy Mihály utca, although the rich marble and tiled interior of the **Zeneakadémia** is also worth seeing. Characteristically curvaceous iron doorways with flower and bird motifs can be spotted all over the centre, notably at **Gresham Palace.** The Metro Klub at VII. Dohány utca 22 is a rare Hungarian example of the more geometric Viennese secessionist style.

The decorative arts and fine craftsmanship were integral to art nouveau. The Hungária mosaic rising above V. Szervita tér on the former Turkish Banking House (now Black Point Jeans & Shoes at ground level) is particularly striking.

A PLACE OF ONE'S OWN

Questions of national identity preoccupied intellectuals throughout the nineteenth century and

were paralleled by attempts to develop a national style of architecture. Disillusionment after defeat in the Second War of Independence led to the belief that Hungary's salvation lay in its eastern origins and folk culture. Frigyes Feszl's ornamentation for the **Vigadó** included frog fastenings from Hussar's uniforms, the faces of moustachioed Hungarian peasants and Tibetan heads.

The **Central Synagogue** is also in the Moorish and Turkish-inspired Romantic style. Orientalism resonated later in the designs of the **Párizsi udvar** and the **Museum of Applied Arts.** Zsolnay tiles, manufactured in Pécs, were important in creating a distinctive sense of place and frost-resistant glazes ensured that their rich colours survived. The deep blue wallpaper-like façade of Lechner's Thonet House (V. Váci utca 11a) is particularly beautiful. Ancient middle eastern symbolism is evident in Béla Lajta's mausoleums in the Jewish part of **Újköztemető cemetery** and in his motifs on the Parisiana nightclub, now the **Új Szinház.**

Ödön Lechner made it his life's cause to develop a distinctive Hungarian architecture. He believed that the new idiom should emerge with the use of modern materials and structural applications, yet also made a serious study of Hungarian folk art which he brought to life in three dimensions. The gracious curves in the Museum of Applied Arts, the Geological Institute on XIV. Stefánia út 14 and the magnificent former **Royal Post Office Savings Bank** are enhanced by soft colours and light that give his buildings a magical aura. The playful surreality of his decoration is comparable to that of Antoni Gaudí.

A group of architects called A Fiatal Csoport ('The Young Ones'), originally students of Lechner's, looked to medieval folk architecture as the 'true' basis for an authentic national style and conducted detail-collecting expeditions much like the musical odysseys of Bartók and Kodály. Their style has become known as the 'National Romantic' and can be seen in the **Werkerle Estate** in Kispest built between 1909-14.

Béla Lajta, on the other hand, another student of Lechner's, pursued an urban version of the Hungarian idiom. His 1911 Rózsavölgyi House (now the **Rózsavölgy** music shop) is a forerunner of internationalist avant garde architecture. Here the use of folk art is purely decorative, confined to patterns on the copper skirting.

The tension between these two trends – urban modernist versus rural romantic – continued to dominate the architecture of the interwar period.

Between the Wars

The Hungarian utopian avant garde was centred around the journal *Ma* (*Today*), edited by the poet and painter Lajos Kassák. The Horthy dictatorship forced Kassák (whose futurist poems and constructivist paintings reside at the **Kassák Museum**) and other leading avant gardists into exile. László Moholy-Nagy and Marcel Breuer found fame at the Bauhaus, as did Ernst Kállai in the Der Stijl group. But many important figures, such as Lajos Kozma and the Bauhaus-trained Farkas Molnár, remained.

Kozma's **Atrium cinema** and apartment block can be found at II. Margit körút 55. The former Manfred Weiss Pension Office apartment block at Margit körút 17 is notable for the lifts in glass tubes centred in the eliptical staircase. Molnár's houses can be found in District II, particularly along Pasaréti út. Both architects were among those who designed the 1931 **Napraforgó utca experimental housing estate**.

Not all modern architects were leftists, however. An enormous Nietzschean superman looks down with disdain from the apartment block at VI. Bajcsy-Zsilinszky út 19, built in 1940.

FAMILY VALUES

Garden suburb developments were common under the Horthy regime, constructed mainly for refugees fleeing territories lost after Trianon. The residents of Szent Imre Kertváros in Pestszentlőrinc (District XVIII) paid for the construction of the garden suburb themselves, which was planned to reflect the traditional communities they had left behind. Though now in a sad state of disrepair, many of the tiny houses mimic the neo-Baroque mansions of the aristocracy.

Public buildings of the Horthy era, such as the enormous Szent Imre Church on XI. Villányi út 23-25, as well as many of the larger mansions on Gellérthegy, were also designed in a neo-Baroque style, a reaction to the liberalism and supposed immorality of the city.

Post-World War II

Shock at war devastation was intensified by subsequent social upheaval. Rebuilding Budapest became a national priority of psychological and political importance. The policy of reconstruction, which took decades, was to restore historic buildings to their prewar state. Restoration of the Mátyás templom, for instance, faithfully executed Schulek's original design.

The need for a sense of historical continuity followed through during the Rákosi regime. The radical replanning of Budapest didn't get very far, but the regime did attack the 'the visual landscape of everyday life'.

Streets were renamed rather than obliterated and the names of Communist leaders were used alongside those of Hungarian national heroes. Street corners sometimes still display the old street signs, crossed through since the demise of Communism. Shopfronts were another battle ground. The campaign to end competition between individual shops led to the destruction of many Art Nouveau interiors. Király utca still sports several painted glass shop signs of the Rákosi era, all in the same gold typeface and dark backgrounds.

Kozma and Molnár both worked on the 1931 **Napraforgó utca experimental housing estate**.

Rákosi-era architecture was a relatively restrained version of totalitarian classicism. The elegant porticos of the Hungarian Optical Factory (MOM) on XII. Csörsz utca 35-47 are reminiscent of 1930s Italian modernism. The College of Fine Arts at II. Zugligeti út 9-25 and the Dubbing Film Studio at II. Hűvösvölgyi út 68 have been recommended for national protection.

Architecture was actively used as propaganda. Housing estate and factory design were promoted as monuments of working class achievement. The workshops of the Csepel Car Factory (Autogyár tér, Szigethalom) have an almost organic form, their skylights curved like shark fins. Fifty thousand people laboured 'voluntarily' to build the **Népstadion** with its Stalinist statues, the major monument of the Rákosi regime.

Tenement blocks sprang up to cope with the postwar housing crisis. They were comfortable but small, the absence of privacy compounded by thin walls. Social activity was meant to take place in the workplace and in the specially built culture houses which are still important in city life.

Soviet war memorials turned Budapest into a necropolis. Tombs were built in public places such as the park on XII. Csörsz utca and Ludovika Gardens in Csepel (District XXI). Separate areas for Soviet soldiers were also laid out in **Kerepesi cemetery.**

The **Liberation Memorial** on Gellérthegy and the memorial to Soviet soldiers in **Szabadság tér** symbolised Hungarian military defeat. Statues of Stalin and Lenin once standing in the Városliget were infused with an almost religious significance. Stalin was pulled down in 1956, but other statues, including the Soviet soldier from the Liberation monument, can now be found in the **Statue Park.**

1956 AND ALL THAT

The Kádár government was quick to eradicate most signs of the uprising, although bullet holes can be seen down many side streets and the **New York Kaveház**, its façade smashed into by a tank, is still unrepaired today.

The thaw after Stalin's death in 1953 gradually worked its way into the architecture of the city. Eszpresszó interiors celebrated with rock 'n' roll décor. The Origo Eszpresszó in the bus terminus at II. Pasaréti tér still has groovy 1960s light fittings, and is kitted out in the ubiquitous brown and orange. Neon signs from this period still grace the shopfronts of Margit körút and the Buda waterfront near Margit híd. Many say simply 'shoeshop' or 'food', but look out for the cartoon waiter advertising the Pinguin bar on XI. Bocskai út 33 and the daring typography of the Sztár Fodrász on VI. Király utca 72 – the politically correct place to get your hair done.

Kádárism was a disaster for architecture, which was relegated to a subsection of the building industry. Prefabricated concrete housing estates such as József Attila Housing Estate on IX. Üllői út were the result, though the Óbuda Experimental Housing Estate on III. Bécsi út is still acclaimed for its varied housing and attention to detail.

Ironically it is the work of Imre Makovecz, then excommunicated from the profession, that has brought modern Hungarian architecture international renown. He claims to invoke the magic latent in peasant folk culture. His yurt houses on Sashegy in Districts XII and II. Törökvész lejtő draw on the symbolic form of Siberian nomad shelters. His approach is best suited to metaphysical exploration, as in his interior for the Mortuary Chapel in **Farkasréti cemetery**.

CONSUMING PASSIONS

These days the spotlight has returned to Budapest's shopfronts and interiors. Western retail logos and brash fast food chains now dominate the Nagykörút. Multinational neon hoardings are replacing the Inca Orion mask and the glorious Casco revolving tyres (examples of both still shine above the Buda foot of Margaret Bridge, flanking a new Philips sign).

Old-style shop fronts and signs are again symbolising resistance, this time to rampant commercialism. Erma's at VII. Erzsébet körút 62 suggests a 1930s elegance, the genteel place to buy your underwear. The 1920s typography of the Otthon Bútorház (VI. Teréz körút 27) sign harks back to the days when quality still mattered. Ancient dingy eszpresszó bars such as the Majakovszkij at VII. Király utca 103 hold out against the tide of change, while the brass-and-mirror tack in newer bars feigns membership of the affluent West. **Café Mozart**, the ultimate in postmodern indelicacy, reduces a vibrant coffeehouse culture to a mythologised 'central European experience'. But a local sense of irony prevails in the pastiche. **Marxim** pizzeria, serves up Stalinist kitsch with tomato ketchup. The Statue Park attempts to construct a critique of Stalinism while treating the statues themselves with dignity in their obsolescence.

The city has been reduced to theatrical backdrop. Juxtaposed with crass western commercialisation, crumbling nineteenth-century architecture achieves a dignity it would have lacked in its prime. The 1994 collapse of an apartment building on Ó utca in the centre of Budapest highlighted the poor state of the city's infrastructure. Little maintenance has been done since World War II although several of the most important buildings have been renovated in the past few years.

While George Morriose's French Institute at I. Fő utca 17 enhances the Buda waterfront, the only real monuments for the 1996 Magyar Millennium celebrations are high-tech hotels catering to a foreign élite, such as József Finta's gleaming and monumentally proportioned **Kempinski Hotel.**

Budapest by Area

Budapest
by Area

Combining one of the most magical urban landscapes in the world with shabby, bullet-pocked façades and overgrown inner courtyards, Budapest is like any other major European city – only more so.

In **Clark Ádám tér**, near the funicular that leads up to the **Castle District**, stands a thing like a giant, elongated doughnut. This is the Zero Kilometre Stone, the point from which all distances to Budapest are measured and thus the official centre of town. And centre it is, between the Danube, central Europe's main waterway, and the Castle District, the rocky promontory that throughout history offered a controlling vantage over the river – together the main reason why there was ever a settlement here in the first place. From this square the Chain Bridge stretches over the Danube into Pest. Completed in 1849, it was the first permanent crossing over the river (before that were only rickety pontoon bridges in summer, occasional ferries or perilous treks across thin ice in winter). It was this bridge that allowed the subsequent incorporation of Buda, Pest and Óbuda into one single city in 1872. Other routes from here prod north and south along the Danube, while the tunnel conveys traffic beneath Castle Hill and into Buda beyond.

The Danube sweeps by strong and wide, though here it is at its narrowest and currents are relatively weak. The river, too, is one area of Budapest – the only city on its long course between Black Forest and Black Sea where the Danube flows straight through the middle of a city. There are quiet parks on its Margaret and Óbuda islands. Spectacular views from its bridges – upstream from Szabadság híd or downstream from Margaret híd – form part of the urban landscape. Always present in the panorama from the Buda Hills, the Danube asserts itself even when out of sight. Come down one of the Pest streets leading to the embankment and the light changes as you approach the river, a result of reflection off the water and the sudden open space. The Danube is never blue, however. More usually it's a dull and muddy brown.

Buda

Older than Pest, more conservative and residential, and notably devoid of decent bars, Buda is sort of disjointed. The Castle and Gellért Hills carve up the central area into a patchwork of separate parts. The continuation of the Nagykörút runs round the back of these two urban hummocks, losing definition between Moszkva tér and Móricz Zsigmond körtér, the north and south hubs of public transport on this side of the river. To the north and west of the central area, smart residential districts amble up into still higher hills – green and spotted with villas in a way that, from a distance, are reminiscent of Los Angeles.

Castle District

Wandering around the streets at the north end of the Vár – the Castle District – you'll see surnames against the doorbells of small Baroque houses. This is perhaps the most surprising thing about this whole historic area: people still live here. Without that reminder, the Vár appears to be nothing but one big tourist attraction – and certainly no visit to Budapest is complete without at least one afternoon up here. Apart from the obvious major landmarks – the former **Royal Palace** complex, the **Mátyás templom** and the **Fisherman's Bastion** – the narrow streets and open squares that top this 60-metre hill also contain no fewer than nine museums, from the dreary waxworks in the **Panoptikum** through oddities such as the **Museum of Commerce & Catering** to national institutions such as the **Széchenyi Library** and the **National Gallery**, as well as assorted other churches, mansions and statues. Practically every building, as the ubiquitous stone plaques with their Hungarian-only inscriptions indicate, seems to have been declared a Műemlék – an historic monument.

The air of unreality is abetted by the quiet. You have to have a permit, or else be staying at the awful **Hilton Hotel** to bring a car into the Castle District, and though there are plenty of parked

*The most surprising thing about the Vár – the **Castle District** – is that people still actually live there.*

vehicles, there is no through traffic. A few souped-up horses and carts with traditionally costumed coachmen (you can rent them at Szentháromság tér) clatter along backstreets bearing parties of sightseers. The small Várbusz comes up from Moszkva tér to circle the district every few minutes. But otherwise the only street noises are the prattle of tour groups and the whirr of Japanese video cameras. Most of the shops are tourist-orientated, selling lacy folk items, overpriced antiques, 35mm film, postcards and strings of dried paprika. Locals have to dive downhill to Moszkva tér or **Déli station** to buy their bread and túró.

But the feeling that all here is not really real is an accurate one. Buda Castle has been destroyed and rebuilt so many times that virtually nothing historically authentic remains. Though it was inhabited in celtic times, the first major settlement on this hill was in the thirteenth century. That was promptly trashed by the Mongols.

King Mátyás built a renaissance palace, then the Turks showed up in 1541 and wrecked the place again. Everything they built was in turn destroyed when Habsburg-led armies chased them back out in 1686. Rebuilt once more, it was damaged during the 1848-49 War of Independence, rebuilt again in the latter half of the nineteenth century, somehow managed to get through World War I unscathed, and was pounded back into rubble in 1945.

Postwar reconstruction, which took decades, has followed the way things were before the war, and incorporated earlier bits and pieces unearthed in wartime ruins. Many Baroque houses were built on medieval foundations, and all this has been faithfully reproduced.

A lot of it was only simulated history anyway. Bits of the Mátyás templom date back to the thirteenth century, but the nineteenth-century reconstruction by Frigyes Schulek, who also designed the phony ramparts of the Fisherman's Bastion, romanticised the thing according to then current notions about Hungarian national identity. Add touches such as the **Sikló** – funicular – and the **Turul Statue**, and what you get is a sort of historical theme park: Dual Monarchyland.

The Royal Palace, which looks splendid from over the river, is pretty boring up close. Nothing here now but the musuems. Even the Habsburgs, for whom it was originally built, never stayed here much. The crenellated Fisherman's Bastion, guarded by a statue of St Stephen, offers fantastic views across the Danube and Pest, but isn't quite the same now one can't wander at will, and instead must pay an entrance fee to help save 'this internationally recognised value of Hungarian architecture'. Here one can sit and drink the worst and most overpriced beer in Budapest – we'd swear it must be watered down – and listen to competing musics from the violinist in one of the turrets, and

cocktail piano drifting up from the terrace behind the horrible mirror glass Hilton which has somehow managed to worm its way into this UNESCO-protected area.

Tóth Árpád sétány, the promenade on the other side, overlooks ugly Déli station, the houses of Krisztinaváros, and a telecommunications centre that looks like something out of *Thunderbirds*. It's pleasant under the chestnut trees, especially at sunset. Relatively tourist-free, this is where the old folk of the Castle District come to stroll.

If you walk up to the north end of the hill, along the Anjou Bastion past the artillery pieces behind the Museum of Military History, you'll find the Memorial to the last Pasha of Buda. Vizir Abdurrahman Abdi Arnaut Pasha was killed and buried here in 1686. 'A valiant foe,' reads the inscription, 'may he rest in peace.' People still sometimes leave fresh flowers at his grave. The nearby Vienna Gate, which looks much older, was built in 1936 to commemorate the 250th anniversary of the victory over the Turks.

In a way the only real piece of history in the whole Castle District is the wrecked stump of the former Ministry of Defence, down at the south end of Dísz tér, unrestored and bullet-pocked from the last desperate battles between Nazis and Soviets. Little happens up here at night, although it can all be very atmospheric in the dark. The **Király** is the only restaurant we'd recommend. If you want to pause for a coffee or beer in the middle of all this relentless sightseeing, the **Café Miró** is refreshingly unhistorical.

The Tabán, Gellért Hill & Surrounds

Krisztinaváros sits below the Castle District to the west. Apart from the enormous, and enormously ugly, Déli pályaudvar – the station for trains to the Balaton, Croatia and other points south-west – there isn't much noteworthy about the area.

South of here, between Castle Hill and **Gellért Hill**, is the Tabán. Now a public park, this was once an ancient and disreputable quarter inhabited by Serbs, Greeks and Gypsies, most of whom made their living on the river. The Horthy government levelled it in the 1930s and only a few bits and pieces remain. Appropriately enough for an area once renowned for its gambling dens, one of these is the **Várkert Casino**, housed in a Miklós Ybl-designed neo-Renaissance-style pump house (it used to furnish water for the Royal Palace) near the **Semmelweis Museum of Medical History**. Ybl also designed the nineteenth-century exterior of the **Rác baths**, over on the other side of the park below Gellért Hill. The original domed Turkish pool survives within.

On the other side of the roads which feed traffic on and off Erzsébet híd (Elizabeth Bridge), the only

*The little park beyond Móricz Zsigmond körter boasts a supposedly **bottomless lake.***

building between Gellért Hill and the Danube, stands the **Rudas**, most beautiful, atmospheric and (though men-only) least gay of all the Turkish bathhouses. It doesn't look much from outside, though. On the cliff behind it, over the road from the number 7 bus stop, plaques note several springs that emerge from the hill at this point, variously christened Rákóczi, Gül Baba, Beatrix, Kinizsi and Musztafa. This last is named for Sokoli Mustapha, pasha from 1566-78, who caused the Rudas to be constructed.

Gellért Hill rises steep at this point. Looking up you'll sometimes see rock climbers scaling the limestone cliffs with ropes. An easier route is the path that leads up to the **statue of martyred Archbishop Gellért**, enclosed by a colonnade and brandishing a crucifix at motorists crossing Erzsébet híd. Paths meander up and around the hill and it's easy to find your way to the top. Villas dot the south and west slopes but here there are only trees, through which one catches steadily more spectacular views of the Danube and Pest rooftops beyond. Once this hill was covered in vines, but a nineteenth-century epidemic of phylloxera destroyed them all. Some fig trees still flourish, though, brought here by the Turks in the sixteenth century.

The grim **Citadella** on the 230-metre summit was built by the Austrians to assert their authority after the 1848-49 War of Independence. Its artillery were never used against the city and portions of it were symbolically dynamited when Budapest and Vienna kissed and made up with the Ausgleich of 1867. It's now a quiet spot with extraordinary views and contains a variety of tourist amenities, although the Hungarian army still sets up camp here every August to supervise the **St Stephen's Day** fireworks. The **Liberation Monument**, a figure apparently doing some form of aerobics with a palm frond, towers above the ramparts, flanked below by sprightly statues of Progress and Destruction.

From here any number of paths lead down the other side of the hill. On the way you might pass the **Cave Church**, an odd and somewhat spooky place of worship run by monks of the Hungarian Paulite order. The white-robed brothers live in the pseudo-historical monastery just around the hill facing the river. At the Buda foot of Szabadság híd (Freedom Bridge) stands the four-star **Gellért Hotel**, an imposing Art Nouveau edifice with a complex of thermal baths and swimming pools behind. This is Budapest's most famous hotel, built 1912-18. The first-class eszpresszó is one of the city's few decent spots for breakfast, although the terrace is rather noisy. Even if you don't want to swim or soak, it's worth poking your head round the **Gellért baths**' entrance in Kelenhegyi út just to clock the impressively ornate secessionist foyer.

The **Technical University** stands to the south of here on what was once a marsh, and Bartók Béla út runs round the south side of the hill. From about 200 metres down, the view of Szabadság híd's green metal girders sweeping across the line of the road is a unique piece of cityscape. This busy shopping street and some of the roads off it (Mészöly utca, Lágymányosi utca) also have an assortment of interesting turn-of-the-century buildings, notably Ödön Lechner's number 40, and József Fischer's numbers 15B and 49.

Roads off to the right lead up to the residential district of Gellért Hill, where the former School of State Management, academy for the Communist elite, stands tall and still somehow a little proud. A statue of **Géza Gárdonyi**, famous for authoring an adventure novel about the 1552 Siege of **Eger**, one of Hungary's few famous victories, occupies the triangle where Bercsényi utca meets the main road.

Just beyond Móricz Zsigmond körtér, terminus for assorted trams and buses and very much the border between the city centre and the outlying industrial suburbs to the south, is a small park, venue for the annual **World Music Festival** each June. This has an austere statue of Bartók and a supposedly bottomless lake (actually four metres deep). The Baroque façade of Szent Imre's church over the way on Villányi út lends some historical atmosphere, but like so much else in Budapest, it's a bit of a fake, built in 1938.

The Víziváros (Water Town)

From the north-east side of the Castle District, ancient streets cascade down towards the Danube. The Víziváros (Water Town) is one of Budapest's oldest districts. It's a quiet and conservative area where nothing very much happens, stretching about a mile north from Clark Ádám tér to the foot of Margaret Bridge, gradually widening west away from the river and towards Moszkva tér.

Main street is Fő utca (it means just that: 'main street') a thoroughfare of Roman origin that runs parallel to the Danube-hugging Bem rakpart. Down here are medieval houses, Baroque churches, small squares and narrow roads leading up to the Castle. George Mauroius's French Institute at number 17 is one of the city's few decent postmodern buildings, with an impressive and prominent waterfront location.

The space in front of it somehow invites you to stroll across and wonder whether the French are trying to make amends for 1920, when their support for the Little Entente was instrumental in Trianon's dismemberment of Hungary, or just ostentatiously asserting Gallic culture. The flashy fireworks they let off here every 14 July, Bastille Day, suggests the latter.

Batthyány tér is the centrepiece of this area, opening from Fő utca out on to the Danube where Parliament looms rather largely on the opposite bank. It's a busy and interesting square, with a desultory flea market in the middle and an assortment of notable, mostly eighteenth-century architecture round the edges. The **Church of St Anne**

on the southern side is one of Hungary's finest Baroque buildings, with a decidedly camp interior. The middle-class ladies of Buda gather for coffee and cakes in St Anne's former presbytery, now the **Angelika** café, where light seeps in through atmospheric stained glass windows. Number 4 was built in 1770 as the White Cross Inn and is these days called the Casanova House – he supposedly once stayed here – while number 3 next door is a rare example of a late Baroque style called copfstil. The 1902 market hall now houses a modern supermarket with depressing piped Muzak.

Batthyány tér is also a public transport hub: various buses leave from here, and underground there is both a station on the M2 line and the southern terminal of the HÉV line that runs north to **Szentendre**. The station boasts Budapest's first privately owned public convenience, which has clean towels and plastic flowers.

Further north along Fő utca at 70-72 is the forbidding Military Court of Justice, used as a prison and headquarters by both the Gestapo in the Nazi times, and the secret police in the Stalinist 1950s. Here Imre Nagy and associates were tried in secret and condemned to death after the 1956 revolution. A block away are the **Király baths**, another leftover from the Turkish days and, unlike the others, interesting to view from outside as well as in.

The street ends at Bem tér, where there's a statue of General Joseph Bem. A Pole, Bem led the Hungarian army in the War of Independence. On 23 October 1956, this small square was the site of a huge demonstration – partly because people wished to express their approval of political changes in Poland. It was the beginning of the revolution that was to end so starkly just three blocks back down the road.

Moszkva tér & the Rózsadomb

Coming up the escalator from Moszkva tér metro, you see concrete supports which fan beautifully across the ceiling above the mouth of the tunnel. Outside, though, the station building looks tired and tatty. On the terrace above, where you can sit, drink a beer and watch the action in the square from the rooftop eszpresszó, grass grows up from cracks in the concrete.

Ugly and delapidated, Moszkva tér, a major public transport hub connecting the Buda Hills to the rest of town, bustles with lowlife. From 5am it's an unofficial labour market: Romanians and Gypsies gather outside the station, waiting for someone to come along and hire them for a day's work. All day long, as trams going in several directions pull in and out and small buses nip up to the Castle District, police check the papers of anyone sitting around who looks like they might be an illegal immigrant. Hungarians from rural areas also cluster here, selling flowers, fruit and lace tablecloths to rush hour crowds.

Over the road in Ostrom utca, the **Várlak** is a friendly gay pub that always seems to be full of straight people. In nearby Retek utca, the **Szent Jupát** restaurant serves cheap and hearty platefuls deep into the night. A short walk on to Kis Rókus utca, up the side of a large tram factory, leads to the **Marxim**, where pizzas are served up with Stalinist kitsch. But despite all the bustle there's not really much life around here. Moszkva tér is mainly a tawdry transition zone where people pass through but rarely stop.

And very different from the Rózsadomb, which it serves. Down near the Buda foot of Margaret Bridge, you can walk up the narrow, cobbled Gül Baba utca and come to the **tomb of Gül Baba**. The northernmost Islamic holy place in Europe and a peaceful spot, this is the resting-place of a Turkish dervish credited with introducing roses to Budapest. It's also the foot of the Rózsadomb – Rose Hill – Budapest's most fashionable residential district.

This villa-speckled hill has long been known as the 'millionaires' district'. Whereas in cities such as London, Paris and Berlin the rich settled in western areas while prevailing winds blew industrial effluents towards working-class east ends, in Budapest avoiding the smoke has always been a matter of altitude. It was said in Communist times that inhabitants of the airy Rózsadomb had the same life expectancy as in Austria, while the citizens of polluted Pest below had the life expectancy of Syria: two continents in one city.

Unless you're either staying here or visiting one of the area's many restaurants – places such as the **Vadrózsa**, **Remix** or **Kikelet**, all with beautiful gardens for summer dining – there aren't many reasons to go to the Rózsadomb. The yurt houses designed by Imre Makovecz on Törökvész utca are one architectural attraction. The fascinating Napraforgó utca experimental housing estate, where each house has been built in a different style of the modern movement, is another. Near the picturesquely decayed concrete bus terminal at Pasaréti tér is the **Bartók Memorial House**, the composer's former residence, now a concert venue as well as a museum. The Szépvölgy and Pálvölgy caves burrow beneath the outskirts of this area. But otherwise you'll see a lot of embassies, flash cars, tasteless new villas and a huge variety of Hungarian 'Beware of the Dog' signs.

The Buda Hills

From opposite the cylindrically ugly Budapest Hotel on Szilágyi Erzsébet fasor, you can catch the cog railway up to the summit of Széchenyi Hill, a ride of about 20 minutes. There's no view to speak of, unless you count the large building festooned with radar dishes, but you immediately feel as if you're out of the city. It's quiet and in summer there's a cool breeze.

There are wooded hills all around the western fringes of Buda, most of them criss-crossed with hiking trails. At weekends these can get quite crowded. You can ramble all you like, but take a good map, a strong pair of hiking boots and keep a sharp eye out for rampaging wild boar.

Otherwise, you can walk across the park from the cog railway terminal and hop on the narrow-gauge **Children's Railway**. This was formerly the Pioneers' Railway, named for the Communist youth organisation whose membership supplied the conductors and ticket collectors. Its charming trains, open to the breeze and still manned by children, snake hourly through the Buda Hills. The line meanders through woodland and retains a vaguely socialist flavour: the kids wear uniform hats and neckerchiefs, salute guards at stations, punch all tickets conscientiously and insist you remain seated when the trains are in motion. Many of the stations still sport murals of idealised socialist youth diligently enjoying their leisure time.

Near the end station of Hűvösvölgy you'll find a small amusement park and the popular **Náncsi Néni** restaurant. Or you can get off earlier at János-hegy, from where it's a brisk 15-minute walk up to the 527-metre summit of Budapest's highest hill. Here the view from the Erzsébet lookout tower puts the city in context: the Buda Hills roll around and behind; Castle Hill looks small and barely significant down below; the Danube bisects the entire landscape; way over on the other side, the outskirts of Pest shade into a patchwork of fields that in turn disappear into a flat, dusty horizon – the beginning of the Great Hungarian Plain.

From a terminal by the buffet below, the **libegő** – chair-lift – will convey you back down into urban Buda, the city spread grandly before you as you ride. Be warned, though: if you get the last Children's Railway train, you won't make it over the hill in time to catch the final chair-lift.

Pest

Though the south part of District V, the Belváros (Inner City), dates back to medieval times, the current shape of Pest – as resolutely flat as Buda is jaggedly hilly – is essentially nineteenth century. Its great boulevards were laid out in 1872, the same year that the three towns of Buda, Pest and Óbuda were merged to form one single city.

The main lines can be quickly drawn: a concentric series of semi-circular boulevards is cut through by several avenues that radiate from the centre. The spaces outlined by these major roads contain the various different districts. The two big circular roads – Kiskörút and Nagykörút (Small and Great Boulevards) – both have their own atmosphere and take on some of the character of the districts they traverse. A journey along them is thus an introduction to the whole of central Pest.

Kiskörút

The southern half of the Kiskörút follows the line of the old city walls – extant portions of which can be seen in Bástya utca behind Vámház körút and also a few yards down Ferenczy István utca off Múzeum körút. The Kiskörút begins at Fővám tér at the Pest foot of Szabadság Bridge, Gellért Hill standing craggily opposite. Marxist philosopher and literary critic George Lukács used to live just by here, in a fifth-floor flat at Belgrád rakpart 2. On the south side of the small square are two buildings: the **Budapest University of Economic Science**, facing the Technical University over the river; and the recently restored **Nagy Vásárcsarnok** (Great Market Hall), an indoor emporium of stalls selling every kind of meat, fish, vegetable and fruit. The former, designed by Miklós Ybl in neo-Renaissance style, was originally the Main Customs Office (hence Fővám – 'main customs'). The latter was in those days the city's main wholesale market. At one time an underground canal ran from the Danube, taking barges through the customs house and into the market.

Vámház körút leads up to Kálvin tér, named after the ugly Calvinist church on the square's south side. This was once the city's eastern gate and, with the ugly pink, postmodern Korona Hotel bridging Kecskeméti utca (its saving grace is the **Korona Passage** pancake place on the ground floor), still feels somewhat gate-like. From here two roads stab out eastwards into the city: Baross utca, which runs through the heart of District VIII, and Üllői út, which forms the border of Districts VIII and IX and leads eventually to Ferihegy airport. Ráday utca, a narrow commercial street leading off to the south-west, has some interesting shops and bars, including the **Paris, Texas**.

The next stretch is Múzeum körút, named for the **National Museum** on the east side. The fourth institution of its kind in the world when it was built between 1837-47, it was then so far out of town that cattle are said to have once wandered in. St Stephen's rather bent Crown is the main treasure here. Every 15 March the neo-Classical building gets decked out in red, white and green and crowds fill the forecourt to hear speeches from the steps. This is to commemorate the moment in 1848 when Sándor Petőfi launched the revolt against the Habsburgs by standing here and reading out his evidently inflammatory National Song. On the next corner is the century-old **Múzeum restaurant**, while over the road are some of Budapest's biggest antiquarian booksellers.

Múzeum körút ends at **Astoria**, where the grand but faded 1912 hotel dominates the inter-

*Souvenir shops and Western retail chains line main shopping drag **Váci utca** – too expensive for most Budapesters.*

section It has christened. Westwards, Kossuth Lajos utca leads towards the Danube and Elizabeth Bridge. East of here it continues as Rákóczi út towards **Keleti station** which, on a clear day, you can spy in the distance. The Népstadion, Hungary's biggest sports arena, lies beyond it.

Károly körút continues on up to Deák tér, passing on the right the enormous **Central Synagogue** which guards the entrance to District VII, and a huge apartment block, bridging Madach út, that looks like 1950s Soviet architecture but was actually built in the late '30s. It was intended as the start of a new avenue, but never got further than a couple of blocks.

The 47 and 49 trams run this far up the Kiskörút and Deák tér is the central hub of Budapest's transport network: all three metro lines intersect in the station below, where there's also the cute little **Underground Railway Museum**. Sütő utca, off Deák tér to the south-west, has the austerely neo-Classical Lutheran Church, has the main office of **Tourinform** – best place in town to pick up free maps, find details of cultural events and answer such niggling little queries as this book may not already cover.

The old city walls here curved west to meet the river at Vigadó tér. The Kiskörút, however, flattens out and continues on up north past the **Basilica of St Stephen** and down Bajcsy-Zsilinszky út, a drab boulevard named after a right-wing politician who turned anti-fascist. His half-sitting, half-standing statue in Deák tér supposedly depicts the moment he was arrested in Parliament. With grasping hand outstretched, he looks like a man outraged because his pint of beer has just been stolen.

Bajcsy-Zsilinszky út is boring and undistinguished, save for the enormous figure who languishes on top of a building at the corner of Ó utca, and the startling glimpse of the **former Royal Post Office Savings Bank** afforded by looking left down Nagysándor utca. On the corner of Alkotmány utca, just before the Kiskörút joins the Nagykörút at Nyugati tér, stands **Becketts** – the huge Irish pub and restaurant that provides expensive beer and bad music for Budapest's expatriate business community.

Nagykörút

At exactly 4,114 metres, the Nagykörút is the longest thoroughfare in the city, running from Petőfi Bridge in the south to Margaret Bridge in the north and passing through Districts IX, VIII, VII, VI and XIII en route. Trams 4 and 6 run the whole distance, starting at Móricz Zsigmond körtér in Buda, and ending up back on that side of the river in Moszkva tér.

A busy commercial boulevard built, like much of nineteenth-century Pest, entirely in eclectic style, it is curiously lacking in two things: decent bars or restaurants, and any kind of shop where you might actually want to buy something. Nevertheless it's here, rather than on upmarket Váci utca, that the real day-to-day business of downtown takes place. American fast food franchises thrive on every other corner, but new Western logos haven't quite driven out all the beautifully dated neon signs.

On the Ferenc körút stretch you'll see people dressed in green and white – supporters of **Ferencváros FTC**, the local football club, currently Hungary's most successful team and known for its right-wing following. The ugly concrete building on the south-west corner of the Üllői út intersection is known as the Lottóház – its apartments were given away as prizes in the 1950s. The contrast with Ödön Lechner's extraordinary and colourful **Museum of Applied Arts** round the corner couldn't be more complete. The building on the south-east side is a former army barracks. This and the **Corvin cinema** tucked away in Corvin köz behind the intersection were the scenes of fierce fighting during the 1956 revolution.

Continuing north as József körút, the boulevard acquires a disreputable air as it passes through District VIII. Sleazy bars advertise 'leszbi sex shows', a bingo hall does a brisk trade and prostitutes ply their wares day and night around Rákóczi tér. One shop on this stretch (it's on the west side, near the Baross utca tram stop) sells absolutely nothing but soda syphon chargers.

At Blaha Lujza tér, Népszínház utca runs away south-east towards **Kerepesi cemetry** and the vast and seedy **Józsefvárosi piac**, the place to buy Chinese tat. Rákóczi út runs back towards Astoria and on up to Keleti station, its façade quite distinct from this vantage. Frank Zappa fans will appreciate **Z Hangelemez** in the courtyard of Rákóczi út 47, one of Budapest's curiouser record shops. 'Blaha', as it's universally known, has the **Centrum Corvin** department store (now unfortunately updated from the intriguing Communist cornucopia of old) and an M2 metro station.

As it passes into District VII and its name changes to Erzsébet, the körút gets noticeably glitzier. Cinemas and theatres begin to appear. This is the best stretch for elegantly quaint neon. A block up from Blaha the venerable **New York Coffeehouse**, rammed by a tank in 1956, stands in dire need of renovation. A few blocks further on the other side, its postmodern grandchild, the dreadful **Café Mozart**, stands in equally dire need of demolition. You almost wish Soviet tanks would come back just to ram this place, too. The **Fészek restaurant** and artists' club, a block away down Dob utca, has managed to survive the twentieth century intact, and offers peaceful summer dining in a picturesquely tatty inner courtyard, formerly a monk's cloister.

Crossing Király utca, a lively street worth delving into, Erzsébet changes into Teréz körút as it stumbles into District VI. The **Zeneakadémia**, Budapest's principal concert hall, is a block west down Király on the corner of Liszt Ferenc tér.

Oktogon, where the Nagykörút intersects broad Andrássy út, is the grandest intersection, once lined with coffee houses but now sadly dominated by burger joints. In the Communist days this was November 7 Square; under Horthy it was named after Mussolini. The M1 metro stops here, on its way underneath Andrássy út to Heroes' Square and the Városliget (City Park) beyond.

Teréz körút is the flashiest segment of boulevard and brightest at night. Here there are more cinemas and the respectable **Béke Radisson Hotel** in the run-up to the Nagykörút's most magnificent landmark: **Nyugati station**. Built by the Eiffel company in 1874-77 (in the low-rent shopping complex underneath, everything seems to be named after Eiffel: tacky shops, amusement arcades, dowdy coffee bars) it's a pale-blue palace of iron and glass. The panes in front allow you to see inside the station, making arriving and departing trains part of the city's street life. In the early 1970s this became literally so, when one engine crashed through the façade and came to rest at the tram stop. Over the road, the mirror glass frontage of the Skála is by contrast oddly forbidding for a department store, despite attempts to enliven the square with summer lunchtime concerts. Behind the station on Váci út, **Bahnhof**, housed in an old train shed, is currently Budapest's most happening nightclub, and employs its most evil bouncers.

Views of Nyugati from Szent István körút are spoilt by the unsightly road bridge carrying traffic over Nyugati tér between Bajcsy-Zsilinszky út and Váci út, which leads on up to the busy Lehel tér produce market. The only stretch that isn't named after a Habsburg, Szent István körút is also the only part where there's very much of interest at night. **Okay Italia** does a roaring trade. **Sziesta** purveys pizzas until 4am. The **Franklin Trocadero** is a decent Latin disco on a good night. The streets beyond in Újlipótváros have a number of busy bars, including the **Ipoly**, **Tam-Tam** and **Yes**, making this an admirable locality for late-night pub-crawling.

Built in the 1930s and originally a middle-class Jewish district, Újlipótváros and its main thoroughfare, Pozsonyi út, is also lively by day, with lots of small shops, a busy street life and the Szent István Park opening out on to the Danube. There's nothing in particular to go to see, but these are amiable streets for an afternoon stroll.

Centrepiece of this last stretch of körút is the stubbily Baroque **Vígszínház** (Comedy Theatre). Built in 1896 and renovated in 1995, this has pretensions of grandeur, but in a certain light looks like nothing so much as a tawdry end-of-the-pier attraction. Szent István körút ends at Jászai Mari tér, terminus of the number 2 tram. Here traffic sweeps on to Margit hid (Margaret Bridge), a Y-shaped construction that leads not only to Buda and the Rózsadomb, but also to the traffic-free and wooded park of **Margaret Island**.

Belváros

Trace the line of the Kiskörút as far as Deák tér. Now move your finger west along Harmincad utca, past the Erzsébet tér bus station and the **Kempinski Hotel**, past the British Embassy and the neighbouring **Sushi** bar. Dogleg into Vörösmarty tér, sweep by the **Gerbeaud** patisserie and the M1 terminus, and go down to the Danube at Vigadó tér. The area you have outlined, bounded by the river to the west, is the Belváros, or Inner City.

The area south of Kossuth Lajos utca is one of Pest's most appealing quarters. Though the Danube is mostly invisible (one or two streets that run out on to it offer sudden, startling views of Gellért Hill) its narrow, quiet streets feel like a waterfront district. Apart from the old Customs House (now the Economic University) on the Kiskörút– the dock for international Danube traffic (notably **jetfoils to Bratislava and Vienna**), complete with customs area, is on this stretch of riverfront. The still-functioning gear-repair shop at Belgrád rakpart 18, with its beautiful old sign and window display of cogs, cogs and more cogs, is a relic from an earlier era of river travel.

Though it's never too busy, either by day or night, this area offers a host of decent restaurants and bars: **Taverna Dionysios, Nautilus,** **Amstel Bar, Hause & Trogers, Fregatt, Chan-Chan, Fatál** and the **Adria** are all within a block or two of each other. The restful **Bécsi Kávéház** is on the lower end of Váci, as is the ridiculous **Barbados**. The **Janis Pub, Old Amsterdam** and the **Irish Cat** are all also nearby, making this perhaps Budapest's premier district for pub-crawling – particularly as the streets are so atmospheric at night.

The **Serbian Orthodox Church** nestles in a garden up Szerb utca, near the **Rhythm 'n' Books** shop which offers world music and English-language reading materials, but this is a quarter for quiet strolling rather than serious sightseeing. Váci utca is nothing like the stretch north of Elizabeth Bridge, and despite slow redevelopment, still contains many curious old shops.

All this changes at Ferenciek tere (named for the Franciscan Church which stands near the University Library). The extraordinary 1913 **Párizsi udvar** on the other side of Kossuth Lajos utca heralds the beginning of Budapest's prestige shopping district, though around here there are also more notably ancient monuments, including the **Inner City Parish Church**, Pest's oldest building, down towards the bridge. From here on up to

Vörösmarty tér, Váci and its environs are pedestrianised and bustle with street hustlers and expensive shops, both aiming their pitch at the equally numerous tourists.

Although the Westerner will not find it very impressive (it's mostly souvenir shops and drab Western retail chains) Hungarians are proud of Váci utca. It's what they think the tourists want. Budapesters will invariably bring visitors to Váci, although they rarely shop here (too expensive) and more or less visit as tourists themselves. Brash, tacky, full of life and, five years after Communism still remarkably bare of decent clothes shops, it remains interesting principally for anthropological reasons: grab a table outside Gerbeaud or the **Anna Café**, prepare yourself for a heftier bill than you'd receive elsewhere in town, and settle back to study the holidaying habits of the lesser spotted Austrian package tourist.

At night, it's a different story. A few restaurants and bars stay open, but after about 11pm the area is mostly deserted save for sex bar touts handing leaflets to such foreigners as remain on the streets. Vörösmarty tér, which on summer days now always seems to be hosting some wacky product promotion event, at night is patrolled by prostitutes, who'll cheerfully approach any passing male. There's nothing threatening about the atmosphere, though. In Budapest even the sex industry seems vaguely conservative and respectable.

The area west of Váci, between Petőfi Sándor utca and the Károly körút, is mostly pretty dead, dominated by two huge bureaucratic complexes: the Budapest City Hall and the Pest County Hall. Narrow streets and small squares lead through to Deák tér. Szervita tér has the Hungaria mosaic topping number 5 and Béla Lajta's **Rózsavölgyi House** next door, still occupied by a Communist-era **music shop** offering, among a stock of modern CDs, an assortment of bizarre vinyl bargains.

The Danube Korzó, Budapest's premier promenade, is almost as busy as Váci. It begins at the convergence of Március 15 tér, with its stubby Roman ruins, and Petőfi tér, with its statue of the stern, finger-pointing poet. From here up until Vigadó tér is the city's main **gay cruise**, though you'd not notice if you weren't looking for it. At Vigadó tér are buskers, stalls selling folkloric souvenirs, the excellent **Marco Polo** restaurant and the **Vigadó** itself, Budapest's second-best concert hall. The Korzó continues from here on up to Roosevelt tér, where statues of Deák and Széchenyi stand among the trees and the **Gresham Palace** faces off against the Chain Bridge.

On the river side of this main stretch is the track for the number 2 tram and various odd attractions – an Irish restaurant on one moored boat, a Renault car showroom on another – while above them tower many of Budapest's most prestigious hotels, including the **Marriott** and **Atrium Hyatt**, all of them architecturally quite uninspiring. But these need not spoil the view of the Chain Bridge ahead and Castle District opposite. Particularly when lit up at night and reflecting in the river, whether under a clear, starry sky or softened by trails of autumn mist, these form one of the most magical urban landscapes in the world.

Lipótváros

The northern part of District V – the Lipótváros – is Budapest's quarter for business and bureaucracy. There are few shops in this area, though **Bestsellers** bookstore on Oktober 6 utca is an obvious rallying-point for Anglophones. There are few restaurants too, save for the business-orientated **Szindbád** and the Polynesian-themed **Luau** with its hourly fake thunderstorms. Relatively busy by day, at night these broad, blocky late-nineteenth century streets, almost Prussian in feel, are dead and deserted.

The remarkably ugly Basilica of St Stephen points its façade down Zrínyi utca towards Gresham Palace and the river. There's nothing much to see inside, save for the mummified right hand of St Stephen, contained in a box and lit up for Ft20 like something in a fairground sideshow. József Finta's glossy new postmodern building for the national bank, cousin to his Kempinski Hotel a few blocks south, is adding a blue glass and polished granite sheen to the south-east corner of **Szabadság tér**, Budapest's late nineteenth-century financial centre. It's dominated by the National Bank, the American Embassy, the huge and authoritarian Magyar Televízió headquarters (formerly the Stock and Commodity Exchange) and the Soviet obelisk which stands on the site of the former Sacred Mound of soil from territories lost at Trianon. It's an unappealing space which, for all its size, is easily missed as no major roads pass through.

Note, though, on the east side, the small statue of US General Harry Hill Bandholtz. An officer of the peace-keeping force in 1919, he saved the treasures of the National Museum from rampaging Romanian soldiers by 'sealing' the doors with the only official-looking seals he had to hand: censorship seals. The Romanians saw the American eagle, and backed off down the steps. A mirror-image of this ruse is sometimes performed by today's Romanian street hustlers.

One will approach, offering to change currency, and then his partner will harass you, pretending to be the police and aiming to get hold of your money. Ask for identification and you'll probably get shown some kind of Bucharest bus pass – official-looking enough to fool many out-of-towners. In the backstreets round here you might also be approached by Transylvanian village women selling illicitly imported lace.

Apart from General Bandholtz, every notable landmark in this part of town seems to have some kind of nationalist function. A diagonal block away from the institutions of Szabadság tér, the Eternal Flame burns on the corner of Hold utca and Báthory utca to commemorate Count Lajos Batthyány, Prime Minister in the Revolutionary Government, and executed by Habsburgs at this spot on 6 October 1849. Even the brightest spot of this sombre, officious quarter – Ödön Lechner's startlingly ornate and colourful former Royal Post Office Savings Bank – was built around forms Lechner considered to be 'original' pre-Christian Hungarian patterns and thus the basis for a new nationalist architecture. Behind the US Embassy and a block south of the Eternal Flame, it's one of the city's most extraordinary buildings. The only pity is that there's nowhere to step back and take a good look at it.

The same can't be said of the **Parliament**, one of Budapest's most conspicuous structures. Built, like the rest of Lipótváros, at a time when Hungary, getting its first and only taste of empire, was in a position to boss around a few Slovaks, Romanians and Croats, it was the largest parliament in the world when in opened in 1902 – larger even than the British Parliament (whose neo-Gothic style and riverside location it aped) then still administering the biggest empire the world has ever seen. Its 691 rooms have never been fully utilised, even in the 16 years before Trianon dismembered Hungarian imperial pretensions. The business of governing Hungary today takes up only 12 per cent of the space. (Offices for the various parties are down the road in the Fehérház – 'White House' – at Széchenyi rakpart 19, formerly the Communist Party headquarters.)

The whole building is appealingly ridiculous. In Communist times a red star topped the crowning spire, much like a giant Christmas tree. Today you feel it needs something new up there, a symbol to counterpose all the Hungarian mythology and bring the building back down to postmodern reality – perhaps a giant corporate advertising umbrella designed by Claes Oldenburg.

The **Museum of Ethnography**'s positioning, opposite on Kossuth Lajos tér and looking pretty governmental itself, says much about how seriously Hungarians take their folk traditions.

Andrássy út, District VI & the Városliget

Andrássy út, built between 1872-85 with the continent's first electric underground railway running underneath, is the spine of District VI. Intended as

*Miklós Zrinyi, hero of sixteenth-century battles against the Turks, watches over the once splendid **Kodály körönd**.*

Budapest's Jewish community has its heart in **District VII**, *which has several synagogues.*

Budapest's answer to the Champs-Elysées, it stretches for 2.5 kilometres and has had a variety of names: Sugárút (Radial Avenue), Andrássy út (after the nineteenth-century statesman), Sztalin út and the tongue-twisting Népköztársàság útja (Avenue of the People's Republic) before being renamed Andrássy once more in 1989.

Like much of Dual Monarchy Budapest, Andrássy út today seems a little too grand for its own good: there isn't enough wealth and power in contemporary Budapest to flesh this avenue out with the kind of shops and businesses that might do its proportions justice. Even on the liveliest stretch – between Bajcsy-Zsilinszky út and Oktogon – there isn't much save banks and supermarkets, stationery chains and electrical stores. The venerable **Művész** coffeehouse and **Irók Boltja** (Writers' Bookshop) are down here, though, as are the **Belcanto** and **Bombay Palace** restaurants.

Few individual buildings stand out from the uniform eclectic style, with two notable exceptions: Miklós Ybl's **Opera House**, where the appeal of the architecture is perhaps greater than the quality of the productions, and Béla Lajta's extraordinary 1910 Parisiana nightclub (now **Új Színház**), a worthwhile 50-metre detour down Dalszinház utca.

Nagymező utca, with the main **MÁV office** on the corner (best place to get advance train tickets), is known as Budapest's Broadway – a name echoed on a couple of shop signs. There are some West End-style theatres (including the **Operetta**) and a couple of nightspots, notably the **Piaf**, after-hours hangout for the older arty set. This area to the north and west of Andrássy – a triangle also bounded by Teréz körút and Bajcsy-Zsilinszky út – is by day a dull commercial district (although it does include Wave and Trance, two the city's better specialist record shops) but by night offers a cluster of eccentric bars and restaurants. **Off-Broadway**, **Kétballábas**, **Balett Cipő**, **Picasso Point** and **Crazy Café** are all around here.

More nightlife can be found on Liszt Ferenc tér, which leads from Andrássy up to the Zeneakadémia. **Incognito** is the trendiest café in town, and the opening of the **Cafe Mediterran** opposite means the square now bustles with outdoor drinkers on a summer night.

One curiosity on this stretch. In the courtyard of Andrássy út 27 there's the Esperanto centre. Hungary is the only country in the world with state exams in Esperanto, and where the 'universal tongue' (modelled on Romanian and invented by a Pole) is accepted as a second language for university entrance requirements.

It's taught in about 30 schools and an estimated 50,000 Hungarians speak it – meaning, ironically, they have not one language nobody else in the world understands, but two. At the shop you can buy 'Saluton el Hungario' postcards and Bulgarian 7-inch Esperanto singles.

The middle stretch of Andrássy út – between Oktogon and the Kodály körönd – is the most boring part, mainly institutional and bureaucratic buildings. The unprepossessing number 60, though, was once feared enough to make people cross the road to avoid it. These days sporting a Chemokomplex sign, it was secret police headquarters for both the Horthy and Communist regimes. The Lukács at number 70 was until recently one of the city's best surviving coffee houses. Closed to the public for a while in the 1950s, when it became the secret police cafeteria, it is now apparently closed for good. Over the road at number 69 there's the neo-Renaissance Képzőművészeti Főiskola (Old Exhibition Hall), now the College of Fine Arts, which also contains the State Puppet Theatre.

Kodály köröud is the Rond-Point of Andrássy út, and was clearly once very splendid. The four palatial town houses that enclose it are dilapidated but still fascinating. The composer Zoltán Kodály used to live in the turreted number 87-89, and his apartment is now a musuem.

The final stretch of Andrássy út is wider than the rest, mostly occupied by villas set back from the road. This is Budapest's diplomatic quarter and many embassies are here and on the surrounding streets (Benczúr utca is shady and quiet and full of Art Nouveau mansions). The Yugoslav embassy where Imre Nagy holed up for a while in 1956 is the last building on the southern corner by Hősök tere. This stretch also houses the incongruous **FMK** and **Made Inn** complex – an alternative arts centre and shiny nightclub.

Hősök tere (Heroes' Square), flanked by the **Museum of Fine Arts** and the **Műcsarnok** (Exhibition Hall) and offering the Archangel Gabriel amid a pantheon of Hungarian heroes, is a monumental celebration of mythic Magyardom, these days mostly inhabited by skateboarders. The **Városliget (City Park)** beyond is Pest's most interesting park, with a boating lake, the **Széchenyi baths**, the **Zoo**, **Vidám** (Amusement) **Park** and **Petőfi Csarnok** concert hall among its amenities. Once the site of the 1896 Magyar Millennium exhibition, the theme-park feel of the place survives in the Disneyfied mock-Transylvanian design of Vadjahunyad castle, now home for the **Agriculture Museum**. This and Hősök tere form the heart of Dual Monarchyland, while the **Gundel** restaurant nearby offers an expensively recreated taste of the old days.

District VII

Like so much else in Budapest that dates from the latter half of the last century, the Central Synagogue on Dohány utca is grandiose and simply enormous – so big it's impossible to heat and has never been used in winter. Though tucked discreetly behind the junction with Károly körút – you don't see the thing until you're almost upon it – the building stands like some twin-domed Moorish fortress, guarding the district behind.

District VII, or Erzsébetváros, between the Kiskörút and the Nagykörút, Andrássy út and Rákóczi út, is Budapest's Jewish quarter, established here in the eighteenth century when Jews were still forbidden to live within the city walls. These days people call it 'the Ghetto', although it never was one until 1944-45, when Arrow Cross

*Tucked away on **Dob utca** is Fröhlich Cukrászda – your best bet for kosher pastries.*

*In **Klauzal tér** old men play cards and chess in the summer, while children expend energy.*

fascists walled off this whole area and herded the Jewish community inside. The junction by the Central Synagogue was one of two entrances.

It's not as picturesque or as ancient as Prague's Jewish quarter, but although 700,000 Hungarian Jews were murdered in the Holocaust, enough survived to mean that District VII is still the heart of a living community. You can hear Yiddish spoken on Kazinczy utca, or eat a kosher pastry at the **Fröhlich Cukrászda** on Dob utca. Several synagogues in the area are still active – the small Heroes Temple behind the now almost-renovated Central Synagogue, the Orthodox synagogue on Kazinczy utca and a hidden Hasidic prayer house in the courtyard of Vasvári utca 5 – and a number of Jewish organisations have their headquarters at Síp utca 12.

This community has survived both an exodus of younger, wealthier Jews into less noisy and congested districts, and postwar attempts by the Communist government to homogenise the area. If you'd survived the Holocaust, you got to keep your flat. Workers brought into Budapest to work on the reconstruction of the city were housed in the empty properties.

Many of these were Gypsies and District VII is now also the Gypsy quarter – although the heart of Gypsy territory is beyond the Nagykörút, an area of broken phone boxes, repair shops and dingy borozós where people have wine for breakfast. In that area there's the hideous **Nemzeti Színház**, which looks more like a National Car Park than a National Theatre, as well as the **Stamp Museum**, but otherwise it's pretty devoid

of particular things to see. Ármin Hegedűs's 1906 Primary School at Dob utca 85 is definitely worth a detour, though.

The heart of the Jewish quarter is Klauzál tér, with the **Shalom** kosher restaurant, assorted other Jewish businesses, and the District VII market hall on the east side. In summer, old men play cards and chess under the trees. The best taste of how it once was is afforded by the **Gozsdu udvar** – a linked series of courtyards running between Dob utca and Király utca, still inhabited by workshops and labs, barbers and violin-makers.

Király utca was 70 per cent Jewish at the turn of the century. It's still full of character and commotion, with old Communist-style shop signs, curious courtyards, one or two excellent bars and an informal market for dodgy goods on the corner of Kis Diófa utca. The backstreets round here are dark, narrow, tatty and full of odd detail. Síp utca has some fascinating buildings, including the secessionist Metro Klub on the corner of Dohány utca sporting one of Budapest's best old neon signs, and a number 11 with neo-Gothic doorways, gargoyles and the statue of a seventeenth-century halberdier. Kazinczy utca is intriguing too, with the stretch between Wesselényi utca and Király utca containing the 1930s **Hungarian Museum of Electrotechnics** in a sort of junior totalitarian style, the Orthodox synagogue, angled to the bend of the street, and a final stroll up to the **Wichmann** bar, a lonely but welcoming tavern that by night casts an almost medieval glow.

A fine mini-pub crawl can be had around here, taking in the Wichmann, **Zöldség-Gyümölcs** and Incognito and Café Mediterran up on Liszt Ferenc tér, and then maybe moving over Andrássy to Piaf and beyond. If walking alone, though, be just a little bit wary at night.

District VIII

Although its tabloid nickname, Csikagó (Chicago), originated with the fast construction rate round here late last century, District VIII is indeed what it also suggests: a crime-ridden, run-down area that is Budapest's red light district and heartland of the mafia, both Ukrainian and Chinese. (If Pest ever acquires a Chinatown, this is where it will be.)

Bounded by Üllői út and Rákóczi út, the pie-slice shape of Józsefváros, as it's also known, has its point at the National Museum. In Pollack Mihály tér behind, former mansions rub shoulders with the ugly socialist-realist Magyar Rádió headquarters, scene of much bloodletting in 1956. Mikszáth Kálmán tér in the streets beyond is where you'll find the **Tilos az Á**, the club and venue that is alternative Budapest's main institution. **Nothing But The Blues** is a few yards down the road and jazz venue **Big Mambo** a short walk away down Mária utca near the corner of Pál utca. This short, unprepossessing street was the scene of Ferenc Molnár's well-known novel *The Paul Street Boys*.

On Rákóczi út and in the streets beyond the Nagykörút, District VIII is at its seediest. Grass grows up through cracks in the pavement. Prostitutes work the squares and street corners. Many of the shops are Chinese discount stores or sad old repair shops. Eclectic façades are shabby, bullet-pocked and crumbling while overgrown inner courtyards, many still with their racks for beating carpets, buzz with a ragged, almost medieval life. It's a fascinating area, and not as dangerous as it sounds, as long as you look as if you know what you're doing. Venture into a bar or two and you'll find a warm, though starkly impoverished, neighbourhood atmosphere. Just don't knock over any drinks or wave your wallet around, and remain a little watchful on the streets.

Óbuda

The oldest part of the city (in archeological terms, at least), Óbuda was a separate village until 1873 and still feels very different from the rest of Budapest. The Romans established the town of **Aquincum** here, although no one knew it had been there until late in the nineteenth century. The Magyars set up shop here when they arrived in the ninth century, christening it Buda, which got changed to Óbuda (Old Buda) when the first Royal Palace went up on Castle Hill.

Apart from the Communists erecting clusters of tower blocks and a flyover right over Flórián tér

and its Roman baths, the area has been pretty much forgotten about ever since. Locals consider themselves independent of Budapest – the chant of Óbuda's second division football club (III. kerület TVE) is 'Come on you district!' In the last century there was some industry – mainly shipbuilding and viticulture – but all you'll see now are rows of rickety old peasant houses and run-down bars, with some new shops going up in plastic neo-Baroque style.

Apart from Aquincum's Roman ruins and a couple of art museums (the **Kiscelli**, the **Vasarely** and the **Budapest Galéria**) the only reasons to come up here are for the stretch of bars and stalls selling cheap fish on the Danube by Római Fürdő, and the **Maharaja**, Budapest's second-best Indian restaurant. For a week or so every August, the area buzzes as Hungary's rocking youth crams out Óbuda island for the **Diáksziget** festival.

Csepel

Budapest's industrial District XXI perches at the very tip of Csepel Island, to the south of the centre. Militant and independent-minded, it was known as 'Red Csepel' in the interwar years, in 1944 held one of the few successful acts of mass resistance to the Nazis as locals refused to be evicted en masse, and in 1956 its local workers' council was one of the longest to hold out against the Soviets.

It's easily reached by the HÉV from Boráros tér, an interesting ride running down by the Danube and then over the area of waste ground that might have housed Expo '96, had Hungary not fessed up to the fact that it couldn't afford it.

Szent Imre tér is the centre. Down the end of Tanácsház utca is the main gate for the enormous Csepel Iron and Metal Works. Founded as the Manfred Weiss Works and for a while in the 1950s named after Mátyás Rákosi (the huge Lenin statue which once stood outside the gates is now a feature of the Statue Park), it's no longer one monolithic state enterprise but still employs thousands of people in the area.

Although it is not strictly speaking allowed, it's easy to get inside: tell them you're visiting the Gyártörténti Múzeum (which exists on Központi út inside, but is invariably closed) and they'll issue you with a pass resembling a raffle ticket. After that, feel free to poke around among this cornucopia of ducts and chimneys, back lanes with corrugated tin roofing and ivy-covered brick, desolate workshops full of interesting debris, and odd old Communist displays of nuts and bolts. There's even some street life in the complex, including a few cafés and a bicycle shop.

Around Béke tér, near the terminus of the HÉV, various run-down but friendly bars provide a delapidated dose of the local pride.

Eating & Drinking

Restaurants

Sup with singing waiters at the Belcanto and football commentary at the Kétballábas; dine under an hourly drenching at the Luau or lurid rock formations at the Crystal Palace. No two Budapest dinners need be the same.

Although Hungary, unlike most of its neighbours, does have a distinct and developed (if second-rank) cuisine, and although eating out in Budapest has improved immeasurably in the last half-decade, no one would ever come here just for the food.

Which isn't to say you can't eat well in Budapest. From the humble caff-like étkezde to the exceedingly classy Gundel, you can lunch simply but heartily for next to nothing, or splash out big and get some genuinely handsome dining in return. The arrival of capitalism hasn't just meant the absurd proliferation of brand-name burger joints. There's also been an upsurge in restaurants offering every kind of cuisine, from first-rate Italian to street-corner falafels and kebabs.

Still, unless you're prepared to pay top dollar, don't expect too much. Hungarian food is heavy, bland, rich and, contrary to legend, generally under-spiced. Especially in cheaper places, it's sort of central European school dinners. Aficionados of

game and goose liver will enjoy themselves, though, and the fogas, a pike-perch indigenous to Lake Balaton and featured on many menus, is one of the world's most delicate freshwater fish. But many of the ethnic restaurants are distinctly second-rate. Out of around 50 Chinese places in Budapest, for example, we can only find it in our hearts to recommend four. Even the upmarket establishments, where food and service are of an internationally acceptable standard, tend to lack character – mainly because only tourists and businesspeople can afford them.

We've recommended the best of Hungarian dining at both ends of the price spectrum. For most Hungarians, lunch is the main meal. Dinner in the evening still tends to be accompanied by Gyspy musicians and Hungarian wines that get better by the year (although in restaurants they're often disgracefully overpriced). Service varies from slow to very slow and, where good, is usually quite formal.

*Dream away a summer afternoon in the old monk's courtyard at **Fészek**. See page 119.*

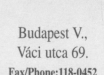

Mid-1990s Budapest can offer a huge variety of dining experiences. From singing waiters at the Belcanto to football commentary at the Kétbal-lábas, from hourly thunderstorms at the Luau to lurid rock formations at the Crystal Palace, from folk jam sessions at the Gyökér to extremely short skirts at the Okay Italia, no two dinners need be the same.

Although you can always find something to eat in the small hours (*see chapter* **Nightlife**), most places tend to wind down before midnight. Vegetarians must work hard to find anything interesting. Hungarian restaurants provide little other than trappist cheese or mushroom caps, boringly breaded and fried (often in goose fat) and served up with tartar sauce. But decent salad bars are on the increase, ethnic cuisine offers some meatless diversity, and contemporary Budapest is more veghead-friendly than ever before.

Averages listed below are for a starter and main course. We've organised restaurants according to price: **Inexpensive** means an average of less than Ft1,000, **Moderate** is between Ft1,000-Ft2,000, and **Reassuringly Expensive** anything upwards of that. Note, though, that prices on any Hungarian menu vary wildly. Even in some of the more expensive places, it's still possible to dine on the relative cheap.

We've also included some of the better étkezdék – cheap and cheerful diners where Hungarians take lunch – and a selection of fast food that you won't already know from back home.

Reassuringly Expensive

Adria Grill
II. Zilah utca 9 (175 7363). Bus 49. **Open** noon-midnight daily. **Average** Ft2,700. **Credit** AmEx, EC, V.
A modern villa in a smart residential area whose main attraction is a nicely maintained garden. All the stranger that the inside bit is decorated with plastic flowers. Vast lumps of grilled meat are the specialities and the leg of veal, recommended for two, would be enough for four normal people. The potato soup is a meal in itself.

Amadeus
V. Apáczai Csere János utca 13 (118 4677). M1 Vörösmarty tér. **Open** noon-midnight Mon-Fri; 6pm-midnight Sat, Sun. **Average** Ft2,100. **No credit cards.**
The owner has decorated the place with his own artwork, including eccentric metal coat racks and odd, intricate light fittings. The food, by contrast, is simple but good, centring around grilled meat and fish (scampi weighs in most expensively at Ft2,800, a mixed grill is Ft1,700, chicken Ft700) and an excellent salad bar. The beer glasses are chilled, the staff are friendly and the beautiful main room has a table for large parties. Pop radio droning in the background at lunchtimes is the only real drawback.

Barokk
VI. Mozsár utca 12 (131 8942). M1 Oktogon. **Open** noon-midnight daily. **Average** Ft2,500. **No credit cards.**
A theme restaurant complete with staff in period costume, taped Baroque music and metal platters on the table. Gilt-framed paintings and Louis-XV style chairs lend a luxurious feel. The menu is in extraordinary language: 'Grilled lifer from Kosmarok', 'The eatable of Grudinovich in salsa and ginger' and 'roste of cu'. Fortunately there are elaborations in modern English. In spite of the weird dishes the menu is broad and user-friendly, and despite the gimmicks this is a really good restaurant.

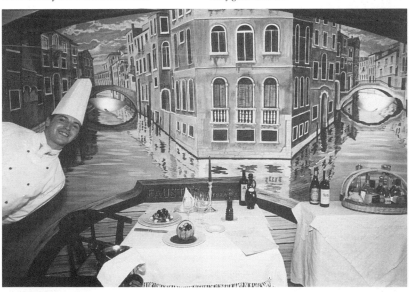

*The wine list's great, but remember, you're in **Fausto's**, Budapest, not Venice. See p112.*

Uncork some Chinese regional cooking at **Hong Kong Pearl Garden.** *See page 115.*

Belcanto

VI. Dalszínház utca 8 (269 3101/269 2786). M1 Opera.
Open 6pm-2am daily. **Average** Ft3,000. **Credit** AmEx,
DC, MC, V.

In a splendid baroque room, with unique entertainment: stars from the Opera next door wander around delivering hits of the 1890s and standards of the 1980s. Just when you think the coast is clear, the entire waiting staff appears as a chorus line. The menu is upmarket, in keeping with the furs and jewels which appear as the Opera finishes, but not really first-class. Their various steak options are the best bet. Service is pretty good, considering the waiters have to remain aware their cue might be coming up at any moment. Best time is just before the Opera tips out. A special place, and a wonderful spot for a party. Booking essential.

Chan-Chan

*V. Váci utca 69 (entrance in Pintér utca) (118 0452). Tram
47, 49.* **Open** noon-4pm, 6pm-midnight, daily. **Average**
Ft2,500 **Credit** AmEx, V.

Well-established Thai joint offering a long and highly Hungarianised menu with items such as Grilled Boar's Leg in Thai Sauce. Slim pickings for vegetarians. Even the spring rolls contain so much pork you can't taste anything else. They are fairly flexible, but if you try to order the Kay Xam Yang (mixed Thai spices with peanuts) they'll stubbornly insist this dish is not suitable for Europeans. A well-lit no smoking restaurant with Buddhas and an aquarium or two.

Crystal Palace

III. Szépvölgyi út 21 (250 4808). Tram 17. **Open** noon-
3pm, 6pm-2am, daily. **Average** Ft2,200. **Credit** AmEx,
DC, MC, V.

A bizarrely themed restaurant with glass spires outside and coloured crystals everywhere within. By day this is hard to appreciate; by artificial light you start wondering if it is only Marlboros you are smoking. But the place is comfortable enough and the menu is good Hungarian international with a few original items, including a vegetarian section. Strange, but a lot better than many similarly priced restaurants.

Fausto's

VII. Dohány utca 5 (122 7806). M2 Astoria/tram 47, 49.
Open noon-3pm, 7pm-11pm, Mon-Sat. **Average** Ft2,500.
Credit AmEx, MC.

Possibly the best restaurant in Budapest just now. Owned by the chef who forged Marco Polo's reputation for the best Italian eats in central Europe, Fausto's is small, slick, elegant, unpretentious and offers inventive Italian dishes that make good use of local ingredients. Excellent wine list, too. Booking recommended, as is sitting with your back to the disconcerting perspectives of the Venetian canal mural.

Gundel

*XIV. Állatkerti út 2 (321 3550/fax 342 2917). M1 Hősök
tere/trolleybus 72, 75, 79.* **Open** 7pm-midnight daily.
Average Ft5,000. **Credit** AmEx, DC, MC, V.

Still the city's most famous restaurant, in the interwar years this was the focal point for elegant, aristocratic Budapest and the international wealthy who came here to play. Originally opened in 1894 as the Wampetics, it was taken over by chef Károly Gundel in 1910 who proceeded to Frenchify Hungarian cuisine, inventing many now standard Hungarian

Treat yourself to the **Gundel** *experience.*

The Hungarian menu

If you're coming to Hungary for its spicy food, prepare for disappointment. The typical menu (*étlap*) relies on heavy, bland portions of pork (*sertés*) or chicken (*csirke*), garnished with over-cooked vegetables. Meats are mainly stewed (*pörkölt*) or breaded (*rántott*). Salads (*saláták*) are often sour, pickled affairs. Even the goulash (*gulyás*) is a thin disappointment, soup rather than stew. Bean soup (*bableves*) is a better bet.

Starters (*előételek*) feature breaded cheese (*sajt*) or mushrooms (*gomba*); *Hortobágyi palacsinta*, a pancake in meat sauce, and goose liver, *hideg libamáj*, are hardy perennials. Soups (*levesek*) are based on rich meat stock. Only cold fruit soup, *gyümölcsleves*, pass the veggie test. Spicy fish soup, *halászlé*, is worth investigating.

Main courses (*főételek*) may feature *töltött káposzta* (stuffed cabbage rolls in meat sauce); *paprikás csirke* (chicken in sour cream and paprika sauce); *sertésborda* (pork chops with different fillings); *vaddisznó pörkölt* (wild boar stew) and *fogas* (pike-perch from Balaton). Tournedos Rossini and Beefsteak (*marhabélszín*) Budapest Style (with stewed paprika) are very common. These will be served with a side dish (*köretek*) of potatoes (*burgonya* or *krumpli*), rice (*rizs*) or noodles (*galuska*). Hungarians go to town on desserts (*desszertek*). *Somlói galuska*, sponge cake soaked in cream, rum and chocolate sauce, and Gundel pancakes (*palacsinta*), fruit-filled, covered in chocolate sauce and flamed in rum, are ubiquitous. Some menus have strudel (*rétes*) and most offer *fagylalt*, ice cream.

Useful Phrases

I'd like a table for two. *Két fő részére kérek egy asztalt.*
Are these seats taken? *Ezek a helyek foglaltak?*
I'd like the menu, please. *Kérem az étlapot.*
I didn't order this. *Én nem ezt rendeltem.*
I am a vegetarian. *Vegetáriánus vagyok.*
I am diabetic. *Diabetikus vagyok.*
Do you have...? *Van...?*
Bon appétit! *Jó étvágyat!*

Basics

Ashtray *Hamutartó*
Bill *Számla*
Bread *Kenyér*
Cup *Csésze*
Fork *Villa*
Glass *Pohár*
Knife *Kés*
Milk *Tej*
Oil *Olaj*
Pepper *Bors*
Salt *Só*
Spoon *Kanál*
Sugar *Cukor*
Water *Víz*

Meats (*Húsok*)

Bárány Lamb
Bográcsgulyás Thick goulash soup
Borjú Veal
Comb Leg
Jókai bableves Bean soup with pork
Kacsa Duck
Kijevi pulykamell Cheese-filled turkey in breadcrumbs
Liba Goose
Marha Beef
Máj Liver
Mell Breast
Nyúl Rabbit
Pulyka Turkey
Sonka Ham
Szarvas Deer

Fish/Seafood (*Hal/tengeri gyülmölcs*)

Halfilé roston Grilled fillet of fish
Homár Lobster
Kagyló Shellfish, mussels
Lazac Salmon
Pisztráng Trout
Ponty Carp
Rák Crab, prawn
Tonhal Tuna

Salads (*saláták*)

Cékla Beetroot
Fejes saláta Lettuce salad
Paradicsom Tomato
Uborka Cucumber
Vitamin saláta Mixed salad with mayonnaise

Vegetables (*Zöldség*)

Karfiol Cauliflower
Kukorica Sweetcorn
Lencse Lentils
Paprika Pepper
Sárgarépa Carrot
Zöldbab Green beans
Zöldborsó Green peas

Fruit (*Gyümölcs*)

Alma Apple
Dinnye Melon
Dió Nut, walnut
Eper Strawberry
Gesztenye Chestnut
Meggy Sour cherry
Narancs Orange
Őszibarack Peach
Szilva Plum

Drinks (*Itallok*)

Ásványvíz Mineral Water
Bor Wine
Édes bor Sweet wine
Fehér bor White wine
Kávé Coffee
Narancslé Orange juice
Pálinka Fruit brandy
Pezsgő Champagne
Sör Beer
Száraz bor Dry wine
Vörös bor Red wine

THE JOHN BULL® PUB™

GOURMET FOOD SELECTION

◆

TRUE VICTORIAN EXPERIENCE WITH THE
BEST CUISINE IN TOWN

◆

JOHN BULL BITTER, DOUBLE DIAMOND, TETLEY,
SKOL AND GUINNESS ON TAP

◆

THE BEST ATMOSPHERE TO RELAX IN BUDAPEST

Not to be missed when in Budapest!

Several locations to serve you:

The John Bull Pub
1052 Budapest Apáczai Csere János u. 17. Tel: 138-2168

Víghajós John Bull Pub
1118 Budapest Budaörsi út 7. Tel: 209-1713

Klotild John Bull Pub
1056 Budapest Szabadsajtó u. 6 Tel: 118-3600

John Bull Pub Vadász
1054 Budapest Podmaniczky tér 4. Tel: 269-3116

Automobile John Bull Pub
1122 Budapest Maros u. 28. Tel: 156-3565

Palota John Bull Pub
1157 Budapest Erdökerülö u. 3-5. Tel: 271-8205

Little Horse John Bull Pub
2092 Budakeszi Fö tér 5. Tel: 176-6949

dishes, such as the ubiquitous Gundel pancakes. A tourist trap under Communism, in 1991 it was acquired by Hungarian-American restaurateur George Lang and given a multi-million-dollar makeover with the aim of recreating the glory days. It's a huge place, in an art nouveau mansion by the Zoo, with a ballroom, garden and terrace, and several private dining rooms as well as the large main room hung with paintings by nineteenth-century Hungarian masters. Tables are laid with Zsolnay porcelain and sterling silver and the Gypsy band is slick. The menu is, not surprisingly, a little old-fashioned, and starters and desserts tend to outshine the main courses, but award-winning chef Kálmán Kalla has created fine versions of Hungarian standards, and Hungarian-ised versions of international dishes, such as the Tournedos Franz Liszt, made with local goose liver. A long and authoritative list of Hungarian wines is rounded off with excellent sweet Tokaj from the restaurant's own vineyard. Service is smooth and formal, if at times a little glib, and dining at Gundel is always a memorable experience. If you're only going to splash out once in Budapest, this is the place to do it, but don't expect to escape for less than Ft10,000 a head.

Hong Kong Pearl Garden

II. Margit körút 2 (212 3131). Tram 4, 6. **Open** noon-2.30pm, 6.30-11.30pm, Mon-Fri; noon-11.30pm Sat; noon-11pm Sun. **Average** Ft2,200. **Credit** AmEx, DC, V.
The huge Hong Kong skyline is a mite tacky and the one big room lacks atmosphere, but this place on the Buda foot of Margaret Bridge offers the best Chinese food in town. The extensive menu spans many regional styles, with a big selection of seafood, excellent duck, lobster fresh from the tank by the door and a couple of interesting vegetarian items. Set menus for two range from Ft2,200 to Ft5,800 for the Imperial Seafood Platter, but it's also possible to eat quite cheaply. Service occasionally scatterbrained.

Japán

VIII. Luther utca 4-6 (114 3427). M2 Blaha Lujza tér/tram 4, 6/bus 7. **Open** noon-2.30pm, 5pm-11pm, daily. **Average** Ft2,500 **Credit** AmEx, DC, JCB, MC, V.
Before the same crew opened the Sushi downtown, this was long the only Japanese place in town. These days the tatami is looking a little tatty. Frequented both by Japanese and by 'businessmen' from the former Soviet Union, it has a long menu offering every Nipponese favourite, from cheap Yakitori (Ft450) to Sukiyaki dinners cooked at the table (Ft3,500). Sushi, at the restaurant or separate sushi bar, comes at Ft450-Ft1,600 a piece. Poor by international standards and sadly no Japanese beer.

Kaviár Gourmet Bár (KGB)

II. Csatárka utca 54 (06 30 441 028/250 1492). Bus 11, 29. **Open** 4pm-2am daily. **Average** Ft3,500. **Credit** AmEx.
Strange is the word for this place hidden away at the top of the Rózsadomb. The name both identifies the main speciality and harks back to the days when owner Attila used to serve the real KGB at a restaurant near the Vár. The dining room is windowless and features running water, an icon and office chairs. Surprisingly friendly and worth the effort to find. The average price would drop considerably if you ate one of their Hungarian standards instead of caviar.

Király

I. Táncsics Mihály utca 25 (156 9891/156 8565/fax 201 3767). Várbusz. **Open** noon-midnight daily. **Average** Ft4,000. **Credit** AmEx, DC, JCB, MC, V.
Every place in the Castle District tends to be tourist-orientated and overpriced, but here the service and food (mostly well-prepared Hungarian standards) are to a genuine standard. Tread carefully with the outrageously expensive wine list, though. The main room is a pleasant semi-circular space with stone walls and heavy furnishings. Strange floor show with gypsy band and dancing girls in kilts.

Kisbuda Gyöngye

III. Kenyeres utca 34 (168 6402). Tram 17. **Open** noon-midnight Mon-Sat; noon-3.30pm Sun. **Average** Ft2,500. **Credit** AmEx.
Sidestreet favourite with Óbuda locals. Walls are panelled with parts of old wardrobes and the seating is an assortment of old and not always terribly comfortable kitchen chairs. A pretty general Hungarian menu with some interesting daily specials. The venison fillet with wild mushrooms and a brandy sauce is a real plateful and demonstrates the best of the kitchen.

Légrádi Testvérek

V. Magyar utca 23 (118 6804). M3 Kálvin tér/tram 47, 49. **Open** 6pm-midnight Mon-Fri. **Average** Ft2,500. **Credit** AmEx.
One of the oldest upscale restaurants in Budapest. The basement is a comfortable drawing room which sells very similar contemporary Hungarian food to its sister restaurant, Légrádi Antique. Friendlier than the Antique although the kitchen isn't quite as good.

Le Légrádi Antique

V. Bárczy István utca 3-5 (266 4993). M1, M2, M3 Deák tér/tram 47, 49. **Open** noon-3pm, 7pm-midnight, Mon-Fri. **Average** Ft2,500. **Credit** AmEx, DC, V.
Difficult to find (it's hiding in an antique shop – take the staircase opposite the door), this special restaurant – one of the best in town – is elegant and comfortable, with heavy antique furniture and waiters wearing tails. The hors d'oeuvres trolley selection is limited but represents a true taster session of the best of Hungarian cooking, including fish terrine, foie gras, miniature portions of steak tartar and quails' eggs. The main courses include pork stuffed with goose liver, excellent steaks and a wide selection of game and local fish. Gypsy music in the evenings.

Marco Polo

V. Vigadó tér 3 (138 3925). M1 Vörösmarty tér/tram 2. **Open** noon-3pm, 7.30pm-midnight, Mon-Sat. **Average** Ft2,800. **Credit** AmEx, DC, JCB, MC, V.
A polished and mature establishment, Italian-owned and run, which imports many of its ingredients and nearly all of its wine from the Old Country. Service and food are excellent: for its cuisine alone this would rank as a first-class Italian restaurant anywhere in the world. Daily specials often feature toothsome home-made pasta and soups are especially good. The décor is pretty bland – beige walls and polished wood – and the place often lacks atmosphere, but the small terrace on Vigadó tér, just yards from the Danube, is an enjoyable spot on a summer evening.

Margitkert

II. Margit utca 15 (155 3883). Tram 4, 6. **Open** noon-midnight daily. **Average** Ft2,200. **Credit** AmEx, DC, JCB, MC, V.
At the foot of the Rózsadomb, with a spacious courtyard for summer dining, a menu of heavy Hungarian standards and a Gypsy band generally considered to be one of the very best in town. Not a place to go if you want to avoid the music.

Robinson

XIV. Városliget, tósziget (343 0955). M1 Hősök tere. **Open** noon-4pm, 6pm-midnight, daily. **Average** Ft3,000. **Credit** AmEx, DC, JCB, MC, V.
So-called presumably because of its location on an 'island' (about a yard from the shore) in the Városliget duckpond, Robinson has an agreeable waterside terrace but is otherwise overpriced, overrated and inflexible. The long menu – Hungarian with a French accent – contains a few unusual items, but the food is unspectacular for the price and the service simply infuriating. Once regarded as one of the best restaurants in Budapest, these days Robinson doesn't cut it. Avoid.

Szindbád

V. Markó utca 33 (132 2966/132 2749/fax 112 3836).
M3 Nyugati tér. **Open** noon-3.30pm, 6.30pm-midnight,
Mon-Fri; 5pm-midnight Sat, Sun. **Average** Ft3,000.
Credit AmEx, DC, JCB, MC, V.
In Budapest's business district and very much a business
venue. The bar area is full of heavy chesterfields and the dining room is comfortable in a formal sort of way. The menu
contains a few surprises such as a chop suey dish, but the
main emphasis is on Hungarian international cuisine and
this they do well. Not a spot to relax 'a deux' but good for a
more formal dinner.

Vadrózsa

II. Pentelei Molnár utca 15 (135 1118/fax 115 0044).
Bus 91. **Open** noon-3pm, 7pm-midnight, daily. **Average**
Ft3,000. **Credit** AmEx, DC, JCB, MC, V.
In a beautiful small villa halfway up the Rózsadomb, this
was once one of the few top-flight restaurants in Budapest,
but is these days just its best. Their custom of eschewing a
written menu, and inviting guests to choose from a plateful
of raw ingredients such as goose liver, fogas, wild boar, venison, filet mignon and Russian caviar, harks back to black
market days when so much fine meat was something pretty special. The resulting meals are well-prepared but a little
plain. In the main wood-panelled room a mournful pianist
plays with the air of one who has seen regimes come and go.
Elegant garden for summer dining.

Moderate

Acapulco

VII. Erzsébet körút 39 (322 6014). Tram 4, 6. **Open**
noon-midnight daily. **Average** Ft1,500. **Credit** AmEx,
DC, MC, V.
The best Mexican food in Budapest, although that isn't saying much. The ambience approximates that of an American
shopping mall theme restaurant: Mexican tat, useless mari-
achi music, offhand service, and frozen margarita so weak
it ought to arrive with a note from its mother. Certain staples – meatball soup, guacamole – will not disappoint, but
tacos and quesadillas are served up drearily dry. Non-smoking section.

Bagolyvár

XIV. Állatkerti út 2 (next door to the Gundel) (321
3550/fax 342 2917). M1 Hősök tere. **Open** noon-11pm
daily. **Average** Ft1,500. **Credit** AmEx, DC, V.
In a mock Transylvanian castle attached to the Gundel and
owned by the same people. Locals refer to it as 'Junior
Gundel'. It's run by women because proprietor George Lang
reckons that they are the best home cooks and this place is
all about home cooking. The menu varies daily and features
some very good soups and other basic offerings. A roulade
of fresh breads, served with various spreads, is part of the
starter. A good inexpensive restaurant.

Beckett's

V. Bajcsy-Zsilinszky út 72 (111 1035). M3 Arany János
utca. **Open** noon-midnight daily. **Average** Ft1,800.
Credit AmEx, DC, MC, V.
The restaurant operation of this Irish pub (see also chapter
Cafés & Bars) has confused many by being a mess of Irish,
French and Hungarian dishes. A new chef, appointed as this
book goes to press, seems finally to be making the food passable. Despite the kitchen's dodgy reputation, Beckett's
restaurant is normally full and for foreigners is the user-
friendliest place in town. Fry-up brunch on Sundays.

Bombay Palace

VI. Andrássy út 44 (132 8363/131 3787). M1
Oktogon/tram 4, 6. **Open** noon-3pm, 6pm-midnight,
daily. **Average** Ft1,900. **Credit** AmEx, DC, JCB, MC, V.

A local branch of the international chain in suitably palatial
premises with marble floors, chandeliers and so many service staff they mostly sort of mill around aimlessly. The fare
is excellent, displaying no particular regional bias. There's
a good tandoori selection, many vegetarian options and a
fine basket of assorted nan breads to clean your plate afterwards. The weekend lunch buffet offers all you can eat for
Ft1,400.

Carmel Pince

VII. Dob utca 31 (entrance from Kazinczy utca) (322
1834/342 4585). **Open** noon-11pm daily.
Average Ft1,500. **Credit** AmEx, DC, JCB, MC, V.
Outside the sign announces that this is not a Kosher restaurant but, right next door to the Orthodox synagogue, it is
defiantly Jewish. The vaulted cellar is comfortable and
shows the maturity of age, with an easy ambience afforded
by stained glass and interesting nick-nacks. The food is traditional Hungarian Jewish with goose as the speciality. The
cooking is all right and the service normally helpful.
Reasonable vegetarian section, too.

Cyrano

V. Kristóf tér 7-8 (266 3096). M1 Vörösmarty tér. **Open**
11am-5pm, 6.30pm-midnight, daily. **Average** Ft1,700.
Credit AmEx, DC, MC.
Just off the brash end of Váci, and offering an imaginative
selection of French-accented Hungarian and international
dishes with some good vegetarian options. The service can
be shocking, though. In summer the terrace is great for
people-watching as passers-by pause to splash in the small
fountain outside. Booking recommended.

Fatál

V. Váci utca 67 (entrance in Pintér utca) (266 2607).
Tram 2, 47, 49. **Open** 11.30am-2am daily. **Average**
Ft1,100. **No credit cards.**
No, you won't get food poisoning – the name means 'wood-
en platter' and Fatál is a country-style restaurant with mock
stained-glass windows serving hearty portions of well-
cooked traditional food that even includes a few vegetarian
choices. The Vetrece, chicken soup served in a hollowed-out
half-loaf, is particularly interesting. Service is indifferent,
though. Watch they don't pad your bill. Nice location off the
quiet end of Váci.

Hax'n Király

XI. Király utca 100 (267 2304). Trolleybus 70, 78. **Open**
noon-midnight daily. **Average** Ft1,500. **Credit** AmEx,
DC, MC.
Authentic and entertaining Bavarian restaurant which
serves delicious pig hocks spit-roasted in full view of the
assembled carnivores. Both the limited starter selection and
the main courses are all about meat and lots of it. The hocks
are the speciality and one between two is a massive portion
of high-fat food. At least nobody around you will be mut-
tering about cholesterol, they will just be tucking in and
enjoying themselves.

Kárpátia

V. Károlyi Mihály utca 7 (117 7305). M3 Ferenciek tere.
Open noon-3pm, 6-11pm, daily. **Average** Ft1,500.
Credit AmEx, EC, JCB, MC.
As downtown tourist-orientated Hungarian restaurants with
Gypsy bands go, this one is pretty good. Slack service, but
a decent terrace, a beautiful neo-Gothic interior and the odd
vegetarian option lurking among all the goose liver, game
and pike-perch dishes. The food is adequate, the Gypsy band
more enjoyable than most.

Kéhli

III. Mókus utca 22 (250 4241). HÉV Árpád híd/tram 1.
Open noon-midnight daily. **Average** Ft1,900. **Credit**
AmEx.

*Craving a curry? Then try **Maharaja**. Just don't expect fireworks.*

Kéhli is rated by many residents and visitors as Budapest's very best Hungarian restaurant. The main area with its Gypsy band is difficult to get into without booking, but there are several other rooms in which to perch and which also fill up every night. One of the best specialities is a rich bone marrow soup: first drink the soup, then scrape out the marrow and spread it on toast with garlic. Portions are mountainous. There are normally a few tourists looking for the real Hungarian experience, but the great atmosphere is provided by the largely Hungarian clientèle – so maybe this is the real Hungarian experience.

Kétballábas

VI. Teréz körút 36 (entrance in Dessewffy utca) (269 5563). M1 Oktogon/tram 4, 6. **Open** noon-midnight daily. **Average** Ft1,300. **Credit** AmEx, EC, JCB, MC.
No gourmet paradise, but not bad considering it's owned by a footballer – György Bognár, capped 50 times for Hungary. The décor is soccer kitsch with mementoes from Bognár's career. It's an interesting place to catch major matches on television, when György often invites along old football stars and sports journalists. The menu is a blend of Hungarian and international, perhaps leaning a little heavily on the microwave, but the 'butter footed salad bowls' are excellent at around Ft400.

Leroy's Country Pub

XIII. Visegrádi utca 50 (140 3316). M3 Lehel tér. **Open** noon-2am daily. **Average** Ft1,500. **No credit cards**.
An American theme bar decked out with old enamel signs, wire netting and a load of ramshackle furniture. The clientèle tend to be local entrepreneurs who double park their motors as near to the door as possible and spend most of their time on the mobile phone. The accompanying molls spend fortunes on blond rinses and very little on cloth. Despite all this, the food is wholesome, the steaks are just about the best in Budapest and there is normally a good buzz in the air.

Les Amis

II. Rómer Flóris utca 12 (212 3173). Tram 4, 6. **Open** 10am-1am Mon-Sat. **Average** Ft1,500. **No credit cards**.
A tiny, popular neighbourhood place on a quiet street. Flock wallpaper, banquet seating and lots of greenery add up to a décor unusual for Budapest – even without the name, Les Amis would remind you of northern Europe. The menu reflects the limited cooking facilities that the chef has behind the small bar. The only hot starter options are soups, followed by a section of 'frying pan foods', 'grill foods' and a small range of fogas dishes. A friendly spot. Tables outside in summer.

Luau

V. Zoltán utca 16 (131 4352). M2 Kossuth tér. **Open** noon-11pm daily. **Average** Ft1,500. **Credit** AmEx, DC, JCB, MC, V.
A Polynesian place, and the first theme restaurant to open in contemporary Budapest. The black main room has cane furniture, fish nets and large pictures of Pacific beaches. A defiantly naff cocktail menu lists things such as Fluffy Duck and Potted Parrot. The food ranges widely and has as much to do with New Orleans as Polynesia. There's an extensive fish section and the Shrimp Jambalaya at Ft950 looks good value. The general standard of cooking is poor, but the daft décor and some very different dishes make a detour worthwhile if only to enjoy the hourly artificial thunderstorm.

Maharaja

III. Bécsi út 89-91 (188 6863). Tram 17. **Open** noon-midnight Tue-Sun. **Average** Ft900. **Credit** AmEx, MC, V.
Many expats make the trek up to Óbuda to dine at Budapest's second-best Indian restaurant, though on any UK high street you'd find somewhere just as good, and probably better. The garlic soup is excellent and samosas get the thumbs-up but much of the food here is both underspiced and a mite too greasy. Cheap, though, and cheerful too.

Múzeum

VIII. Múzeum körút 12 (138 4221). M3 Kálvin tér.
Open 10am-2am Mon-Sat. **Average** Ft1750. **Credit**
AmEx.
High ceilings, tiled walls, tall windows providing plenty of
light and well-spaced tables add to the fin de siècle ambience
at the ever-popular Múzeum, founded in 1885. The menu is
generally impressive with an enormous difference in price
from one dish to another – you can spend a fortune here or
you can dine very cheaply. The Hungarian-international food
is good, if unexceptional. Vast, well-presented portions,
smooth service and the pleasant surrounds keep this old
place buzzing.

Náncsi Néni

II. Ördögárok út 80 (176 5809). Tram 56 then bus157.
Open noon-11pm daily. **Average** Ft1,100. **Credit**
AmEx, MC, V.
City-dwellers flock here at weekends, pretending it is in the
country, although actually it is now well into suburbia. Both
location and food retain a rustic charm, with a leafy garden,
extravagant portions and very reasonable prices. The food
is Hungarian home cooking and excellent home-made soups
are a speciality.

Okay Italia

*XIII. Szent István körút 20 (131 6990). M3 Nyugati/tram
4, 6.* **Open** noon-midnight daily. **Average** Ft1,100. **No
credit cards.**
The Szent István körút branch was a revelation for Budapest
when it opened in late 1993: simple, good, reasonably priced
Italian food in an unpretentious atmosphere. Staffing the
place with good-looking women in very short skirts was also
part of a strategy which proved so popular they opened up
a second branch round the corner, universally known as
'Okay 2'. The branches have slightly different menus but in
both there's a good general selection of familiar dishes. Not
the best Italian in town, but certainly the best value. So
popular with foreigners, some call it 'Okay Expatria'. In the
evenings book or expect a wait.
Branch: V. Nyugati tér 6 (132 6960).

Old Amsterdam

V. Királyi Pál utca 14 (117 9257). M3 Kálvin tér. **Open**
noon-2am Mon-Fri; 6pm-2am Sat, Sun. **Average** Ft1,100.
No credit cards.
A pleasant corner bar that would not look out of place in the
city it is named after. The menu is basic and sensible: a well-
chosen selection of meat and fish grill dishes (the beefrib
steak is excellent), six omlettes (four of them without meat)
and a few sandwiches. The only place in town that serves
Old Gouda.

Paletta

II. Erőd utca 22 (201 2928). Tram 4, 6. **Open** 4pm-
midnight Mon-Sat. **Average** Ft1,500. **Credit** AmEx,
MC, V.
This appealing place has recently been changed from an elegant Hungarian-international restaurant to a fun modern
restaurant serving some interesting and different dishes (at
least for Budapest). Some quite striking contemporary art on
the walls, a good vegetarian section and seven different types
of fondue.

Remiz

II. Budakeszi út 5 (275 1396). Bus 22. **Open** 9am-
midnight daily. **Average** Ft1,500. **Credit** AmEx.
A few summers' old and with an enviable reputation for its
wonderful sheltered garden and separate grill kitchen that
churns out summer barbie-type food. There are a few vegetarian dishes and the Russian caviar is the cheapest in town.
The grills, proudly borne around the room on wooden platters, tend to be murdered rather than cooked. Patchy service
but the staff normally speak good English.

Rózsalugas Restaurant

*Udvarház, III. Hármashatárhegyi út 2 (188 8780/188
6921). Bus 65.* **Open** May-Oct 11am-11pm Tue-Sun. Nov-
Apr 5-11pm Tue-Fri; 11am-11pm Sat, Sun. **Average**
Ft1,900. **Credit** AmEx, DC, JCB, MC, V.
Main attraction is the fine view from the top of this large
Buda Hill: on a summer's day the peaceful terrace is perfect.
The food is better than one expects from a place that also
runs a large folklore operation next door, with tourists getting bussed up to see some dancing. The Rózsalugas is separate from the tourist bit and the menu is typically
Hungarian-international. The foie gras (described as 'Goose
liver pie') is particularly good. Best to stick to the menu's
plainer items.

Seoul House

I. Fő utca 8 (201 7452). Tram 19/bus 2, 86, 105. **Open**
noon-11pm Tue-Sun. **Average** Ft1,900. **Credit** AmEx,
DC, JCB, MC, V.
The better of Budapest's two Korean restauarants. Décor is
a mite bleak, but it's usually full – popular not only with local
Koreans but also regarded as one of the best Far Eastern
restaurants in town. Table-top barbecues allow those in the
know to order strange and wonderful dishes they can cook
themselves. A favourite is bulgogi, marinated beef.
Modumjeon, Korean stuffed vegetables, fried tempura-style,
is a recommended starter and arrives at the table cooked.

Taverna Dionysos

V. Belgrád rakpart 16 (118 1222). Tram 2, 47, 49.
Open noon-midnight daily. **Average** Ft1,200. **Credit**
AmEx, V.
The hyperreal whitewashed and blue interior looks more
Greek than Greece; the terrace, on the Danube overlooking
Gellért Hill, can be noisy but boasts a unique view. The ser-
vice is apt offhand, but it's a well-run place offering accept-
able versions of all the Aegean standards. Non-carnivores
will enjoy picking among the starters.

Tian Tan Chinese Restaurant

V. Duna utca 1 (118 6444). M3 Ferenciek tere. **Open**
noon-midnight daily. **Average** Ft1,900. **Credit** AmEx,
DC, JCB, MC, V.
With its labyrinthine interior of dark lacquer and back-lit
multicoloured panels, dotted with fountains, fish tanks and
jade sculptures, entering this place is like stepping into some
kind of Chinese computer game. The menu is huge, with 14
categories of main course including good duck and shrimp
and some tasty tofu variations, but by international standards the food is acceptable rather than outstanding.
Possible to eat cheaply if you lay off the seafood.

Sushi

V. Harmincad utca 4 (117 4239). M1 Vörösmarty tér.
Open 11.30am-3pm, 4-11pm daily. **Average** Ft1,200. **No
credit cards.**
Surprisingly good sushi and sashimi in this simple, clean,
traditionally styled sushi bar next to the British embassy
and down the road from the Kempinski Hotel. Vegetarian
seaweed rolls also on the short menu, along with miso soup
and one excellent tofu dish. Attracts a cosmopolitan crowd,
including many Japanese. No alcohol served, alas.

Vörös Sárkány

VI. Andrássy 80 (131 8757). M1 Kodály körönd.
Open noon-midnight Mon-Sat. **Average** Ft1,100. **Credit**
AmEx.
The Red Dragon opened more than ten years ago, way before
anybody else thought of ethnic food in Budapest. After an
initial period when Chinese chefs trained the locals, the staff
has remained totally Magyar. Food and service are not bad
compared to some very ordinary Chinese places in town. The
spring roll, a cross between the Chinese version and the
Hungarian palacsinta, is worth trying.

Just desserts & bloody hangovers

Hungary is a major wine producer. The two best-known wines are Tokaj, a dessert-style wine that's inspired hundreds of poetic eulogies, and Bull's Blood, a heavy red blend that has received thousands of curses the morning after. But there are wine regions all over the country, and, apart from the large regional wine companies, now also many boutique wine producers as well as thousands of private vintners growing anything from a few litres for private use to a few thousand for public sale.

It is possible to visit a borozó (wine cellar – *see chapter* **Cafés & Bars**) and drink something called wine for as little as Ft100 a litre. There are also some very fine, and very expensive, Hungarian wines on offer.

Most are named after their grape variety and area of production. The main white wine areas are Balaton, Etyek and Szekszárd. The best grape varities are Chardonnay, Riesling (Olaszrizling) and Pinots Gris and Blanc. All should provide dry, reasonably fruity wine. Etyek Chardonnay can be particlularly good, and Balaton rizling is on most menus.

The main red grapes are Cabernet Sauvignon, Merlot and Kékfrankos – though check that this last is *száraz* (dry) rather than *félédes* (half-sweet). The region with the best reputation for reds is Villány; those of Szekszárd and Eger are also worthwhile. Hungarian reds are often drunk chilled – which at least kills the taste of some poor, high-tannin varieties.

As for brand names, some of the best Villányi comes from Bock or Gere. Bátapáti and Morcseny wines dominate Szekszárd. Some very pleasant Balaton wines are produced under the label 'Volcanic Hills', and the Dörgicse vineyard has a growing reputation.

The fabled Bulls' Blood is called Egri Bikavar in Hungarian. It is a strong, dry and reasonably consistent red blended from Cabernet Sauvignon, Cabernet Franc, Merlot and Kékfrankos.

The origins of Tokaji go back to an inconvenient Turkish invasion which delayed the vendange until the 'noble rot' had reduced the grapes to raisins. A vintage Tokaji Aszú with 5 or 6 *puttonyos* (a measure of sweetness), drunk as a dessert wine, is an experience both for the palate and, if you're not wary, the wallet as well.

Inexpensive

Chinatown Restaurant
VIII. Népszínház utca 15 (113 3220). M2 Blaha Lujza tér/tram 4, 6. **Open** noon-midnight daily. **Average** Ft700. **No credit cards.**
A menu of largely familiar dishes and a small fortune's worth of pagodas, lattice-work and red dragons. The food is merely average, but it's cheap and in a useful location.

Falafel
VI. Paulay Ede utca 53 (no phone). M1 Oktagon/tram 4, 6. **Open** 10am-8pm Mon-Fri; 10am-6pm Sat. **Average** Ft160. **No credit cards.**
Build your own falafel or fill your own salad bowl from the excellent salad bar. Takeaway cartons available if you feel like eating on a bench in nearby Liszt tér; otherwise there are tables upstairs. Best and healthiest value for money of any place in town.

Fészek
VII. Kertész utca 36 (corner of Dob utca) (322 6043). Tram 4, 6. **Open** noon-1am daily. **Average** Ft700. **Credit** AmEx.
An artist's club since the turn of the century but in practice open to anyone (with a Ft100 entrance fee in the evening), Fészek offers very elegant dining at bargain prices. The ornate high-ceilinged main room is attractive enough, but the real bonus is the appealingly delapidated Venetian-style courtyard, formerly a monk's cloister and one of the most beautiful places in central Budapest to wile away a long summer lunchtime. Service can be suffocatingly slow and sullen, but the food is all right and the atmosphere deeply relaxing.

Gyökér
VI. Eötvös utca 46 (153 4329). M3 Nyugati. **Open** 4pm-2am Mon-Thur; 4pm-4am Fri; 6pm-4am Sat; 6pm-2am Sun. **Average** Ft700. **No credit cards.**
The name means 'roots', which explains tree stumps dangling from the ceiling and refers to the fact that, owned by a musician, this is the folk scene's favourite restaurant. Late evenings there is often some sort of jam session as musicians drop by for a bite of the inexpensive and unusually greasefree Hungarian food. Almost every night there are also more formal concerts in a separate room, including a Friday night táncház (dance house) led by Transylvanian group Újstílus. Cover charge for concerts about Ft150. (*See also chapter* **Folklore**.)

Karagöz
VII. Nefelejcs utca 27 (121 4114). M2 Keleti. **Open** 11am-midnight daily. **Average** Ft600. **No credit cards.**
Friendly if typically tacky Turkish restaurant that offers kebabs galore, a good selection of salads and many vegetarian starter options. Once known for wild raki parties, these days it's more sedate, with nice touches including free tea from the samovar and finger bowls of rose-scented water.

Kikelet
II. Fillér utca 85 (212 5444). Bus 49. **Open** noon-11pm daily. **Average** Ft950. **No credit cards.**
In a strangely out of place log cabin, but it's the rustic, shady garden that attracts. The furniture has seen better days and the food is basic: a few typical Hungarian dishes, mostly prepared to order with that essential local cooking utility, the frying pan. Main attractions are affordable prices and the ambience, which is wonderful on a balmy summer's evening. Cheap, cheerful and unpretentious.

Gypsy violinists 1: Where they come from

Of all the Hungarian stereotypes, one has been disappearing with alarming speed – the Gypsy violinist, strolling amongst the tables entertaining diners with wild and romantic music. Though many Budapest restaurants still have them, particularly the more touristy places, violin bands are fast becoming a thing of the past, victims of changing tastes, lost in the headlong charge towards Europe.

Gypsy musical prowess has long been noted, and families of musicians tended to settle in areas where there was demand for their art. While preserving their own percussive and vocal music, to make a living, Gypsies adopted the instruments and repertoire of the non-Gypsy majority. While Hungarian peasants sang and danced to the music of the bagpipe, flute and hurdy-gurdy,

Gypsies were often hired by the nobility to play fashionably western violins, violas and cellos. They added the cimbalom, a hammered dulcimer with a long tradition in the orient.

Large professional Gypsy orchestras began to appear in the first half of the nineteenth century. About this time the saying arose that all a Hungarian needed to get drunk was a glass of water and a gypsy fiddler. Garden restaurants, hotels, wine gardens all provided a good living to musicians. Famous lead fiddlers were treated as royalty, and extravagant tipping of musicians was common.

These days finding a good Gypsy band in a restaurant is getting harder. The **Kulacs** comes close to the original spirit of the classic restaurants, as does the more upmarket **Margitkert**.

Krónikás

XIII. Tátra utca 2 (269 5048). Tram 4, 6. **Open** noon-midnight daily. **Average** Ft900. **No credit cards.**
The name means 'chronicler' and this dingy cellar is decorated with a procession of scenes from the history of mankind. Dark wood and maroon trimmings abet the sober atmosphere. The fare is a huge selection of reasonably priced Hungarian basics plus one or two rather desultory vegetarian options. Excellent service, acceptable cooking, nice prices.

Kulacs Étterem

VII. Osvát utca 11 (267 0735). M2 Blaha Lujza tér. **Open** 10am-4am daily. **Average** Ft800. **Credit** AmEx, MC, V.
This is the place where, in 1927, László Jávor wrote the song 'Szomorú Vasárnap'. Translated as 'Cloudy Sunday', it became a huge hit for Billie Holiday. For a while it was the fashion for young men to dress in black, pin the lyrics to their clothes as a suicide note, and throw themselves off the nearest Danube bridge. Less melodramatic these days, Kulacs offers a good but straightforward Hungarian menu, a pianist in one room, and some of Budapest's best and most authentic Gypsy music in the other.

Marquis de Salade

VI. Hajós utca 43 (153 4931). M3 Nyugati. **Open** noon-midnight daily. **Average** Ft400. **No credit cards.**
Cooks from six countries provide Budapest's most imaginative selection of salads, augmented by falafels and Chinese dumplings, samosas and spring rolls heated to order. The self-service salad bar is badly lit and the contents often past their best by the evening, making this a better spot for a light lunch than a sit-down dinner, though vegetarians will sigh with relief at any time of day.

Marxim

II. Kisrókus utca 23 (115 5036). Tram 4, 6. **Open** 11am-1am Mon-Fri; 11am-2am Sat; 6pm-1am Sun. **Average** Ft350 **Credit** AmEx, DC, JCB, V.
In an appropriately industrial setting behind a Buda tram factory, the theme of this pizzeria is Communist kitsch.

There's a small showcase of Stalinist trinkets by the door, red flags and trades union banners festoon the interior, chicken-wire separates the tables and the pizzas have names such as Anarchismo and Gulag. Alas, it isn't only the décor which harks back to Communist days: the pizzas are so tough they can bend the cheap cutlery.

Off-Broadway

VI. Zichy Jenő utca 47 (131 5920). M1 Oktogon/tram 4, 6. **Open** noon-1am daily. **Average** Ft900. **Credit** AmEx, DC.
Owned by film-maker Gábor Dettre and actress Kathleen Gáti, and just around the corner from Budapest's Broadway, Nagymező utca, this small, friendly and comfortable cellar place appeals to the film and theatre crowd. The eclectic, New York-accented menu is mostly vegetarian (excellent quiches, salads, soups and pancakes) and there's a formidable selection of American-style desserts.

Taverna Ressaikos

I. Apor Péter utca 1 (212 1612). Tram 19/bus 2, 86, 105. **Open** noon-midnight daily. **Average** Ft850 **Credit** AmEx, MC.
The city's second-best Greek place and bit of a dive, although there are some interesting menu items and it's a useful spot if you're stuck down the Lánchíd end of Fő utca. Five per cent added to your bill when the 'orchestra' (a small and not terribly good Greek folk group) is playing.

Semiramis

V. Alkotmány utca 20 (111 7627). M3 Nyugati/tram 4, 6. **Open** noon-9pm Mon-Sat. **Average** Ft550. **No credit cards.**
Small, friendly Syrian joint offering usual spread of middle eastern stuff: lentil soup, lamb and chicken dishes, salads, kebabs. Cheap and cheerful without frills or pretensions.

Shalom

VII. Klauzál tér 2 (322 1464). M2 Blaha Lujza tér. **Open** noon-10pm Mon-Thur, Sat, Sun; noon-5pm Fri. **Average** Ft900. **No credit cards.**

Right on the central square of the Jewish quarter, a comfortable, friendly establishment offering kosher versions of Hungarian standards with a few Jewish classics: goose liver (Ft1300) rubs shoulders with gefilte fish (Ft310). Service excellent, food average but inexpensive, atmosphere relaxing.

Tabáni Kakas
I. Attila út 27 (175 7165). Tram 18. **Open** noon-midnight daily. **Average** Ft950. **Credit** AmEx, MC.
This no-frills local restaurant has been around a long time and changed little, although somebody did recently buy a pot of paint. The trad Hungarian menu is balanced between cooked-to-order fries and pre-cooked stews.

Vegetárium
V. Cukor utca 3 (267 0322). M3 Ferenciek tér. **Open** noon-10pm daily. **Average** Ft800. **Credit** AmEx, JCB, MC, V.
Long Budapest's only vegetarian restaurant, but now poultry and fish have arrived on a menu 'prepared in accordance with dietary principles carefully worked out with the help of foreign consultants'. There is beer and wine, a few vegan and macrobiotic dishes among more standard vegetarian fare, and strictly no smoking. The atmosphere is austere, the food plain and solid. Usually a queue in the evenings when a classical guitarist entertains diners at booth tables.

Étkezdék

The étkezde is the Hungarian equivalent of the English caff: small, cheap and often family-run places which provide simple home cooking. They have few vegetarian options but offer a hearty lunch for between Ft350-Ft500 for two courses. Staff tend to be friendlier than in restaurants.

Házias Étkezde
I. Várfok utca 8 (115 2931). Várbusz from M2 Moszkva tér. **Open** noon 5pm Mon-Fri; noon-4pm Sat. **Average** Ft400. **No credit cards.**
Five minutes' walk from the Castle District, the Házias is a tiny eaterie with a limited menu and no alcohol. The food is standard, but you will welcome the lack of tourist kitsch.

Kisharang Étkezde
VI. Október 6 utca 17 (no phone). M3 Arany János utca. **Open** 11am-8pm Mon-Fri; 11.30am-3.30pm Sat, Sun. **Average** Ft400. **No credit cards.**
The Little Bell bustles near Budapest's business quarter: quick, clean and efficient. You're as likely to sit next to a chap in a pinstriped shirt as a granny gulping goulash. Main dishes are not for the meek and are served with rice, parsley potatoes and salad. They can be ordered in half-portions or the staff will lovingly wrap leftovers for Ft15. Vegetable porridge, *főzelék*, is the ideal winter warmer.

Lukrécia Snackbar
V. Váci utca 65 (118 1098). Tram 2, 47, 49. **Open** 10am-6pm Mon-Fri. **No credit cards.**
In the unfashionable end of Váci utca and run by a batty woman who would be perfectly at home running a Torquay boarding house. Go early because some of the main dishes disappear before mid-afternoon. Draught light and dark beer.

Karcsi Ételbár
VI. Jókai utca 20 (112 0557). M1 Oktogon/M3 Nyugati/tram 4, 6. **Open** 11am-9pm Mon-Fri. **Average** Ft400. **Set menu** Ft195. **No credit cards.**
Two menus, one changed weekly, the other the chef's regular specialities. Two set menus also change weekly, Ft195 for a soup, a main course and a pudding. Service a little slow but the customers seem to have time to spare.

Kádár Étkezde
VII. Klauzál tér 10 (no phone). Trolleybus 74. **Open** 11.30am-3.30pm Tue-Fri. **Average** Ft300. **No credit cards.**
Signed celebrity photos plastering the walls testify to Kádár's former glory. Menu changed daily to keep the regulars' interest, with a fair selection of puddings. Pay at the cash desk by the door.

Tüköry Söröző
V. Hold utca 15 (269 5027). M3 Arany János utca. **Open** 10am-11pm Mon-Fri. **Average** Ft400. **No credit cards.**
A cheap restaurant rather than the beer hall its name suggests. Tables fill from around noon. Grab one by the window and watch shoppers come and go at the indoor market next door. Menu changes weekly.

Gypsy violinists 2: Getting rid of them

Many diners are surprised the first time a Gypsy band leader approaches the table. Some, intent on quiet conversation, are simply appalled. Many enjoy the mournful folk melodies and just-about-recognisable renditions of old movie hits and ancient pop songs. Some, however, do not.

The band don't care either way. They are there for the tips and, like it or not, you are going to provide them. Even if you pick a table miles from the band, sooner or later they'll ooze over and accost you with their dying art form. The following scenarios are then possible. Do not tip, and the violinist will position his instrument a few millimetres from your face and bash out

something loud and grating. Tip well, and the entire band virtually camp at your table, playing ever more frenzied music in the hope of further offerings.

The answer is the insult tip: just enough to be serious but well below expectation. The band will look at it, take it, and hopefully plunge off in search of more rewarding victims.

The exact amount varies from place to place. If you want to keep them (the after-dinner period is the traditional time) Ft500-Ft1,000 is about right. If you want to get rid of them, Ft100-Ft200 should do the trick. And remember to look as though you feel very generous.

Fast Food

Brand-name burgers, doughnuts and pizzas dominate Budapest fast food to a ridiculous degree, making indigenous street eats ever harder to find. You'll find small Prima Pék bakery kiosks selling cakes and rolls at many main metro stations. Butchers have small stand-up eating areas for grilled chicken and sausages (*see* **Let's have a butcher's** *below*). At markets and stations you'll also find *lángos*, deep-fried dough served with sour cream and cheese.

Duran Szendvics
V. Október 6 utca 15 (132 9348). M3 Arany János utca. **Open** 8am-6pm Mon-Fri; 8am-1pm Sat. **No credit cards.**
This Viennese Imbiß boasts more than 20 kinds of small, delicately made open sandwiches at around Ft50. Excellent *cappuccino* at Ft65. Takeaway boxes for up to 25 items.

Házi Rétes
VII. Király utca 70 (no phone). Tram 4, 6. **Open** 9am-6pm Mon-Fri; 9am-1pm Sat. **No credit cards.**
As the sign outside says, 'Ahogy Nagymama Sütött' – just how Grandma used to make. The best takeaway strudel in Budapest: apple, cherry, plum and cabbage at Ft50 a throw.

Korona Passage
V. Kecskeméti utca 14 (117 4111). M3 Kálvin tér. **Open** 10am-10pm daily. **No credit cards.**
Upmarket cafeteria with the best takeaway pancakes in town. Cottage cheese pancakes at Ft260, apple at Ft190, cheese at Ft240. Impressive salad bar.

Lángos úr és Társai/Sandwich Box
VIII. Keleti pályaudvar (342 9720). M2 Keleti pályaudvar. **Open** *Lángos* 8am-8pm daily; *Sandwich Box* 24 hours daily. **No credit cards.**
Well-positioned for observing the bustle of Budapest's main station, these neighbouring stand-up snack bars offer sour cream and cheese *lángos* at Ft53, chicken sandwiches at Ft92, mozzarella sandwiches at Ft85 and draught beer at Ft110 a korsó.

Marie Kristensen Sandwich Bar
IX. Ráday utca 9 (218 1673). M3 Kálvin tér. **Open** 10am-9pm Mon-Fri. **No credit cards.**
Budapest's first sandwich bar could still do with a little more variety. Turkey salad baguettes at Ft150, salmon salad baguettes at Ft349.

New York Bagel
VI. Bajcsy-Zsilinszky út 21 (111 8441). M3 Arany János utca. **Open** 7am-10pm Mon-Fri; 9am-10pm Sat, Sun. **No credit cards.**
Eight different kinds of bagels, ten types of topping. Tuna salad bagels Ft127, lox bagels Ft349, tuna melts Ft149.
Branch: V. Károly Mihály utca 9 (266 5011).

Pizza Kuckó
VII. Károly körút 1 (no phone). M2 Astoria. **Open** 9am-9pm Mon-Fri; 9am-2pm Sat. **No credit cards.**
Popular Hungarian kiosk standing proudly on Astoria. Mushroom pizza slices for Ft80, Salami at Ft85. Slowest fast food in town, though.

Seherezádé Büfé
IX. Üllői út 40 (no phone). M3 Ferenc körút. **Open** 9am-10pm Mon-Fri. **No credit cards.**
Small, friendly takeaway falafel joint. Falafels at Ft130, swarma at Ft 170. Fair selection of meats and grilled chicken.

Istanbul
VII. Király utca 17 (267 0836). M1, M2, M3 Deák tér/tram 47, 49. **Open** noon-11pm Mon-Sat. **No credit cards.**
Busy hatch serving kebabs, böreks and Turkish sweetmeats on the Jewish quarter's main drag. Inconsistent sit-down restaurant attached.

Let's have a butcher's

Hungarians often eat lunch at the *hentesáru*, or butcher's shop. For one thing, it's cheap. Very cheap. And anyway, all Hungarians eat *kolbász* (sausage) and there is only one place to eat *kolbász* besides your own kitchen: the butcher's shop.

Disregard the menu listing and look around for the steaming trays and vats containing the day's offerings. You will usually find *kolbász*, smoked sausage that looks a lot like, well, a sausage. It is best boiled (*főtt*) or roasted (*sült*). You may also find shorter links of *debreceni kolbász*, a spicier version native to the eastern plains. Often there are *virsli* (hot dogs), *szafaládé* and *krinolin* (knockwursts). There may be *főtt tarja* (steamed smoked ham) or maybe *főtt fej* (boiled pig's head). A grease-filled tray may contain shrivelled *hurka*, either the black *véres* or grey *májas* (blood filled or liver filled, mixed with spiced rice.) Blood *hurka* resembles the black puddings of northern England while liver *hurka* is none other than the pricey Louisiana boudin in Magyar guise.

Order by specifying the amount you wish. 'Tíz deka kolbászt, kérek' and you get a snack portion of 100 grams of sausage. Twenty dekas (*húsz deka*) is a lunch-sized serving. Bread (*kenyér*), rolls (*zsemle*) and mustard (*mustár*) are classic accompaniments, but there are also bowls of pickled cucumbers (*uborka*) and vinegared peppers (*ecetes paprika*). The butcher will tally up your order on a sheet of paper, which you then take to the cashier, pay, and return it to the counterman.

It takes skill to stack and carry your messy purchase to the nearby counter. Most Hungarians carry a pocket knife for al fresco butcher shop dining. Sausages, particularly *debreceni kolbász*, have a tendency to splatter indelible paprika grease, so take care.

Cafés & Bars

There are wine bars as far removed from Knightsbridge as it's possible to get, coffeehouses that serve beers and wines in addition to beans, and a national drink that'll make you believe you're Jesus Christ – if you knock back enough of the stuff.

Hungarians take both their boozing and their coffee drinking seriously, and while Budapest isn't bar heaven, it does have everything from elegant baroque coffeehouses to scuzzy late-night dives. Modest prices will also appeal to Western visitors.

The city's savage drinking culture is fuelled by cheap wine. But Hungary's position at the crossroads between spirit-drinking Slav countries and the beery endeavours of Germanic Europe has also affected local customs. Add six years of Western influence and you get a mixed bag of drink habits and places to indulge them. The mainstays are: the borozó, unpretentious cheap wine cellar; the söröző, a beer bar inferior to those in Germany or

the Czech Republic; the kávéház, a coffeehouse which served as an upmarket pub before its demise 50 years ago; and the eszpresszó, the tacky café which took its place. Apart from a remaining few coffeehouses, sophisticated they're not. Background music is dire and some décor should carry government health warnings. Hungarians aren't that bothered either way as long as they've got a drink in front of them. Standing at counters is rare and table service, although the norm, varies from slow to virtually stationary. Excellent cakes can be had in the kávéház, but bar snacks are starchy and simple, such as the ubiquitous *pogácsa*, a salty scone that fills you up and fires your thirst.

Think Before You Clink

In the company of friends, faced with a clutch of freshly poured beers, you may be tempted to clink glasses.

Don't even think about it.

Any attempt at clinking beer mugs will get you nasty looks or, worse, an intoxicated historical lecture. The story you'll hear, however, depends on who you're talking to. All versions agree that it was at the end of the failed 1848 rebellion against Habsburg rule. Some then say that victorious Austrians, the night before executing the Hungarian generals, clinked beer glasses to toast their vile sentence of death. Others claim the Austrians were drinking beer even as the brave generals were dangling from the gibbet, clinking glasses as each victim was carried off to the great Puszta in the sky.

Whatever the truth of the matter, if there is indeed any at all, Hungarians never, repeat never, clink beer glasses. You can clink pálinka, wine, Unicum, whisky or Champagne, but clinking such non-beery beverages might still get you evil looks as people swivel to see if it was beer glasses they just heard being clinked.

Polite ways around this problem are simply to raise your glass, or to touch the proffered

glass with an outstretched finger, or else just tap it on the table.

In the meantime, a Hungarian historian has recently put forward the theory that actually it was Champagne, not beer, that the Austrians were drinking.

Coffee Culture

At the turn of the century there were around 600 coffeehouses in Budapest. Now there are about six. In those days the coffeehouse was a vital part of the city's social and intellectual life. The survivors now mostly cater for tourists, a shadow of their formerly vibrant selves.

The habit of coffee drinking arrived in Budapest with the Turks, and coffeehouses were a feature of the city long before they appeared in Vienna or Paris. Their golden age lasted as late as 1940, but Communism managed to kill them off, replacing the grand old establishments with downmarket eszpresszó bars.

Combining the neighbourliness of a local pub, the facilities of a gentlemen's club and the intellectual activity of a free university, coffeehouses flourished in the nineteenth century. The 1848 Revolution was started from the Café Pilvax, now a shoddy branch of a Hungarian fast-food chain.

Without the coffeehouse, wrote Jenő Rákosi, 'the education of a young man would be imperfect and incomplete'.

One could eat a full meal or linger for hours over one cup of coffee. Writers were provided with free pens and paper. Playwrights and sculptors, painters and musicians would congregate at particular tables. A journalist didn't need to leave his regular spot to catch the very latest stories and scandals, compose his article or even dispatch it to the paper – coffeehouse regulars could even send and receive messages.

The cream of the crop patronised the grandiose **New York Kávéház** (also known as the Café New York), designed by Alajos Hauszman, which still more or less stands today. Its century-long demise epitomises the sad fate of coffeehouse culture. Having thrived between the wars, when visiting Hollywood moguls were as vital to the atmosphere as the literary set, the New York was closed by the Communists, then housed a sports shop for a while, and later reopened as the Café Hungaria, but was never fully to recover.

Apart from the coffeehouse, the Communists also destroyed the social classes and literary scene which had brought them life. Eszpresszós, smaller and seedier, which had risen in popularity in the 1930s depression, were encouraged in their place. The eszpresszó's heyday was the 1960s, when they became the domain of bored youngsters seeking solace in their neon lights, chrome coffee machines, jukeboxes and lurid décor. Fine tatty examples of the genre, such as the Majakovszkij or Ibolya, can still be found.

The Művész, meanwhile, is the best surviving coffeehouse, and still retains a semblance of some literary life. Its prettier sister, the Gerbeaud, now a tourist trap on Vörösmarty tér, has recently been privatised in a deal that guarantees its continuing existence as a coffeehouse for the next decade. The New York Kávéház, as it has now been re-renamed, also has not quite fallen down yet.

Hungarian beer is acceptable if cold. Borsodi is your best option on draught, otherwise Austrian and German brews are widely available. Beers are either light (*világos*) or, more rarely, dark (*barna*). The younger generation have taken to drinking pints (*korsó*, a smaller glass is a *pohár*) instead of the wine their dads drink.

Both generations will chase their tipple with shots of Unicum, the national drink, or pálinka, fruit brandy. These fierce spirits are not mixed with anything, just tinged with gushes of melancholy, soul-searching and memory lapses.

Hungarians drink like brushmakers, as they say here. The borozó clientèle can get pitifully drunk for a handful of coins; beer drinkers will be paying Ft100-Ft150 for their pint. Pubs appealing to Budapest's expatriate crowd happily charge double that. Beware of Hungarians bearing pub signs.

The narrow dusty area either side of the grubby sound end of Váci utca is good for bar-crawling: there are a dozen good dives in these atmospheric streets. The patch around Oktogon and the Opera offers a more refined crawl, taking in old-style coffeehouses and beery boltholes. For those into starting the party late and finishing as day breaks, the crumbling Jewish quarter of Újlipótváros, between Szent István körút and Szent István Park, offers enough human flotsam and jetsam, death-wish drinking and animated conversation to keep anyone entertained until dawn. And then the borozós open up. (*See also chapter* **Nightlife**.)

Akali Borozó

XIII. Szent István körút 2 (112 2861). Tram 2, 4, 6. **Open** 5.30am-11.30pm Mon-Fri; 8am-10.30pm Sat; 7am-9.30pm Sun. **No credit cards**.
Friendly borozó on the Pest side of Margaret Bridge. Wine tureens, bread and dripping, and a clientèle with faces like let-down balloons. Ground-level wine bar, so good for late-afternoon views of Nagykörút action from the doorway.

Opposite: mogul magnet between the wars, then closed by the Communists, the **New York Kávéház** *is back in business.*

Amstel Bar

*V. Váci utca 61 (267 0296). M3 Ferenciek
tere/tram 47, 49.* **Open** 8am-6am Mon-Sat; 10am-6am
Sun. **No credit cards.**

It's been here for ever, this small corner place, and despite
a better selection of alcohol brands, remains largely unchanged in atmosphere since Communist times. The circular bar is beautiful, the atmosphere is relaxed and it's open
until the crack of dawn.

Angelika

I. Batthyány tér 7 (212 3784). M2 Batthyány tér. **Open**
10am-10pm daily. **No credit cards.**

In the former crypt of St Anne's Church on Battyhány
tér, the Angelika is a refined café where the ladies of
Buda come to gossip. When the sun streams through the
stained-glass windows on a September afternoon, it's a most
atmospheric venue for coffee and cakes. There's a terrace
which is open in summer.

Anna Café

V. Váci utca 5 (118 2016). M1 Vörösmarty utca/tram 2.
Open 8.30am-2am daily. **Credit** AmEx.

On the corner of Türr István utca round about where
bustling Váci runs into just as bustling Vörösmarty tér,
Anna Café is pricey, touristy and somewhat characterless
but does offer an excellent spot to watch the ceaseless flow
of shoppers. The pastries and coffee are pretty good too.
At night the crowd in here, like those roaming the street
outside, begins to get a little dodgy.

Astoria Café

*V. Kossuth Lajos utca 19 (117 3411). M2
Astoria.* **Open** 7am-11pm daily. **Credit** AmEx,
DC, JCB, MC, V.

Elegant without being either overbearing or overpriced, the
high-ceilinged café of the Astoria Hotel has big, comfortable
leather chairs and offers basic coffee, cakes and snacks. Once
the haunt of both Nazi (1944-45) and Soviet (1956) official-
dom, and despite being part of a state hotel chain for decades,
the Astoria has somehow managed to retain its turn-of-the-
century feel. Cafés don't come more grandly *mitteleuropäisch*
than this.

Beckett's

V. Bajcsy-Zsilinszky út 72 (111 1033). M3 Nyugati.
Open *bar* noon-2am daily. **Credit** over Ft3000: AmEx,
DC, JCB, MC, V.

Enormous Irish pub and principal watering hole for Budapest's Anglophone expat business community. Although
pricey for Budapest, many Hungarians do wander in too.
Friday night is the liveliest, as financial consultants and
estate agents quaff away the cares of the week, and the place
also heaves when major sporting events of interest to
English-speakers are piped in by satellite. Hardly a place to
experience the 'real' Hungary, although one could contend
that all these expats in suits, reflecting the degree of post-
Communist foreign investment, are as real an aspect of modern Budapest as anything else. The live music, which usually
starts around 11pm, is loud and often dreadful. (*See also*
chapter **Restaurants**.)

Bécsi Kávézó

V. Váci utca 50 (118 1119). M3 Ferenciek tere.
Open 10am-10pm Mon-Sat; 2-10pm Sun. **No
credit cards.**

The Vienna Café, up on the quiet end of Váci, was an office
building from 1837 until 1991, when the current management
turned it into a tasteful Mitteleuropa-style coffeehouse. With
the Lukács closed and the New York on the skids, it's nice
to see a new place opening in the old central European tradition. Quiet, spacious, comfortable and appealingly plain,
it's a restful spot for good coffee, ice creams and a limited
selection of pastries and liqueurs.

Picasso Point – *food, drink and art events.*

Café Mediterran

*VI. Liszt Ferenc tér 10 (342 1959). M1 Oktogon/tram 4,
6.* **Open** 10am-2am daily. **No credit cards.**

Once Liszt Ferenc tér quietly hummed with students taking
a leafy stroll across to the Music Academy. Now, thanks to
the popularity of this place and the Incognito (*see below*)
across the way, it bustles until the early hours. Of the two,
the Mediterran is preferable. Smaller, less pretentious and
certainly redder than its rival, the Mediterran is a smart,
friendly bar for an Amstel or three. The terrace gets very
popular in summer.

Café Miró

*I. Úri utca 30 (175 5458). Várbusz from M2
Moszkva tér/bus 16.* **Open** 9am-midnight daily. **No
credit cards.**

Although, like everywhere in the Castle District, frequented
mostly by tourists, this new place has resisted the temptation
towards the phonily historical. Décor and furniture has been
designed in the shapes and colours of Joan Miró. The green
metal chairs look crazy but are surprisingly comfortable;
extraordinary sofas and hatstands impel you to pause and
admire. Campari umbrellas outside spoil the effect somewhat, but service is cute and there's a fine selection of snacks,
salads, sandwiches and cakes.

Café Mozart

VII. Erzsébet körút 36 (267 8586). Tram 4, 6.
Open 9am-11pm Mon-Fri, Sun; 9am-noon Sat. **No
credit cards.**

Laughable simulation of coffeehouse culture: waitresses in
Baroque costume, phony period furniture, crap *mitteleuropäisch* murals, inept portraits of Mozart and 62 different
kinds of coffee, all with straight-faced descriptions so absurd
it's almost worth going in just to deride the menu. ('Espresso:
strong, black coffee made out of carefully selected coffee

beans, served in a small cup'). Overlit, sterile and naff as ninepence, this is the unacceptable face of capitalist Budapest. Avoid also its sister establishment, the equally asinine Café Verdi at Astoria.

Calgary

II. Frankel Leó út 24 (115 9087). Tram 4, 6, 17. **Open** 11am-2am daily. **No credit cards.**
From the outside the Calgary, in the shadow of Margaret Bridge, looks like any corner bar. Step inside and it's like Steptoe and Son's front room. Run by a radio star from the 1950s, the Calgary attracts a variety of faded actresses, antiques collectors and misplaced alcoholics. Downstairs among the ornaments you'll find a record player and Hungarian pop hits from the 1960s. There's no menu, but ask if the fish soup is on.

Captain Cook Pub

VI. Bajcsy-Zsilinszky út 19A (269 3136). M3 Arany János utca. **Open** 10am-2am Mon-Sat; 6pm-2am Sun. **No credit cards.**
Pleasant watering hole in an area where few others exist. Run by a Hungarian who spent six years Down Under, the Captain Cook has a maritime and antipodean theme. An Australian flag, Foster's adverts and nautical signal flags deck the walls. A drop of the amber nectar on draught. Expect a crowd on the tables outside in summer. Stays open until the early hours seven nights a week.

Cotton Club

XIII. Pannónia utca 7 (131 1599). M3 Nyugati pu. **Open** noon-midnight daily. **Credit** EC, MC.
The best of the American-style pub-diners. Full Latin American-style menu, a selection of regular cocktails at Ft450, Guinness, Heineken, Stella, Gösser and Plöchinger on draught and a fabulous collection of old drinks posters on the wall. The theme is prohibition.

Crazy Café

VI. Jókai utca 30 (153 1110). M3 Nyugati pu. **Open** 11am-1am daily. **No credit cards.**
Its name and the long row of beer signs outside refer to the ridiculous choice of drinks: up to 18 types of draught beer, nearly 100 types of bottled beers, and some 50 cocktails. There are two restaurant areas serving pizzas and various Hungarian standards, two bars and an area for live music and karaoké.

Fregatt

V. Molnár utca 26 (118 9997). Tram 2, 47, 49. **Open** 3pm-midnight Mon-Fri; 5pm-midnight Sat, Sun. **Credit** AmEx.
For years before and after the fall of Communism this was the main hangout for Anglophone expats and those who wished to meet them. On a Friday night you'd have trouble getting in the door. But life has moved on from Budapest's first English-style pub and though the barmen still ring a bell when one of them gets a tip, the thing doesn't chime so often. Quiet, air-conditioned, some rudimentary food and a depressing tendency to play the Gypsy Kings.

Fröhlich Cukrászda

VII. Dob utca 22 (121 6741). M2 Astoria/tram 47, 49. **Open** 10am-5pm Mon-Thur; 7am-2pm Fri. **No credit cards.**
Entertainingly decrepit bakery café still serving kosher pastries in the heart of Budapest's Jewish quarter. A couple of Israeli tourist posters brighten up an otherwise drab interior; ancient customers sip coffee at battered tables where the dirty plates rarely get cleared. Every guide book will tell you to try the traditional apple flodni, but last time we were there they claimed no longer to bake it: too expensive for their clientèle. Go now before staff and customers alike all finally fade away.

Gerbeaud

V. Vörösmarty tér 7 (118 1311). M1 Vörösmarty tér **Open** 9am-9pm daily. **Credit** AmEx, DC, JCB, MC, V.
The much vaunted café once frequented by Empress Elisabeth 'Sissi' Habsburg has the largest selection of patisserie items in the city. Other cities would be lucky to have such an elegant café, though these days it's mostly just tourists who stop by. Service runs from rude to efficient. Privatised at press time, so its future is uncertain.

Hause & Trogers

V. Havas utca 2 (267 0260). Tram 2, 47, 49. **Open** 6pm-2am daily. **No credit cards.**
Wandering into this cosy bar just off the Belgrád rakpart, you're greeted by the smell of wood and a beautiful, misspelt neon 'Coctail'. Walls are covered with logs and seating is on carved tree stumps – faced with a forest of these, the route to the toilet, through drink-fuddled eyes, can look like a game from *It's a Knockout*. The young couple who run the place are two of the best barkeepers in Budapest and take

The Hungarian National Accelerator

Unicum baffles the first-time imbiber. In a bottle that looks like an old-style anarchist's bomb, Hungary's national drink is a dark-brown liquid that smells like a hospital corridor and packs a wallop like Biffa Bacon. 'Uuch!' is a normal first reaction, followed by the feeling that it must be good for you since it tastes so foul. Cough medicine that tasted this way went out with the bubble car.

But, made from a secret recipe that was smuggled out of the country during the Communist era and has now been brought back, Unicum has a taste that is easy to acquire: vaguely sweet and minty, but bitter as a midwinter night. A good rule of thumb is not to drink more than three in a night, but of course everyone does and the hangovers can be spectacular. No problem, however, as Hungarians consider Unicum (along with sour cabbage juice) to be the premier hangover cure.

Italians may favour Fernet Branca, Germans might hymn the praises of Jägermeister, but the taste and effect of these digestifs is belittled by the mighty Unicum. Unicum settles the stomach. Unicum keeps out the cold. But above all else Unicum is The Accelerator. Drink five beers and feel bloated. Drink five beers and whack back one Unicum and feel like five more beers – and several more Unicums. After that, forget the holes in the feet and walk across the Danube.

an enjoyable pride in their work. They also play music which, if not always brilliant, is at least of a recognisably consistent taste. Friendly, relaxed, entertaining, largely undisovered and though not among the cheapest, certainly one of the very best bars in town.

Ibolya eszpresszó

V. Ferenciek tere 4 (267 0239). M3 Ferenciek tere. **Open** 7am-10pm Mon-Sat; noon-8pm Sun. **No credit cards.**
Just opposite the ELTE University Library, Ibolya is among the best and certainly the most central of the surviving Communist-era eszpresszós: staff are a little slow, but you can have fine salads, sandwiches and drinks. Avoid the microwaved meat. Take a seat on the small terrace if you prefer traffic fumes to cigarette smoke.

Incognito

VI. Liszt Ferenc tér 3 (267 9428). M1 Oktogon. **Open** 10am-midnight Mon-Fri; noon-midnight Sat, Sun. **No credit cards.**
The trendiest café in town. Its success has turned the formerly quiet Liszt Ferenc tér into a major thoroughfare of nightlife. Large bar area with walls covered in classic jazz LP sleeves. Although it can boast an adventurous drinks menu – 20 types of coffees including carajillo, ten types of teas, 20 types of cocktails – the Incognito isn't as cool as it thinks it is. It could be the loud jazz, it could be the dim lighting, it could be the extortionate price charged for draught Heineken. It's at its best in summer, when the outside tables fill up regularly night and day.

Ipoly

XIII. Pozsonyi út 28 (270-2923). Trolleybus 78, 79. **Open** 7am-11pm Mon-Fri; 9am-11pm Sat, Sun. **No credit cards.**
Successfully modernised spit-and-sawdust pub. Extensive cocktail menu, HB beer, selection of salads and snacks, friendly staff. Flashy clientèle despite its low-key setting although an old regular occasionally sneaks in for a swift Unicum behind the bleep of mobile phones.

Irish Cat

V. Múzeum körút 41 (266 4085). M3 Kálvin tér. **Open** 11am-2am daily. **No credit cards.**
Every major European city seems to have an Irish pub that functions as a meat market. This is Budapest's. Crowded bar area with intimate wooden booths and back section for over-spill and smooching. Packed after midnight.

Janis Pub

V. Királyi Pál utca 8 (266 2619). M3 Kálvin tér. **Open** 4pm-2am Mon-Fri; 4pm-3am Sat. **No credit cards.**
Quiet pub tucked away in the narrow academic backstreets between Kálvin tér and Ferenciek tere. Ms Joplin would have been pretty disappointed if someone had dragged her here, although Southern Comfort can be had to chase the Guinness. Attracts an expatriate and native crowd, decent bar counter, chili and pub grub on offer.

Litea Bookshop & Tea Garden

I. Hess András tér 4 (175 6987). Vár Bus Szentháromság tér. **Open** 10am-6pm daily. **Credit** AmEx, DC, EC, JCB, MC, V.
Indifferent bookshop whose main attraction is the opportunity to sip any one of 25 different teas under a beautiful glass dome.

Majakovszkij

VII. Király utca 103 (342 5732). Trolleybus 70, 78. **Open** 6am-10pm Mon-Fri; 7am-8pm Sat, Sun. **No credit cards.**
Classic eszpresszó that would fit well with the Stalinist edifices in Statue Park. Today the Majakovszkij still stands proudly among the dust, filth and neon of Király utca, a street once also named after the Russian revolutionary. (*See* also chapter **Architecture**.)

Móri Borozó

I. Fiáth János utca 16 (no phone). M2 Moszkva tér. **Open** 2pm-11pm Mon-Fri; 2-9pm Sat, Sun. **No credit cards.**
Comfortable wine bar singled out by its younger clientèle.

The recently privatised **Gerbeaud** *has the largest selection of patisserie items in the city.*

Inside the Borozó

Borozós are wine bars: dark, dank and about as different from those in Knightsbridge as can possibly be imagined. God gave grapes to Hungary and its people were wine-drinkers long before heathens ever brought them beer. As well as providing a laughably cheap form of intoxication, the borozó offers a skewed glimpse of everyday Hungarian life.

The wine cellars of the nation start filling before dawn. Step down, and you'll see a whole lot of shaking 'twixt lip and glass, sense a slow shuffling of feet – most borozós are stand-up joints – and hear a storm of coughing.

The formula is always much the same. On the counter will be three metal lids, similar to those guarded by the Soupdragon in *The Clangers*. These ones cover tureens of sweet white wine (*fehér édes bor*), dry white wine (*száraz édes bor*) and red wine (*vörös bor*). The white will often be a Rizling, the red a Burgundi or Egri Bikavér. Labels on the lids indicate the type and price per litre, generally around Ft150.

At the controls will usually stand a baggy-eyed, friendly fellow who has left his bed before dawn to service Hungary's drink problem. His right-hand man is a long metal soda syphon, used to dispense spritzers (*fröccs*). These are measured in deciliters. Red is often served with cola and mixed drinks have imaginative nicknames, such as *hosszúlépés*, a big step – 1dl wine and 2dl soda. No combination will cost more than Ft50, nor mess up your insides. Much.

By around 9am many drinkers have already had their fill and are dealing with the problem of lying down. All types will drift through in the course of the day. By mid-afternoon, the borozós are hives of activity, buzzing until the honey takes hold again and it's time to fly off home. Most close around 8pm.

The food may only be bread and dripping, the furniture bare and toilets primitive, but at least you can say you've been to Hungary.

There'll usually be a borozó within stagger ing distance. The Móri behind Moszkva tér and the Akali on the Pest side of Margaret Bridge are two of the best.

In the 1970s Moszkva tér was a major meeting place for young rockers with nowhere else to go. It still attracts the leather waistcoat brigade, one generation down from the messy mac merchants who usually frequent these joints. Friendly atmosphere, Innstadt beer on draught, and the wine is cheap and plentiful.

Művész

VI. Andrássy út 29 (267 0689). M1 Opera. **Open** 9am-midnight daily. **No credit cards.**

Perhaps the last real turn-of-the-century coffeehouse in Budapest, with excellent coffee, unpretentious period décor, a good, though limited, selection of cakes, savouries and ice creams, and some genuine life apart from the tourist trade. The name means 'artist' and you still see people annotating manuscripts at corner tables, next to gaggles of gossiping old ladies. It's also a haunt of the less business-orientated expat crowd. On Pest's grand boulevard, not quite opposite the Opera, the outside tables are a grand spot in summer. A few years back it narrowly avoided being turned into a car showroom. Now it's a protected establishment, and rightly so.

New York Kávéház

VII. Erzsébet körút 9-11 (322 3849). M2 Blaha Lujza tér/ tram 4, 6. **Open** 9am-11pm daily. **Credit** AmEx, DC, MC, V.

Budapest's most famous coffeehouse is now only a sad ruin of its former magnificent self. Once the main haunt of Pest's artistic and literary life, it's been run down by decades of Communism and these days is too expensive for the locals. Tourists who can afford what is now more of a museum than a living coffeehouse (and can find their way in through the wooden scaffolding that's been holding up the façade since 1956 when a Soviet tank slammed into it) are meanwhile greeted with some of the surliest and most indifferent service in town. The beautiful Baroque detailing of the interior is still worth a look, even though spoilt somewhat by horrible Communist-era light fittings. But unless someone buys up the state-run hotel chain of which this is a part, it's only likely to deteriorate even further. A tragedy. (*See also chapter* **Sightseeing.**)

Old Amsterdam

V. Királyi Pál utca 14 (117 9257). M3 Kálvin tér. **Open** noon-2am Mon-Fri; 6pm-2am Sat, Sun. **No credit cards.**

One of the better foreign-style pubs. You may not feel you're anywhere near Holland, but the Old Amsterdam can boast a decent selection of bottled Belgian beers, grilled meats and coffees. Guinness and Kilkenny on draught to complement the Amstel and Heineken. Drop in for a Mort Subite and a reasonable drop of funk and soul. Ruinous prices, though.

Paris, Texas

IX. Ráday utca 22 (218 0570). M3 Kálvin tér. **Open** 10am-2am Mon-Fri; 4pm-2am Sat, Sun. **No credit cards.**

The area this side of Kálvin tér has come up of late, reflected in the increased popularity of this pleasant bar, which is decorated with dozens of period portrait photos. Upstairs is a relaxed bar area ideal for afternoon drinking, downstairs there's a pool table and the occasional jazz or blues gig. Cheap beer on Sundays and Mondays.

Picasso Point

VI. Hajós utca 31 (269 5544). M2 Opera. **Open** 9am-2.30am Mon-Thur, Sun; 9am-4am Fri, Sat. **No credit cards.**

Just as popular as it was when it opened in the autumn of 1992, though no longer so fashionable. Picasso's once mainly attracted a pseudo-arty expat crowd. What's left of them now tend to sit in the comfortable large upstairs bar, while Hungarians drink in the darker downstairs bar/disco. Bar food available, occasional live acts and arts events.

Rózsadomb

II. Margit körút 7 (212 5145). Tram 4, 6. **Open** 9am-2am daily. **No credit cards.**

A humble eszpresszó offering the simple pleasures of beer, cakes and pinball, it's an inaccurate reflection of its namesake – the posh and barless residential area in the hills. Furthermore it has a jukebox. The downside is the Flintstones pinball machine, which interrupts your mood with the Hungarian for Fred's immortal exclamation: 'Subi-dubi-duu!'

Talk Talk

V. Magyar utca 12-14 (267 2878). M2 Astoria. **Open** 24 hours daily. **No credit cards.**

A young crowd frequent this Israeli-owned round-the-clock café and bar. It's a stylish place, in a good downtown location, with a small selection of sandwiches, a long menu of coffees and teas, and 18 different beers. It's popular enough to mean you might have trouble finding a table mid-evening, and there isn't really anywhere to stand about, but it gets very quiet again in the small hours. Sometimes the music is so loud it might as well be renamed Listen Listen.

Tam Tam Klub

XIII. Csanády utca 19 (270 3026). Trolleybus 76. **Open** 2.30pm till the last guest leaves Mon-Fri; 5pm-late Sat. **No credit cards.**

Intimate students' club attached to an art gallery and a private dance studio in the same building. Entrance by membership only, arranged for free at the bar. Lively place for cultural debate, fancy dress and romance.

Tik-Tak

XII. Böszörményi út 17C (212-3762). Tram 59/bus 21, 201. **Open** 9am-midnight Mon-Fri; 9am-10pm Sat, Sun. **No credit cards.**

A gorgeous old presszó fronted by a neon cuckoo clock overlooking a leafy terrace a few tram stops up from the seedy outskirts of Déli Station. Inside there's a raised area at the back of the snug bar for intimate conversation and cheap pints of Dreher beer.

Tilos Kávézó

VIII. Mikszáth Kálmán tér 2 (118 0684). M3 Kálvin tér/tram 4, 6. **Open** 10am-9pm Mon-Fri; 3-9pm Sat, Sun. **No credit cards.**

Attached to the Tilos az Á next door (*see chapters* **Nightlife** *and* **Music: Rock, Roots & Jazz**) and management have had to apply the same silly alcohol regulations to this quiet kávézó: wine, champagne and Martini only. All the same, a reasonable place to waste the afternoon. French windows open out on to the square, allowing customers fresh air and plenty of opportunity for human observation. Treat your hangover to the freshly made lemonade. Coffee is average.

Wichmann

VII. Kazinczy utca 55 (142 6074). M1, M2, M3 Deák tér/tram 47, 49. **Open** 6pm-2am daily. **No credit cards.**

Owned by former world champion canoeist Tamás Wichmann, this rough and smoky bar with no sign outside (it's just south of the corner with Király utca) seems largely untouched by recent history. Only a couple of yellowing West cigarette ads testify to the advent of capitalism. Wine is appallingly cheap, young customers cluster around big and sociable wooden tables, and the staff have a daft sense of humour. This is the place to toast Oscar Wilde with Transylvanian English Lit students, or hear the staff singing the Hungarian equivalent of rugby songs. A fine establishment.

Zöldség-Gyümölcs

VII. Király utca 13 (267 2206). M1, M2, M3 Deák tér/tram 47, 49. **Open** 11am-2.30am Mon-Fri; 11am-4am Fri; 6pm-4am Sat; 6pm-2.30am Sun. **No credit cards.**

One of the focal points of young, alternative Budapest. Comfortable by day, and offering simple meals as well as a range of drinks, at night the action spills on to the street or fills up the big cellar space, otherwise occupied by games machines. Jazzy hip hop throbs beneath the buzz of conversation. The staff are sweet-tempered, there are interesting people to talk to, and the prices are nice too. The only black mark is for the neanderthals who come in late to order everyone off home: these bouncers more often provoke fights than prevent them.

*One of the best surviving eszpresszós of the Communist era, the **Ibolya** is centrally located.*

Shopping & Services

Shopping

You need a new stovetop espresso maker, a piece of Zoltán Ács glassware and a self-adhesive fun moustache, but do you know where to go? You soon will.

The number of private shops in Budapest has grown dramatically in the last five years. The retail boom and a flood of foreign products mean that formerly hard-to-find items such as functional condoms and non-polyester shirts are now readily available, although you may have to settle for unfamiliar brands. Most of the city's shops are in Pest and the central shopping district is the upmarket pedestrian area around Váci utca. Other major shopping areas are along the two ring roads and Rákóczi út. For international labels, head for Váci utca. For everyday needs, old-style speciality shops compete with Hungarian and Austrian chains that have branches throughout the city.

Though the days of amazing bargains are over, there are still interesting shopping opportunities. Hungary's folk art culture remains very much alive and textiles and craft items are still a relatively good buy. Hungary also has a tradition of fine hand-painted porcelain from names such as Herend, Zsolnay and Hollóháza – not cheap but nevertheless a bargain compared to similar china from western European firms. On the contemporary scene, Hungarian fashion is on the up as new designers explore their recently found freedom. And for a peek into everyday life, Budapest's markets – whether you're looking for fresh produce or discount antiques – offer entertainment value as well as good deals. Note: for children's clothing and toys *see chapter* **Children**.

Opening Hours

Standard opening hours are 10am-6pm Monday-Friday and 10am-1pm on Saturdays. Many corner shops, selling basic groceries, tobacco and booze, stay open later. For a selection of 24-hour 'non-stops' *see chapter* **Nightlife**.

Late opening on Thursdays is beginning to catch on around Váci utca, where many shops now stay open until 7pm. Saturday afternoon and Sunday remain sacrosanct with only a few hardy corner shops still open. The Castle District is one exception, with many stores and boutiques open 10am-6pm daily. Note that smaller shops and repair places may keep somewhat irregular hours. A *rögtön jövök* (back in ten minutes) sign on the door could mean the shop will not reopen for hours,

if at all. Most places will be closed around major holidays, including 15 March, 20 August and 23 October. Everything closes at Christmas.

Antiques

Antiques shops are dominated by the eighteenth- and nineteenth-century Habsburg style. Though wares are competitively priced compared to Vienna, dealers here do know the value of their collections. Dedicated bargain hunters and collectors of Communist kitsch should head to **Ecseri** or the **Bolhapiac** (*see below* **Flea Markets**). Antiques shops are concentrated in the Castle District, on Váci utca and in the traditional antiques district on Falk Miksa utca. *See also chapter* **Services: Auctions**.

BÁV

BÁV is a state-owned chain of pawn shops recognisable by the Venus de Milo signs outside. Each outlet has a different speciality and several auctions are held each year. Prices are lower than in many antiques shops, though the chances of running across a genuine collector's item are slim. For information on auctions (*árverés*) call 217 6072 extension 287 and talk to Buryán Imréné. Auctions take place at IX. Lónyay utca 30-32 (M3 Kálvin tér).
V. Bécsi utca 1-3 (117 2548). M3 Ferenciek tere. Jewellery, silver, furniture.
V. Ferenciek tere 12 (118 3381). M3 Ferenciek tere. Porcelain, bronze.

Nagyházi Gakléria – *largest antiques dealer.*

*V. Kossuth Lajos utca 1-3 (117 8855/117 3718). M3
Ferenciek tere.* Porcelain, furnishings.
V. Szent István körút 3 (131 4534). Tram 4, 6.
Furniture, porcelain, paintings.
V. Párizsi utca 2 (118 6217). M3 Ferenciek tere.
Jewellery.
VI. Andrássy út 43 (342 9143). M1 Opera. Gold.
All branches open 10am-6pm Mon-Fri; 9am-1pm Sat.
Credit AmEx, EC, DCI, JCB, MC, V.

Judaica Gallery

*VII. Wesselényi utca 13 (267 8502). M3 Astoria/tram
47, 49.* **Open** 10am-6pm Mon-Thur; 10am-2pm Fri.
Credit AmEx, MC, V.
New and antique merchandise related to Hungarian Jewish
culture. Expect somewhat ratty old prayer books, Korond-
style pottery with Hebrew sayings, Black Sea mud face
masks, silk-screened T-shirts of the Great Synagogue and
hand embroidered Challah covers.

Moró Antik

V. Szent István körút 1 (112 7877). Tram 4, 6. **Open**
11am-6pm Mon-Fri. **No credit cards.**
Owner Lajos has a 25-year-old love affair with ancient
weapons – particularly eighteenth-century swords and guns.
He collects other militaria as well as Far Eastern pieces that
were in vogue here at the turn of the century.

Nagyházi Galéria

*V. Balaton utca 8 (131 9908/112 5631/fax 131 7133).
Tram 2.* **Open** 10am 6pm Mon-Fri; 10am-1pm Sat.
Credit AmEx, EB, DCI, JCB, MC, V.
The largest antiques dealer in Budapest. A cavernous shop
full of furniture, porcelain, glass, carpets and paintings from
all periods. They hold three catalogue auctions per year plus
smaller auctions in the shop every month.

Relikvia

*I. Fortuna utca 14 (175 6971/fax 156 9973). Várbusz
from M2 Moszkva tér, bus 16.* **Open** 10am-6pm daily.
Credit AmEx, DC, EC, JCB, MC, V.
Three sister shops hold one of Budapest's highest-quality
and most interesting collections of antique furniture, paint-
ings, porcelain and a variety of smaller knick-knacks.
Fortuna utca is located in prime tourist territory in the Castle
District, so you won't find many bargains. The third shop is
located in the Hilton Hotel.
Branch: I. Fortuna utca 21 (156 9973).

Art Supplies & Stationery

Ápisz

*VI. Andrássy út 3 (122 6347/268 0534). M1 Bajcsy-
Zsilinszky.* **Open** 10am-6pm Mon-Fri; 9am-1pm Sat. **No
credit cards.**
The main Hungarian chain of stationery stores. Branches of
Ápisz carry paper, pens, pencils, crayons, band-aids, floppy
disks, aluminum cooking tins, packing tape and string –
much is Hungarian-manufactured and cheap.
Branch: VII. Rákóczi út 64 (142 1228).

Interieur Studio

V. Vitkovics Mihály utca 6 (137 7005). M2 Astoria.
Open 10am-6pm Mon-Fri; 10am-2pm Sat. **Credit**
AmEx, MC, V.
Handmade paper, fine stationery, gift wrapping service and
tasteful home accents by local crafts people. Also essential
oils and neat bath supplies.

Leonart

VI. Bajcsy köz 3 (153 3750). M3 Arany János utca.
Open 9am-5pm Mon-Fri. **No credit cards.**
International brand names for painting, graphic arts, silk

Interieur Studio *– supports local craftsmen.*

screening, watercolour, drawing and other art supplies.
Framing and matting materials as well as a large selection
of fine papers and other arty stuff.

Pirex

VI. Paulay Ede utca 17 (322 7067). M1 Opera. **Open**
8.30am-5pm Mon-Fri. **Credit** AmEx, EC, MC, V.
Diskettes, printer paper and other computer supplies along
with the most complete selection of paper, notebooks, fold-
ers, pens and other miscellaneous office products under one
Budapest roof. Basic graphic art supplies, too.

Books

Bestsellers

V. Október 6 utca 11 (112 1295). M3 Arany János utca.
Open 9am-6.30pm Mon-Fri; 10am-6pm Sat. **Credit**
AmEx, DC, MC, V.
Bestsellers stocks contemporary fiction and books on history and politics as well as a wide selection of newspapers
and periodicals in English. Their selection of local history
and literature is probably the best in Budapest. Efficient
ordering service.

Corvina Books & Music

V. Kossuth Lajos utca 4 (118 3603). M3 Ferenciek tere.
Open 10am-6pm Mon-Fri; 10am-2pm Sat. **Credit** AmEx,
DC, EC, JCB, MC, V.
Corvina is the primary publisher of English-language books
in Hungary. A broad selection of picture and guide books,
and Hungarian authors translated into English.

*Secondhand and antique books – and a warm welcome – await you at **Ulysses Antikvárium**.*

Írók Boltja

VI. Andrássy út 45 (322 1645). M1 Oktogon/tram 4, 6.
Open 10am-6pm Mon-Fri; 10am-1pm Sat. **Credit** AmEx,
DC, EC, JCB, MC, V.
On the site of the former Japan Café, favourite watering-hole of the turn-of-the-century literary scene, the so-called Writers' Bookshop is spacious, hosts readings and signings and has tables where you can enjoy a cup of tea while you browse. There's not that much in English, but it's good for art and photography.

Rhythm 'N' Books

V. Szerb utca 21-23 (266 3311). M3 Kálvin tér. **Open**
10am-6pm Mon-Fri. **No credit cards.**
In the same courtyard as the University Theatre, an interesting mish-mash of new and secondhand books in English and a selection of world music on CD and cassette. They'll buy and exchange books and CDs.

Térképbolt

VII. Nyár utca 1 (322 0438). M2 Blaha Lujza tér/tram 4, 6. **Open** 9.30am-5.30pm Mon-Fri. **No credit cards.**
Maps from all over the world, street maps of Budapest and county maps of Hungary.

Antiquarian Bookshops

Font Antikvárium

VI. Andrássy út 56 (132 1646). M1 Oktogon/tram 4, 6.
Open 10am-7pm Mon-Fri. **Credit** AmEx.
Not much in the way of English books, but an excellent source for art, graphic art and architecture books, including much Communist-era stuff, plus a lot of old travel books.

Forgács

V. Stollár Béla utca 12C (111 6874). M3 Nyugati. **Open**
10am-noon, 3-7pm, Mon-Fri; noon-4pm Sat. **Credit**
AmEx, DCI, EC, JCB, MC, V.
Budapest's oldest antiquarian bookshop, Forgács has art and graphics books in several languages and a small but interesting shelf of English material. A second location in the Kempinski hotel has foreign-language books and rare editions.

Kollin Antikvárium

*V. Bajcsy-Zsilinszky út 34 (111 9023). M3 Arany János
utca.* **Open** 9.30am-5.30pm Mon-Fri. **Credit** AmEx, EC,
JCB, MC, V.
Upstairs the hallway is lined with old prints with more in cabinets against the window. The German section is much larger than the English, but lots of other odds and ends grab your attention, including tins, postcards, maps, travel books and a small section of Judaica.

Központi Antikvárium

V. Múzeum körút 15 (117 3514). M2 Astoria/tram 47, 49. **Open** 10am-6pm Mon-Fri; 10am-3pm Sat. **Credit**
AmEx, EC, MC, V
Spacious, convivial, century-old shop with the best selection of English-language secondhand books in Budapest. Also many old posters and postcards, Hungarian rarities and good German and Russian sections.

Ulysses Antikvárium

VIII. Rákóczi út 7 (138 0247). M2 Astoria. **Open** 10am-6pm Mon-Fri; 10am-1pm Sat. **No credit cards.**
An odd mix of secondhand and antique books in English, a cosy coffee shop and extensive collection of art picture books including many obscure exhibition programmes.

Department Stores

Centrum Áruház – Corvin

*VIII. Blaha Lujza tér 1-3 (138 4160/266 0708). M2
Blaha Lujza tér.* **Open** 10am-6pm Mon-Fri; 10am-2pm
Sat. **Credit** AmEx, DC, EC, JCB, MC, V.
One of the last of the Communist-era department stores, where the décor remains tacky and you still have to queue several times to pay for your purchase. Today the shelves are mostly full of Western-style goods, but you can still find polyester granny dresses, boarskin rugs and cheap berets.

Luxus Department Store

*V. Vörösmarty tér 3 (118 2277/118 3550/fax 118
3555). M1 Vörösmarty tér.* **Open** 10am-7pm
Mon-Wed, Fri; 10am-5pm Thur; 10am-2pm Sat. **Credit**
AmEx, EC, JCB, MC, V.

The sometimes over-eager staff will help you sort through three floors of Europe's top names in men's and women's fashion, accessories, cosmetics, perfumes and jewellery.

Fontana

V. Váci utca 16 (138 2004/118 9166). M1 Vörösmarty tér. **Open** 10am-6pm Mon-Fri; 10am-1pm Sat. **Credit** AmEx, EC, MC, V.

Less upmarket than Luxus with younger, trendier clothing. Highlights are kids' clothes by Bambino, an extensive luggage department and a roof-top café.

Design & Household Goods

Antique Pine Wood Furniture Store

II. Pasaréti út 53 (176 3120). Bus 5. **Open** 10am-6pm Mon-Fri; 10am-2pm Sat. **No credit cards.**

Charming, simple peasant-style bureaux, wardrobes and bedsteads are collected from Hungarian villages, restored and tastefully displayed here.

Hephaistos Háza

VI. Zichy Jenő utca 20 (132 6329). M3 Arany János utca. **Open** 11am-6pm Mon-Fri; 10am-2pm Sat. **Credit** AmEx.

One of the most original design shops in Budapest: wrought iron meets crushed velvet and hand-blown glass in innovative furniture and decorative pieces. Pick from stock, or talk to one of the artists and design your own metal fantasy.

Opal Art

I. Hess András tér 4 (Fortuna passage) (06 30 446 178). Várbusz from M2 Moszkva tér, bus 16. **Open** 11am-5pm daily. **Credit** AmEx, DC, EC, JCB, MC, V.

Zoltán Ács is currently the only glass artist in the world using the craft of layered glass sculpture invented by Gallé of France. There are intricate Art Nouveau flowered lamps and delicately landscaped vases.

Household Goods

Bigrav

V. Váci utca 75 (137 6226). Tram 47, 49. **Open** 10am-5pm Mon-Fri. **No credit cards.**

American appliances need a transformer to cope with European 220 voltage; this is the only shop that sells them.

Kátay

VI. Teréz körút 28 (111 0116). M1 Oktogon. **Open** 9am-6pm Mon-Fri; 9am-2pm Sat. **Credit** AmEx, DC, EC, MC, V.

A centrally located stop for appliances, kitchen utensils, garden tools and miscellaneous DIY supplies.

1,000 Aprócikk

V. Bajcsy-Zsilinszky út 1 (322-6420). M1, M2, M3 Deák tér. **Open** 9am-6pm Mon-Fri; 9am-1pm Sat. **No credit cards.**

If you melt the rubber gasket in your stovetop espresso maker, this is where to find a replacement, along with 999 other small but useful household gadgets.

IKEA

XIV. Örs vezér tere (221 9444/fax 251 9154). M2 Örs vezér tere. **Open** 10am-8pm Mon-Fri; 10am-5pm Sat; 10am-3pm Sun. **No credit cards.**

IKEA is nothing new to most Europeans, but when you decide to throw out the god-awful furniture in your apartment, it's the place to go for moderately priced, moderately tasteful replacements. The huge store, some way out of the city centre, has underground parking, an adult-supervised playroom for children, several cafés and a smoking lounge upstairs.

Keravill

V. Kossuth Lajos utca 2B (118 5008/117 6422). M3 Ferenciek tere. **Open** 9am-5pm Mon-Fri; 9am-2pm Sat. **Credit** EC, MC.

Beautiful Art Nouveau flowered lamps and landscaped vases are featured at **Opal Art**.

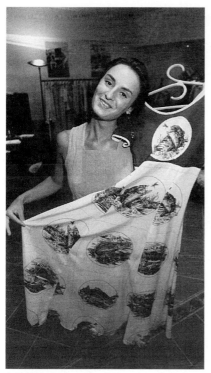

Artista – cutting edge funky togs all the rage.

Appliances and electronics are generally less expensive in Budapest than in other major European cities. Keravill has outlets all over the city and each carries a different mix of items.
Branches: VI. Teréz körút 27 (132 7175); V. Kossuth Lajos utca 8 (117 6080).

Fashion

Hungarian fashion has come a long way from the days of polyester suits and smuggled Western Levi's. But even though major fashion names have entered the market, poorly designed Italian rip-offs dominate the fashion scene. There is some hope for the future as young designers begin to make their mark. Local fashion a bargain and a one-of-a-kind creation can cost the same, or even less, than a comparable piece off the rack.

Accessories & Jewellery

Marácz Kalap
VII. Wesselényi utca 41 (no phone). Tram 4, 6. **Open** 10am-6pm Mon-Fri. **No credit cards.**
An old-fashioned milliner. The essential Hungarian-style fedora and ladies' hats for all occasions.

Manu-Art
VI. Bajcsy-Zsilinszky köz 3 (132 0298). M3 Arany János utca. **Open** 10am-6pm Mon-Fri; 10am-1pm Sat. **No credit cards.**
Highlights here are *cloisonné* jewellery by Béla Szerényi and other funky jewellery by local artists as well as simple, homey dresses, ceramics and other handicrafts.

Ómama Bizsuja
V. Szent István körút 1 (112 6812). Tram 4, 6. **Open** 10am-6pm Mon-Fri; 10am-2pm Sat. **No credit cards.**
Owner Zsuzsa has an astonishing collection of antique bijoux from all over Hungary – ask for a peek in the cabinet on the right by the door. Rhinestones, beads and semi-precious costume jewellery plus some old clothes and selected antiques.

Clothing

Artista
V. Párizsi utca 1 (118 2724). M3 Ferenciek tere. **Open** 10am-7pm Mon-Fri; 10am-1pm Sat. **No credit cards.**
Six-designer collective churns out a mixed bag of funky togs on the cutting edge of youth fashion. Loud colours and flashy designs are the key for the small but growing number of Hungarians brave enough to step beyond strict good taste.

Christina Designer Shop
V. Semmelweis utca 8 (118 5006/266 8009). M2 Astoria. **Open** 10am-6pm Mon-Fri; 10am-1pm Sat. **Credit** AmEx, DC, EC, MC, V.
Two neighbouring shops. In the first are Christina's line of fine-quality linens, hand-crocheted tablecloths and select antique Transylvanian textiles. Next door are bath and beach accessories. From sexy to-be-seen-on-the-strand wear to cute children's robes, everything is 100 per cent cotton and made to last. Accessories include beach bags, embroidered towels and slippers.

Divat Ház
V. Kecskeméti utca 11 (117 7190). M3 Kálvin tér. **Open** 10am-6pm Mon-Fri; 10am-2pm Sat. **Credit** AmEx, DC, JCB, MC, V.
Featuring well tailored men's suits from Hungarian, Austrian and Italian designers, it's a good all-round haberdashery, specialising in the somewhat putrid shades favoured by young Hungarians with mobile phones. Cotton shirts by Gio-M, ties, belts and other Pierre Cardin accessories.

Greti
V. Bárczy István utca 3 (117 8500). M1, M2, M3 Deák tér. **Open** 10am-6pm Mon-Fri; 10am-1pm Sat. **No credit cards.**
Elegant, conservative looks for women by one of Budapest's Grande Dames of fashion. Seasonal dresses and evening wear with a small selection of shoes and nifty under-things. Anything in the shop can be made to order, or they'll help design something special.

Home Boy
V. Irányi utca 5 (266 4601). M3 Ferenciek tere. **Open** 10am-6pm Mon-Fri; 10am-1pm Sat. **No credit cards.**
Gang wear and clothes for clubbing from Billabong, Cross-Colors, Dready, Fresh Jive, Gang, Karl Kani, Stoopid and Third Rail. Hats, flannel, and the obligatory hooded sweat-shirts plus a tattoo and piercing studio downstairs.

Manier
V. Váci utca 48 (118 1812). M3 Ferenciek tere. **Open** 10am-6pm Mon-Fri; 10am-2pm Sat. **Credit** AmEx, EC, MC, V.
Daring fashion by Anikó Németh and jewellery by Ágnes Légrádi. While it's not exactly street wear, Németh's recent

designs have a baroque feel unique in Budapest – and probably Europe. Also, any piece from their previous collections can be made to order.

Monarchia
V. Szabadsajtó út 6 (118 3146). M3 Ferenciek tere. **Open** 10am-6pm Mon-Wed, Fri; 10am-7pm Thur; 10am-1.30pm Sat. **Credit** AmEx.
The window displays change daily to show off chic women's suits and daring evening wear from five local designers. Fabric swatches and sample books are on hand for custom orders for 26 per cent extra.

Munkaruházati áruház
VIII. Üllői út 14 (133 1509). M3 Kálvin tér. **Open** 8am-5pm Mon-Thur; 8am-4pm Fri. **No credit cards.**
Just one of many shops in town that keep workers in overalls and waitresses in their famous lace-up boots, but there are other interesting duds to be found such as heavy-duty jeans and inexpensive winter coats. Also a good place for cheap linens and tea-towels.

New Boxer-Stefano Classico
VI. Podmaniczky utca 20 (131 1543). M3 Nyugati. **Open** 10am-6pm Mon-Wed, Fri; 10am-7pm Thur; 10am-1pm Sat. **Credit** MC.
The slick clean lines are what you'd expect from the Italian name. Men's suits, shirts and accessories with underwear by New Boxer.

Nouvo Naomi
V. Károly körút 10 (137 2772). M2 Astoria. **Open** 10am-6pm Mon-Wed, Fri; 10am-7pm Thur; 10am-1pm Sat. **No credit cards.**
Women's dresses and suits by Klára Farkas have a youthfully clean and elegant look. Hungarian designers Lilifo, Adoni, and Rubidiász too, plus Björn Borg's designer underwear. Look upstairs for a collection of cocktail and evening dresses, all of which can be made to order.

The London Store
V. Semmelweis utca 14 (137 7453). M1, M2, M3 Deák tér. **Open** 10am-6pm Mon-Fri; 10am-1pm Sat. **No credit cards.**
A fashion pacifier for the homesick with the largest selection of Doc Martens in Budapest and clubbing clothes by Lonsdale, BTKA, Have a Nice Day and Boy.

V50 Design Art Studio
V. Váci utca 50 (entrance on Nyáry Pál utca) (137 5320). M3 Ferenciek tere. **Open** 1-6pm Mon-Fri. **No credit cards.**
Valéria Fazekas's true passion is hats and her big glass case is full of nifty, if sometimes slightly impractical, headgear. Fazekas also scours local shops to find interesting textiles to create an ever-changing collection of minimalist women's clothes. Straight, severe lines still manage to be feminine, cleverly mediated by oversized buttons and subtle softer accents.

Ecseri Piac – *best place in town for small collectibles and all sorts of interesting junk.*

Porcelain & Ceramics

Porcelain and pottery are still cheap compared to similar western European work. The folk pottery style was developed to supply Transylvanians who traditionally set out plates of food on the graves of deceased relatives. Notable are plates from the village of Korond and black ceramics from Hódmezővásárhely. Both can be found at the Folkart Centrum. Be warned though: this stuff was designed only to look good hung on walls and heavy metals in the glaze will rub off into food.

Hollóháza and Alföldi, however, use similar colourful patterns to make non-toxic dinnerware, available at Haas & Czjek.

In another tradition, the works at Herend has been turning out hand-painted porcelain since 1826 and by the end of the nineteenth century had developed its own meticulous style. At the 1896 Paris exhibition they introduced a delicate flower-and-butterfly design which ended up gracing none other than Queen Victoria's table.

Less formal in style and using different glazing techniques, the Pécs factory of **Zsolnay** is famous for the glazed tiles on the Mátyás templom roof and their dinnerware designs are more free-flowing than Herend's.

Zsolnay also produces garden statuary glazed with iridescent pigments in turn-of-the-century and contemporary styles. Ask the sales staff at the Zsolnay Márkabolt.

Haas & Czjek
VI. Bajcsy-Zsilinszky út 23 (111 4094). M3 Arany János utca. **Open** 10am-6pm Mon-Fri; 9am-1pm Sat. **Credit** AmEx, DC, EC, JCB, MC, V.

Herend Porcelain
V. József nádor tér 11 (117 2622). M1 Vörösmarty tér.
V. Kígyó utca 5 (118 3439). M3 Ferenciek tere. **Open** 10am-6pm Mon-Fri; 9am-1pm Sat. **Credit** AmEx, DC, EC, JCB, MC, V.

Zsolnay Porcelain
V. Kígyó utca 4 (118 3712). M3 Ferenciek tere. **Open** 9am-6pm Mon-Fri; 9am-1pm Sat. **Credit** AmEx, DC, EC, JCB, MC, V.

Shoes & Leather Goods

Bagaria Leather
V. Váci utca 10 (118 5768). M1 Vörösmarty tér. **Open** 10am-6pm Mon-Fri; 10am-1.30pm Sat. **Credit** AmEx, MC, V.
Bagaria Leather has a wide selection of imported and locally crafted leather goods. Tucked into a courtyard, the shop is worth a visit for their display of antique leather suitcases and bric-à-brac.

Hisztéria
VII. Wesselényi utca 11 (322 4074). M2 Astoria/tram 47, 49. **Open** 10am-6pm Mon-Fri. **No credit cards.**
Though it looks like an abandoned store from outside, some of the most interesting footgear in the city rests humbly within on stacks of boxes – mostly Italian imports with some Hungarian brands. The owners have a good eye for the latest trends.

Kaláka Studio
V. Haris köz 2 (118 3313). M3 Ferenciek tere. **Open** 10am-6pm Mon-Wed, Fri; 10am-7pm Thur; 10am-2pm Sat. **No credit cards.**
Local designer Bodor Ágnes creates affordable and interesting shoes in soft suedes available at Kaláka Studio. Pick out a pair to go with something from their small selection of women's clothing (also by local designers) on the other side of the shop.

Krokodil
V. Kossuth Lajos utca 11 (137 2619). M3 Ferenciek tere. **Open** 10am-6pm Mon-Wed, Fri; 10am-7pm Thur; 9.30am-1.30pm Sat. **No credit cards.**
A step up from the stodgier competitors Salamander or Humanic, with fashionable shoes at sensible prices. Better than their Váci utca location.

Vízió
V. Türr István utca 8 (118 5620). M1, M2, M3 Deák tér. **Open** 10am-6pm Mon-Wed, Fri; 10am-7pm Thur; 10am-2pm Sat. **No credit cards.**
Krokodil's exclusive shoe shop carries stylish treads by international names such as Fendissime and Yves St Laurent.

Vintage & Secondhand Clothes

In a country obsessed with Western fashions, vintage clothes have yet to catch on. But Ecseri market is a treasure trove with stalls specialising in antique cloths and good pickings on tables outside.

Bazaar
V. Molnár utca 12. M3 Ferenciek tere. **Open** noon-6pm Mon-Fri. **No credit cards.**
The owner's a bit batty, but that's the key to the odd assortment of clothes and bric-à-brac collected in her shop. One of the few stores with a true junk-shop feel.

Nostalgia
VI. Podmaniczky utca 43 (112 4609). M3 Nyugati. **Open** noon-6pm Mon-Fri. **No credit cards.**
Every nook and cranny of this tiny courtyard shop is crammed with wonderful old clothes, shoes and an astounding collection of accessories – spats, gloves, parasols and rhinestones. Make friends with other customers trying on lacy Victorian underwear behind the suit rack.

Flowers

For late night romantics, the flower stand on the Pest side of Margaret Bridge is open 24 hours daily. (*See also chapter* **Services**.)

Sasad Virág
V. Haris köz 3 (118 4415). M3 Ferenciek tere. **Open**
9am-6pm Mon-Fri; 9am-2pm Sat. **Credit** AmEx, V.
Small flower shop offering Interflora service for within
Budapest and abroad.

Yucca
V. Váci utca 54 (137 3307). M3 Ferenciek tere. **Open**
9am-6pm Mon-Fri; 9am-2pm Sat. **No credit cards.**
The smell of orchids is the first thing you encounter as you
walk into this shop filled with unusual fresh and dried flowers available by the stem or for creative custom bouquets.

Folklore

See also chapter **Folklore**.

Folkart Centrum
V. Váci utca 14 (118 5840). M1 Vörösmarty tér. **Open**
9.30am-4am daily. **Credit** AmEx, DC, EC, JCB, MC, V.
Purveyor of cute folk costumed dolls, factory-produced
weavings, and machine-tooled woodwork – mostly kitsch
though some offerings are worthwhile. A hint: if 900 follows
the third digit of the serial number, the article is hand-made
by a local craftsperson.

Holló Folkart Gallery
*V. Vitkovics Mihály utca 12 (117 8103). M2 Astoria/
tram 47, 49.* **Open** 10am-6pm Mon-Fri; 10am-1pm Sat.
Credit AmEx, MC, V.
László Holló reproduces hand-carved, hand-painted furniture and wooden objects in a style that blends traditions from
several west Hungarian villages.

Vali Folklore Souvenir
*V. Váci utca 23 (118 6495/137 6301). M3 Ferenciek
tere.* **Open** 10am-7pm Mon-Sat; noon-5pm Sun. **Credit**
AmEx, DC, MC, V.
Virtually the only store that stocks genuine Hungarian and

Transylvanian folk costumes. Beaded and embroidered
skirts, blouses and leather vests, pottery and hand-carved
wooden things.

Food & Drink

Nagy Tamás Sajtüzlete
*V. Gerlóczy utca 3 (117 4268/137 7014). M1, M2, M3
Deák tér.* **Open** 9am-6pm Mon-Fri; 9am-1pm Sat. **No
credit cards.**
Choose from 150 kinds of cheese from Hungary and Europe
in one of the only places to stock cheddar or good-quality
Parmesan. Selected wines, too.

Coquan's Kávé
IX. Ráday utca 15 (215 2444). M3 Kálvin tér. **Open**
8am-6pm Mon-Fri; 9am-2pm Sat. **No credit cards.**
Hungary's first and only speciality coffee roaster, Coquan's
friendly English-speaking staff will serve you up a steaming *latté* or custom-mix whole beans roasted fresh every day
to take home.

Kóser Élelmiszer
VII. Nyár utca 1 (322 9276). M2 Blaha Lujza tér. **Open**
10am-6pm Mon-Fri. **No credit cards.**
Kosher foods including meats, Israeli cup-a-soups, fresh
salads, baked goods, an extensive collection of real cream
cheese spreads and the perennial matzoh crackers.

Ázsia Bolt
IX. Vámház körút 1 (217 7700). Tram 47, 49. **Open**
7am-6pm Mon-Fri; 7am-2pm Sat. **No credit cards.**
In the basement of the central market hall, oriental spices,
miso, noodles, woks and 10kg bags of rice.

Piramis
VII. Garay tér 9 (121 7488). M2 Keleti. **Open** 11am-
10pm Mon-Fri; 11am-10pm Sat; 3-10pm Sun.
No credit cards.

Bringing it all Back Home

Magyar Posta is the cheapest way to send stuff
home, but be prepared for a head-on collision
with the full weight of Hungarian bureaucracy.

Packages up to 2kg with a maximum value
of Ft10,000 can be sent overland to any destination for Ft720. Bring your own packed box
or buy one from the *Csomagfelvétel* window
(they come in three sizes and cost between Ft45-
Ft80). Next, have a go at tackling the blue
Vámáru-nyilatkozat (customs form – conveniently in both Hungarian and French) which
is found at the window labelled *Levélfelvétel*.
Itemise the contents of your package and the
value of each item.

After the forms are filled out, the last step is
to seal the box with both the packing tape and
the string you have remembered to bring with
you, then lug it back to the *Levélfelvétel* window
for final processing.

Sending larger parcels by post is so complicated that it's hardly worth the bother. Instead,

try one of the carriers listed below, who will
handle normal customs for everything but
antiques. Officially, any object over 70 years
old requires registration with the Ministry of
Culture and a special customs stamp before it
can be taken out of the country. Your antiques
dealer will have the details.

AmExS Transport
*XIII. Szent István körút 20 I/1 (269 2725/269
2467/fax 269 2466). M3 Nyugati.* **Open** 8am-6pm
daily. **No credit cards.**
Packing materials and customs clearance available for
international air freight. Helpful English-speaking staff.
Express service airport to airport: to UK $3.75/kg; to
US $2.90/kg; minimum 45kg. Standard service: to UK
$1.50/kg minimum 100kg.

TNT Express
*VII. Nagy Diófa utca 7 (269 6464). M2 Blaha Lujza
tér.* **Open** 8am-6pm Mon-Fri. **No credit cards.**
Contact Tibor Berzsepi for British Airways unaccom-
panied luggage rates; 10kg to UK approx Ft13,000; to
USA, Ft19,000.

Open-air Markets

Open-air markets are one of the best places to peek into everyday Hungarian life. Old ladies in traditional costumes hawking garden produce, the freshest sheep cheese, local honey, cheap kitchen gadgets and discount clothing are just some of the attractions.

There's some kind of open-air market in every district, but the most interesting are at XIII. Lehel tér (M3 Lehel tér), II. Fény utca (M2 Moszkva tér), and XIV. Bosnyák tér (Bus 7

Bosnyák tér). They open early to provide fresh meat and produce to bleary-eyed shoppers at 7am. Consequently, most merchants begin packing up around 2pm except on the days leading up to major holidays.

If you're not an early riser, the grand old (and recently renovated) Nagycsarnok (central market hall) at Fővám tér (M3 Kálvin tér/tram 47 49) has longer opening hours (7am-6pm Mon-Fri; 7am-1pm Sat).

All the supplies for a Middle Eastern feast: fresh feta cheese, pitta, olives, home-made frozen falafel mix, dried beans and okra, tahina and the tastiest Baklava this side of Istanbul.

Supermarkets

Super Közért

I. Batthyány tér 5-7 (202 5044). M2 Batthyány tér. **Open** 6am-8pm Mon, Tue, Thur, Fri; 6am-7pm Wed; 7am-4.30pm Sat; 7am-1pm Sun. **No credit cards**.
In a restored market hall, a full-service supermarket with key-cutting, shoe repair and other stalls, including a café and ice-cream joint.

Csemege Julius Meinl

VIII. Rákóczi út 59 (133 1061/134 3500).
M2 Blaha Lujza tér/tram 4, 6. **Open** 6am-9pm Mon-Fri; 7am-2pm Sat. **Credit** AmEx, EC, JCB, MC, V.
There are branches of this Austrian chain all over town. Extended evening hours and credit card facilities are available at this location.

Kaiser's

VI. Nyugati tér (132 2531). M3 Nyugati/tram 4, 6. **Open** 7am-8pm Mon-Fri; 7am-3pm Sat. **No credit cards**.
This German supermarket chain offers the best grocery

assortment in Budapest, including a decent deli section and fruit and vegetables.
Branch: VII. Klauzál tér 11 (322 8031).

Rothschild
VII. Károly körút 9 (342 9733). M1, M2, M3 Deák tér.
Open 7am-10pm Mon-Fri; 8am-6pm Sat; 9am-5pm Sun.
Credit DCI, EC, JCB, MC, V.
This location is open on Sunday, takes credit cards and will deliver free for orders of over Ft2,500.

Vegetarian & Health Food

Vegetarianism hasn't really caught on in Hungary, but an increasing number of shops offer the basic supplies for meat-free cooking. Look to **Kaiser's** (*see above* **Supermarkets**) for crackers, interesting varieties of bread, muesli, soy and hot sauces. The best places for vitamins are body-building shops, such as **Mini-Mix Gyógynövény**.

The Trafik – Home of Tack

Most Continental towns are dotted with handy corner kiosks plying a quick trade in small daily necessities: stamps, cigarettes, bus tickets, lottery coupons. Useful places, the Roman tabbachi and Parisian tabac. But not the Hungarian trafik. Okay, these humble establishments do stock a few brands of cigarettes and occasionally even matches. Sometimes they have cheap soap and malodorous colognes.

But otherwise it's useless tack: toy Trabants, rubber spiders and joke false teeth. If you're caught short without a self-adhesive fun moustache, this is the place to go. Once, trafiks were exciting places where grown men would buy flints for their lighters, boys purchase caps for their guns and girls spend their pocket money on *nyalóka* (lollipops). Now trafik owners no longer have the right to sell stamps and rarely stock BKV tickets, while flints, cap-guns and lollipops have since gone the way of all flesh. Still, could the Frenchman find a wind-up Barney Rubble in his corner tabac?

Bio-ABC

VI. Teréz körút 32 (269 3298). M1 Oktogon. **Open**
10am-7pm Mon-Fri; 10am-1pm Sat. **No credit cards.**
A friendly shop offering tofu, soy milk, organic grains and
other vegetarian essentials plus natural cosmetics, essential
oils, dried medicinal herbs, fresh-baked wholegrain breads
and pastries, and filtered water.

Egészségbolt

XII. Csaba utca 3 (212 2542). M2 Moszkva tér.
Open 9am-7.30pm Mon-Fri; 8.30am-2pm Sat. **No
credit cards.**
The smell of fresh wholegrain breads and pastries will
lead you to this basement shop. Vegetarian staples, organic grains and produce, dried herbs and a wide assortment
of Hungarian natural beauty and health products.

Mini-Mix Gyógynövény

VI. Oktogon 4 (no phone). M1 Oktogon/tram 4, 6. **Open**
8.30am-7pm Mon-Fri; 8.30am-2pm Sat. **No credit cards.**
Hungarian vitamins are unreliable and often, in normal pharmacies, inaccessibly located behind the counter. This place
is different. American and German brands of vitamins as
well as medicinal herbs, natural cosmetics and other health
food products. Staff are helpful, too.

Wine

Hungary is a country of wine-lovers and -makers.
While it's easy to drop into your local ABC for a
two-litre soda bottle of last week's vintage *házibor*

(home-made), wines of much higher quality (less
likely to give you a hangover) are not that much
more expensive. (*See chapter* **Restaurants.**)

Demijohn

*V. Cukor utca 4 (tel/fax 118 4467/118 6509). M3
Ferenciek tere.* **Open** 10am-6pm Mon-Fri; 10am-4pm Sat.
Credit AmEx, MC.
Hungarian wines in all price ranges fill half the shop while
the other half is a mix of international vintages. Free wine
tasting of three or four features every Saturday and consul-
tation for large parties. (Also free delivery for orders of at
least one case.)

La Boutique des Vins

*V. József Attila utca 12 (117 5919). M1, M2, M3
Deák tér.* **Open** 10am-6pm Mon-Fri; 10am-3pm Sat.
Credit AmEx.
Hungary's premium vintages are the speciality in Hungary's
oldest private wine shop opened by the former sommelier of
the Gundel restaurant. Look for the owner's own 'Sommelier'
label for the best reds and rosés from the Villány region. Free
delivery for orders of two cases or more.

Clinique, Estée Lauder and Christian Dior are on
Váci utca between numbers 8-12. Guerlain is nearby at Petőfi Sándor utca 8, and Yves St Laurent
can be found in the Kempinski Hotel.

Gift Rap

Searching for small Hungarian-style presents
for the folks back home? The tide of foreign goods
hasn't quite washed away every last little Hungarian product. Here are a few suggestions for
filling those small gaps in your suitcase.

The two national drinks, unicum and pálinka, are available in an assortment of sizes.
Pálinka is fruit brandy. Choose from *szilva*
(plum), *barack* (peach), *körte* (pear) or *cseresznye*
(cherry), but read your labels. Bottles listing *etil
alkohol* as the principal ingredient are simply a
raw alcohol base with water and a little flavour-
ing. The best szilva pálinka is kosher and comes
aged three, six or 12 years.

Unicum, a dark green bitter herb liqueur, is
known locally as both the best cure for a hangover and as the chief cause of many. This is
fierce stuff, but the taste for it is easy to acquire.
The spherical green bottle is splendid, and, with
its red cross label (a reference to the drink's supposed medicinal properties), resembles a holy
anarchist's bomb. Any size over half a litre is
difficult to pour from, but the miniatures are cute.

Unicum and pálinka are cheapest at grocery
stores, where all sorts of other Hungarian good-
ies may be found. Paprika, either *csípős* (strong)

or *édes* (sweet), is found as strings of dried
peppers, as packets of ground powder, as a
puree in tubes and in combination with other
spices in jars – look for the Csípős János
(Spicy John) brand of sharp paprika relish.
Garlic purée (*fokhagyma krém*) and sweet horse-
radish (*torma*) are other popular spices that
come in cheap and easy-to-squeeze tubes.

At Hungarian sweet counters, Balaton bars
offer a cardboardy chocolate crunch named
after Europe's largest puddle. Look out also for
Negro, the politically incorrect boiled sweet. A
Túró Rudi can be found in the fridge of any
supermarket, and is basically chocolate-covered
sweet cottage cheese. Don't try packing one of
these in your luggage.

Last but not least, the Hungarian experience
can instantly be recreated back home with genuine eastern European cigarettes. Sopianae (best
of the worst) has recently been trying to upgrade
its image with new light, menthol and mysteri-
ous 'extra' varieties, but the old fashioned brown
packets give the most authentic 'gravel-fag'
flavour. Symphonia is another old-style brand
and, for the truly hard-core smoker, try a pack
of filterless Munkás ('worker's') cigarettes.

Azúr

V. Petőfi Sándor utca 11 (118 5391). M3 Ferenciek tere.
Open 8am-8pm Mon-Fri; 9am-2pm Sat. **Credit** AmEx,
DC, MC, V.
For all your general health and beauty needs, Azúr has
branches throughout the city. Most also carry home clean-
ing supplies, Dr Scholl's foot-care products and Western-
brand condoms.
Branch: VIII. Rákóczi út 30 (342 1909).

Herbária

II. Margit körút 42 (201 6093). Tram 4, 6. **Open** 10am-6pm
Mon-Fri; 9am-1pm Sat. **No credit cards.**
Hungarians are very herb-conscious, and this chain stocks
a big selection of herbal remedies and related products.
British baby-boomers may be intrigued to rediscover a taste
from their childhood: *csipke szörp* – rose hip syrup.
Branch: V. Bajcsy-Zsilinszky út 3 (322 6003); VIII.
Rákóczi út 49 (113 4678).

Kállos Illatszer és Fodrászcikk

VII. Nagy Diófa utca 1 (268 0930). M2 Blaha Lujza tér.
Open 10am-6pm Mon-Fri; 9am-1pm Sat. **No credit cards.**
An assortment of imported natural cosmetics and Western
brands such as Freeman.

Flea Markets

Ecseri Piac

XIX. Nagykőrösi út 156. Bus 52 from Boráros tér.
Open 7am-early afternoon Mon-Sat. **Admission** free.
No credit cards.
Budapest's most famous antiques market is no longer quite
the bargain basement it once was and many merchants tend
to inflate their prices for Westerners, so be prepared for some
tough haggling. The tables outside often yield unusual finds
and Ecseri Piac is still the best place for folk costumes and
textiles, Communist artefacts, small collectibles and all sorts
of interesting junk. Arrive early Saturday morning for the
best pickings.

Józsefvárosi Piac

VIII. Kőbányai út 21-31. Tram 28, 36. **Open** 6am-6pm
daily. **No credit cards.**
The shoppers are mostly Polish and Romanian, the stallholders mostly Chinese and their assistants mostly Gypsy.
You'll find no antiques here, but stall after stall of cheap
clothes, shoes, electronics and kitchen equipment. There are
Chinese shops all over Budapest, and most of them get their
stock from here. Truly international – bargain in sign language and choose from Turkish, Vietnamese or Hungarian
for lunch.

Városligeti Bolhapiac

*XIV. Zichy Mihály út (251 2485). M1 Széchenyi
Fürdő.* Open 7am-2pm Sat, Sun. **Admission** Ft20. **No
credit cards.**
Ecseri's smaller cousin and considerably easier to get to
(it's in the Petőfi Csarnok in the middle of the park), the
Bolhapiac has Communist relics, a contingent of peasant
ladies from Szék, miniature Trabis and lots of other really
interesting junk.

Music

See also chapters **Music: Rock, Roots & Jazz**
and **Music: Classical & Opera.**

CD Bar

VI. Székely Mihály utca 10 (142 8380). M1 Opera.
Open 10am-8pm Mon-Fri; 10am-4pm Sat. **Credit**
AmEx, EC, MC.

The best place to find contemporary and classic jazz on disk,
though some classical, pop and rock music also in stock.
There are CD players to check your selection, and free
coffee or tea while you listen.

Concerto

VII. Dob utca 33 (121 6432). M1 Opera. **Open** noon-
7pm Mon-Fri; noon-4pm Sun. **Credit** AmEx, DC, EC, V.
Charming small shop with knowledgeable staff dealing in
new and used classical CDs and vinyl.

Fotex

V. Szervita tér 2 (118 3395). M1 Vörösmarty tér. **Open**
10am-9pm daily. **Credit** AmEx, DC, JCB, MC, V.
Budapest's biggest record shop has a large but depressing-
ly mainstream and unimaginative selection, although it's
useful to be able to shop for all genres in one store.

Hungaroton

V. Vörösmarty tér 1 (138 2810). M1 Vörösmarty tér.
Open 10am-6pm Mon-Fri; 10am-1pm Sat. **Credit** AmEx,
DC, EC, JCB, MC, V.
Classical music buffs will find works by Hungarian com-
posers and local ensembles at reasonable prices. (*See also*
chapter **Music: Classical & Opera.**)

Liszt Ferenc Music Shop

VI. Andrássy út 45 (322 4091). M1 Oktogon. **Open**
10am-6pm Mon-Fri; 10am-1pm Sat. **Credit** AmEx, EC,
MC, V.
Extensive imported classical CDs with some world music,
Euro-pop and Hungarian bands thrown in. Sheet music
downstairs. The staff emanate a sombre mood to go with the
serious music.

Rózsavölgyi

V. Szervita tér 5 (118 3312). M1 Vörösmarty tér. **Open**
9.30am-7pm Mon, Tue, Thur, Fri; 10am-7pm Wed; 10am-
3pm Sat. **Credit** AmEx, DC, JCB, MC, V.
Rózsavölgyi has three floors brimming with books, sheet
music, cheap records and more or less normally priced cassettes and CDs, with the emphasis pretty much on classical,
but including other stuff too.

Wave

VI. Zichy Jenő utca 17 (112 9477). M1 Opera. **Open**
10am-8pm Mon-Fri; 10am-2pm Sat. **No credit cards.**
The first alternative music shop in Budapest, its stock is
erratic and often misleadingly racked but offers a good
spread of non-mainstream guitar-orientated music. Tell them
you want to tape a CD, and they'll sell you it for Ft200 above
the normal price, and buy it back off you the next day. Their
tiny sister shop Trance, round the corner at Révay köz 2 (269
3135, same opening hours), has a selection of techno, trance
and ambient CDs.

Sporting Goods

Magic Football Shop

VI. Teréz körút 40 (112 1332). M1 Oktogon. **Open**
10am-1pm, 2-6pm, Mon-Fri; 10am-1pm Sat. **No credit
cards.**
Hungarian football souvenirs galore, particularly for top
teams Ferencváros and Újpest, plus a good selection of
Italian and Spanish gear.

Mallory Sport

VII. Király utca 59 (342 0744). Tram 4, 6. **Open** 10am-
6pm Mon-Wed, Fri; 10am-7pm Thur; 10am-1.30pm Sat.
Credit EC, MC.
Named after the famous climber, Mallory carries indoor and
outdoor sporting supplies covering everything from aerobics to racquet sports.

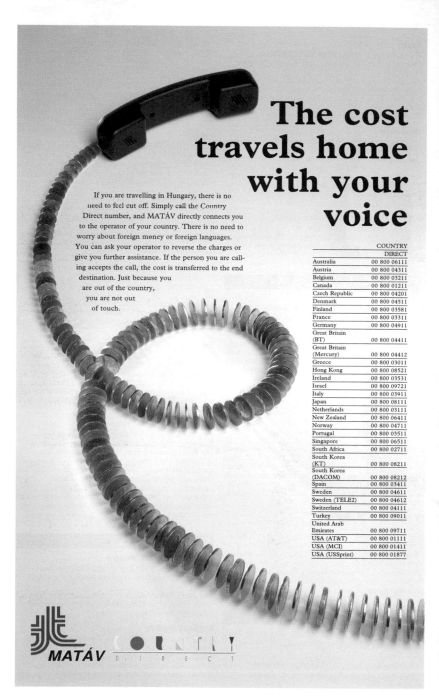

The cost travels home with your voice

If you are travelling in Hungary, there is no need to feel cut off. Simply call the Country Direct number, and MATÁV directly connects you to the operator of your country. There is no need to worry about foreign money or foreign languages. You can ask your operator to reverse the charges or give you further assistance. If the person you are calling accepts the call, the cost is transferred to the end destination. Just because you are out of the country, you are not out of touch.

	COUNTRY DIRECT
Australia	00 800 06111
Austria	00 800 04311
Belgium	00 800 03211
Canada	00 800 01211
Czech Republic	00 800 04201
Denmark	00 800 04511
Finland	00 800 03581
France	00 800 03311
Germany	00 800 04911
Great Britain (BT)	00 800 04411
Great Britain (Mercury)	00 800 04412
Greece	00 800 03011
Hong Kong	00 800 08521
Ireland	00 800 03531
Israel	00 800 09721
Italy	00 800 03911
Japan	00 800 08111
Netherlands	00 800 03111
New Zealand	00 800 06411
Norway	00 800 04711
Portugal	00 800 03511
Singapore	00 800 06511
South Africa	00 800 02711
South Korea (KT)	00 800 08211
South Korea (DACOM)	00 800 08212
Spain	00 800 03411
Sweden	00 800 04611
Sweden (TELE2)	00 800 04612
Switzerland	00 800 04111
Turkey	00 800 09011
United Arab Emirates	00 800 09711
USA (AT&T)	00 800 01111
USA (MCI)	00 800 01411
USA (USSprint)	00 800 01877

MATÁV

COUNTRY DIRECT

Services

Yes, you can get served in Budapest. Eventually.

The customer is always right? Under Communism it was more like the customer was an unwarranted irritation, awkward and in the way, someone to be got rid of as soon as possible. Any slightly unusual request would be met with a brusque shake of the head.

Inevitably, such attitudes die hard, and service in Budapest remains erratic, off-hand and at times laughable. The surliness of some service staff is only aggravated if you start speaking in broken Hungarian and sign language. Take along a pocket dictionary or, if possible, a Hungarian-speaking friend for anything more complicated than basic requests.

On the other hand, the quality of most services is both quite high and comparatively cheap, if often slow by Western standards. Services such as dental care, optical work and watch repair can still be obtained relatively inexpensively. Because of this, Austrians and Slovenes spill over the open borders into western Hungarian towns such as Sopron all year round for root canals and new glasses.

For anyone staying beyond a brief visit, *The Phone Book*, a privately published directory in English, is an invaluable tool for finding services of all types. This is on sale at some bookshops and international newsagents, or else available free from CoMo Media, XIII. Váci út 6, Floor 2 (132 3364/fax 131 0794), open 9am-5pm Mon-Fri. Updated each year, it's much easier to use than the cumbersome Hungarian version and contains all kinds of useful information.

See also **BÁV** in *chapter* **Shopping**.

Information Services

Tourinform
V. Sütő utca 2 (117 9800). M1, M2, M3 Deák tér/tram 47, 49. **Open** 8am-8pm daily; *15 Nov-1 Mar* 8am-3pm Sat, Sun.
Officially, Tourinform is an agency to promote events in Budapest and the countryside, but the staff at one of the few truly helpful information centres in Budapest will also look up phone numbers and make suggestions to meet most travellers' needs.

Taverna Tourist Service
V. Váci utca 20 (tel/fax 118 1818/118 7287). M3 Ferenciek tere. **Open** 8am-7pm Mon-Sat; 8am-1pm Sun. **Credit** AmEx, DC, EC, MC, V.
Part of the Taverna Hotel. The staff speak good English and will give friendly assistance in booking concert tickets and tours, help you find your way around town and answer any odd questions.

Vass: *good for the sole.*

Auctions & Appraisals

See also **BÁV** in *chapter* **Shopping**.

Nagyházi Galéria
V. Balaton utca 8 (131 9908/112 5631). Tram 2. **Open** 10am-6pm Mon-Fri; 10am-1pm Sat. **Credit** AmEx, DC, EC, JCB, MC, V.
Budapest's largest antiques dealer holds small auctions every month in the shop. Bids start as low as Ft1,000 for all types of antiques, art and jewellery. Three or four catalogue auctions every year turn over up to Ft40 million's worth of more valuable pieces.

Blitz Gallery
V. Falk Miksa utca 30 (132 0401). Tram 4, 6. **Open** 10am-6pm Mon-Fri; 10am-1pm Sat. **Credit** AmEx, DC, EC, JCB, MC, V.
Blitz is Hungary's largest art auction house turning over up to Ft30 million at its bi-annual auctions held in April and November at the **Kempinski Hotel**. Specialises, but not exclusively so, in twentieth-century Hungarian painters.

Profila
VII. Szentkirályi utca 6 (267 2494/267 2495). M2 Blaha Lujza. **Open** 10am-4pm Mon-Fri. **No credit cards.**
Stockists of stamps, postcards, old phone cards, coins and other valuable paper things. The main office in Szentkirályi holds the most interesting stuff. Catalogues for the bi-annual auctions are available from the Kazinczy utca branch.
Branch: VII. Kazinczy utca 3A (268 0198).

Clothing & Shoes
Costume Rental

Női és Férfi Jelmezkölcsönző
V. Irányi utca 18-20 (117 5491). M3 Ferenciek tere. **Open** 8am-4pm Mon-Thur; 8am-noon Fri. **No credit cards.**
A Hungarian ID card or letter of guarantee from your place of work is needed as deposit for costumes. Renaissance and nineteenth-century garb, formal attire and folk costumes available inexpensively for weekend hire.

Laundry & Dry-cleaning

Not long ago, most foreign residents would cringe at the thought of having to get something dry-cleaned in Hungary. Now a number of companies have moved in guaranteeing service to Western standards. If you want to do it yourself, the word for laundry is *patyolat* and most places will charge a minimal fee to wash and fold your clothes.

Ametiszt American-Hungarian Dry Cleaning

East-West Business Center, VIII. Rákóczi út 1-3 (266 7770). M2 Astoria. **Open** 8am-5pm Mon-Fri. **No credit cards.**
Almost, but not always, next-day service on most dry cleaning. The staff is almost, but not quite completely unintercstcd. And the prices, for the acceptable quality of the cleaning, are almost (but not quite) the best in town. Dry-cleaing a standard women's dress will cost about Ft400 and a shirt Ft200.

The Home Laundry

II. Radna utca 3 (156 4230). Bus 5. **Open** 9am-7.30pm Mon-Fri; 9am-1pm Sat. **No credit cards.**
You can entrust your delicate items to The Home Laundry. Services include folding, hanging and starching for shirts and other pieces charged by the piece. Underwear and linens are charged by the kilo. Pick up and delivery in inner Budapest costs a flat fee of Ft375, and Ft700 for outer districts. Dry-cleaning is finished within three days, or there's an express 24-hour service. English-speaking staff.
Branch: XII. Németvölgyi út 53B (155 3696).

Crystal

V. Arany János utca 34 (131 8307). M3 Arany János utca. **Open** 7am-7pm Mon-Fri; 8am-1pm Sat. **No credit cards.**
Next-day dry-cleaning, as well as leather clothing and winter jackets within a week.

Nádor Patyolat

V. József nádor tér 9 (117 1542). M1, M2, M3 Deák tér/tram 47, 49. **Open** 7am-3pm Mon, Wed, Fri; 11am-7pm Tue, Thur. **No credit cards.**
Leave your laundry, they'll do it for you.

Shoemakers

The two shops listed below use fine-quality materials to make handsome men's dress shoes for around Ft30,000 per pair.

Vass

V. Haris köz 2 (118 2375). M1, M2, M3 Deák tér, tram 47, 49. **Open** 10am-6pm Mon-Fri; 10am-1pm Sat. **Credit** AmEx, DC, EC, JCB, MC, V.

Zábrák Shoes

V. Erzsébet tér 7-8 (266 8175). M1, M2, M3 Deák tér, tram 47, 49. **Open** 9am-6pm Mon-Fri; 9am-2pm Sat. **Credit** AmEx, DC, EC, JCB, MC, V.
In the Grand Hotel Corvinus Kempinski.

Shoe Repair

See also below **Luggage Repair.**

Mister Minit

Skála Metró Áruház. VI. Nyugati tér (153 2222). M3 Nyugati. **Open** 9am-6.30pm Mon-Fri; 8am-3pm Sat. **No credit cards.**

The American chain has 14 branches in major shopping centres in Budapest for while-you-wait key copying, sharpening and shoe repairs.
Branch: *Corvin. VIII. Blaha Lujza tér 1-3 (138 4160 ext 28). M2 Blaha Lujza.* **Open** 10am-6pm Mon-Fri; 9am-12.30pm Sat. **No credit cards.**

Tailors

See also chapter **Shopping: Fashion.**

Kiskakas Butik

VII. Síp utca 6 (141 6020). M2 Astoria. **Open** 10am-6pm Mon-Fri; 10am-7pm Thur; 10am-1pm Sat. **No credit cards.**
A 50-year-old Jewish family tailoring business in the heart of the Jewish quarter. The boutique stocks large-size suits and jeans for men. Owner Gyula Nádas's English-speaking daughter is usually around in the afternoon to take mea surements for men's suits of any size.

Flowers

LufiLand

VII. Andrássy út 5 (342 6989). M1 Bajcsy-Zsilinszky út. **Open** 9am-8pm Mon-Fri; 9am-5pm Sat, Sun. **No credit cards.**
Balloons, flowers and customised gift baskets can be delivered to all parts of the city.

Sasad Virág

V. Haris köz 3 (118 4415). M3 Ferenciek tere. **Open** 9am-6pm Mon-Fri; 9am-2pm Sat. **Credit** AmEx, V.
Interflora service is offered at this small, central flower shop.

Yucca

V. Váci utca 54 (137 3307). M3 Ferenciek tere. **Open** 9am-6pm Mon-Fri; 9am-2pm Sat. **No credit cards.**
The English-speaking owner delivers beautiful bouquets of exotic fresh and dried flowers.

Food Delivery

New York Bagel

VI. Bajcsy Zsilinszky út 21 (118 4415). M3 Arany János utca. **Delivery** 10am-7.30pm Mon-Fri. **No credit cards.**
Two Americans set up their own bagel bakery here in 1993, though now it's Hungarian-owned. For 25 per cent extra they'll deliver anywhere in town in under 45 minutes for most destinations. Choose from sandwiches, salads, American-style carrot cake and chocolate chip cookies.

Kentucky Fried Chicken

Districts V, VI, VII, XIII: *VII. Erzsébet körút 53 (351 7926).*
Districts VIII, IX, XIV: *VII. Thököly út 6 (322 0180).* **Delivery** 11am-10pm daily. **No credit cards.**
The Colonel awaits your pleasure.

Pink Cadillac

IX. Ráday utca 22 (216 1412). M3 Kálvin tér. **Delivery** 11am-11pm Mon-Thur; 11am-1am Fri; 1pm-1am Sat; 1-11pm Sun. **No credit cards.**
Easily the best pizza/pasta delivery in town. Fifty different varieties of pizza, pasta, salads and desserts. Delivery within about 30 mins to most central locations for an extra Ft100.

Pizza Hut

District II: *Budagyöngye Bevásárlóközpont, II. Szilágyi Erzsébet fasor 121 (275 0860). Tram 56.*
Districts V, VI, VII, XIII: *VII. Erzsébet körút 58 (322 4434). M1 Oktogon.*

Districts VIII, IX, XIV: *VIII. Baross tér 15 (267 9523).*
M2 Keleti
Districts I, III, XI, XII:*XII. Alkotás utca 7B (175 8186/155 9377). M2 Déli.*
Delivery 11am-11pm daily. **No credit cards.**

Il Treno Pizzeria

Districts V, VI, VII, VIII, IX, XII, XIII, XIV: *VIII. József körút 60 (269 9223). M3 Ferenc körút.*
Districts I, II, III, X, XII, XIII: *XII. Alkotás utca 15 (156 4251). M2 Déli.*
Delivery 11am-10pm daily. **No credit cards.**
Full-service Italian-style restaurant with pizza, pasta, salads and desserts. Home delivery to listed districts included.

General Services

Bicycle Repair

B Bike

VII. Wesselényi utca 14 (322 5667). M2 Astoria. **Open** 10am-6pm Mon-Fri; 10am-1pm Sat. **No credit cards.**
Reliable and professional staff repair mountain and touring bikes for serious bikers. You'll also find accessories, parts for DIY repairs and a small stock of new bikes.

Computer Repair

Mr Mac

III. Kalászi út 11 (160 9299/160 8995). HÉV Rómaifürdő. **Open** 8am-4pm Mon-Fri. **No credit cards.**
Authorised service and sales of Apple computers with English speakers on staff.

Service in a flash at **Fotolux.**

EXE

XIII. Párkány utca 20 (173 1272/06 20 348 874). M3 Árpád híd. **Open** 9am-5pm Mon-Fri. **No credit cards.**
In-shop and on-site service for IBM-compatible PCs, laptops and printers.

Electrical Appliances

Getting electrical appliances repaired in Hungary is not necessarily expensive, though the process can be time-consuming. The company Telinformix (269 3333)/open 8am-8pm daily, can recommend the nearest repair shop for various appliances. Only some of their staff speak English, so have a Hungarian speaker nearby.

Bigrav

V. Váci utca 75 (137 6226). Tram 47, 49. **Open** 10am-5pm Mon-Fri. **No credit cards.**
Will repair stereo equipment, convert appliances to 220v current, and make transformers for larger appliances.

Luggage Repair & Key-cutting

See also above **Shoe Repair.**

Flekk GMK

VI. Podmaniczky utca 19 (111 0316). M3 Nyugati. **Open** 9am-6pm Mon-Fri; 9am-1pm Sat. **No credit cards.**
This little family-run shop will take care of most repair jobs efficiently and inexpensively. They handle shoe, zip and luggage repair within a few days as well as key-cutting while you wait. There's also an eclectic jumble of DIY supplies and kitchen bric-à-brac.

Mountex

IX. Üllői út 7 (217 2426). M3 Kálvin tér. **Open** 10am-6pm Mon-Fri. **Credit** AmEx, DC, EC, JCB, MC, V.
A mountaineering store with equipment for climbing, caving and hiking, they also have a repairman on staff for back pack blowouts and other equipment repairs.

Opticians

Ofotért-Optinova Magyar-Amerikai Optikai KFT

V. Múzeum körút 13 (117 3559/266 2137). M2 Astoria. **Open** 10am-6pm Mon-Fri; 10am-1pm Sat. **Credit** AmEx, DC, EC, JCB, MC, V.
English-speaking examinations for glasses/contacts. Contact cleaning supplies, a large selection of international (expensive) and Hungarian (cheaper) frames, and lens treatments.

Photocopying & Printing

Copy General

V. Semmelweis utca 4 (266 6564/fax 266 6563). M2 Astoria. **Open** 7am-10pm Mon-Fri; 9am-6pm Sat. **No credit cards.**
Fast and friendly service from eight shops in Budapest. All do b&w and colour copying, binding and other finishing services and will pick up and deliver (Ft500 each way). The Lónyay utca branch is open round the clock with desktop publishing and computer rental (by the hour) in addition to its regular services. The self-service centre is next door.
Branches: I. Attila út 12 (175 9047/fax 175 9083). **Open** 7am-10pm Mon-Fri.
IX. Lónyay utca 36 (218 9052/fax 217 5304). M3 Kálvin tér. **Open** 24 hours daily; self service 8am-11pm daily.

Photography

Ofotért
*V. Károly körút 14 (117 6313/fax 117 5986). M2
Astoria.* **Open** 10am-6pm Mon-Fri; 9am-1pm Sat. **Credit**
EC, MC.
Local photographers now recommend Ofotért over its competitor Fotex for the best-quality prints, though you won't
find film processing any cheaper here than at home. In fact,
Americans will find it much more expensive. B&w, colour,
and slide developing are offered, as well as Kodak photography supplies.

Fotolux
V. Károly körút 21 (342 1538). M1, M2, M3 Deák tér.
Open 8am-9pm Mon-Sat; 9am-7pm Sun. **No credit
cards.**
Budapest's certified Nikon dealer has camera supplies,
colour and slide processing and will help you find camera
repair services.

Watch & Jewellery Repairs

Orex óraszalon
V. Petőfi Sándor utca 6 (137 4915). M3 Ferenciek tere.
Open 10am-6pm Mon-Fri; 10am-1pm Sat. **Credit** AmEx,
DC, EC, MC, V.
Almost any jewellery store in Budapest will replace old batteries or repair watches in-house for a negligible fee.
However, this Orex location specialises in watches, carries
most international names and has an experienced and reliable repair staff.

Hair & Beauty

Beauty Salons

Lancôme Beauty Salon
*V. Vörösmarty tér 3 (118 2277/118 3550). M1
Vörösmarty tér.* **Open** 10am-6pm Mon-Fri; 10am-7pm
Thur; 10am-2pm Sat. **Credit** AmEx, EC, MC, V.
You'll find the salon on the bottom floor of the Luxus
Department Store. The entire staff speaks English and provide short and long facials, body treatments, waxing and
make-up consulting.

Picurka Salon
VII. Lövölde tér 2 (141 2339). Tram 4, 6. **Open** 6am-
8pm Mon-Fri. **No credit cards.**
The extra-special cosmetic treatment is much less expensive
than at downtown salons and Picurka is reputed to have the
best face massage in town. Women's hair stylists as well,
but no English-speakers.

Vivien Talpai
II. Fillér utca 10B (213 1445). M2 Moszkva tér. **Open**
8am-6pm Mon-Fri; 8am-noon Sat. **No credit cards.**
Taking advantage of the booming business in orthopaedic
footwear in Budapest, Vivien Talpai does good things for
your feet with pedicures, foot massage and computer assisted examinations for custom-fit insoles. These cost Ft1,600
and are ready within a week.

Hair Salons

It is possible to get some sort of haircut here for as
little as Ft200, but there's always the risk of a
dreadful breakdown in communication if you're
after anything but the simplest of cuts. For a reliable trim, the Hilton, Grand Hotel Hungaria,
Fórum, Atrium Hyatt and Gellért all have salons

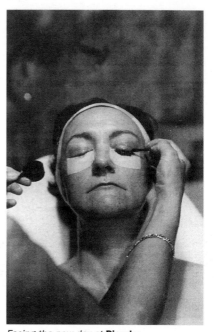

Facing the new day at **Picurka**.

with English-speaking hairdressers that cater to
men, women and children (for addresses, *see chapter* **Accommodation**).

Jaques Dessange
*V. Deák Ferenc utca 10 (266 8167/266 1000 ext 885).
M1, M2, M3 Deák tér/tram 47, 49.* **Open** 9am-8pm
Mon-Fri; 9am-4pm Sat. **Credit** AmEx, MC.
A full-service salon in the **Kempinski Hotel**. All of the
receptionists are multi-lingual as are most of the staff.
Fashionable cuts, Dessange hair-care products, facials, body
treatments, manicure and makeovers by, they claim, 'award-winning' make-up consultants.

Removals

For information on Budapest's postal system, *see
chapter* **Survival**.

Allied Pickfords
*II. Margit körút 8-10 III/24 (135 2602/06 30 461 160).
Tram 4, 6.* **Open** 9am-5pm Mon-Fri. **No credit cards.**
International removals through 12,000 offices worldwide.
Individual price quotes only.

AES Transport
*XIII. Szent István körút 20 I/1 (269 2725/269 2467/fax
269 2466). M3 Nyugati.* **Open** 8am-6pm Mon-Fri. **No
credit cards.**
The special 'You pack, we ship' service provides door-to-door
delivery, packing materials, and handles all customs. Rates
to the UK are $100 plus $4.50/kg. To US $150 plus $6/kg.
Minimum 100kg.

Museums & Galleries

Art Galleries

From György Galántai to Gilbert & George, Budapest's art scene is anything but parochial.

Where once there wasn't much except state-owned galleries with strictly censored art, these days new galleries are popping up all over Budapest – most privately owned, some run by foundations or institutions. Although many don't last too long, there are currently over 70 spaces devoted to twentieth-century art.

Galleries can be divided into several different categories; a few, such as Galéria '56, specialise in international art; others seem to be stores of over-rated and expensive contemporary work – Körmendi Galéria, for example. A growing number of galleries prefer a more specific profile, featuring special artists, groups or themes.

Smaller than in other parts of Europe, the Hungarian art scene seems to be on the verge of complete chaos. Individualism is far more important than inspiration through cooperation, resulting in lone-ranger artists and feebly outlined movements. The experimental, alternative and 'young artist' galleries are the most interesting and active. Look out for the Artpool-organised part of the annual Budapest Autumn Festival: a blissfully different series of events on Liszt Ferenc tér. The Gallery by Night performances and happenings at the Stúdió Galéria are also interesting.

Although there is no real artists' quarter, the north end of District V around Jászai Mari tér, Falk Miksa utca, Parliament and the Nagykörút is

particularly lively, with auction houses, antiques shops and expensive galleries in abundance. The galleries around Deák tér, Vörösmarty tér and Castle Hill are more tourist-orientated, although it's still possible to find Hungarian art of genuine quality. Current information about the art scene and temporary exhibits can be found in *Pesti Műsor*, *PestiEst*, *Budapest Week* or the Friday edition of any newspaper.

Public Galleries & Spaces

Budapest Galéria Kiállítóterem
V. Szabad sajtó út 5 (118 8097). M3 Ferenciek tere.
Open 10am-6pm Tue-Sun. **Admission** Ft50; Ft25 children. **No credit cards**.
Apart from nineteenth-century masters, all genres of modern and contemporary art are exhibited here, including photographs, architecture, installations and graphic design. The Budapest Galéria also runs the **Budapest Galéria Kiállítóháza** (*see below*) and some smaller galleries including the **Imre Varga Collection** (*see below* **Collections**). It's also responsible for the caretaking and installation of all public statues and monuments in the capital.

Budapest Galéria Kiállítóháza
III. Lajos utca 158 (188 6771). Tram 1. **Open** 10am-6pm Tue-Sun. **Admission** Ft50; Ft25 children. **No credit cards**.
Exhibition space for the Budapest Galéria. There are no differences between the two galleries, only the space and the material decides what goes where; because of the garden most sculptures are displayed here rather than downtown. It also houses a collection of classicist sculptures and statues by Imre Varga's tutor Pál Patszay.

Dorottya Galéria
V. Dorottya utca 8 (118 3899). M1 Vörösmarty tér.
Open 10am-6pm Mon-Fri; 10am-2pm Sat. **Admission** free. **No credit cards**.
A small exhibition space opened in the early 1960s and today rented by the Műcsarnok for smaller pieces of art and experimental work.

Duna Galéria
XIII. Pannónia út 95 (140 9186). M3 Dózsa György út.
Open 10am-6pm Tue-Sun. **Admission** free. **No credit cards**.
Exhibition space belonging to the Vigadó gallery, it deals mainly with the work of younger artists.

Ernst Museum
VI. Nagymező utca 8 (341 4355). M1 Opera. **Open** 10am-6pm Tue-Sun. **Admission** Ft50; Ft25 children; free Tue. **No credit cards**.
In 1912 the private collector Lajos Ernst created this exhibition space in a building full of artists' studios. The showroom is these days rented by the Műcsarnok and devoted to

This way for **Budapest Galéria Kiállítóterem.**

The **Ernst Museum** – *that's private collector Lajos rather than Dadaist and Surrealist Max.*

Hungarian contemporary art. Eventually it will house the Műcsarnok's permanent collection, accumulated over the years as donations and currently languishing in storage.

Fényes Adolf Showroom
VII. Rákóczi út 30 (322 5818). M2 Blaha Lujza tér. **Open** depending on exhibit. **Admission** depending on exhibit. **No credit cards.**
Up until recently owned by the Műcsarnok, this salon now serves as an independent space which artists or groups can rent for shows or happenings.

Kempinski Galéria
Grand Hotel Corvinus Kempinski, V. Erzsébet tér 7-8 (266 1000). M1, M2, M3 Deák tér/tram 47, 49. **Open** 8am-8pm daily. **Admission** free. **No credit cards.**
In the carpeted corridors of the Kempinski's first-floor gallery, domestic rural art as well as foreign contemporary works co-exist in well-balanced shows of a high standard.

Kilátó Galéria
Margitsziget, Víztorony (112 7472). Tram 1, 4, 6/bus 26. **Open** *May-Oct* 10am-6pm Tue-Sun. **Admission** Ft60; Ft40 children. **No credit cards.**
On the green island in the Danube, the UNESCO-protected water tower is now an exhibition space for hitherto unshown contemporary work. Organised by the Gönczöl Foundation, a diversity of art shows – including textiles, art groups, modernist painters and puppet-makers – have taken place over the last ten years. Open from May until late September or, weather permitting, October. A fascinating venue.

Ludwig Múzeum
Wing A, Buda Palace, I. Dísz tér 17 (175 9175). Várbusz from M2 Moszkva tér/bus 16. **Open** 10am-6pm Tue-Sun. **Admission** Ft100; Ft50 children; free Tue. **No credit cards.**
In 1989, Peter Ludwig, a German businessman, donated parts of his enormous contemporary art collection to the Hungarian state, which then was placed in the halls of the National Gallery. Now in a separate wing, the Ludwig museum contains some international pieces, some loans from Aachen (the centre of the Ludwig collection) and some temporarily exhibited pieces. The oldest painting is a Picasso from the 1950s, and the collection also includes a whole set

of American pop art by Warhol, Lichtenstein and Oldenburg, together with modern Italian, German and Austrian works. There is also a permanent exhibition of Hungarian avant garde art from the 1960s up to the present.

Műcsarnok
Palace of Exhibitions
XIII. Dózsa György út 37 (343 7401). M1 Hősök tere. **Open** 10am-6pm Tue-Sun. **Admission** Ft100; Ft50 children. **No credit cards.**
This magnificent and recently renovated neo-classical building, dating from 1896, houses the most renowned public gallery in Budapest. Originally a private institution, since 1945 it has belonged to the Ministry of Education and deals exclusively with contemporary art, both foreign and Hungarian. Andy Warhol, Gilbert & George and an assortment of Hungarian pop artists have been on show. It has a reputation for showing the very best of modern art. There are no permanent exhibits, but phone or check the listings press for up-to-date information.

Vigadó Galéria
V. Vigadó tér 2 (117 6222). M1 Vörösmarty tér/tram 2. **Open** 10am-6pm Tue-Sun (sometimes closed Sun when exhibitions are set up or taken down). **Admission** free. **No credit cards.**
A fin-de-siècle building designed by Frigyes Feszl that houses not only Budapest's second-best concert hall, but also a prominent exhibition space for members of the Hungarian Creative Artists' Assembly, who present their latest work in the spacious two-floor gallery. Together with its two other venues (the Duna Galéria and a small gallery in Újpest), the Vigadó has the largest number of exhibitions in Budapest – around 50 a year.

Commercial Galleries

Art-X Gallery
II. Pasaréti út 65 (393 1190). Bus 5 from Moszkva tér. **Open** 10am-6pm Mon-Fri; 10am-2pm Sat. **Admission** free. **Credit** AmEx, DC, JCB, MC, V.
The exhibition space in the green belt of Buda displays contemporary Hungarian painters as well as objects of applied

art: from dresses and pottery to icons, graphic art and furniture. Young talent finds a place alongside established artists. Art-X also has operations at the Hilton and in Szentendre, but these are more like gift shops than galleries.

BÁV Kortárs Művészeti Galéria
V. Bécsi utca 3 (118 4403). M1, M2, M3 Deák tér/tram 47, 49. **Open** 10am-6pm Mon-Fri; 10am-2pm Sat. **Admission** free. **Credit** AmEx, DC, JCB, MC, V.
A new venture by the country-wide BÁV chain of commission shops (*see chapter* **Shopping**), this gallery deals mainly with furniture, paintings, graphic art, engravings and sculpture by Hungarian contemporary artists. Close by, their Mese Galéria (Fairytale Gallery) on Károly körút 22 (117 7843/open 10am-6pm Tue-Fri) has popular illustrations for children's books, paintings and puppets. It's worth visiting even just for Károly Reich's graphic art and paintings.

Csontváry Terem
V. Vörösmarty tér 1 (118 4594). M1 Vörösmarty tér/tram 2. **Open** 10am-6pm Mon-Fri; 10am-2pm Sat. **Credit** AmEx, DC, JCB, MC, V.
The only worthwhile branch of the city-wide Képcsarnok chain of galleries – most of the others are little more than tourist shops. Housed in a hideous socialist-realist building, it's full of high-quality work, such as graphic art by Tot Amerigo and sculptures by Miklós Melocco.

Dovin Galéria
V. Galamb utca 6 (118 3524). M1 Vörösmarty tér. **Open** Mon-Fri noon-6pm; 11am-2pm Sat. **Admission** free. **Credit** AmEx, MC, V.
Established in 1993, the Dovin deals with work by young up-and-comers and provides an exhibition space for Hungarian artists with a reputation abroad, but unheard of at home, such as Péter Gémes and Márton Barabás.

Galéria '56
V. Falk Miksa utca 7 (269 2529). M3 Nyugati. **Open** noon-6pm Tue-Sat. **Admission** free. **No credit cards.**
Opened in 1992 and famous for being owned by Yoko Ono, this gallery focuses on internationally established artists such as Robert Mapplethorpe, Andy Warhol, Keith Haring and László Moholy-Nagy.

Gulácsy Galéria
V. Semmelweiss utca 4 (117 8245). M2 Astoria/tram 47, 49. **Open** 10am-6pm Mon-Fri. **Admission** free. **No credit cards.**
Owned by a collective of 15 modern painters and sculptors – including abstract colourist Ignác Kokas and expressionist Lajos Sváby – this acclaimed gallery adequately represents the contemporary Hungarian art scene.

Kieselbach Galéria
V. Falk Miksa utca 13 (112 2071). Tram 2, 4, 6. **Open** 10am-6pm Mon-Fri; 10am-1pm Sat. **Admission** free. **Credit** EC, MC, V.
This art-dealing salon was established in April 1995 by well-known art historian and connoisseur Tamás Kieselbach and his wife. They focus on Hungarian art from the turn of the century to World War II.

Koller Galéria
I. Táncsics Mihály utca 5 (156 9208). Várbusz from M2 Moszkva tér/bus 16. **Open** 10am-6pm Tue-Sun. **Admission** free. **Credit** AmEx, DC, JCB, MC, V.
With the ambience of an art lover's apartment, this hidden-away gallery (go through the gates and up the stairs on the

The Műcsarnok's exhibits of foreign and Hungarian contemporary art have included Andy Warhol and Gilbert & George.

right) is crowded with high-quality early-twentieth-century Hungarian art, plus works by Imre Varga and Endre Szász.

Körmendi Galéria
II. Nagybányai út 25 (266 4857). Bus 11. **Open** by appointment only.
V. Deák Ferenc u 15 (266 4857). M1, M2, M3 Deák tér/tram 47, 49. **Open** 10am-6pm Mon-Fri; 10am-2pm Sat. **Admission** free. **Credit** AmEx, MC, V.
A private collection of contemporary Hungarian art – incorporating grand masters such as Tot Amerigo and Victor Vasarely – was the basis on which the Körmendi was established in 1992. Exclusive and airy, these downtown showrooms contain an extensive bookshop and a café. Probably the only gallery for modern Hungarian altar-paintings.

Qualitás Galéria
V. Haris köz 1, 4th floor (118 4438/fax 266 3508). M3 Ferenciek tere. **Open** 10am-6pm Mon-Fri; 10am-1pm Sat. **Admission** free. **Credit** AmEx, DC, JCB, MC, V.
Specialists in seriously expensive work by twentieth-century Hungarian masters such as post-Impressionist József Rippl-Rónai, secessionist László Mednyánszky, fauvist Béla Czóbel and modernist Hugó Scheiber. In bright, stylish rooms overlooking Váci utca, true expertise and discretion await the serious buyer.

Rózsa Galéria
I. Szentháromság utca 15 (155 6866). Várbusz from M2 Moszkva tér/bus 16. **Open** 11am-6pm Tue Fri; noon-6pm Sat, Sun.* **Admission** free. **Credit** AmEx, EC, JCB, MC, V.
Established by 'folkart-educator' Csilla Szabó in 1992, the Rózsa is unique in promoting contemporary naive art. It's all evaluated by a jury and categorised as folk art, which means foreign buyers get their VAT back. The best-known of their artists is probably Pál Homonai, whose works appear almost every year on UNICEF Christmas cards.

Experimental & Alternative

Artpool Art Research Centre
VI. Liszt Ferenc tér 10 (268 0114/fax 121 0833). M1 Oktogon/tram 4, 6. **Open** 2-6pm Wed, Fri. **Admission** free. **No credit cards.**
A unique centre for the research and documentation of the Hungarian avant garde, Artpool began as an illegal private institution in 1979, lead by Júlia Klaniczay and visual artist György Galántai. Now supported by the local council, the centre highlights different themes each year, such as Fluxus or mail art. A gallery is opening sometime in 1996. Meanwhile the library, the sound and video archives and the bookshop are open to the public two days a week.

Várfok 14 Gallery
I. Várfok utca 14 (115 2165). M2 Moszkva tér. **Open** 10am-6pm Wed-Sun. **Admission** free. **No credit cards.**
One of the first experimental galleries in the city now also displays well-known modern artists such as El Kazovszkij and Imre Bukta. On the slopes of Castle Hill, a diminutive and friendly space full of the latest art in town.

Collections

Imre Varga Exhibit
Varga Imre Állandó Kiállítás
III. Laktanya utca 7 (250 0274). HÉV Árpád híd. **Open** 10am-6pm Tue-Sun. **Admission** Ft50; Ft35 children. **No credit cards.**
Hungary's most renowned living sculptor has a tainted reputation as a favoured artist of the Communist regime, but his unquestionable talent is demonstrated in this wonderful

collection (minus, of course, the Lenin statues he had to do). His figures – usually in impressionistically worked bronze or sheet metal – evoke warmth and amusement (a portly grandmother) and sadness (the headless soldiers series). The garden houses some of his most touching portraits, those of martyred poet Miklós Radnóti, and sculptor Alajos Stróbl. Varga himself, now in his mid-seventies, is often here on Saturday mornings.

Kassák Museum
Zichy Mansion, III. Fő tér 1 (168 7021). HÉV Árpád híd. **Open** 10am-6pm Tue-Sun. **Admission** Ft40; Ft20 children. EB Ft200, texts in German.
Lajos Kassák (1887-1967), one of the country's main avant garde artists and poets, led Hungary's constructivist movement and was also editor of the journal *Ma* (*Today*). He spent most of his life both on the cutting edge of current cultural and political trends and inevitably in opposition to them as they became popular. There are permanent and temporary exhibits of his art, plus documents that won't mean much if you don't know anything about him, but the museum also has good, temporary exhibitions on twentieth-century artists and photographers, sometimes with English text.

Molnár C Pál Gyűjtemény
XI. Ménesi út 65 (185 3637). Tram 61. **Open** 3-6pm Tue-Thur; *Oct-Apr* 3-6pm Tue-Thur, 10am-1pm Sun. **Admission** Ft90; Ft50 children. **No credit cards**.
In the former studio of graphic artist, painter and illustrator Pál C Molnár (1894-1981) you can have the pleasure of meeting his daughter, Eva Csillag, who entertains visitors with stories about Hungary's most famous Surrealist painter and graphic artist. M-C P, as he signed his paintings, was

preoccupied with Christian themes and created many altarpieces. This private collection also contains many of his best-known graphic works.

Vasarely Museum
III. Szentlélek tér 6 (188 7551/250 1523). HÉV Árpád híd/tram 1. **Open** 10am-6pm Tue-Sun. **Admission** Ft50; free children. **No credit cards**.
In the historical part of Óbuda, Count Zichy's baroque eighteenth-century castle houses a unique exhibition of works by the Hungarian-born graphic artist and op-art painter Victor Vasarely (born Győző Vásárhelyi, 1908). Nearly 400 paintings and pieces of graphic art were donated by the artist, who these days lives in Paris, on condition that they should never be returned to France. There are temporary exhibits of other Hungarian-born artists living abroad.

Szentendre

Beer-drinking tourists, picnicking families, tacky giftshops and 'genuine' Hungarian restaurants are not all that the Szentendre of today has to offer. This picturesque town 20km to the north of Budapest has been an artist's colony since the early 1920s when Impressionists fleeing the big city moved out to nearby villages for peace and inspiration. The Szentendre Artists' Society was formed in 1928, and the town was inhabited by Naturalists and Impressionists as well as Modernists. The most significant settlers, such as Realist János Kmetty and

---

The Young Ones

The work of young artists – Fiatal Művészek – has long been the most vital sector of the Budapest scene. It's almost a movement, despite its lame name, and operates quite independently from the official art establishment. Unusual and uncompromising exhibits, readings, performances and installations – some of them actually quite good – can be found all over the city, if you know where to look.

The FMK – Fiatal Művészek Klubja, or **Young Artists' Club** – has been a centre of alternative action since the early 1960s. Closed down several times during the Communist years, these days it may have lost some of its dissident thunder but it's bigger than ever and welcomes not only artists, but anyone who just wants to hang out and mingle with what's left of the underground. On weekdays the club functions as a studio, with exhibits, installations and performance events, while at weekends there are often parties (concerts, a busy bar and some of the city's better DJs).

The young ones (and some older ones too) also congregate at the **Stúdió Galéria**, which hosts some of the most entertaining exhibitions in the city, including the Gallery by Night events at the Budapest Spring Festival (*see chapter* **Budapest**

By Season). These one-night performances can be anything from happenings to poetry readings and attract a self-consciously cool clientèle.

The Fiatal Iparművészek Stúdiója Galéria – **Young Applied Art Artists' Studio & Gallery** – has a different kind of profile. Members exhibit fanciful handmade dresses, mesmerising works of glass and exquisite, unwearable jewellery.

Stúdió Galéria
V. Képíró utca 6 (267 2033). M3 Kálvin tér. **Open** 2-6pm Mon-Fri when there's a show. **Admission** free. **No credit cards**.
Check local listings press for details of the Stúdió Galéria's springtime Gallery By Night events.

Young Applied Art Artists Studio & Gallery
Fiatal Iparművészek Stúdiója Galéria
V. Kálmán Imre utca 16 (111 3051). M3 Nyugati/tram 4, 6. **Open** noon-5pm Mon-Thur; noon-3pm Fri. **Admission** free. **No credit cards**.

Young Artists' Club
Fiatal Művészek Klubja
VI. Andrássy út 112 (131 8858). M1 Bajza utca. **Open** 10am-6pm Mon-Fri. **Admission** free. **No credit cards**.
See chapter **Music: Rock, Roots & Jazz**.

Owned by Yoko Ono, Galéria '56 exhibits Robert Mapplethorpe, Keith Haring and others.

Impressionist Károly Ferenczy, have their own museums. Still a refuge for many artists, Szentendre has several worthwhile studios and galleries.

Anna Margit – Ámos Imre Múzeum

2000 Szentendre, Bogdányi utca 10 (no phone). HÉV Szentendre. **Open** 10am-4pm Wed-Sun. **Admission** Ft60; Ft20 children. **No credit cards.**
Two very different personalities, lyric painter Imre Ámos and his partner Surrealist Anna Margit, lived together at this address before the Holocaust swallowed Ámos in 1944. The work of both artists is clearly inspired by Jewish themes, but while Ámos kept to dreams and visions, Anna Margit painted themes from life. Inspired by Chagall, Anna Margit was also one of the founders of the shortlived European School.

Arteria

2300 Szentendre, Rákóczy Ferenc utca 5 (26 310 111). HÉV Szentendre. **Open** 10am-6pm daily.
Founded by painters who left the Műhely Galéria, Arteria has wilder art than its neighbour. The one-room gallery is crammed with 'alternative' paintings, such as overrated works by István ef Zámbó & László fe Lugossy, and abstracts by Pal Deim, Imre Bukta and Imre Bak.

Czóbel Béla Múzeum

2000 Szentendre, Templom tér 1 (26 312 721). HÉV Szentendre. **Open** 10am-4pm Tue-Sun. **Admission** Ft60; Ft20 children. **No credit cards.**
One of Hungary's most prominent 20th century painters, Béla Czóbel (1883-1976) lived a long time in Paris, where he joined the Fauvist movement and hung out with Matisse before retreating to the artist colony of Szentendre. Here, influenced by the surroundings, he created his best work, such as *The Venus of Szentendre*, on display here along with earlier work.

Ferenczy Múzeum

2000 Szentendre, Fő tér 6 (26 310 790). HÉV Szentendre. **Open** 10am-4pm Tue-Sun. **Admission** Ft60; Ft20 children. **No credit cards.**

The works of the artist family Ferenczy spread over four bright and spacious floors. Károly Ferenczy's early works reveal traces of fine Naturalism but he later turned towards Impressionism. His wife Olga Fialka was an established Wiener Biedermeier painter. His eldest son Valér Ferenczy was only a mediocre talent but the twins Béni (who moved from Art Deco to Cubism and Naturalism in sculpture) and Noémi Ferenczy (who created Symbolist gobelin works) both earned a reputation as exalted as their father's.

Kmetty János Múzeum

2000 Szentendre, Fő tér 21 (26 310 790). HÉV Szentendre. **Open** 10am-6pm Tue-Sun. **Admission** Ft60; Ft20 children. **No credit cards.**
Apart from Béla Czóbel, János Kmetty (1889-1975) was the only Hungarian representative of the French school. He experimented with Pointilism, Impressionism and Expressionism before settling for Cubism in the late 1920s. His fame finally made its way out of Hungary when he took part in the 1962 Venice Biennale.

Kovács Margit Múzeum

2000 Szentendre, Vastagh György utca 1 (26 310 790). HÉV Szentendre. **Open** 10am-6pm Tue-Sun. **Admission** Ft120; Ft30 children. **No credit cards.**
Margit Kovács (1902-77) was probably the most popular Hungarian sculptor ever. Over the years she created small porcelain figures and beautiful statues as well as decorated glazed wall panels and oven tiles. Her naive and personal works, collected in this eighteenth-century house just behind Fő tér, recall popular Hungarian traditions and mythology.

Műhely Galéria

2300 Szentendre, Fő tér 20 (26 310 139). HÉV Szentendre. **Open** 10am-6pm Mon-Sat. **Credit** AmEx, DC, V.
Some 20 painters, sculptors, silversmiths and graphic artists collectively own this gallery. A friendly place with surprisingly interesting stuff – including mosaics by György Hegyi, sculptures by Róbert Csikszentmihályi and paintings by Piroska Szántó, last representative of the European School.

Museums

*Transylvanian mummy powder, Cherokee Bibles and raw
sewage – where else could you hope to see such sights?*

If anything characterises a Hungarian museum,
it's the museum *néni* – the elderly female attendant
at every door. Elderly and poorly paid, the *néni* (or
male *bácsi*, at technical museums) is incredibly
proud of the exhibits in her charge and eager to
explain all in minute, gushing, Hungarian-only
detail. She exudes nostalgia for pre-war Hungary
but has been worn grey by Communist rule – not
unlike the relics she guards. Although she's unable
to catch up with modern times, you'll get a warm
reception for showing interest in 'her' museum.

With the post-Communist tourist boom you'd
imagine museums would make certain improve-
ments, such as printing texts in English, publicising events, updating exhibits or dusting the
display cases. You'd be wrong. The problem is
mainly financial. Like their OAP attendants, the
museums are poorly financed – cut off from government support, culture, like old people, becomes
a category forgotten in the mad scramble for fast
bucks. Cash shortages aside, more than a few institutions suffer from old-guard, unimaginative and
indifferent management. Many have vast amounts
of space they're unwilling to utilise, preferring to
keep things in the basement; or they use spaces
without publicising them, so you wander through
a museum and miss half of its treasures. Many
exhibits are crammed into dim, musty rooms while
historical displays tend to ignore most of the twentieth century and Jewish and Gypsy participation
in Hungarian society.

Nevertheless, things are looking up for the
major institutions – and you'll find museums in
Budapest on just about any subject imaginable.
The **National Museum** and **Budapest History
Museum** have recently been restored, reorganised
and expanded. Others, such as the **Ethnographic**,
Applied Arts, **György Ráth**, **Kiscelli** and
Music History museums offer excellent permanent displays despite other shortcomings. Even
the blandest have important or amusing highlights. The Socialist-era desire to promote working-class occupations and culture has resulted in
some exhibits you'd probably never find outside
the former Eastern bloc (though maybe you would
not want to).

Temporary exhibitions and small museums
rarely provide adequate English translations, if
any at all. Where indicated below, there's an
English booklet (EB) available – an Ft80 booklet,

for example, is noted as EB Ft80. Most are an inexpensive investment, given how low museum
admission prices usually are in Budapest. For the
exceedingly penurious, the large institutions often
have one free day a week.

Opening times are typically 10am-6pm from
Tuesday-Sunday, with last tickets given out 30-45
minutes before closing. Almost all (notable exceptions being the **Budapest History Museum**, the
Jewish Museum and **Statue Park**) are closed
Mondays. Between November and March, most
close an hour or two earlier than indicated below,
and some small museums shut entirely for the
winter, as well as in July or August. Art and music
are frequently combined, with concerts held in
the grander buildings or, of course, other music-
related museums – especially during the spring
and autumn festivals and in the summer.

The *Budapest Week* and *Budapest Sun* carry
information on hours, concerts and temporary
exhibitions.

National Institutions

Museum of Applied Arts
Iparművészeti Múzeum
*IX. Üllői út 33-37 (217 5222). M3 Ferenc körút/tram 4,
6.* **Open** 10am-6pm Tue-Sun. **Admission** Ft80; Ft20
concs; free Tue. **No credit cards.**
Established in 1872 to showcase Hungarian art objects and
furnishings which had won acclaim at international exposi-
tions, it found its permanent home in this magnificent Ödön
Lechner-designed building opened at the 1896 Millennium.
The permanent exhibition of furniture and objets d'art, 'Style
Periods of the Applied Arts in Europe', is clearly explained
in English with much historical context. Mainly nineteenth-
century, the items range from a Viennese ivory cigar holder
and a rose-festooned Rococo vase from St Petersburg to
Parisian gowns and mother-of-pearl inlaid furnishings from
Turkey. The colours and style of a dazzling Zsolnay stove
resemble those of the Zsolnay-tiled building itself. Other
important items are collecting dust in the back – few visitors find out about the Fabergé eggs, Tiffany glass and
Lalique crystal in a back room near the staircase.

Museum of Ethnography
Néprajzi Múzeum
*V. Kossuth Lajos tér 12 (132 6340). M2 Kossuth
tér/tram 2.* **Open** 10am-6pm Tue-Sun. **Admission**
Ft100; Ft30 concs; free Tue. Call to arrange guided tour in
English, Ft2,000.
Despite its poor planning and unwillingness to rotate an
enormous collection (too much of which languishes in the
basement), this extremely worthwhile museum offers a com-
prehensive illustration of Hungarian village and farm life,

The **Statue Park** *is a dumping ground for monuments that have had their Marxing orders.*

folk customs and gorgeous folk art. Each display is accompanied by good English text, rendering the rented cassette from the front desk unnecessary. The exhibition starts one flight up on the left with regional folk costumes. A 1909 map gives a colour-coded breakdown of the many ethnic minorities in the region. The museum also usually has two or three temporary photo exhibitions on at a time – recent topics included Gypsies in the twentieth century, current peace movements in Serbia, and the Khazakhs of Western Mongolia. It also usually hosts the World Press Photo exhibition every March. The building is anything but folky – a monumental, gilt-columned edifice with ceiling frescoes by Károly Lotz, constructed in 1893-96 to serve as the Supreme Court, though it never did. The management appears to do more catering than curating – on many days you'll find the centre hall set up for banquets for visiting dignitaries.

Museum of Fine Arts

Szépművészeti Múzeum
XIV. Hősök tere (268 0090). M1 Hősök tere. **Open**
10am-5.30pm Tue-Sun. **Admission** Ft200; Ft100 concs.
English tours (Ft1,500 for up to five people) can be arranged on the spot in summer, otherwise contact Zoltán Bartos on ext 137.
While the National Gallery is Hungary's chief venue for Hungarian art, the country's major display of European art is here: a world-class including a dozen El Grecos and Goyas, an excellent Venetian collection (particularly Titian and Giorgioni), as well as ancient Egyptian and Greco-Roman artefacts, Dutch and Flemish art (Breugel, Rembrandt and Memling), Baroque statues, and works – though not the best ones – by the main French Impressionists. The

vast collection of drawings and graphics from the Renaissance to the present is generally rotated in small, temporary exhibits. The museum also stages major temporary exhibitions in the grand, eclectic halls leading from the entrance.

Hungarian National Gallery

Magyar Nemzeti Galéria
I. Buda Palace, Wings B, C, E (175 7533 ext 423).
Várbusz from M2 Moszkva tér/bus 16. **Open** *Apr-Oct*
10am-6pm Tue-Sun; *Nov-Mar* 10am-4pm. **Admission**
Ft100; Ft40 concs; guided tour Ft1,200 up to five people.
This vast museum's purpose is to chronicle art by Hungarians since the founding of the state, and requires more than one visit to take in all of the permanent exhibits of paintings, sculptures, ecclesiastical art, medallions and graphics. The two collections considered most important are its fifteenth/sixteenth-century winged altarpieces (so-called because of their ornately carved pinnacles which create a light, soaring effect); and its mid-nineteenth- to early twentieth-century art. Most of the work here is derivative of major European art movements such as Classicism, Impressionism, Fauvism, Art Nouveau. There are depictions of Hungarian history by Viktor Madarász and lively sculptures of Hungarian peasants by Miklós Izsó. Three prominently represented artists are Mihály Munkácsy, a Courbet-influenced Realist who was world-famous in his time, Pál Szinyei Merse, the 'Hungarian Impressionist', and László Pál, known for his Barbizon School-influenced landscapes. The Gallery, along with the Museum of Fine Arts (devoted to non-Hungarian works) also hosts important temporary exhibitions. For a separate, 50Ft entrance fee, one can enter (with a guide only) the Palatine Crypt beneath the museum, built in 1715 as part of the Habsburg reconstruction of the palace.

National Museum

Nemzeti Múzeum
VIII. Múzeum körút 14-16 (138 2122). M3 Kálvin tér/tram 47, 49. **Open** 10am-6pm, *winter* 10am-5pm, Tues-Sun. **Admission** Ft40.

The oldest museum in Budapest was also the site of the reading of Petőfi's 'National Song' on 15 March 1848, which heralded the start of the revolt against Habsburg domination. At the time of writing, its most famous item – St Stephen's Crown – is the only thing on view while the museum undergoes much-needed restoration and reorganisation. But it's due to reopen bit by bit on key holidays throughout 1996: The History of Hungary in the Eighteenth and Nineteenth Centuries on 15 March (National Day); The History of Hungary from the Establishment of the State up to the Seventeenth Century on 20 August (St Stephen's Day); and The History of Hungary in the Twentieth Century on 23 October (Remembrance Day). From 15 March until the end of 1996 there'll also be a temporary exhibit, The Magyars of the Conquest Period. The Hungarian Crown and Other Regalia is always open.

National Széchenyi Library

Országos Széchenyi Könyvtár
I. Buda Palace, Wing F (175 7533). Várbusz from M2 Moszkva tér/bus 16. **Admission** 40Ft, 20Ft concs, for exhibits; passport required to enter library. **Open** 10am-4.30pm Mon, Tue; 10am-6pm Wed-Fri.

The seven-storey national library houses over 2 million books plus even more manuscripts (as well as collections on music, theatre history, graphics, newspapers and journals), with the aim of gathering anything related to Hungary or in Hungarian published anywhere in the world. If you wish to conduct research there or just look round, bring your passport and ask for English-speaking staff who will help you with the interesting (if a bit noisy) retrieval system by which books are sent down on automated carts. The library is named after Count Ferenc Széchenyi (father of the nineteenth-century reformer, István) who donated his library to the state in 1802. The institution possesses volumes (codices, or *corvina* in Hungarian) which belonged to King Mátyás, who owned one of the largest libraries in Renaissance Europe. These are rarely displayed, however. The exhibits on the first floor usually concern Hungarian and German writers, but there are occasional displays of book illustrations. The library also offers an interesting way to reach the Castle if you're coming from the west side of Castle Hill; there's an elevator (Ft10) that takes you from the bottom of the hill (near buses 78 and 5 or tram 18 in the Tabán) into the library wing of the palace.

History

Agriculture Museum

Mezőgazdasági Múzeum
XIV. Vajdahunyad Castle in Városliget (343 8573). M1 Hősök tere. **Open** 10am-5pm Tue-Sat; 10am-6pm Sun. **Admission** Ft60; Ft20 concs. EB Ft100. **No credit cards.**

Antique ploughs and the history of cattle breeding sit oddly inside the mock-Baroque wing of a fake Transylvanian castle. The dozen exhibits range from snoozers such as the History of Grain Production to one on the Hungarian rural ritual pig killing. The hunting hall has rows of stuffed stags and shelved antlers beneath a magnificently vaulted and painted ceiling.

Aquincum Museum

Aquincumi Múzeum
III. Szentendrei út 139 (250 1650). HÉV Aquincum. **Open** *ruins (Apr-Oct)* 9am-6pm Tue-Sun; *museum* 9am-5pm Tue-Sun. **Admission** Ft100; Ft60 concs. EB Ft400. Workers' housing estates and a highway dwarf the numer-

ous Roman ruins scattered throughout Óbuda. The largest concentration is at this site, where most of Aquincum's 4,000 or so residents lived. Don't expect to find anything very grand; most of the ruins are just crumbling walls. There's a small amphitheatre across the road by the HÉV station, usually open the same hours, or by request at the museum. The museum has one remarkable item: a replica of a second-century Roman water organ found at the site in 1931 – the only one ever found that was complete enough to be replicated. Within the vast Flórián tér underpass, the so-called Baths Museum – ruins of Roman baths – are closed indefinitely but you can pretty much view these unexciting remnants from outside the glass enclosure. Likewise, the Hercules Villa is out of the way on a suburban street and merely comprises what little is left of a Roman official's villa, with a few faded pieces of mosaic depicting the legendary strongman.

Hercules Villa, *III. Meggyfa utca 19-21 (250 1650).*

Banknote & Coin Collection of the Hungarian National Bank

Magyar Nemzeti Bank Bankjegy-és Éremgyűjteménye
V. Szabadság tér 8 (153 2600 ext 1532). M3 Arany János utca. **Open** 9am-2pm Thur or by appointment. **Admission** free (plus English-speaking guide).

In a room at the National Bank, a display of 1,200 coins from nearly every kingdom, principality and government since King Stephen, as well as one or two cases of commemorative issues.

Budapest History Museum

Budapesti Történeti Múzeum
I. Buda Palace, Wing E (155 8849). Várbusz from M2 Moszkva tér/bus 16. 10am-6pm Mon, Wed-Sun. **Admission** Ft100; Ft50 concs; free Wed. **No credit cards.**

The main exhibit on Budapest starts from the earliest tribal settlements, with lots of interesting artefacts, photos of excavations and good descriptions in English. Until recently the '2,000 years of Budapest' exhibit was actually about three-quarters of that – it ended with the Turkish occupation. By the time you read this, though, it should have been updated to the present. A dark room is full of ghoulish Gothic statues pre-dating King Mátyás unearthed at the castle. The lower levels are partially reconstructed remains of his palace, including a vaulted chapel and music room. The upper floor houses temporary exhibits, usually on other historical topics. They're not always well-documented in English but the museum seems to be improving in that respect.

Catacombs & Wax Museum

Panoptikum
I. Úri utca 9 (175 6858). Várbusz from M2 Moszkva tér/bus 16. **Open** 10am-6pm Tue-Sun; closed Dec-Jan. **Admission** Ft250; Ft120 concs. **No credit cards.**

The worst – and most expensive – exhibit in Budapest unfortunately offers the only way into Castle Hill's 10km network of underground caves and manmade passageways (*see also chapter* **Sightseeing**). This poor excuse for a museum, for which there are mandatory tours in bad English every 15 minutes, offers mouldy, sloppy wax figures of medieval Hungarian historical figures and a few torture instruments.

Museum of Military History

Hadtörténeti Múzeum
I. Tóth Árpád sétány 40 (156 9522). Várbusz from M2 Moszkva tér. **Open** 10am-5pm Tue-Sat; 10am-6pm Sun. **Admission** Ft100; Ft50 concs; free Sat; Ft500 guided tour. **No credit cards.**

Though there's lots of room in this eighteenth-century barracks you won't find much here other than rows and rows

Opposite: under restoration, the **National Museum** *is due to reopen bit by bit in 1996.*

of boring cases full of Hungarian documents, photos and unremarkable weapons from the 1791 and 1848 revolutions and the two World Wars. The temporary exhibits usually aren't up to much either.

Óbuda Local History Exhibit
Óbudai Helytörténeti Gyűjtemény
Zichy Mansion, III. Fő tér 1 (250 1020). HÉV Árpád híd.
Open 2-6pm Tue-Fri; 10am-6pm Sat, Sun. **Admission** Ft50; Ft15 concs.
A single corridor of the mansion displays old photos and artefacts on Óbuda, plus rooms set up in Secession and Sváb (ethnic German) styles, and a delightful room full of toys, including a Herend tea service for dolls.

Semmelweis Museum of Medical History
Semmelweis Orvostörténeti Múzeum
I. Apród utca 1-3 (175 3533). Tram 18. **Open** 10.30am-5.30pm Tue-Sun. **Admission** Ft60; Ft20 concs; Ft400 tour in English.
Known as the 'saviour of mothers', Dr Ignác Semmelweis (1818-63) discovered the cure for puerperal fever, blood poisoning contracted during childbirth. He was born in this building and it displays his possessions, but more interesting is the exhibit on the history of medicine. The items, from all over the world, include a medieval chastity belt, eighteenth-century beeswax anatomical models and a portrait of Hungary's first female doctor, Vilma Hugonai. Another room contains the 1786 Holy Ghost Pharmacy transported whole from Király utca.

Statue Park
Szobor Park
XXII. Balatoni út (227 7446). Yellow bus for Érd from Kosztolányi Dezső tér/tram 49. **Open** *May-Sept* 8am-8pm, *Oct-Feb* 10am-dusk, daily. **Admission** Ft100.
One of Europe's most unique museums is a dumping ground on the south-west edge of the city for the politically undesirable monuments of the Communist era. The outdoor museum was opened in 1993 after the 42 works were removed from prominent positions in the city. Most are in blocky socialist-realist form, and some are quite massive – such as a terrifying sailor modelled on a call-to-arms poster by the 1919 Communist government, and a Soviet soldier that used to guard the Liberation Monument. With your ticket you'll get a sheet outlining the statues' layout, date, artist and former location, but for further information you'll need to purchase the Ft400 catalogue. The ticket booth also sells commie kitsch and drinks such as the 'Molotov cocktail'.

Arts

Ferenc Hopp Museum of Eastern Asiatic Arts
Kelet-Ázsia Művészeti Múzeuma
VI. Andrássy út 103 (322 8476). M1 Bajza utca. **Open** 10am-6pm Tue-Sun. **Admission** Ft40; Ft10 concs; free Tue. EB Ft470.
One of two major Asian art collections in Budapest (the other is at the **György Ráth Museum** nearby), this features ancient works, including Buddhist art in China dating as far back as the tenth century; Lamaist scroll paintings; and Gandhara sculpture, third- to sixth-century Indian art influenced by ancient Greece. By the end of his life and after five trips round the world, Hopp (1833-1919), a successful businessman turned collector, had amassed over 4,000 pieces.

György Ráth Museum
VI. Városligeti fasor 12 (342 3916). Trolleybus 70, 78. 10am-5.45pm Tue-Sun. **Admission** Ft 40; free concs & Tue.
Chinese and Japanese works make up this excellent collec-

tion in the former home of the artist and art historian who collected them. The displays are accompanied by English texts more detailed than most in Hungarian museums. Note the wonderful snuff bottles, scroll paintings and tools in the Chinese collection, and the miniature shrines, Samurai armour and finely carved lobster on a laquer comb in the Japanese rooms upstairs. There are also temporary exhibitions from other Far Eastern countries.

Kiscelli Museum
III. Kiscelli utca 108 (188 7817). Tram 17 then bus 165. **Open** 10am-6pm Tue-Sun. **Admission** Ft100; Ft30 concs.
This Baroque Trinitarian monastery (built 1745) atop a wooded hill in Óbuda houses an important collection of Hungarian art from about 1880-1990. The works, displayed upstairs, include late nineteenth- to early twentieth-century masters and paintings influenced by the Impressionists, pre-Raphaelites, Cubists and Surrealists. Among them are Rippl Rónai's *My Parents After 40 Years of Marriage*, János Kmetty's cubist *City Park*, and works by Alajos Ströbl, Károly Ferenczy, Margit Anna and many others. There are also engravings of eighteenth- to nineteenth-century Budapest – you'll recognise the vantage point from what is now Petőfi bridgehead in Pest, in a 1866 engraving by Antal Ligeti, showing the newly built Chain Bridge, the church at Kálvin tér, the Castle Hill and Citadella, and the twin domes of the new Dohány utca Synagogue. Downstairs are the Golden Lion Pharmacy (formerly at Kálvin tér), old printing presses, and classical statuary from early nineteenth-century Pest façades. The most atmospheric part of the complex, however, is the ruined church, its bare brick walls left intact after bombing in World War II and transformed into a dim, ghostly gallery.

Zsigmond Kun Folk Art Collection
Kun Zsigmond Népművészeti Gyűjtemény
III. Fő tér 4 (no phone). HÉV Árpád híd. **Open** 2-6pm Tue-Fri; 10am-6pm Sat, Sun. **Admission** Ft60; Ft20 concs. EB Ft30.
'Zsigi bácsi' (Uncle Sigi), as the attendants affectionately refer to him, is a 103-year-old ethnographer who formerly lived in this eighteenth-century apartment. It now serves as a showcase for his charming collection of folk art: about 1,000 pieces from all over nineteenth- and early twentieth-century Hungary, including handpainted furniture, textiles, pottery and carvings. Particularly notable are ceramics from his hometown Mezőtúr in northern Hungary and the replica of a peasant stucco oven.

Literature

Petőfi Museum of Literature
Petőfi Irodalmi Múzeum
V. Károlyi Mihály utca 16 (117 3611). M3 Ferenciek tere. **Open** *Apr-Oct* 10am-6pm Tue-Sun; *Nov-Mar* 10am-4pm Tue-Sun. **Admission** Ft60; Ft20 concs.
Considering the scope of Hungarian literature, Budapest's main museum on the topic does a half-hearted job of demonstrating it. Much of Hungarian literature is lost on the rest of the world because of the obscure language and a hard-to-translate literary idiom. There's also almost nothing in English at this museum about the romanticised portraits and personal effects of Sándor Petőfi and other writers on display. The building warrants some historical explanation but this too is neglected. It was the Budapest mansion of the aristocratic Károlyi family, whose most famous scion, Mihály, was born here and headed Hungary's first, but short-lived,

Opposite: the **Museum of Applied Arts** *was established in 1872 to showcase Hungarian art objects and furnishings.*

Hungarian Museum of Electrotechnics – *men in white coats demonstrate things that go pop.*

democratic government in 1918. There used to be a memorial to him here, but this was removed (possibly because the conservative government elected in 1990 didn't like him). There are also a number of preserved apartments of other late, great and largely untranslated Hungarian writers. These, which have little English documentation, include:
Endre Ady Memorial Room (Ady Endre Emlékszoba) *V. Veres Pálné utca 4-6 (137 8563). M3 Ferenciek tere.* **Open** 10am-6pm Wed-Sun. **Admission** Ft60; Ft20 concs.
Mór Jókai Memorial Room (Jókai Mór Emlékszoba) *XII. Költő utca 21 (156 2133). Bus 21.* **Open** 10am-2pm Wed-Fri; 10am-4pm Sat, Sun. **Admission** Ft60; Ft20 concs.
Attila József Memorial Room (József Attila Emlékszoba) *IX. Gát utca 3 (117 3143). Tram 24.* **Open** 10am-4pm Tue-Sat; Sun 10am-3pm. **Admission** Ft60; Ft20 concs.

Music

Béla Bartók Memorial House
Bártók Béla Emlékház
II. Csalán utca 29 (176 2100). Bus 5. **Open** 10am-5pm Tue-Sun. **Admission** Ft50; Ft20 concs.
The composer lived here with his wife and two sons from 1932 until he left an increasingly fascist Hungary in 1940. The house has some of his original furnishings and an exhibit of Bartók memorabilia, such as commemorative stamps. Chamber concerts are often held here on Fridays (*see chapter* **Music: Classical & Opera**). In good weather they take place outside, by Imre Varga's Bartók statue.

Kodály Memorial Museum & Archive
Kodály Emlékmúzeum és Archívum
VI. Andrássy út 87-89, in courtyard (142 8448). M1 Kodály körönd. **Open** 10am-4pm Wed; 10am-6pm Thur-Sat; 10am-2pm Sun. **Admission** Ft20; Ft10 concs.
This was where Zoltán Kodály lived from 1924 until his death in 1967. His library, salon and dining room were left

in their original state, with an eclectic range of furnishings as well as folk art objects the composer bought while collecting songs. His bedroom displays manuscripts including parts of the *Psalmus Hungaricus* and *Buda Castle Te Deum*.

Franz Liszt Museum
Liszt Ferenc Múzeum
VI. Vörösmarty utca 35 (322 9804 ext 16). M1 Vörösmarty utca. **Open** 10am-6pm Mon-Fri; 9am-5pm Sat. **Admission** Ft50; Ft20 concs; free Mon.
Free concerts most Saturday mornings. Liszt lived here from 1881 until his death in 1886. The three-room apartment is preserved with his furniture and other possessions, including a composing desk-cum-keyboard. Text in English.

Museum of Music History
Zenetörténeti Múzeum
I. Táncsics Mihály utca 7 (175 9011 ext 164). Várbusz from M2 Moszkva tér. **Open** 4-8pm Mon; 10am-6pm Wed-Sun. **Admission** Ft40; Ft20 concs. EB Ft20. **No credit cards.**
Beethoven was a guest here in 1800, when it was the palace of the Erdődy family. Within are many gorgeous, seventeenth- to nineteenth-century classical and folk instruments. These vary from delicately ornamented lyres and a unique, tongue-shaped violin in the classical section, to the gardon (a crude cello), bagpipes and cowhorns in the folk section. The minimalist, orderly arrangement of the exhibit puts the beauty of the instruments in full focus. As well as temporary exhibits of musically themed contemporary art, there is also a collection of Bartók manuscripts.

Theatre

Gizi Bajor Theatre Museum
Bajor Gizi Színészmúzeum
XII. Stromfeld Aurél út 16 (156 4294). Bus 112. **Open** 2-6pm Tue-Thur; 10am-6pm Sat, Sun. **Admission** Ft50; Ft25 concs.

This lovely, turn-off-the-century villa was once home to theatre and film actress Gizi Bajor (1893-1951). The exhibit is devoted to actors of the Hungarian National Theatre and early cinema, with lots of old photographs and Bajor's original furnishings.

Religion

Bible Museum

Biblia Múzeum
IX. Ráday utca 28 (no phone). M3 Kálvin tér. **Open** 10am-5pm Tue-Sun. **Admission** free. EB Ft160.
'3,000 years of the Holy Bible', mainly facsimiles, pictures and texts in a dusty room at a Calvinist seminary, is mostly the sort of exhibit to which reluctant Sunday school students are dragged. There are some interesting items, though, such as a 1534 Hebrew Bible from Basel and a 1599 12-language New Testament from Nuremberg. In the corridor are missionary Bibles in languages such as Tamil, Khmer and Cherokee.

Ecclesiastical Art

Egyházművészeti Gyűjtemény
I. Mátyás Templom, Szentháromság tér (no phone). M2 Moszkva tér then Várbusz/bus 16. **Open** 9am-7pm daily. **Admission** Ft80; Ft30 concs. **No credit cards.**
The exhibit begins in the partially reconstructed medieval crypt (take the stairs down from the south-east aisle of the church), in which there's a red marble sarcophagus containing bones from the Royal Tomb of Székesfehérvár and mediocre photos of the church taken after a 1994 terrorist bomb. A passageway leads back up to the St Stephen chapel, with walls showing scenes from the life of the first Hungarian king. The chapel and gallery above contain ecclesiastical treasures, nothing remarkable since the country's best are at Esztergom.

Jewish Museum

Zsidó Múzeum
VII. Dohány utca 2 (342 8949). M2 Astoria/tram 47, 49. **Open** Apr-Oct 10am-3pm Sun-Fri. **Admission** Ft100.
This small museum displaying mainly eighteenth- to nineteenth-century ritual objects from central and eastern Europe, is located in a wing of the Great Synagogue complex and on the site where Zionist leader Theodore Herzl was born. Everything is well-documented in English, and there are English-speaking staff and tours. The collection is arranged in three rooms according to function: Sabbath, holidays, and life-cycle ceremonies. The fourth room covers the Hungarian Holocaust – one photo shows corpses piled up in front of this same building after a massacre by Hungarian Arrow Cross fascists. What is missing from the museum – actually, from virtually all Hungarian museums – is any historical exhibit on pre-war Hungarian Jewry, though there are plans to open an archives section and create exhibits on the topic. Though the museum was founded in 1931 when Hungarian Jews were feeling fairly secure, many more objects were given to the collection after their owners were murdered in the Holocaust. In 1993, over 80 per cent of the collection was stolen but then recovered eight months later in Bucharest.

The Lutheran Museum

Evangélikus Múzeum
V. Deák tér 4 (117 4173). M1, M2, M3 Deák tér/tram 47, 49. **Open** 10am-6pm Tue-Sun. **Admission** Ft30; Ft10 concs. EB Ft80. **No credit cards.**
Adjoining Budapest's main Lutheran Church, this museum traces the history of the Reformation in Hungary. On display is a fascimile of Martin Luther's last will and testament (the church archive has the original); the first book printed in Hungarian, a New Testament from 1541; and a pulpit cover from 1650 with an embroidered tableau of the 12 apostles (who for some reason all have red noses) – in Lutheran churches usually one item with graven images was permitted. A small display commemorates Gábor Sztehló, a pastor who rescued over 2,000 Jewish children during World War II. There's some English text but also usually an English-speaking attendant who can better describe the exhibits.

Trades

Museum of Commerce & Catering

Kereskedelmi és Vendéglátói Múzeum
I. Fortuna utca 4 (175 6249). Várbusz from M2 Moszkva tér. **Open** Mar 15-Sept 30 10am-6pm Tue-Sun; Oct 1-Mar 14 10am-4pm. **Admission** Ft30; free concs. **No credit cards.**
The Commerce section features advertisements from 1900 through to the middle of this century, including Hungary's first electric billboard (the attendant will turn it on for you). It advertises Buck's Beer, with goats leaping toward a frothy mug. A truly bizarre highlight is a stuffed dog atop a His Master's Voice phonograph – which raps its paws against the glass case. There's little in English (just one page in an Ft90 brochure), but the ads are colourful and visual, and more interesting than the catering section next door with its antique baking tools and photographs of old coffee houses.

Golden Eagle Pharmaceutical Museum

Arany Sas Patikamúzeum
I. Tárnok utca 18 (175 9772). Várbusz from M2 Moszkva tér/bus 16. **Open** 10.30am-5.30pm Tue-Sun. **Admission** Ft60; Ft20 concs. EB Ft300. **No credit cards.**
The Golden Eagle was the first pharmacy in Buda established after the expulsion of the Turks, though it was originally in nearby Dísz tér and didn't move here till the mid-eighteenth century. The house, however, dates from the fifteenth century (one of the oldest in the Castle District). The museum is an eye-catching hodgepodge of Hungarian and pharmaceutical history in the Castle District – jugs and bottles from every era and part of the world, and old, hand-painted Hungarian pharmacy furnishings. Highlights are an excellent reconstruction of an alchemist's laboratory; mummy powder from Transylvania (believed to cure epilepsy); and a large painting of a sweet-faced nun performing, as monks and nuns did in the Middle Ages, the duties of a chemist. The staff speak English, German or French and can show you around.

Industry

Foundry Museum

Öntödei Múzeum
II. Bem József utca 20 (201 4370). Tram 4, 6. **Open** 10am-5pm daily. **Admission** Ft50; Ft10 concs. EB Ft30.
The original building of the Ganz Foundry (1845-1964), one of the big players in Hungary's industrial revolution, displays historical exhibits on metalwork, and cast-iron products from giant tram wheels to a woman-shaped stove.

Milling Industry Museum

Malomipari Múzeum
IX. Soroksári út 24 (215 4118). Tram 2, 4, 6. **Open** 9am-2pm Mon-Thur (or by appointment). **Admission** free. EB free.
The museum's environs – the working class District IX – are a freeze-frame from Hungary's Communist years. There's

Opposite: dial up a dodgy Hungarian pop song on a 1970 blower at the **Telephone Museum.**

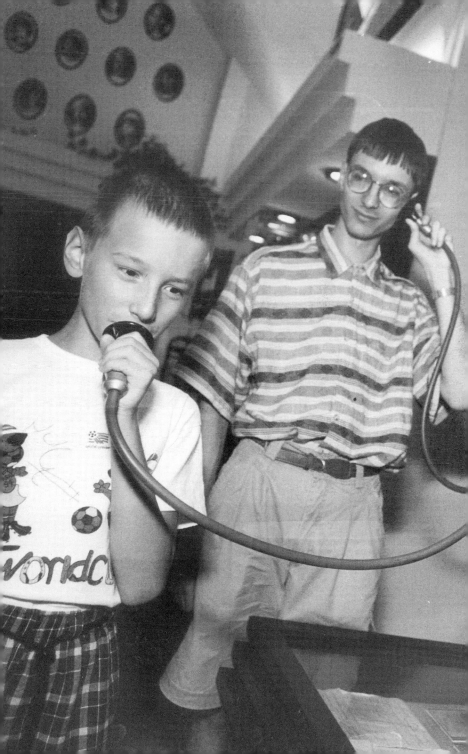

even a quote from Karl Marx right as you enter: 'The history of machinery can be followed through the development of the flour-milling industry'. Inside are lots of nineteenth-to early twentieth-century cylinder mills (*hengerszék*) and charming models (including a wind-operated ship mill).

Capital Sewerage Works Museum

Fővárosi Csatornázási Művek Múzeuma
II. Zsigmond tér 1-4 (188 6572). Tram 17. **Open** 10am-3pm Mon-Fri. **Admission** free. EB free.
Ring bell at gate.
Yes, this place is for real, and even whiffs just a little bit (it's still in operation). The museum is located in a modest, rather pretty brick and stucco building (1912) full of curvy, shiny, black pumps which look like giant snails. There's also a Secession-style Siemens switchboard.

Hungarian Museum of Electrotechnics

Magyar Elektrotechnikai Múzeum
VII. Kazinczy utca 21 (322 0472). M2 Astoria/tram 47, 49. **Open** 11am-5pm Tue-Sat. **Admission** free.
Housed in a 1930s transformer station, the outside of which looks like a set from Terry Gilliam's *Brazil*. Men in white coats demonstrate things that crackle and spark and proudly present the world's first electric motor, designed by a Hungarian Benedictine monk. There are also old household appliances and an exhibit on the electrification of the Iron Curtain. The collection of consumption meters is amusingly tedious, as are the switches throughout the ages.

Leisure

Sport & Training Museum

Testnevelési és Sportmúzeum
IV. Dózsa György út 3 (252 1695, ask for Sport Museum). M2 Népstadion. **Open** 10am-4.30pm Tue-Sun. **Admission** 30Ft; 15Ft concs.
Part of the huge 'People's Stadium' athletics complex. Temporary exhibits on current and past sports themes, in Hungarian only. An exhibit on '100 Years of Olympic History' is due to run until the end of the Atlanta Games.

Stamp Museum

Bélyeg Múzeum
VII. Hársfa utca 47 (342 3757). M1 Vörösmarty utca. **Open** 10am-6pm Tue-Sun. **Admission** Ft20; Ft5 concs.
No credit cards.
Thousands of stamps from every corner of the world. Kept in a large room above a post office, the collection resembles a well-organised card catalogue, with 3,000 pull-out boards of stamps organised by continent and country.

Public Services

Museum of Firefighting

Tűzoltó Múzeum
X. Martinovics tér 4 (261 3586), inside fire station. Tram 28. **Open** 9am-4pm Tue-Sat, 9am-1pm Sun. **Admission** free. EB free.
History of firefighting in Hungary, with items and reproductions from Aquincum, statues of St Florian (the patron saint of firemen), old photos and engravings, and a horse-drawn engine from 1899. By the time you read this the exhibit will have been restored and updated, so who knows what delights are in store?

Géza Kresz Emergency & Ambulance Service Museum

Kresz Géza Mentőmúzeum
V. Markó utca 22 (112 3430, ask for museum). M3 Nyugati. **Open** 8am-2pm Mon-Fri; 9am-2pm Sat, Sun. **Admission** Ft50, concs free.

Dr Kresz (1846-1901) founded Hungary's first volunteer ambulance service in 1887. Medical rescue history here is covered in excruciating Hungarian-only detail. Listed opening hours may prove unreliable.

Postal Museum

Posta Múzeum
VI. Andrássy út 3 (342 7938). M1, M2, M3 Deák tér/tram 47, 49. **Open** 10am-5.30pm Tue-Sun. **Admission** Ft20; free concs.
The richly frescoed and wainscoted former apartment of the wealthy Saxlehaner family now displays all things relating to the Hungarian postal service. The frescoes in the entrance and stairway are by Károly Lotz, whose frescoes also adorn the Opera House. The second room somehow manages both to preserve the appearance of a bourgeois home and to look like a workaday post office. Further on are old delivery vehicles and wartime radio transmitters. The good English text at the front desk will guide you through.

Telephone Museum

Telefónia Múzeum
I. Úri utca 49 (201 2243). Várbusz from M2 Moszkva tér. **Open** 10am-6pm Tue-Sun. **Admission** Ft30; Ft10 concs.
Though this place is touted as being great for kids, you'd have to have a doctorate in engineering to understand the long, dry, techie text in Hunglish (though there's an interesting page of references to phones in Hungarian literature). It might have once been exciting for Hungarian kids, many of whom didn't have phones at home until recent years (an irony since the switchboard was invented by a Hungarian, Tivadar Puskás – and anyone dealing with the Budapest phone system will suspect that they're still using his model). In any case, kids can ring up old-fashioned exchanges, or dial up a bad Hungarian pop song on a c1970 phone, and there are lots of old equipment and photos.

Transport

Transport Museum

Közlekedési Múzeum
XIV. Városligeti körút 11 (343 0565). Trolleybus 72, 74. **Open** 10am-5pm Tue-Fri; 10am-6pm Sat, Sun, holidays. **Admission** Ft60; free concs & Wed. EB Ft170.
Remains of the prewar Budapest bridges are displayed in front of this large museum, which covers every aspect of transport in Hungary in full but Hungarian-only detail. However, guided tours in English can be arranged in advance. Kids should enjoy the antique cars, trams, steam train and model boats, and can try out some of the engines in the big hall on the ground floor. The railroad models include one truly realistic miniature Hungarian countryside, with Stalinist high-rises on the town outskirts and A-frame weekend cottages, demonstrated at the top of the hour. The other part of the museum, Air & Space Travel, is a five-minute walk away, on the second floor of the Petőfi Csarnok concert hall (open 10am-6pm Tue-Sun, closed Nov-Mar, same admission fees). Small planes, gliders and helicopters fill two halls – the oldest a 1921 Junkers F13 and a replica of a 1909 monoplane. The aerospace section is dead boring.

Underground Railway Museum

Földalatti Múzeum
Inside Deák tér metro station, near Károly körút exit. M1, M2, M3 Deák tér/tram 47, 49. **Open** 10am-6pm Tue-Sun. **Admission** Ft35 or one transport ticket; free children.
If you're passing through Budapest's main metro intersection, pop in to have a look at several original carriages from continental Europe's first underground, built in 1896. For the centenary in 1996, Emperor Franz Joseph's reconstructed 'Royal' Carriage in which he test-drove the underground will probably be displayed here.

Arts & Entertainment

Media

The Communist regime forced journalists to write – and people to read – between the lines, but in the mid-1990s fact-based reporting is on the increase.

After more than half a decade of democracy, Hungary is still having problems coping with media freedom. Fifteen national daily newspapers compete for market share in a country of just ten million. Many are either internally divided or else heavily biased towards the conservative or liberal views they represent. The Hungarian press is also often accused of lacking a clear distinction between fact and opinion – a legacy of Communism, which forced journalists to write, and the public to read, between the lines. Fact-based journalism is, however, now becoming more widespread.

While newspapers were privatised after 1990, state TV and radio became the site of bitterly partisan politicking, particularly on the evening news programmes. President Göncz came under fierce attack when he refused to sack the heads of Hungarian TV and radio on the orders of the previous MDF administration. The row which developed, known as the 'media war', dominated Hungarian political discourse for years.

In 1993, fascist skinheads disrupted a speech by Göncz marking the anniversary of the 1956 revolution and the entire episode was broadcast on the national news. Six months later, the pro-government news programme on MTV1 accused the 'liberal' 10pm MTV2 news, *Esti Egyenleg*, of having doctored the videotape. The entire staff of the show was sacked, Hungarian radio was reshuffled and programmes which had not toed the party line were cancelled. Eventually, the courts found the news editors innocent, and the MDF government

paid by losing much public faith, a factor in their dismissal at the 1994 elections.

In late 1995, however, the new government had still not got around to Parliamentary debate on a much-discussed and urgently necessary Media Law. In the meantime, a frequency moratorium continued to hinder the launch of new national and local channels and doubts linger about the independence of state media.

The Press

Press freedom brought Hungary dozens of new publications. Many newspapers were privatised and are now published by foreign media groups; others live hand to mouth, fighting ever-increasing print bills.

Newspapers

Hungary has 15 national daily newspapers. Most are not published on Sundays.

Népszabadság
The most popular of the national dailies, this was once the official mouthpiece of the Communist government and continues to represent left-of-centre views. *Népszabadság* claims a readership of over one million, which implies that it is read by one-tenth of the population. Dry-looking and the closest thing Hungary has to a paper of record, it resembles the French *Le Monde*.

Magyar Hírlap
Bright and colourful, the *Hírlap* has been one of the largest and most influential dailies since 1968. It has a liberal attitude and a sharp focus on economy and finance. Published by the Swiss Marquard group.

Népszava
In the former regime, 120-year-old *Népszava* was the organ of the trades unions and relatively independent in outlook. Sustained by a loyal but ageing readership, it is known for the sharp critical voice with which it addresses the coalition government.

Világgazdaság, Napi Gazdaság
Both these financial dailies report on the stock exchange, shares and bonds, and quote currency exchange rates.

Mai Nap, Blikk, Kurír
The tabloid triumvirate. *Mai Nap* is the smallest, *Blikk* the most colourful and *Kurír* has the most gossip.

Expressz
The national daily classified ads paper and the ultimate place to look for everything from flats to pets. Budapesters, aware

*Same-day editions of the **Herald Tribune.***

Pre-1990, you tuned into TV1 or TV2, run by **Magyar Televízió** *– or you tuned into nothing.*

that the paper is already available the afternoon before official publication, queue up outside the editorial offices to snatch away bargains.

Periodicals

Buksz

Half of the country's best scholars use this literary quarterly to sharpen their pens on the works of the other half; the latter then usually go ahead and take revenge in the next issue. Patterned on the *New York Review of Books, Buksz* (the threatening title, a pun on 'books', actually means 'you'll fail') appears not only in Hungarian, but also in a shorter English version.

Heti Világgazdaság (HVG)

HVG (*Weekly World Economy*) focuses on politics, economics, financial and corporate issues and has been the most influential Hungarian weekly for over two decades. It resembles the *Economist*.

Magyar Narancs

Originally launched by the FIDESZ (Association of Young Democrats) in 1990, *Magyar Narancs* (*Hungarian Orange*) has since become independent. Fresh language, alternative views, a comprehensive listings supplement and an unprecedented tolerance towards minority, gay and drug issues have won it a large, young readership.

Listings Magazines

Pesti Műsor

Budapest's small-format what's-on bible is out every Wednesday. It features comprehensive listings of theatre performances, films, museums, galleries and concerts.

Pesti Est

Can be picked up free at cinemas and bars around town. The emphasis is on films, concerts and nightlife.

Foreign Press

Many British, American and international newspapers and magazines are available at hotels, from vendors on Váci utca and in the Castle district, and at major news kiosks. Apart from the *Guardian International* and *International Herald Tribune* only the previous day's papers will be available. Foreign dailies run out by early afternoon.

English-Language Publications

There are currently three English-language weeklies, written and edited by British and American journalists living in Budapest. These are all long-established, but it's a saturated market and any could still go under at any time.

Budapest Week

The oldest English-language weekly, around since 1991. A colourful tabloid, erratic but full of character, it's strong on news features, cultural events and eccentric columns. There's a business directory, a survival guide and detailed listings.

Budapest Sun

A large-format newspaper launched in 1993. Drier and more business-oriented than the *Week*, it's intensely American in style and focus and tends to treat the expat business community as if it was some kind of local aristocracy. Good for useful tips, though, and with a 'Style' supplement full of social columns and recipes.

Budapest Business Journal

Economy, finance and corporate news are the focus of this weekly, which also keeps an eye on major political events. The paper also runs the official, 24-page catalogue of the State Property Agency.

Hungary Around the Clock

An English news digest compiled from the Hungarian press and faxed or e-mailed to subscribers by 9am each business day. It costs $80 a month for individuals, $100 a month for schools and embassies, $150 a month for businesses. Call 268 1450/fax 322 2245/e-mail 100324.141@compuserve.com.

Econews

A daily economic and business news service with details of shares and bonds on the Budapest Stock Exchange. A three-month subscription costs around Ft25,000 (depending on current exchange rates). Call (118 8683) or fax (118 8204) the Hungarian press agency MTI for details.

The Hungary Report

Free weekly news digest in English e-mailed to subscribers. News shorts, features, political and business stories. E-mail (in the body, not the title of the message) the single word 'subscribe' to: hungary-report-request@hungary.yak.net.

Television

Before the democratic changes of 1990, TV1 and TV2, the two national channels run by Magyar Televízió (MTV), were the only ones available. The appearance of cable and satellite dishes did increase the competition, but MTV's critics make the point that importing *Dallas* and upping the amount of advertising per hour may not be the best response to the challenge. TV1 and TV2 remain the daily bread of Hungarians who do not speak other languages or starve for local and regional news.

TV1

The channel that Hungarians watch and criticise the most. A so-called 'public service' station, it has to meet the demands of all audiences – a virtually impossible mission. Besides the daily news programme *Híradó*, TV1 features minority, religious and children's programs, soap operas, sports, quizzes, talk shows and documentaries. Every night before closedown, the station runs the BBC news in English with Hungarian subtitles. Broadcast begins between 11pm-1am, depending on the length of the preceding programmes.

TV2

Parliamentary sessions live, political debates, sports events and the popular daily news analysis *Objektív* at 10pm.

Cable

Each Budapest district has one or two cable companies. Some offer more channels than others, but a basic selection of ten to 15 is available all over town and in most hotels.

HBO (Home Box Office) is the only movie channel available in Hungarian, mostly featuring dubbed Hollywood movies. The basic menu of unencrypted channels includes: Sky News, NBC Super Channel, CNN, Eurosport and TNT Cartoon Network in English, plus an assortment of German, French, Italian and Spanish services.

Encrypted satellite channels in English are FilmNet, the Discovery Channel, the Adult Channel and, since summer 1995, MTV Europe, which used to be unencrypted but got the hump because most cable companies had refused to pay the requested charges.

Local Cable

Currently about half of Budapest's districts boast a local cable channel, featuring news and music for a couple of hours a day. They borrow programmes from each other to rationalise costs.

A3

Sixteen hours a day broadcast to the Budapest area only. More visible round town than its rival, TV3. Creative director Péter Müller, brains behind the summer Sziget Festival (*see chapters* **By Season** *and* **Music: Rock, Roots & Jazz**), set up live A3 broadcasts in the square opposite Nyugati Station in the summer of 1995. Müller describes A3's policy as 'human TV for a certain group of young, open-minded people'. Music, talk shows, games.

Duna TV

This public satellite channel (disseminated via cable) broadcasts cultural programmes, documentaries and Hungarian films, and is available not only here but also in neighbouring countries with Hungarian minorities.

Top TV

Hungary's answer to MTV with 30 per cent space for Hungarian music. This national music channel, available on most cable networks, plans to present pan-European video clips.

TV3

Twelve hours a day broadcast to Budapest and surrounding area. The channel has run into financial problems since losing local government funding. Live Italian football on Sundays and plenty of international sport.

Radio

Kossuth

66.14-72.98 FM; 540 and 1116 AM; 6025 SW.
Kossuth broadcasts from 4.30am-midnight daily. News on the hour, foreign-language programmes for ethnic minorities, and the everlasting soap opera *A Szabó család* (*The Szabó Family* – Hungary's answer to *The Archers*).

Petőfi

66.02-72.77 FM; 873 and 1350 AM.
News, pop music, sports and political discussion.

Bartók

67.04-72.08 FM.
Classical music, both canned and live.

Radio Bridge

102.1 FM.
A selection of pop, rock and jazz; MTV Europe news in Hungarian several times a day, and the 30-minute news programme *Central Europe Today* in English at 8am Mon-Fri.

BBC World Service

The following are the best frequencies. All times GMT.
5-8.15am 6.195 mHz SW
6-8.15am 9.410 mHz SW
8am-5.45pm 12.095 mHz SW
8am-4.15pm 15.070 mHz SW
4-9.15pm 9.410 mHz SW
4-11pm 6.195 mHz SW
5-6.30am 6.180 mHz SW
5-10pm 6.180 mHz SW

Baths

Stretch out in the sauna or wallow in warm water pools and centuries of history, from Turkish occupation to Communist rule.

The Ottoman mosques, monasteries and schools that once filled the streets of Buda are all long gone, but the Turks did leave one enduring contribution to the life of the town: the bathhouses, several of which, centuries later, continue to offer variations on the theme of an Oriental soaking experience.

It was under the Ottoman empire that the culture of the baths reached its apogee, although bathing in Buda had been a tradition since Roman times. Buda has around 120 thermal springs and mineral-rich waters have long gushed up from the city's bedrock to fill the pools at sites such as the Király and Rudas baths.

This natural and abundant supply, combined with the demands of Islam that its followers adhere to a strict set of rules for ablution before praying five times a day, inspired an aquatic and hedonistic culture that still thrives today. Budapest's baths are some of the finest remains of the city's Ottoman architecture, complete with domed roofs and arches. Lolling in the warm water while the morning sun cuts through the rising steam, it's easy to imagine yourself as an Ottoman Pasha or valide sultan (Sultan's mother) reviewing the new recruits to the harem.

For an English speaker without much command of Hungarian, entering the baths for the first time can be a baffling experience. Most are still state-run and subsidised to keep prices down. Lengthy menus offer such treats as ultra-sound or a pedicure as well as massage. Instructions in Hungarian, German and Russian explain that customers can stay for an hour and a half, although this rule is not strictly enforced.

After buying a ticket you enter a warren of passageways where the entrance is guarded by a white-clothed attendant. Hand over your ticket and you will be given a white (well, it was white once) flap of cloth which is to be tied around your waist for modesty's sake. The ones for women also have an apron-like addition that supposedly covers the breasts, but few women bother to wear them at all. Men tend to keep theirs on, though, sometimes swivelling them round behind to prevent scorched buttocks on the wooden sauna seats.

Once in the changing rooms, either the attendant will show you a cubicle, or else you find one yourself, but each is locked twice and reliably secure. The attendant has one key and you keep the other: tie it to the spare string on your once-white cloth flap thing.

The baths generally have one or two main pools and a series of smaller ones around the perimeter, all of different temperatures, ranging from dauntingly hot to icily cold. The precise drill depends on individual preference, but involves moving between different pools, taking in the dry heat of the sauna and the extreme humidity of the steam rooms, alternating temperatures and finally relaxing in gentle warm water.

An hour or two of this is usually sufficient and extremely relaxing. The waters also ease stiff joints and rheumatic complaints. Afterwards you shower (take soap) and are provided with a towel (so don't bother taking one of those). All the baths have a rest-room, where customers can take a short nap and recover for a while before changing back into street clothes. On the way out, tip the attendant Ft20.

Apart from pools, saunas and steam rooms, most sites also offer a variety of medical treatments such as massages. These come in two types: vízi (water) massage and orvosi (medical) massage. Avoid the former, unless you want to feel as if you have been put through a meat grinder. The medical massage is a gentler experience. Masseurs are professional but inattentive, chatting away to their colleagues as they work. Tip them Ft100 or so.

A full visit to the baths demands a whole morning or afternoon. Ticket offices shut up shop an hour before listed closing times. There's usually

The **Széchenyi Gyógyfürdő és Strandfürdő**.

somewhere in the foyer to get a cold drink or a coffee. Don't expect to have the energy to do much afterwards except settle down for a long lunch or dinner, or head off home to stretch out for a nap.

Apart from the baths listed here, there are also limited thermal facilities at the Palatinus and Dagály strands. (*See also chapters* **Sport & Fitness** *and* **Gay & Lesbian**.)

Rudas Gyógyfürdő

I. Döbrentei tér 9 (156 1322). Tram 18, 19/bus 7. **Open** 6am-7pm Mon-Fri; 6am-1pm Sat, Sun. **Closed** Sun during summer (15 June-31 Aug). **Admission** Ft200.
This is the finest and most atmospheric of Budapest's original Turkish baths (men only, although the swimming pool is mixed), especially when rays of sunlight stream through the windows in the domed roof, cutting through the steam. The first baths on this site dated from the late fourteenth century. The new site was constructed by the Pasha of Buda in the sixteenth century and a plaque in his name still stands in the main chamber. The original cupola, vaulted corridor and main octagonal pool all remain, although they have been heavily restored. The Rudas has three saunas and two steam rooms as a well as six pools of differing temperatures. This is the straightest of the baths, although if you visit alone and someone comes to sit next to you he probably wants to be friends.

Király Gyógyfürdő

II. Fő utca 84 (201 4392). M2 Batthyány tér. **Open** *men* 6.30am-7pm Mon, Wed, Fri; *women* 6.30am-7pm Tue, Thur, Sat. **Admission** Ft170.
Along with the Rudas, the Király is one of the city's most significant Ottoman monuments, particularly the sixteenth-century pool. It takes its name from the nineteenth-century owners, the König family, who changed their name to its Hungarian equivalent – Király. Construction began in 1566 and was finished by Pasha Sokoli Mustapha in 1570. The Király follows the traditional pattern of a main pool, surrounded by small ones of a different temperature, together with saunas and steam rooms, but is not as beautiful as the Rudas. The bath's environs are lighter and airier though and three Turkish-style reliefs mark the entrance corridor. The Király has a reputation for being a gay male pick-up joint.

Rác Gyógyfürdő

I. Hadnagy utca 8-10 (156 1322). Tram 18, 19, 47, 49. **Open** *women* 6.30am-7pm Mon, Wed, Fri; *men* Tue, Thur, Sat. **Admission** Ft170.
Tucked under Gellért Hill, with a pleasant outdoor café, the Rác baths are nicely situated. Named after the Hungarian word for the Serb community that once lived by the river, the Rác also dates back to Turkish times, although the interior area and the main pool are drabber than the Király or Rudas. The Rác offers the same menu of pools, steam and sauna as its two Turkish-built counterparts. It supposedly has the most active gay scene of the all the baths although usually there's little going on except a fair bit of roving eye contact among the elderly and middle-aged clientèle.

Gellért Gyógyfürdő

XI. Kelenhegyi út 4 (185 3555). Trams 18, 19, 47, 49. Open 6.30am-7pm Mon-Sat; 6.30am-4pm Sun. **Admission** Ft600. Mixed.
The most expensive of all the baths, but you do get an Art Nouveau swimming pool chucked in for your money. Probably the best of all the sites, at least in the summer, when your Ft600 also allows access to the several outside pools and sunbathing areas. There was a hospital on this site as early as the thirteenth century and the Turks also had a spa here. Now the beauty of this Art Nouveau extravaganza, built at the turn of the century, is matched only by the surliness of most of its staff, who all seem to be graduates of the

Király Gyógyfürdő – *an Ottoman monument.*

Josef Stalin charm school, class of 1950. The separate thermal pools lead off from the main swimming pool, which also has its own small warm water pool. The secessionist theme continues in the maze of steam rooms and saunas which gives the Gellért a different atmosphere to the Rudas or Király. The clientèle are also quite entertaining, composed mainly of startled tourists and gay men on the prowl, the latter often happily reclining in each others' arms in the warm pools. The rest room is sometimes extremely active.

Széchenyi Gyógyfürdő és Strandfürdő

XIV. Állatkerti körút 11 (121 0310). M1 Széchenyi fürdő. **Open** *strand* 6am-7pm daily. *Mixed thermal baths (Apr-Sept)* 6am-7pm daily; *Oct-Mar* 6am-5pm Mon-Sat, 6am-4pm Sun. **Admission** Ft170.
A very attractive complex of swimming pools and thermal baths, complete with restaurant, the Széchenyi is one of the largest health spas in Europe. Outside stands a statue of Zsigmond Vilmos, who discovered the thermal spring that fills the outdoor pool. The Széchenyi is probably the best choice for a day of watery relaxation as it offers both an outdoor thermal and swimming pool and the usual indoor assortment of thermal baths and steam rooms, so customers can exercise and laze about all on one site. Also, unlike Turkish baths such as the Rudas or the Király, it is open all day on Saturday, when the crowds of customers of all ages give the site an endearing holiday atmosphere, rather than the more medical feel of the Lukács, which also combines a swimming pool and thermal spa. The outside pools are beautifully laid out in a complex of ivy-clad buildings and include a cold water swimming pool as well as an outdoor thermal one, where guests play chess on floating boards, while standing up in the hot water. Drinks and, of course, cigarettes are also available.

Lukács Gyógyfürdő és Strandfürdő

II. Frankel Leó út 25-29 (212 4088). Tram 4, 6. **Open** 6am-7pm daily. **Admission** Ft170.
Like the Széchenyi, a complex of two outdoor swimming pools set in attractive grounds and thermal baths, in this case the Császár Baths, which date back to the sixteenth-century Turkish occupation. The baths are mixed which gives them a different atmosphere to the Rudas or Király and you need to bring a swimming costume. There's something of a medicinal feel to the place which some may find off-putting, but the setting is verdant and restful.

Dandár utcai Gyógyfürdő

IX. Dandár utca 5-7 (215 7084). Bus 33. **Open** 6am-7pm Mon-Fri; 6am-noon Sat. **Admission** Ft120.
Off the tourist trail, in District IX, the Dandár utca mixed thermal baths are small and crowded with locals rather than expats or visitors. They're mixed so bring a swimming costume while you watch a working-class suburb of Budapest take the thermal waters.

Pestszenterzsébet jódos sósfürdő

XX. Vizisport utca 2 (283 1097). Bus 23 from Boráros tér. **Open** *men* 7am-3pm Tue, Thur, Sat; *women* 7am-3pm Mon, Wed, Fri. **Admission** Ft120.

Cheapest and most distant of the thermal baths, way out in District XX. This spa offers salty water and the usual assortment of steam room, sauna and thermal pools.

Thermal Hotel

XIII. Margaret Island (111 1100). Bus 26. **Open** 7am-8pm daily. **Admission** *day ticket* Ft1,200.

A modern luxury hotel in the middle of Margit island, the Thermal offers a squeaky clean complex of three mixed thermal pools, swimming pool, sauna and steam room. A different experience to one of the Turkish baths, more orientated towards sport and fitness than hedonism. The Thermal Hotel also offers a solarium, a pedicure and two sorts of massage – sport and Swedish – which sounds intriguing. Carlos the Jackal apparently used to stay here, though whether or not he used to take the waters is still open to conjecture.

Thermal Hotel Helia

XIII. Karpát utca 62-64 (270 3277). M3 Dózsa György út/trolleybus 79. **Open** 7am-10pm daily. **Admission** *weekday morning ticket to 3pm* Ft800; *weekend or full day ticket* Ft1,200.

Perched by the river, on the edge of a working class suburb, this luxury hotel has a modern complex of swimming pool, thermal pools, sauna, steam room and exercise machines. Massages (Ft950) must be booked in advance. Popular with 'businessmen' from the former Soviet Union discussing contracts as they soak. There is a roof terrace as well.

Thermal Hotel Aquincum

III. Árpád fejedelem útja 94 (250 3360). Tram 1 from M3 Árpád híd. **Open** 7am-9pm daily. **Admission** *weekday tickets purchased before 10am* Ft450; *otherwise* Ft950; *weekend day ticket* Ft1,200

A not-quite-luxury hotel named after the ancient Roman town that once stood in this district. The Romans had baths around here and now the Aquincum offers a modern complex of thermal baths, steam room, sauna, whirlpool, swimming pool and gym.

Gellért Gyógyfürdő – *the most expensive of the baths, but doesn't it look as if it's worth it?*

Film

A city where they roll back the theatre roof in warm weather and haven't yet introduced the multiplex sounds like moviegoers' heaven. Not only that, but it's cheap to get in.

Although Hungarian cinema has attracted international attention with directors such as Miklós Jancsó, Márta Mészáros and István Szabó (whose *Mephisto* won the Oscar for best foreign-language film in 1982), most of the famous directors and cinematographers became successful after they left Hungary. Famous exiles include Mihály Kertész, aka Michael Curtiz, who went to Hollywood and made *Casablanca*, George Cukor (*The Women, A Star is Born*), Alexander Korda (*The Private Life of Henry VIII*), George Pal (*The Time Machine*), Lázsló Kovács, the cinematographer of *Easy Rider*, and Vilmos Zsigmond, who won an Oscar for his camerawork in Spielberg's *Close Encounters of the Third Kind*.

For film-makers who didn't leave the country, things have become even harder since the changes of 1989. Inflation, alternative sources of entertainment and reduced leisure spending hit the Hungarian movie business hard, although the country is in better shape than many others in eastern Europe. Many older film-makers, well adapted to the defunct state system, now feel blocked dealing with commercialism and a distribution policy dominated by American product. Another big problem for Hungarian film is finding private sponsors. There are better investments than film and sponsorships are not tax deductible.

All films released before 1989 were financed by the state and produced at MAFILM, the Hungarian Film Factory. In its 80-year history MAFILM has changed name and ownership structure many times. But since privatisation in 1993 it has become an independent film production company, competing with others such as Novofilm, Hunnia Films, Magic Media or Focus Film.

Financing a film in Hungary is difficult. Many films are co-produced with other countries, mainly Germany and France. (Hungary is also a popular location for international companies, many of which come to shoot here, keeping locals in work.) Still, in a limited fashion, the system of state support continues. The Motion Picture Foundation of Hungary (MMA), set up in 1990, somewhat arbitrarily dispenses Ft800-Ft900 million a year through six advisory boards – a system which is often criticised for a bureaucratic disregard for the actual needs of the film industry.

Despite the 1993 box office success of Róbert Koltai's *Sose halunk meg* (We Never Die), about a coathanger salesman (played by Koltai) who teaches his nephew the facts of life during a countryside odyssey, hopes that the Hungarian film industry will emerge from its doldrums remain faint. Film-makers not only get nostalgic about the 1960s, when Hungarian films captured attention all over the world, but also deplore viewing habits inside the country.

Eighty per cent of all films released in Hungary are American products; only 12 per cent are Hungarian films. In 1994 only 161,000 people (0.2 per cent of all admissions) watched Hungarian films and out of 25 films produced that year, only 18 made it on to the big screen. One of them was János Szász's *Woyzeck*, which won five prizes at the Hungarian Film Festival (Filmszemle) and nine international prizes including the European Felix Film Award for best European Film. Only 3,000 Hungarians went to see it. By contrast, up to spring 1995 more than a quarter of a million people had bought a ticket for Disney's *The Lion King* in Budapest alone.

MOVIEGOING IN BUDAPEST

Budapest has about 51 cinemas (*mozi*), ranging in size from the **Corvin**, the largest, which seats 1,050, to the tiny **Cirko-gejzir** with seating for about 30. Western-style multiplexes don't exist here yet, although a few houses are equipped with more than one screen. The Corvin, now under renovation, will open as a six-screen 1,500-seat cinemaplex on 1 September 1996.

Cinemas are comfortable and, by Western standards, very cheap. Anglophone visitors will feel at home here as mainstream US and UK movies are extremely popular and as many as 85 per week are screened in the original English with Hungarian subtitles.

PROGRAMME INFORMATION

The best guide for US and British films are the cinema sections of the English-language weeklies *Budapest Week* and *Budapest Sun*, on sale in hotels

*Opposite: the very stylish **Művész** cinema.*

The **Uránia**, for a grand night out.

and at newsstands. Both specify times and venues. Other important guides are the magazines *Pesti Műsor* and *Pesti Est* – also available at newsstands – which often list feature films, special screenings, and festivals that may not find their way into other programmes. The entries will state – in Hungarian – if a film is subtitled (*feliratos*) or dubbed (*szinkronizált*). Films in French (*francia*), German (*német*), Russian (*orosz*) and Italian (*olasz*) are also often screened in Budapest. Seats can be reserved ahead of time in most major venues.

In large theatres, seating is assigned by seat and row number. Note that *szék* is seat; *sor* is row; *bal oldalon* designates the left side, *jobb oldalon* the right side, *közép* the middle; and *erkély* is the balcony. In some Hungarian programmes, E refers to show times: n9 is 8.15pm, f9 is 8.30pm, h9 is 8.45pm. *De* means morning, *Du* is afternoon, *este* is evening and *éjjel* refers to late shows.

Cinemas

Atrium
II. Margit körút 55 (212 5398). Tram 4, 6. **Box office** from 10.30am, **last show** 8.30pm, daily. **Tickets** Ft250. **No credit cards.** One screen.
One of the few large houses on the Buda side of the Danube and a major venue for mainstream Hollywood fare.

Broadway
VII. Károly körút 3 (322 0230). M2 Astória, tram 47, 49. **Box office** 3.30pm, last show 8.30pm. **Tickets** Ft250. **No credit cards.** One screen.
Formerly a film museum, this interestingly steep and semi-circular 600-seater, built in the 1930s, specialises in French and Italian features and also screens Hollywood fare.

Corvin
VIII. Kisfaludy köz 1 (113 9897). M3 Ferenc körút. **Box office** from 2.30pm, **last show** 8pm, daily. **Tickets** Ft250. **No credit cards.** One screen.
This baroque-style house, Budapest's largest cinema and soon to be the city's first multiplex, screens mainstream commercial movies. The building was an HQ for resistance during Hungary's uprising in 1956. *See also chapter* **Communism**.

Metro
VI. Teréz körút 62 (153 4266). M3 Nyugati, tram 4, 6. **Box office** from 11 am, **last show** 9pm, daily. **Tickets** Ft250. **No credit cards.** Two screens.

Budapest's most eclectic cinema, Metro's main screen features popular commercial releases, while its second screen (the *Kamaraterem*) mostly plays Hungarian-made movies and foreign art films. The ceiling of the main room is retractable and is often opened on hot summer nights. The Metro number is also the main Budapest office for cinema information, although this service is Hungarian-only.

Puskin
V. Kossuth Lajos utca 18 (118 6464). M3 Astoria. **Box office** from 11 am, **last show** 9pm, daily. **Tickets** Ft250. **No credit cards.** Two screens.
This 420-seat house features major Hollywood releases. Its second screen (*Kamaraterem*) plays previously released movies and art films – both Hungarian and western-made. Constructed at the turn of the century, its upstairs lobby is not as ornate as the nearby **Uránia**'s, but is worth visiting.

Uránia
VIII. Rákóczi út 21 (118 8955). M2 Astória Bus 7, 7A, 78. **Box office** from 11.30am daily. **Last show** 8.15pm Mon-Thur, Sun; 10.15pm Fri, Sat. **Tickets** Ft250. **No credit cards.** One screen.
Built in 1896 as a theatre, the Uránia is one of the grandest cinemas in the country – gold chandeliers and Persian carpets decorate its mezzanine waiting area. Today it is a 684-seat venue for contemporary movies. In 1995, it was the main cinema for Hungary's week-long annual film festival. It gets stifling in the summer.

Art Cinemas

Because of Hungary's tradition of artistic film-making, certain theatres specialise in non-commercial 'art' films. Auteurs Peter Greenaway, John Cassavetes and Hal Hartley are especially popular in Hungary. Most art houses are small venues where seating is not assigned, and all major film guides list their programmes (*see above*).

Blue Box
IX. Kinizsi utca 28 (218 0983). M3 Ferenc körút. **Box office** 3pm, **last show** 9pm. **Tickets** Ft100-Ft200. **No credit cards.** One screen, two in summer.
Former nightclub that now screens everything from Tom & Jerry to Tarkovsky. Seating is removed for occasional events such as jazz concerts and raves. In the summer they also show movies in the garden, convivially equipped with a bar.

Cirko-gejzir
VIII. Lőrinc pap tér 3 (269 9213). M3 Kálvin tér. **Box office** 6pm, **last show** 9pm. **Tickets** Ft150-Ft200. **No credit cards.** One screen.
Formerly the Egocentrum Club, now a tiny cinema with about 30 assorted chairs and sofas and a programme of obscure independent movies, especially Russian ones. Small bar in the front. Occasional photo exhibitions.

Hunnia
VII. Erzsébet körút 26 (322 3471). M2 Blaha Lujza tér, tram 4, 6. **Box office** from 4.30pm, **last show** 9pm, daily. **Tickets** Ft150. **No credit cards.** One screen.
The Hunnia has only one screen, but presents a varied line-up of Hungarian and foreign films that changes daily. It's owned by the Hunnia film studio (one of Hungary's major movie-makers) and is a main venue for Hunnia releases. The café on the second floor is open from 3pm-midnight and is an exhibition space for paintings and photography.

Művész
VI. Teréz körút 30 (132 6726). M3 Nyugati, tram 4, 6. **Box office** from 4.30pm, **last show** 9pm, daily. **Tickets** Ft250. **No credit cards.** Five screens.

Magyar Movies

A dozen Hungarian celluloid greats.

Valahol Európában (Somewhere in Europe), 1947, Géza Radványi

A society of homeless children steal and plunder to survive in wartime and meet a musician in an old castle who shows them the way to a useful life. Impressively modern.

Szegénylegények (The Round-Up), 1965, Miklós Jancsó

Set after the 1848 revolution against Habsburg rule, but this visual masterpiece comments on Nazi concentration camps and Rákosi-era political persecutions.

Apa (Father), 1966, István Szabó

This acclaimed work from the early phase of Szabó's filmmaking is a light, Truffaut-influenced film about a fatherless boy growing up during postwar chaos and revolution.

A tanu (The Witness), 1969, Péter Bacsó

Banned for many years, *A tanu* is a cult political tragicomedy featuring Hungary's first home-grown orange, the 'Magyar Narancs', later to lend its name to a newspaper. Recently director Péter Bacsó made a second part, *Megint Tanu* (Witness Again).

Szerelem (Love), 1970, Károly Makk

Adapted from two stories by Tibor Déri, a dense and atmospheric piece about an old, ill woman. Her contact with the outside world is through her daughter-in-law, while her son, though innocent, is in prison, maintaining the fiction that he is travelling the world. Beautifully shot.

Szindbád (Sinbad), 1970, Zoltán Huszárik (1931-80)

A slow, dreamlike movie about a dying man (Hungarian acting icon Zoltán Latinovits), who remembers his life through colourful flashbacks of the women he has loved.

A kis valentino (The Little Valentino), 1979, András Jeles

A surreal, black and white masterpiece which follows a young drifter through one day. Shot with amateur actors and much affection for its characters. Devastating.

Megáll az idő (Time Stands Still), 1981, Péter Gothár

Dance school lessons, first love and rebellion. Hungarian teenagers in the early 1960s were much the same as teenagers everywhere. This witty movie also looks at social life and politics after the 1956 revolution.

Könnyű testi sertés (Light Physical Injuries), 1982, György Szomjas

Underrated and seldom shown, this impressive comic film looks at working-class life in Budapest's District VIII. Great script and actors, with brilliant camerawork by cinematographer (and sometime director) Ferenc Grünwalski.

A kutya éji dala (The Dog's Night Song), 1983, Gabor Bódy (1946-1985)

A radical film about love, morality and a fake priest who appears in a small village. Full of plot twists, colour changes and experimental sounds.

Az Én XX. századom (My Twentieth Century), 1988, Ildikó Enyedi

At the exact moment Edison invents the electric light bulb in New York, twin sisters are born in Budapest. Enyedi tells the story of their lives and wins the best first feature prize at Cannes.

Sátántangó (Satanic Tango), 1991-93, Béla Tarr

Few have sat all the way through this seven-hour masterpiece on time, lack of self-confidence and a miserable life, but those who do, emerge with an almost religious gleam in the eye.

Strange goings-on in Miklós Jancsó's The Round-Up.

Catch up on Hungarian classics at **Odeon**.

One of the most stylish art cinemas in the city. Its five halls feature previously released classics and contemporary art films. There is a restaurant in the basement, the Federico, after Fellini. This cinema is popular, so get there early.

Örökmozgó Filmmúzeum

VII. Erzsébet körút 39 (342 2167). Tram 4, 6. **Box office** from 4.30pm, **last show** 8.30pm, daily. **Tickets** Ft140. **No credit cards**. One screen and video upstairs. Known for its eclectic weekly schedule of everything from silent classics to documentaries. Foreign films in this small house are often played in their original sound with simultaneous Hungarian translation via headsets. There is a coffee shop in the lobby, and an adjoining book store (main subject headings: art, theatre, cinema) with a few English titles.

Szindbad

XIII. Szent István körút 16 (131 8573). M3 Nyugati, tram 4, 6. **Box office** open 3pm, **last show** 8.30pm. **Tickets** Ft100-Ft200. **No credit cards**. Two screens. Right by the Vígszinház, not as elegant within as it looks from outside, but a decent two-screen art movie house with an interesting programme of independent films. They also have a small video rental outlet. Air-conditioned.

Tabán

I. Krisztina körút 87-89 (156 8162). Tram 18 to Krisztina tér/bus 5, 78, 105 and red 4. **Box office** from 4.30pm-5.30pm, **last show** 8pm, daily. **Tickets** Ft160. **No credit cards**. One screen. Nestled in the old Serbian quarter of the city, this tiny theatre usually plays several English-language gems a week. German and French films also feature. Sound and picture quality are never great, but the lobby and café were recently renovated. They also have a video rental library, including a handful of English-language movies.

Toldi Studio Mozi

V. Bajcsy-Zsilinszky út 36-38 (111 2809). M3 Arany János. **Box office** from 3.30-4.30pm, **last show** 9.30pm, daily. **Tickets** Ft250. **No credit cards**. Two screens. Large venue for contemporary art releases (from Hartley to Tarantino) and Hungarian features both old and new. There is a coffee bar and a hip gift shop (posters, books, postcards).

Video Rental

Budapest has a large number of video rental shops. Most English-language videos are dubbed into Hungarian, but many older releases are available in subtitled form. Video boxes will indicate whether a film is dubbed (*szinkronizált*) or subtitled (*feliratos*) from English (*angol*). Any of the city's video shops will have some titles in English to choose from.

British Council Library

VII. Benczúr utca 26 (321 4039/37/38). M1 Bajza utca. **Open** 11am-6pm Mon-Thur; 11am-5pm Fri; 9.30am-noon Sat.
Membership (Ft3500 per year) is essential for access to this extensive video library. Superb selection of British TV shows: everything from documentaries to sitcoms.

Odeon

XIII. Hollán Ernő utca 7 (131 6776). Tram 4, 6. **Open** 2-9pm daily. **Rental** Ft150 per tape per day (plus refundable Ft1,000 deposit).
Original soundtrack videos of US and UK feature films can be found here. It's highly regarded for its large collection of Hungarian classics subtitled into English, including six of those featured in our box on major Hungarian films (*see page 179* **Magyar Movies**). Videos can be watched in a viewing room on the premises.

Film Festivals

Magyar Filmszemle

c/o Filmunio Hungary, VI. Városligeti fasor 38 (351 7760/61/fax 351 7766).
This is the major event in the Hungarian film calendar. Each February, in one or two different venues, the Magyar Filmszemle (Hungarian Film Festival) shows feature films, documentaries and shorts that have been produced in the previous year. There's a competition with one big prize for the best movie, plus several smaller awards. Some movies are also shown outside the competition. In 1995 there were 14 features and around 30 documentaries. Fear not: simultaneous translation by earphone is available.

Invisible Film Festivale

contact: Tarek Kaszim at Deiss Kaszim Film, Montázs 2000, V. Október 6, utca 14 (131 5402/fax 131 5402).
The Invisible Film Festivale, where no prizes are awarded, shows all kind of films and videos from Hungary and the from rest of the world. The worthy intention is to give mostly young film-makers the opportunity to show their works to a wider audience and 'build a new kind of distribution network'.

Film Studies

Színház- és Filmművészeti Főiskola

H-1088, Budapest, Vas utca 2/c (118 8111/fax 138 4560). Head of Film faculty: János Zsombolyai, or ask for Ferenc Sugár or Péter Linka.
The Hungarian Academy of Drama and Film is the only university-level place of education for dramatic and film arts in the country. In 1991, one year after the fall of Communism, the Academy opened an International class, which, for an annual fee of $8,000, teaches a four-year course in film- and TV-directing and cinematography. Many famous directors and cinematographers come to the Academy to lecture.

Folklore

There's more to Hungary's rich folkloric traditions than factory-produced weaving, machine-carved woodwork and a few costumed dolls – get thee down to a Dance House.

Hungary is renowned for the richness of its folklore. Stubborn loyalty to the traditional values and aesthetics of folklife has helped preserve Hungarian identity through centuries of migrations, foreign invasions, industrialisation and urbanisation. Although visitors to modern Budapest will definitely not feel as if they have been transported to some idyllic village, with a bit of perseverance even a casual visitor can glimpse the traditional life which invades even downtown districts from time to time.

Hungarians have long been aware that their folk culture is a hot tourist commodity. Since Communist times there has been a tendency to pack busloads of tourists out to the Puszta (Great Hungarian Plain) for 'genuine folkloric shows' that include a bit of costumed dancing, a gypsy orchestra, a horse show with traditionally costumed *csikós* cowboys, and dinner at a country *csárda*. One of these trips will radically redefine your concept of kitsch.

If you want to see a village full of peasants in embroidered vests and odd hats dancing to discordant fiddles amidst thatched homes, you will have to do what Hungarians do – go to Transylvania, the multi-ethnic northern region of Romania that has managed to avoid much of the twentieth century. Modern villages in Hungary tend to be much of a muchness since the Kádár era provided cheap loans to build boring, boxlike housing to replace the traditional thatched houses that predominated until the 1970s. Traditions still survive, but only tend to be passed on when there is nothing good on cable TV. Nevertheless, within an hour of Budapest there are several villages that come close to being living museums.

VILLAGES & REGIONS

The village of Hollókő, in the Nógrád hill country, is a well preserved Palóc Hungarian village with old-style wooden houses, a ruined castle and a magnificent wooden church to which the older women still wear folk costumes on Sunday.

*Internationally renowned folk group **Muzsikás** – most famous of the Dance House bands.*

Peasant women sell embroideries and beadwork in front of their houses, and visitors can arrange to stay in peasant homes renovated in traditional style. Hollókő is on the UNESCO list of world treasures, so tour agencies offer bus tours to the region. Check with local travel agents or call **Nógrád Tourinform** for information. Other villages in the Galga valley and Nógrád region are less spectacular, but just as authentic.

Other village regions worth seeing include the Őrség, near Szentgotthárd along the Austrian border, or the Szatmár and Nyírség region near the Soviet border. Closer to home, villages to the north of Buda in the Pilis hills, particularly Csobánka and Pomáz (on the HÉV commuter train near Szentendre) are pleasant for an afternoon walk. Both are home to multi-ethnic populations of Serbian, Slovak, Sváb German, Gypsy and Hungarian backgrounds.

West of Budapest is a series of pleasant villages which are easy to reach by local buses from Moszkva tér. Budakeszi (bus 22 from Moszkva tér) was originally a Sváb German village known as Wudigeiss, but today is more or less a village suburb of Buda, with pleasant restaurants and beer gardens for the Budapest yuppies who are snatching up peasant homes here. You can see ornately carved wooden gates at the entrances to homes built by the Székelys who were settled here from Romanian Bukovina in the 1940s.

But the easiest way to see real live old ladies wearing strange embroidered things on their heads is to go to any of the vegetable markets that ring the downtown. At Bosnyák tér (end of the number 7 bus route in Pest) market, the peasant women who sell in the rear of the market continue to wear folk costumes, as do the women who sell on the terrace of the Skála Open Market in Buda (end of the number 4 tram line)

Nógrád Tourinform

3170 Szécsény, Kulturcentrum, Ady Endre utca 12 (06 32 370 777/fax 06 32 370 170).

*The Palóc Hungarian village of **Hollókő**.*

easier by transporting village homes to Szentendre, this Skansen-like village exhibits peasant homes with original furnishings, wooden churches and farm implements from all over Hungary.

Buying

The State-owned folklore shops (Népművészeti Bolt) cater to the souvenir-hunter who thrives on kitsch. You can find cute little folk costumed dolls, factory-produced weaving and machine-carved woodwork, although some stuff is worthwhile. Ceramic plates painted with floral patterns, or the dull-finished black ceramics of the Great Plains are a good buy, although a visit to the peasant women at Moszkva tér or to a flea market will produce finer-quality pieces, even antiques, for half the price. Some of the embroideries on sale, however, are good buys.

Folk textiles may be the perfect gift: easy to pack, light and impossible to break in transit. Since most of these items are intended for local use, the prices can be shockingly affordable. The embroideries of the Matyó people from the northern Hungarian village of Mezőkövesd are undisputed in richness, while those of the Kalocsa region are light and lacy. In the Kun region, earth tones prevail, with browns, yellows and light blues stitched in yarn, giving a soft, almost fuzzy effect. For everyday use, Hungarians still buy Palóc weavings from northern Hungary for table runners, pillow cases, tablecloths and kitchen towels.

The revival of interest in traditional folklore among young Hungarians has provided a ready market for authentic village costumes and weavings from Transylvania, and Transylvanian peasants now come to Budapest to sell their wares. Try finding the peasant women who sell textiles on the streets, albeit somewhat illegally. Moszkva tér and the area around Parliament offer havens for peasants selling home-made folk arts.

You'll recognise the women by their costumes.

Folk Arts

Seeing & Acquiring

Néprajzi Múzeum

Museum of Folklore
V. Kossuth Lajos tér 12 (132 6340). **Open** 10 am-5.30pm Tue-Sun. **Entrance** Ft100; Ft30 students, children.

Housed in a beautiful nineteenth-century palace that was once the Finance Ministry, the Néprajzi has the most complete collection of ethnographic material in Hungary. The recently opened permanent exhibition of folklore includes costumes, household objects and tools, but most of the accompanying descriptive information is only in Hungarian.

The Open Air Village Museum

Szabadságforrás út, Szentendre (26 312 304). Bus 8 from HÉV terminal. **Open** 1 Apr-31 Oct 9am-5pm Tue-Sun. **Entrance** Ft120; Ft50 children.

Designed in the 1950s to make 'ethnographic' research

White kerchiefs and red skirts signal the women of the Transylvanian village of Szék, while yellow-kerchiefed women in green wool vests and skirts are usually from the Kalotaszeg region. (*See also* chapter **Shopping**.)

Folk Music & Dance

Budapest is one of the few capitals in Europe where you can still find an active traditional music and folk dance scene. Young Hungarians are wildly enthusiastic about their folk music. A visit to a 'Dance House' (Táncház) is one of the best ways to meet Hungarians and learn directly what it is that makes them so, well, Hungarian.

The Dance House Movement, as it is now called, began in the early 1970s among young Hungarians tired of the centrally dictated versions of folklore and the syrupy style of 'restaurant music' favored by State programmers. Fiddler Béla Halmos and singer Ferenc Sebő pioneered the revival by going to the elder village musicians to encourage a direct link to music traditions still strong in the countryside. The search for 'pure sources' of folk music led to Transylvania, where isolation had preserved the context of ancient music which had begun to wither elsewhere in Hungary proper.

Back in Budapest, urban bands opened up 'Dance Houses' based on the Transylvanian model – rented rooms where young people made their own entertainment with fiddles, dancing and lots of illicit plum brandy. The most famous of the Dance House bands, Muzsikás, used the raw, traditional sounds of the Transylvanian string bands, the shepherds' goatskin bagpipes, and the directness of folk song texts sung by Márta Sebestyén to protest against the Hungarian government's strongarm cultural policies, providing a musical voice to the dissident movement in a way local rock never did.

Today the Dance Houses are still going strong. Traditionalist bands that play the capital weekly include Téka, the Ökrös Band, Kalamajka, Méta, and Újstílus. Basic instrumentation includes lead violin, gut-strung bass, and the kontra, a three-string viola with a flat bridge that enables it to play full, rich chords in the skewed rhythms of

Romance and the Roma

Stereotypes of Hungary always include the romanticised nomad Gypsy musician, serenading noblewomen beneath moonlit castle windows. The truth is, Hungary is home to at least a half million Gypsies (in Hungarian, *cigány*), or Roma, as they prefer to be called in their own language, and their life is anything but romantic.

The Roma are essentially a European nationality without a nation. Their language, *Romanes*, is related to northern Indian languages such as Hindi and Punjabi, and it is conjectured that they left India due to war or famine around the eighth century. By the twelfth century they had reached Europe, some claiming to be Egyptian refugees (hence the term 'Gypsy'). Different groups of Roma settled in western Europe, while in eastern Europe many were held as slaves on the estates of the nobility, especially in Romania.

The majority of Roma in Hungary are referred to as *Oláh*, or vlach Gypsies (*vlashiko roma* in their own language) who came into Hungary after the abolition of slavery in Romania in 1855. These Roma tend to guard their traditions closely, and the women continue to wear the traditional voluminous skirts. Many came to Budapest in the postwar period to find work in construction sites.

The Hungarian 'musician Gypsies' form a separate group amongst Roma, with their own dialect of *Romanes* and a hereditary tradition of professional musicianship. Few still speak *Romanes*, and most work in agriculture and industry since the market for violin bands has shrunk.

As in all of Europe, Hungary's Gypsies have faced massive discrimination, and since the fall of Communism things have not really changed very much. Most Gypsies live at or below the poverty level, finding only menial or unskilled employment. Many Hungarians see Gypsies as nothing but a bunch of thieves and beggars, and are not above saying so in public, while police tend to treat all Gypsies as potential criminals. But although the most visible Gypsies may be the women begging coins downtown, the vast majority are busy working in regular, if low-paid, jobs.

Today Gypsies are organising to demand basic rights. There are Roma political parties, local government organisations, and schools for gypsy children taught in *Romanes*. A Gypsy cultural revival has blossomed and bands such as Kalyi Jag, Ando Drom, and Romanyi Rota have produced tapes and CDs of traditional Roma music, predominantly vocal backed with guitars, mandolins and milk-can percussion.

And if you do meet with children begging coins, just say in *Romanes* 'Lasho dyes, t'aves bút bachtalyi' ('Good day and may you have luck') and see how they react.

For these women, Communism has come and gone while traditions remain the same.

Transylvania. Extra fiddles, cimbalom (hammered dulcimer), duda (double chanter bagpipes), hurdy gurdy or reeds may round out the ensemble. Traditional Gypsy string bands from Transylvanian villages also make regular appearances in Budapest's Dance Houses.

Bands such as Kalyi Jag, Ando Drom, and Romanyi Rota perform the music of Hungary's contemporary Roma (Gypsy) communities. Keep an eye on Almássy tér Culture Center for these events. Dance Houses tend to be open from October to the end of May, taking a summer break while festivals go on and bands take time to tour. There is usually a weekly summer Dance House in Budapest (such as the Gyökér Restaurant) but venues change. Check the *Budapest Week* listings for more information. Admission to these events is usually around Ft100-Ft150.

Téka Dance House
I. District Culture House, I. Bem Rakpart 6 (201 0324). Tram 19. **Open** 7pm-midnight Fri.
The Téka band have for years been standard bearers of the traditional music craze. This is a dancers' paradise, and beginners should go early to learn the basic steps from Csidu, one of Hungary's best, and funniest, dance masters. Village guests and concerts all for the same entrance price.

Kalamajka Dance House
Belvárosi Ifjusági Művelődési Ház, V. Molnár utca 9, (117 5928). M3 Ferenciek tere. **Open** 8pm-1am Sat.
The biggest weekend dance, with dancing and instruction on the second floor and jam sessions and serious pálinka abuse on the fourth. The Kalamajka band is led by Béla Halmos, who started the Dance House movement in the 1970s, and usually there are guest performances by traditional village bands.

Méta Dance House
Józsefvárosi Club, VIII. Somogyi Béla utca 13 (118 7930). M3 Blaha Lujza tér/tram 4, 6. **Open** 7pm-midnight Sun.
A small weekend get-together for the serious dance fanatic, held in the basement of a local school. Excellent band which features a woman lead fiddler and plays music from Szatmár on the Hungarian plains.

Csángó Dance House
Marczibányi tér Művelődési Ház, XII Marczibányi tér 5A, (212 5789). M2 Moszkva tér. **Open** 8pm-midnight Wed.

The latest craze among musicians and dancers is Csángó music. The Csángós are two pockets of Hungarians, one in the Gyimes region of Transylvania and one in the Szeret valley of Moldavia, who play a rough, energetic music reflecting the oldest Hungarian traditions. Using instruments such as the gardon (a cello-shaped string instrument hit with a stick), the koboz (similar to the arabic oud but smaller and louder), fiddles and Moldavian flutes, Csángó traditional music has injected the Budapest folk scene with a loud rocking rhythm in the hands of the house band Tatros.

Muzsikás Club
Marczibányi tér Művelődési Ház, XII. Marczibányi tér 5A (212 5789). M2 Moszkva tér. **Open** 8pm-midnight Thur.
Internationally renowned folk band Muzsikás hosts a music-orientated 'club' every Thursday. Not as much dancing, but a chance to hear Muzsikás and friends jam and relax in an informal atmosphere.

Újstílus Dance House
Gyökér Restaurant, VI. corner of Eötvös utca and Szobi utca (153 4329). M3 Nyugati. **Open** 9pm-1am Fri.
The Gyökér was opened by a folk musician to provide a home to Budapest's active folk scene. Some kind of concert goes on almost every day, but Fridays are a treat with Újstilus, the real hard core of the Transylvanian folk scene. Good food. Usually the only Dance House open in summer.

Festivals

The best festivals are held during the summer, especially the Kaláka festivals in Miskolc and Sopron, which also serve as showcases for foreign acts visiting Hungary. The huge National Folk Festival (Országos Táncháztalálkozó) is held annually at the Budapest Sportcsarnok at the end of March. (Information available from the Professional Association of Folk Dancers – Szakmai Ház: 201 3766.)

Performances by professional folk dance troupes, such as the State Folk Ensemble, the Duna Folk Dance Ensemble and the Bartók Dance Ensemble most often take place at the Budai Vigadó, I. Corvin tér 8 (along Fő utca near Batthyány tér in Buda, 201 5928, M2 Batthyány tér) or the FSZMH Fővárosi Culture Center, XI. Fehérvári út 47 (181 1360, tram 47). Almássy tér Culture Center also hosts special folk music events, especially for minorities such as Budapest's gypsies, Serbs, Croats, Jews and Slovaks. They also have a small store in the basement that sells traditional folk instruments and an excellent computer database of cultural events.

Almássy tér Recreation Centre
Almássy téri Szabadidőközpont
VII. Almássy tér 6 (267 8709). M2 Blaha Lujza tér.

Specialist Shop

Kodály Zoltán Music Store
V. Múzeum körút 21 (117 3347). M2 Astoria. **Open** 10am-6pm Mon-Fri; 9.30am-1.30pm Sat. **Credit** AmEx, EC, V.
Budapest's widest selection of Hungarian folk and traditional music, as well as world music from elsewhere. There's also classical music and lots of old vinyl.

Music: Classical & Opera

Over the years Hungary has produced countless masters of classical music, both composers and performers – it's hanging on to them it has found difficult.

Franz Liszt, who is most definitely not *Hungarian. Got that?*

The story of classical music in Hungary is one of migration – out of the country. Despite having one of the most recognisable musical profiles in the world, along with one hell of a music education system, for the last 60 years or so Hungary hasn't been able to provide its talented musicians with either money or recognition enough to keep them here. Solti, Ormandy, Schiff, Éva Marton... all Hungarians who went West.

Many left during the Communist era. The opening of borders in 1989 made it easier for talent to leave, and today there are Hungarians in every major orchestra and opera house in the world. Left behind are hundreds of second rate musicians and an idealistic few genuine talents who are devoted to proving the truth of Hungary's musical legacy.

That legacy consists of two names: Béla Bartók

and Zoltán Kodály (no matter what Hungarians try to tell you, Franz Liszt was not Hungarian). In the early part of the twentieth century Bartók and Kodály ventured out into remote Hungarian villages, documenting the vanishing folk song heritage. Thanks to the fruits of their painstaking research – the system of music education which Kodály developed and the powerfully accessible music composed by Bartók – Hungary is blessed with an elemental sense of its national musical identity. There isn't a Hungarian today who does not know a handful of Hungarian folksongs.

The result is a country of music lovers. Under Communism, classical music was a relatively inexpensive way to satisfy the people, and party leaders gladly provided large state subsidies. When the political system changed in 1989 and subsidies started evaporating, the country was left with an overabundance of orchestras.

Today there are over 20 amateur and professional orchestras in Budapest alone, with more sprouting up, it seems, by the season. Many are still meagrely state-supported and desperately looking for outside help, while a few now hymn the muse of corporate sponsorship. Of all these, only one or two are fine orchestras, but audiences turn up in droves to see every last one of them.

The concert season starts in late September and closes in early June. Repertoire tends to stick to basic German Romantic fare with a smattering of Bartók. Recently, however, a few ensembles have begun playing both more contemporary music and baroque music on period instruments. In the summer, most orchestras pack up and go on either vacation or international tours, allowing smaller chamber groups to take the spotlight.

The free monthly listing of classical concerts, *Koncert Kalendárium* (only in Hungarian), is available at all ticket agencies and some record shops. Complete listings can be found in the English-language *Budapest Week*.

The **Hungarian State Opera House**. *See page 188.*

Principal Orchestras

Of the myriad orchestras in Budapest, the best is also the youngest. The **Budapest Festival Orchestra** was founded in 1983 by conductor Iván Fischer and world-renowned pianist Zoltán Kocsis as an idealistic, thrice-annual ad-hoc gathering of Budapest's best musicians. The BFO became a full-time orchestra in the autumn of 1993, offering its mostly young musicians the best salaries in the country, and its audiences the best orchestral concerts by a local band. Their programming is imaginative, they often have guest conductors and their concerts usually sell out.

The **Hungarian Radio and Television Orchestra** has all the good musicians who didn't defect to the BFO. They are, on average, older and more experienced if not as technically proficient. Conductor is pianist Tamás Vásáry, who was chosen by the orchestra members in 1994. Since his appointment, they've been playing better than ever. Although the HRTO's performances might not be as dazzling as those of the BFO, they are often more mature, especially in readings of the standard repertoire.

Other orchestras, which seem to be stuck playing the same war horses, include the once-mighty **Hungarian State Orchestra**, conducted by the hyperactive and popular Ken-Ichiro Kobayashi, and the **Budapest Philharmonic Society**. The latter is the orchestra of the **State Opera** *sans chanteurs*. The oldest and most prestigious orchestra in Hungary, and perhaps the worst hit by falling state subsidies, they can still be whipped up into an inspired frenzy under the right conductor.

Venues

For a city with so many performing groups and artists (despite the crippling rate of emigration), the number of concert venues in Budapest is decidedly low and most orchestras are homeless. Concerts are given wherever and whenever there is an empty corner, especially in summer when larger venues close.

Principal Concert Halls

Zeneakadémia

VI. Liszt Ferenc tér 8 (342 0179). M1 Oktogon, tram 4, 6. **Open** *box office* 1-8pm Mon-Fri; 10am-noon, 4-8pm, Sat, Sun when there is a concert. **Credit** AmEx, MC, V. Little English spoken.

The Zeneakadémia is the historic Franz Liszt Music Academy, final stop for Hungary's aspiring musicians. Completed in 1907, the building is an eclectic mix of Art Nouveau with Egyptian and Assyrian motifs, dominated by Alajos Stróbl's imposing statute of Liszt. Concerts are held in the Nagy Terem (Large Concert Hall) which, although it seats only 1,200, is still the country's main venue, usually offering performances every night of the week. With gold and silver detailing and cherubs smiling from every corner, the wood-panelled interior provides not only ideal acoustics for orchestral concerts and chamber recitals, but also a treat for the eyes. There is a smaller recital hall, the Kisterem, with much less flattering acoustics. The centre is closed during July and August.

Pesti Vigadó

V. Vigadó utca 5 (138 4721). M1 Vörösmarty tér. **Open** *box office* 10am-6pm Mon-Fri; 10am-2pm Sat; 5-7pm Sun when there is a concert. **No credit cards**. Some English spoken.

Visited by Brahms at the end of the nineteenth century and bombed by the Allies during World War II, the Vigadó is more a historical attraction than a concert venue. Restored after the war, but smaller and less attractive than the Zeneakadémia, the Vigadó's chief redeeming feature is its location on the Danube. Concerts are usually by those who couldn't get the Zeneakadémia that night, though it is used more frequently during festivals.

Other Venues

Budapest Congress Centre

Budapest Kongresszusi Központ
XII. Jagelló út 1-3 (186 9588). M2 Déli, tram 61. **Open**
box office 2pm-6pm Wed, Fri or on day of concert. **No
credit cards.**
A modern convention centre with poor acoustics, BKK is not
suited to concerts. Nevertheless, especially when a large
audience is expected, many performances are given here.

Óbuda Social Circle

Óbudai társaskör
III. Kiskorona utca 7 (250 0288). M3 Árpád híd/tram 1.
Open *box office* 2-6.45pm or one hour before
performance. **No credit cards.**
A charming little building in the middle of a Lego-land housing estate, the Óbuda Social Circle hosts recitals and some
chamber orchestras. Intimate, and often the venue for surprisingly good concerts.

Bartók Memorial House

Bartók Emlékház
II. Csalán utca 29 (176 2100). Bus 5, 29. **Open** no box
office; *museum* 10am-5pm Tue-Sun; *tickets* on sale one
hour before performance and during museum hours.
Closed Aug. **No credit cards.**
Bartók's last residence before emigrating to America, now a
museum, often gives Friday evening chamber concerts by
the best of Hungary's resident musicians. Perhaps a little too
intimate, but the chairs, designed to make an elephant feel
at ease, are the most gratifying of any venue in Budapest.

BM Danube Palace

BM Duna Palota
V. Zrínyi utca 5 (117 2790). **Open** *box office* 1.30-7pm
Mon-Fri. **No credit cards.**
This striking palace with fine acoustics near the Danube is
home to the BM Duna Symphony Orchestra. The Festival
Orchestra also carries an innovative series of chamber con-
certs here, led by Zoltán Kocsis.

Matthias Church

Mátyás templom
*I. Szentháromság tér 2 (no phone). M2 Moszkva tér then
Várbusz.* **Tickets** on sale at the venue one hour before
performance. **No credit cards.**
Organ recitals and choir concerts are often given, especially
in the summer. During the Spring Festival, the church plays
host to larger productions of sacred works with orchestra.

Opera

At present, there is still only one opera company
in the capital, the **Hungarian State Opera**,
which divides its productions between the distinctive Opera House on Andrássy út and the
often-abused essay in Socialist Realism known as
the Erkel Színház.

Where Gustav Mahler and Otto Klemperer once
ruled the Opera House's corridors, today ambles
the spectre of bankruptcy. Drastic cuts in subsidies
and old-style mismanagement have prevented the
State Opera from holding on to any Hungarian
singer or director of better-than-average talent.

Although the State Opera is still able to run
complete seasons, with a yearly repertoire of nearly 60 operas and ballets among the two houses,
including at least seven premières each year, productions are usually tired and under-rehearsed.
But the State Opera is not without a handful of
up-and-coming stars worth seeing. Productions
of Bartók's stage works, all of which were pre-
mièred on the stage of the Opera House, should
not be missed. The Erkel, so enormous it always
seems empty, is usually reserved for less popular
productions.

Mussorgsky's 'Boris Godunov', performed by the Kiev Opera Company.

Operas are listed in the brochure published by the State Opera every month and available at the Opera House.

Hungarian State Opera House

Magyar Állami Operaház

VI. Andrássy út 22 (131 2550). M1 Opera. **Open** box office 10am-7pm Tue-Sat when there is a performance; 10am-1pm, 4-7pm, Sun when there is a performance. **Credit** AmEx. Little English spoken.

Erkel Színház

1081 Köztársaság tér 30 (133 0540). M2 Blaha Lujza tér. **Open** box office 10am-7pm Tue-Sat when there is a performance; 10am-1pm, 4-7pm, Sun when there is a performance. **Credit** AmEx. No English spoken.

Ticket Agencies

Unless there is a major name in town, tickets are almost always both available and enticingly affordable. Tickets for most classical concerts are available at **Nemzeti Filharmónia**. Otherwise your best bet is to buy tickets at the venues an hour or so before the performance. Tickets for the State Opera and Erkel Színház are only available at the Opera House box office. Beware that most places only accept cash. For further information, check *Koncert Kalendárium*, which specifically lists where tickets are available for each event.

Nemzeti Filharmónia

V. Vörösmarty tér 1 (118 0441). M1 Vörösmarty tér. **Open** 10am-1.30pm, 2-6pm, Mon-Fri. **No credit cards.** The state concert agency, this should be your one-stop destination, with tickets for nearly everything and loads of concert schedules and information. Lax service but some English spoken.

Music Mix 33

V. Váci utca 33 (138 2237). M3 Ferenciek tere. **Open** 10am-6pm Mon-Fri; 10am-2pm Sat. **No credit cards.** English spoken.

One of the first private ticket agencies, Music Mix charges a small commission. Usually only handles big-name visiting orchestras and the Festival Orchestra.

State Opera House Organisational Office

VI. Andrássy út 20 (111 9017). M1 Opera. **Open** box office 10am-7pm Tue-Sat when there is a performance; 10am-1pm, 4-7pm, Sun when there is a performance. **Credit** AmEx. Little English spoken.

Festivals

There are two big music festivals in Budapest. The **Spring Festival**, a March-April cultural extravaganza, mainly focuses on classical music, highlighting the best of what Hungary has to offer along with a few international guests. The other is the **Autumn Festival** which focuses on contemporary arts. This only started in 1994 – so it's much too early to tell whether it will become an annual event.

Contemporary music fans shouldn't miss the 25-year-old **Music of Our Time** festival, which presents the best of Hungary's composers and usually has a few big names to boast.

Festival Ticket Service

V. Bárczy I utca 1-3 (118 9570/266 4051). M1, M2, M3 Deák tér. **Open** Feb-Apr 10am-6pm Mon-Fri. **No credit cards.** English spoken.

Set up exclusively to handle the Spring Festival, this is the most reliable for tickets to festival events. Otherwise, it stays closed for the rest of the year.

Hungary On Disc

While imported CDs are even more expensive than in the West, Hungarian recordings on the Hungaroton label remain a good buy. Here we recommend five excellent domestic recordings, all of which should be available at the Hungaroton Record Shop next to Nemzeti Filharmónia on Vörösmarty tér (open 10am-7pm Mon-Fri, 10am-5pm Sat).

1. **Bartók, Béla**: Music for Strings, Percussion and Celeste, Divertimento. Liszt Ferenc Chamber Orchestra. HCD 12531. A cool and biting performance of the Music for Strings... almost gets overshadowed by the deliciously folksy Divertimento. Ignore the newer recording by the same group.

2. **Bartók, Béla**: Six String Quartets. Takács Quartet. Three CDs, HCD 12502-04. Made before the Takács got discovered by Decca, their version of the essence of Bartók's craft is fascinat-

ing in its attention to detail. Near definitive performances.

3. **Bartók, Béla**: Sonata for Two Pianos and Percussion, Two Pictures, Preludio and Scherzo. Zoltán Kocsis & Dezső Ránki, pianos; Gusztáv Cser & Zoltán Rácz, percussion. HCD 12400 (live recording). The two Hungarian giants of the piano, rivals to this day, came up with a performance fraught with intensity.

4. **Kurtág, György**: Works for Soprano. With Adrienne Csengery, soprano; György Kurtág, piano; Ensemble InterContemporain, conducted by Pierre Boulez. HCD 31576. Definitive readings of some representative works by Hungary's greatest living composer.

5. **Bach, J Chr**: Five Symphonies. Concerto Armonico. HCD 31448. Clean and vibrant performances of these rarely heard works by Hungary's première period instrument ensemble.

Music: Rock, Roots & Jazz

From a specialist Zappa store to youth-orientated rock festivals on deserted islands, Budapest's music scene is nothing if not eclectic.

Hungary's rich folk and classical music traditions are not reflected in the world of pop, rock or jazz. Decades of limited access to Western music created a strange pop hybrid which has still to assert its own identity. The main beat bands of the 1970s lost their impact after they were signed to the state label, Hungaroton, and the alternative bands of the 1980s never had an outlet in the first place.

Since 1989, state-sponsored stars, once in a job for life, have struggled against market forces. Hungaroton collapsed. Underground bands, who once had something to kick against, cheap booze to fuel the fire and no job ties to hold them down, have been left as rebels without a cause. Into the vacuum in 1988 rushed MTV, turning Hungarian taste away from bands with relevant Magyar lyrics and on to a generic Anglo-American sound. Unable to beat them, most Hungarian bands don't look very likely to join them either. Some stars, such as rock singer Feró Nagy or Wazlavik Gazember, Hungary's answer to Tiny Tim, turned to nationalism – singing in army camps and supporting the Magyar Democratic Front. Others, such as mainstream rock outfit Sexepil, tried singing in English. The cleverest of these, Rapülők, created a Hungarian sound from an MTV beat and cleaned up in the early '90s before splitting in '94.

Hungary still has no proper infrastructure. Concerts are played, albums released, but there is a serious lack of suitable concert halls, distribution, promotion and just about everything else that oils the wheels of the industry. You might get a decent band together, but you'd be hard pushed to find a good manager. Everyone, from musicians to record company executives, is working in the dark.

Hungarians are not used to the expense of concert tickets, and prices must be kept low if they're to go out at all. That and the shortage of mid-range venues forces major acts to play Vienna or Prague rather than Budapest. Most promoters insist that foreign bands, however humble, only play one concert in Hungary, exclusively theirs, so smaller acts can barely cover their travel costs. Budapest, once a convivial dive across the Iron Curtain, is now an annoying blip on any European tour.

Smaller venues, where people reluctantly fork out some Ft250 on the door to drink, dance and catch a band, have been hit by the 1995 trebling in energy prices. Ticket prices are also affected by a variety of local taxes including a 2 per cent culture tax. Higher prices mean fewer punters which means less money to pay struggling local bands.

The music is mostly still stuck in the white rock tradition which filtered into Hungary during the 1980s. Parents visiting Vienna would be begged to bring back Iggy Pop or Clash LPs. Yugoslavian pressings of independent groups were eagerly sought on the black market. But little of 1980s dance culture found its way here and the influence of hip hop and house culture has been minimal.

The bands worth seeing are those who manage to combine various eastern European, Balkan and Hungarian folk elements without falling under the all-pervasive influence of MTV. Watch out for Kis Pál és a Borz, Korai Öröm, Uzgin Üver, Üllői Úti Fuck and Ápolók, who each possess a distinctive

Made Inn Music Club – *convivial if over-lit.*

*Most mid-range Western acts passing through Budapest stop off at the **Petőfi Csarnok**.*

sound, sing in Hungarian and gig regularly in Budapest. The folk-influenced rock of Budapest four-piece Kampec Dolores, which sounds as good on CD as it does on stage, deserves a listen – try their *A Tű Fokán* album. But even the best bands remain trapped with a language they can't export and a sound they haven't the financial means to improve. Most get no further than playing for peanuts in the hamster wheel of Budapest nightlife.

It is not only live music which is suffering. When the major Western labels all suddenly set up shop here in early 1993, they ate up most of the larger independents and flooded the market with Western back catalogue material, superior to Hungarian imitations. Before the flood, Rapülők had to sell 100,000 units to earn a gold disc. Now a band need only sell 25,000 and most can't manage that.

This implies there is a modern retail industry. There isn't. There is one chain of stores, Fotex, and a handful of halfway decent specialist shops (*see chapter* **Shopping**). Outside Budapest it's mostly just Mum-and-Dad corner shops with a rack of CDs and cassettes among the groceries and cleaning products. Pirate tapes abound, especially outside Budapest, despite strict laws introduced in 1992. Promotion is difficult at best. Despite a few teeny magazines and some talk of a Hungarian edition of *Spin*, there is no real music press and even the majors have little or no promotional material. Whispers and posters carry what news there is of upcoming concerts and releases.

This word-of-mouth culture worked fine in the mid-1980s, when the thriving alternative scene threw up art-punk bands such as Balaton, VHK and Európa Kiadó. Important in their day, these have all recently found a second wind and are worth making the effort to see, if only for the buzz

of an audience who still know all the words to every tune. Dissident musician turned media magnate Péter Müller – who used to play with URH and Kontroll Csoport – these days tries to recreate this scene at Hungary's largest music festival, **Diáksziget** (*see page 193*).

In 1994, after a few false starts, a techno scene started around a small group of Hungarian DJs, led by the duo X-Lab. Still learning from mistakes and feeling its way, this movement is the first genuinely underground happening for ten years. It remains to be seen whether it will be able to throw up any marketable artists, but there are raves aplenty; pick up flyers at Underground, Wave and Trance. Summer dance parties on Danube islands are particularly convivial.

Tickets & Information

Concert details and previews can be found in *Budapest Week*, *Budapest Sun* and *Pesti Műsor*. Concerts rarely sell out but advance tickets can be bought at:

Music Mix
V. Váci utca 33 (138 2237). M3 Ferenciek tere. **Open** 10am-6pm Mon-Fri; 10am-2pm Sat. **No credit cards**.

Venues

Large venues include **Népstadion** and **Budapest Sportcsarnok** (*see chapter* **Sport & Fitness**). Certain smaller venues in *chapter* **Nightlife** will also feature live music.

Budai Parkszínpad
XI. Kosztolányi Dezső tér (166 9849). Bus 7. **Open** from 7pm. **Admission** Ft300-Ft1,000.
The main outdoor venue in summer, the Parkszínpad comprises a few hundred chairs facing a huge stage in the small

park area between Kosztolányi Dezső tér and Móricz Zsigmond körtér. Concerts tend to be Hungarian mainstream pop, although the venue hosts the annual World Music Festival in June (see chapter **Budapest By Season**) and various folk dancing events. The stewards can get a bit rough with screaming teenagers.

Guillotine

IX. Üllői út 45/47 (no phone). M3 to Ferenc körút. **Open** 11pm-3am Mon-Thur, Sun; 11pm-4am Fri, Sat. **Concerts** midnight. **Admission** Ft200.
Opened in the summer of 1994 by the same people who made a success out of the Saigon, this venue has a medieval dungeon theme. Two dance floors, live music four times a week, mainly blues and rock.

Made Inn Music Club/FMK

VI. Andrássy út 112 (Made Inn111 3437/FMK131 8858). M1 to Bajza utca. **Open** from 8pm. **Admission** Ft150-Ft500.
Both venues are situated in the same Young Artists' Club that broke ground in the 1980s. When there was nowhere else for alternative bands to play in town, a select group of influential artists and musicians would regularly meet and occasionally play at the FMK. Entry was by membership only. This was where seminal underground outfit Bizottság made their mark. By 1990, the FMK had lost its thunder, and now concerts there are low-key affairs. The Made Inn downstairs opened in 1990, appealing to a wider audience. Mainstream blues and rock were the order of the day. Now the Made Inn is a convivial if over-lit disco with two bars and a summer terrace also open during the day. The FMK can still boast more adventurous live music and a cooler crowd. Both venues can create a buzz.

Petőfi Csarnok

XIV. Városliget, Zichy Mihály út 14 (251 7266). M1 Széchenyi Fürdő. **Open** from 8pm. **Admission** Ft500-Ft2,000.
Large events hall in City Park. Indoor arena too large for most Hungarian bands but most mid-range Western acts passing through Budapest will invariably stop off here. The PeCsa started life as the Metropolitan Youth Centre in 1984 and still provides the Depeche Mode Fan Club with a venue for their monthly events. The main hall is a soulless barn with poor sound; in summer, the outdoor concert area has a better atmosphere. Both hold around 2,500 people.

Rockland

VIII. Golgota utca 3 (113 0607). Tram 23, 24/bus 99. **Open** from 8pm when there is a concert. **Admission** Ft300-Ft2,000.
Former Vörösmarty Culture House redesigned as a rock venue next to Budapest's oldest punk club. The city's only decent mid-range venue although stuck out in the wilds of District VIII and fairly inaccessible by public transport. Fight for a place at the bar.

Saigon

V. Arany János utca 13 (no phone). M3 to Arany János utca. **Open** from 11pm. **Admission** Ft200.
Medium-sized club and rock venue with an *Apocalypse Now* theme. Camouflage colours and mosquito nets mingle with promotional mirrors and posters. Two dance floors, occasional techno, live music three times a week.

Tilos az Á

VIII. Mikszáth Kálmán tér 2 (118 0684). M3 Kálvin tér/ tram 4, 6. **Open** 9pm-2am Mon-Thur; 9pm-4am Fri, Sat; 9pm-1am Sun. **Concerts** 11pm. **Admission** Ft300.
Budapest's leading venue for alternative music, the Tilos has been an institution since its opening on New Year's Eve 1990. The name is the Hungarian version of the 'Trespassers W' sign from *Winnie-the-Pooh*, and means 'the forbidden A',

which also works as an anarchist symbol. Despite constant battles with the District VIII council, Tilos has maintained a defiant stance. In August 1995 it was closed down on a technicality, and got around this by opening back up as a wine bar a month later. Alternative Budapest turned up in force for the reopening, and quaffed celebratory Champagne. By the time you read this, the Tilos may or may not have been closed down again, but it will definitely be missed if it goes under. Live bands play in a low, smoky cellar – if it's weird and passing through Budapest, it'll appear here. There's a big dance floor upstairs, two bars and mezzanine chill-out enclosure. On a good night, there's nowhere else like it. (See also chapters **Cafés & Bars** and **Nightlife**.)

Titanic

VII. Akácfa utca 58 (342 7569). Tram 4, 6 to Királyi utca. **Open** 6pm-1am Mon-Wed; 6pm-4am Thur-Sat. **Concerts** 9pm or midnight. **Admission** concerts Ft250.
Large three-room venue rarely even half-full. Live music features mainly blues and jazz acts, with dancing until the early hours. Full menu and comfortable bar area.

VMH

VIII. Golgota utca 3 (113 0607). Tram 23, 24/bus 99. **Open** from 7pm. **Admission** Ft300-Ft750.
Former home to the Black Hole, Budapest's punk venue of yesteryear, VMH now mixes thrash with cash, featuring popular Hungarian rock bands with a tune or two in surroundings where you are not likely to get vomit on your trousers.

Jazz Venues

The resurgence of jazz in the 1990s persuaded club owners to limit the number of pool tables and invest in live music. With no language barrier, the music is less baffling to the foreign community. Unfortunately most clubs are too small to warrant top Western acts fitting Hungary into their schedules, so most of the music on offer is home grown. Major tobacco and spirits companies sponsor regular jazz festivals, so good domestic talent can be nurtured. The Dresch Quartet are not to be missed, nor their saxophone player Mihály Dresch when he is playing solo. Trio Midnight are worth checking out, as are solo shows by their pianist Kálmán Oláh. Aladár Pege is Hungary's king of the double bass. Gyula Babos, former leader of seminal group Saturnus and jazz chair at the Liszt Ferenc Music Academy, is the one Hungarian artist who has

Big Mambo! *Jazz, pizza – you need more?*

Eating & Drinking

Film

Music

Nightlife

Art

Sport

Theatre

Shopping

Comedy

Your passport to London

Time Out

At newsagents every Wednesday

earned major recognition abroad. He played with Frank Zappa and James Moody then released *Blue Victory* in 1995, featuring Victor Bailey and Terri Lyne Carrington. He regularly gigs in Europe.

Big Mambo!

VIII. Mária utca 48 (210 3436). M3 Ferenc körút. **Open** 4pm-2am Mon-Fri; 6pm-2am Sat, Sun. **Concerts** 9pm. **Admission** free.

Huge cellar with two rooms and main bar area, small corner stage for jazz acts, and modest menu of pizzas and omelettes. Pleasant atmosphere but not that much room for dancing.

Jazz Café

V. Balassi Bálint utca 25 (269 5506). Tram 2, 4, 6. **Open** 6pm-3am daily. **Live music** 8-10pm Tue-Sat. **Admission** free.

The trendiest jazz venue in town with blue lights, draught Kronenbourg, pool in the back room and trendy statues in the main room. Stage area a little cramped for the musicians. Generally decent background music after showtime. Cool atmosphere almost despite its efforts to engender one.

Old Man's Music Pub

VII. Akácfa utca 13 (322 7645). M2 Blaha Lujza tér. **Open** noon-2am daily. **Concerts** 9pm. **Admission** free.

Strange décor for a jazz bar, more like the set for an Ovaltine advert: dim lights, plenty of woodwork, old wireless sets and telephones. An older clientèle can enjoy their pizzas in peace, washed down with a choice of six draught beers including Guinness.

Specialist Shops

Underground Records

VI. Hegedű utca 6 (141 0000). M1 Opera. **Open** 10am-6pm Mon-Fri. **No credit cards.**

Budapest's best source for dance music is primarily a DJ shop, stocked with groove, hip hop, techno, trance, jungle and ambient 12 inch singles, though they also have a few CDs. Black Market in the same space serves up lighter-weight pop disco. Good place to pick up flyers advertising local raves and parties.

Z Hanglemez

VIII. Rákóczi út 47 (133 0143). M2 Blaha Lujza tér/tram 4, 6. **Open** 1pm-6pm Mon-Fri. **No credit cards.**

Tiny courtyard shop devoted exclusively to the works of Frank Zappa: LPs, CDs, cassettes and videos. The friendly proprietor bears more than a passing resemblance to FZ himself and will cheerfully try to track down rarities he doesn't happen to have in stock.

Diáksziget

'We try to stage something that simply doesn't exist any more,' is how Diáksziget (Student Island) organiser-in-chief Péter Müller describes the ethos behind the annual week-long festival of rock and performance arts on a deserted island in the Danube.

His idea harks back to a time when there was a genuine youth community in Hungary. Ten years ago, pre-pop teenagers could spend their summer at a Communist Pioneer camp. Meanwhile, the post-pop generation of underground musicians, headed by Müller himself as leader of bands URH and Kontroll Csoport, could hang out with other groups around Budapest and the Balaton. Both cultures died with the changes of 1989.

In an attempt to recapture the spirit, each August Müller and hundreds of co-workers put together seven days of music on eight stages, plus films, videos, dance, theatre and cabaret performances. Camping prices are kept low.

The result is something like a rock theme park: a small town of peaceful, drunken music fans staggering from stage to stage, sleeping where they drop, waking up next to whomever they dropped off with. Although some bands are invited, most of the headliners tend to be Hungarian groups from the 1980s. Look out for guest acts from neighbouring countries.

Though the overall standard of music is nothing to shout about, there's still plenty of fun to be had. Beer is copious and dangerously cheap. There's also a funfair, a football pitch and a wedding tent. One fan married his beer in 1994.

Nightlife

The Pest side is teeming with strip joints, sex bars and casinos – or you might just about prefer toasted cheese sandwiches in an all-night bar in Buda.

If you were changing trains in the middle of the night, had a full wallet and a few hours to kill, left your luggage at Keleti and wandered into town, Budapest would seem pretty damn disappointing. But there's plenty enough to do if you know where to look. What Budapest nightlife lacks in soul or bright lights, it makes up for in convenience. You can dance, drink and shop till the early hours, but whether the experience will be a memorable one depends on your mood and your company.

Budapest is not a great clubbing city. You might go to meet friends, or catch a live band (generally uninspiring rock music) but there isn't much excitement out there, either on or off the dance floor. Except for a techno scene still in its infancy and devoid of regular venues (look out for flyers advertising irregular raves), dance culture here is somewhat lame. A more prominent black community or gay scene would work wonders, but neither is likely to materialise in the near future. (*See also* chapter **Music: Rock, Roots & Jazz.**)

Bars range from the cosy eszpresszó to the seedy topless joint with many acceptable hangouts in between. Games machines play a major role in the lives of many late-night types.

Getting around at night is easy. There is a decent night bus service, public transport starts running from 4.40am and taxis, if chosen wisely (*see chapter* **Getting Around**), are cheap and reliable. At the end of a long night there can be no more welcoming sight than the oval glow of a Főtaxi sign appearing round the corner.

Conversely there can be no more harrowing sight than a Budapest nightclub bouncer in full swing. Provoking one of these bruisers, or even answering back, is likely to be hazardous to your health – many places only employ them because they're part of an organised mafia who would otherwise cause them trouble. But apart from these frustrated neanderthals, you should be fairly safe in night-time Budapest. Mugging, although not unheard of, is pretty rare.

The city is well stocked with 24-hour stores, non-stops, which sell basics such as tampons, milk and warm beer.

Hungarians dine fairly early and most restaurants are closed by midnight, but in town you won't have problems finding a pizza or pancake.

Clubs

Aztec
VI. Mozsár utca 9 (153 0729). M1 Oktogon/tram 4, 6/night bus 6É. **Open** 7pm-4am Tue-Sat. **Admission** Ft200. **No credit cards.**
Large but ludicrous dance club done out in sun gods and blue neon. Weekend entrance fee covers live music and passable DJing. Karaoké on Tuesdays. Full menu of Hungarian and international standards. Pleasant enough if you're with the right, youngish crowd.

Bahnhof
VI. Váci út 1 (no phone). M3 Nyugati/tram 4, 6/night bus 6É, 182É. **Open** 6pm-4am Mon-Sat. **Admission** Ft200. **No credit cards.**

Formerly a Nyugati Station outbuilding, this was the place to be in the summer of 1995. There's more to this place than two dance floors crowded with beautiful young things. The railway theme is imaginatively brought out by model trains under the glass bar counter and old compartments instead of tables and chairs. Czech Staropramen beer at Ft200 a korsó is better than you'll get on Hungarian State Railways, the music is almost always danceable, and there's a back room for smooching. Watch out for the brutish bouncers, though.

Bamboo
VI. Dessewffy utca 44 (112 3619). M1 Oktogon/tram 4, 6/ night bus 6É. **Open** 3pm-2am Mon-Thur; 3pm-4am Fri; 7pm-4am Sat; 7pm-2am Sun. **Admission** free. **No credit cards.**
Small cellar done out like a Bounty advert. Free admission attracts a particularly young crowd, but draught Guinness and Weizenbier are almost prohibitively expensive. One of the few places in town where, midweek, you're bound to hear golden disco hits of the 1970s. Occasional live jazz.

Franklin Trocadero
VI. Szent István körút 15 (111 4691). M3 Nyugati/tram 4, 6/night buses 6É, 182É. **Open** 9pm-4am Mon-Thur, Sun; 9pm-5am Fri, Sat. **Admission** Ft250. **No credit cards.**
The best Latin disco in town – in fact the only Latin disco in town – with live acts from Wednesday to Sunday. Large dance floor area downstairs with a small bar in the corner; mezzanine bar upstairs offers a good vantage point for perusing the action below. Bright, metallic and clean, it attracts an appealingly multinational crowd.

Hully Gully
XII. Apor Vilmos tér 9 (175 9742). Tram 59/bus 105, 112. **Open** 9pm-5am daily. **Admission** Ft500. **Credit** AmEx, MC, V.
Any foreigner heeding the taxi driver's promise of a 'wery good deesko with wery larvely girls' will immediately be whisked here – usually by the scenic route. A fair way up from Moszkva tér and the biggest meat market in town, the Hully Gully has all the clichés: goons on the door, go-go girls, hookers at the bar, two-level disco and laser show. If this is what you want, Ft300 is not an unreasonable entrance fee. Drinks aren't too bad either, although the taxi drivers outside will shamelessly rip you off again on the way home.

Piaf
VI. Nagymező utca 25 (112 3823). M1 Oktogon/tram 4, 6/night bus 6É. **Open** 10pm-6am daily. **Admission** Ft250. **No credit cards.**
A venerable institution, Piaf is the after-hours hang-out of the older arty crowd on Budapest's old Broadway. Upstairs it looks like a whorehouse: red velvet, candlelight and wobbly seating. Down a dangerous narrow staircase you'll find a dark cellar bar and minuscule dance floor, with music ranging erratically from old blues tunes through classic soul, funk and punk. Best place in central Pest for that one, last drink. Your admission price covers this.

Tilos az Á Borozó
VIII. Mikszáth Kálmán tér 2 (118 0684). M3 Kálvin tér/tram 4, 6, 47, 49/night bus 6É, 182É. **Open** 9pm-2am Mon-Thur; 9pm-4am Fri, Sat; 9pm-1am Sun. **Admission** Ft300. **No credit cards.**
Now technically a wine bar, to get round the District VIII council's attempts to close them down, Budapest's main alternative club isn't just a place to catch some raucous local band in the cellar space. People also come here just to drink, dance and – you never know – find someone to take home. The DJing is usually lousy and pretty much always the same – Gypsy Kings meets The Stranglers – but weekend nights there's a good mood out on the high-ceilinged dance floor, decorated with an inept but likable Manhattan street scene mural. (*See also chapter* **Music: Rock, Roots & Jazz.**)

Sex Bars

Take a walk down Váci utca after dark. Within 20 yards you'll be handed a leaflet about a topless bar. It'll promise 'the companionship of extremely pretty girls' and warn you to ignore the recommendations of taxi drivers or touts from rival establishments. Walk around a while and you can collect dozens of these things, and probably also get approached by a hooker or two.

Sex tourism is big business in this town. There are literally hundreds of topless bars and strip joints around Budapest, the busiest making up to $500,000 a year from foreign businessmen and tourists on junket trips. Many, but by no means all, are fronts for prostitution. Even in those that aren't, overcharging is the name of the game, and the girls take a large cut of the expensive 'cocktails' you're encouraged to buy them. Many of the women are Ukrainian or Russian and adept at negotiating customers back to the nearest hotel or a flat hired by the club. Most of the trade is controlled by the Ukrainian mafia.

If a bunch of lads are in town, wedged up and on the hoy, chances are they'll be in the Blue Angel (VIII. Baross utca 5), which is open from 9pm-5am daily and charges no entrance fee. If you must try one of these places, that one's as good (or as useless) as any of them. And we're not getting a cut from them. Honest.

Bars

See also chapter **Cafés & Bars.**

Alkotás Presszó

XII. Alkotás út 47 (212-3745). M2 Déli/tram 61. **Open** 24 hours daily. **No credit cards.**
A short walk up from the naff bars alongside Déli Station lies possibly the best all-night bar in town. A terrace, a large bar area and back room for pool await the visitor, with a piano and two pinball machines tucked away behind large velvet curtains. Flaking paintwork, worn carpet, tacky lightshades, a good choice of bottled beers and bar snacks such as casino eggs and toasted cheese sandwiches – it all seems so romantic on a rainy night with the right companion.

Balett Cipő

VI. Hajós utca 14 (269 3114). M1 Opera/night bus 182É. **Open** 2pm-4am Mon-Fri; 10pm-4am Sat. **No credit cards.**
Former haunt of ballet dancers from the Opera House nearby – hence the name and the shoes hanging from the mirrors inside – now a cosy, seedy late-night dive perfect for loners and lovers. Cocktails to order. Slavia Prague mug and thermometer courtesy of the football-mad Czech boss.

Barbados

V. Váci utca 56-58 (267 0207). M3 Ferenciek tere/night bus 78É. **Open** 8am-8am daily. **No credit cards.**
Ridiculous but bearable girlie bar at the unfashionable end of Váci utca. Despite the pimps, hookers and ill-clad dancers, the Barbados is far less repugnant than others of its kind downtown and at least offers HB beer at Ft90 a pint. Enjoy the lowlife and don't step on anyone's toes on the way to the toilets.

Dreher Játékterem

XIII. Váci út 6 (153 4765). M3 Nyugati/tram 4, 6/night bus 6É, 182É. **Open** 24 hours daily. **No credit cards.**
Opposite the bleeping games machines of the Westend Shopping Centre. The Játékterem (amusement arcade) has fruit machines in the back room, but the main bar area is a reasonable spot for a beer at a silly time of the morning. Billions of satellite channels on the television, but they all seem to show soft porn or motor sports around 4am.

Museum Cukrászda

VIII. Múzeum körút 10 (266 4526). M2 Astoria/tram 47, 49/night bus 78É, 182É. **Open** 24 hours daily. **No credit cards.**
Unless you're in the mood for a munch, the main attraction of this all-night overlit cake store is the reasonably priced draught Innstadt beer and bottles of dark and weizen beers. This fact is not lost on the Tilos crowd, many of whom nip in here after that place closes. Salads also available.

Talk Talk Café

V. Magyar utca 12-14 (267 2878). M2 Astoria/tram 47, 49/night bus 78É, 182É. **Open** 24 hours daily. **No credit cards.**
Not a lot happens here in the small hours, but at least it's always open and still serving coffee and sandwiches as well as Czech beers and cocktails. (*See also chapter* **Cafés & Bars.**)

Nothing But The Blues

VIII. Krúdy Gyula utca 6 (no phone). M3 Kálvin tér/tram 4, 6, 47, 49/night bus 6É, 182É. **Open** noon-3am Mon-Sat. **Admission** free. **No credit cards.**
Smoky haunt of serious drinkers unable to face the entrance fee or the cellar stairs at the Tilos down the road. The décor is risible – titles of blues standards stencilled in brown on the pine beams, a paper maché Hendrix, a preposterous mural of Morrison – but draught Stella (Ft150 a pint) and Leffe (Ft200) make up for it. Modest menu of breaded meats and cheese.

Yes

XIII. Hegedűs Gyula utca 1 (269 3105). M3 Nyugati/tram 4, 6/night bus 6É, 182É. **Open** 8am-4am daily. **No credit cards.**
Daft late-night haunt of alcoholics and company-seekers. An intimate two-floor bar near Vígszínház best experienced after a skinful around Újlipótváros, Yes answers all questions: 'Do I really want that one last beer?' 'Yes.' 'Am I bashing the hell out of the downstairs pinball machine?' 'Yes.' 'Aren't those mafia types in the corner amusing?' 'Oh God, did I really spend Ft5,000?' 'It can't be 4am already?' 'Yes.'

Restaurants

Berliner

IX. Ráday utca 5 (217 6757). M3 Kálvin tér/tram 47, 49/night bus 182É. **Open** 9am-4am Mon-Sat; 10am-midnight Sun. **Average** Ft700. **No credit cards.**
Spacious wooden beer hall and restaurant serving Hungarian and international standards at reasonable prices. Small upstairs bar can get a little heavy if the crop-haired, right-wing brigade show up.

Casino Restaurant

V. Vigadó utca 2 (118 4576). M1 Vörösmarty tér. Night bus 18?F. **Open** 10am-4am daily. **Average** Ft1,500. **Credit** AmEx, DC, MC, V.
Tourist-trap restaurant attached to the casino between Vörösmarty tér and the Danube. Large menu of heavy stews and meats, beer Ft400 the korsó, terrace open in the daytime.

Don Pepe Pizzeria

V. Nyugati tér 8 (132 2954). M3 Nyugati/tram 4, 6/night bus 182É. **Open** noon-6am daily. **Average** Ft600. **No credit cards.**
Acceptable alternative to sleeping rough in Nyugati Station, the Don Pepe serves acceptable pizzas and draught Amstel to the sleepless parked on its green wooden benches.

Nagymama Palacsintázója

I. Hattyú utca 16 (no phone). M2 Moszkva tér/night bus 6É/night tram 49É. **Open** 24 hours daily. **No credit cards.**
All-night pancakes more savoury than the clientèle consuming them.

Stop Bisztró

V. Váci utca 86 (267 0273). Tram 47, 49/night bus 182É. **Open** *Apr-Oct* 9am-4am, *Nov-Mar* 10am-1am, daily. **Average** Ft700. **Credit** DC, JCB, MC, V.
Acceptable backpacker trap at the Fővám tér end of Váci utca. Not even Germans are caught out by the faded numbers on the window saying '0 Ft – korsó'. It's Ft150 for a pint of Kaiser to wash down your Ft485 tourist menu. Reasonable selection of Hungarian standards.

Faites vos jeux at the **Várkert Casino.**

Szent Jupát

II. Retek utca 16 (212 2928). M2 Moszkva tér/night bus 6É/night tram 49É. **Open** 8am-4am daily. **Average** Ft550. **No credit cards.**
Named after a Hungarian boat that sailed round the world, the Szent Jupát is an institution for late-night swillers. Massive dinners are served on large, oval wooden platters deep into the night, complemented by reasonably priced draught beer. Bring an appetite.

Szieszta Pizzéria

XIII. Szent István körút 10 (131 8180). M3 Nyugati/tram 4, 6/night bus 6É, 182É. **Open** 8am-4am daily. **Average** Ft600. **No credit cards.**
The Szieszta buzzes deep into the night when diners can observe action on the Nagykörut from the upstairs restaurant. Music usually seems to be early 1980s dance classics. Pizzas are generally acceptable; the pasta is crap. Try the leek soup.

Arcades

West End Shopping Centre

VI. Nyugati Station (no phone). M3 Nyugati/tram 4, 6/night bus 6É, 182É. **Open** 24 hours daily. **No credit cards.**
All-night big-screen arcade games, pinball machines and other games. Loads of neon, noise and nearby fast-food joints.

Labirintus

VI. Teréz körút 55 (06 30 403 351). M3 Nyugati/tram 4, 6/night bus 6É, 182É. **Open** 2pm-6am daily. **No credit cards.**
All-night laser games in Nyugati's shopping arcade, promising 'Adventures in the Twentieth Century'.

Casinos

Budapest has nine casinos – five on the strip between Roosevelt tér and Elizabeth Bridge – all of which take only Western currency, usually US dollars. The best by far is the Várkert, worth visiting for the building, a neo-Renaissance former pump-house for the Royal Palace designed by Miklós Ybl. Its chief rival, the Las Vegas, offers glitz rather than glamour.

Bring your passport or you won't get in.

Várkert Casino

I. Ybl Miklós tér 9 (202 4244). Buses 86, 116/tram 19. **Open** 2pm-5am daily. **Admission** $10. **Games** American roulette, poker, blackjack, punto banco, dice. **Credit** MC, V.

Las Vegas

Atrium Hyatt Hotel, V. Roosevelt tér 2 (117 6022). Tram 2/bus 16, 105. **Open** 2pm-5am daily. **Admission** $10. **Games** American roulette, poker, blackjack, punto banco, dice. **Credit** AmEx, DC, JCB, MC, V.

Non-stops

Non-stops, 24-hour grocery and liquor stores, had their heyday in the early 1990s when many owners made a killing from new-found custom. Now, with the economy down the tubes and staying up late no longer a novelty, they're thinner on the ground. If you're in Pest, there'll be a non-stop

Non-stops *are 24-hour grocery and liquor stores – invaluable for late-night essentials.*

within a ten-minute walk. Some have delicatessen counters, others even keep their beer chilled. Because of rising crime, some (though none listed here) now have a grille on the door and a little gap to trade through. At these you'll probably need a Hungarian speaker to help with anything more complicated than bread and beer.

Super Sarok
II. Retek utca 15 (no phone). M2 Moszkva tér. Night bus 6É/night tram 49É. **Open** 24 hours daily. **No credit cards.**

Non-stop ABC
II. Déli Station (no phone). M2 Déli/night tram 49É. **Open** 24 hours daily. **No credit cards.**

Dóm Market
V. Bajcsy-Zsilinszky út 24 (no phone). M3 Arany János utca/night bus 182É. **Open** 24 hours daily. **No credit cards.**

Nyugati ABC
VI. Nyugati Station (no phone). M3 Nyugati/tram 4, 6/night bus 6É, 182É. **Open** 24 hours daily. **No credit cards.**

Non-stop ABC
VI. Nagymező utca 14 (no phone). M1 Oktogon/tram 4, 6/night bus 6É. **Open** 24 hours daily. **No credit cards.**

Dreher
VII. Rákóczi út 17 (no phone). M2 Astoria/tram 47, 49/night bus 78É, 182É. **Open** 24 hours daily.
Useful, despite surly staff. Tucked between Blaha Lujza tér and Astoria, one half is a bakery, with a night-time counter-service, the other a bar serving draught beer and some runny salads. Tables outside, even.

Novák Delikát
VIII. Üllői út 2 (no phone). M3 Kálvin tér/tram 47, 49/night bus 182É. **Open** 24 hours daily. **No credit cards.**

Non-stop ABC
VIII. Baross tér 3 (no phone). M2 Keleti/night bus 78É. **Open** 24 hours daily. **No credit cards.**

Non-stop ABC
XI. Móricz Zsigmond körtér 9 (no phone). Tram 6/night bus 6É, 153É. **Open** 24 hours daily. **No credit cards.**

Non-stop ABC and Pizzeria
XIII. Hegedűs Gyula utca 20A (140 0454). M3 Nyugati/tram 4, 6/night bus 6É, 182É. **Open** 24 hours daily. **No credit cards.**
This non-stop has a rudimentary all-night pizzeria with salad bar attached. Take the food away (Ft200-Ft300 for pizza or pasta), or sit on stools and munch from a shelf. Alcohol to wash it down can be bought in the shop.

Stalls

Florists
V. Margaret Bridge Pest side. Tram 4, 6/night bus 6É. **Open** 24 hours daily. **No credit cards.**
All-night florists also selling cigarettes and chewing gum.

After a heavy night's drinking why not top up your vitamin C levels at one of Budapest's many 24-hour greengrocers?

Déli Station Florists
XII. Alkotás utca 2 (no phone). M2 Déli/night tram 49É. **Open** 24 hours daily. **No credit cards.**
Roses in abundance for those late-night Déli winos who hit a romantic patch.

Greengrocers

Zöldség Gyümölcs
V. Jászai Mari tér (no phone). Tram 4, 6/night bus 6É. **Open** 24 hours daily. **No credit cards.**
Two stalls on either side of the körút selling fruit, vegetables and cold drinks.

Ínyenc Zöldség Gyümölcs
VI. Oktogon (no phone). M1 Oktogon/tram 4, 6/night bus 6É. **Open** 24 hours daily. **No credit cards.**
Standard if expensive supply of fruit and vegetables.

Zöldség Gyümölcs
VI. Teréz körút (corner of Podmaniczky utca). M3 Nyugati/tram 4, 6/night bus 6É, 182É. **Open** 24 hours daily. **No credit cards.**
Exotic range of late-night fruits. If you want a mango or a star fruit at 4am, this is the place to come.

Other Shops & Services

Folkart Centrum
V. Váci utca 14 (118 5840). M1 Vörösmarty tér/M2 Ferenciek tere. **Open** 9am-4pm daily. **Credit** AmEx, DC, EC, JCB, MC, V.
For reasons best known to the management, but probably not unconnected to the roulette tables and horrid café upstairs, this tacky, unpleasant tourist shop is open while the rest of Váci sleeps or hustles. It makes little sense, as their attitude seems to be that if you're up this late, you're probably a shoplifter who must be watched, hawk-like, by a surely uneconomic plethora of surly assistants. Nothing in here worth nicking anyway: just overpriced strings of dried paprika and nasty folkloric ornaments.

Copy General
IX. Lónyay utca 36 (218 9052/fax 217 5304). Tram 4, 6/night bus 6É. **Open** 24 hours daily. **No credit cards.**
Round-the-clock photocopying and related services.

Fotifon Videotéka
XIII. Pannónia utca 13 (132 5027). M3 Nyugati/tram 4, 6/night bus 6É, 182É. **Open** 24 hours daily. **No credit cards.**
Roughly 200 English-language movies in stock. Six-month membership costs Ft500, but you need Hungarian ID, so the only option is to get a friend to join on your behalf. Videos are Ft60 for eight hours.

Ibusz Travel Agency
V. Apáczai Csere János utca 1 (118 5776). M3 Ferenciek tere/night bus 78É. **Open** 24 hours daily. **Credit** AmEx.
Can arrange accommodation at all hours.

Ibusz Bank
V. Petőfi tér 3 (118 5707). M3 Ferenciek tere/night bus 78É. **Open** 24 hours daily.
Non-stop change service.

Car Wash
XIII. Hegedűs Gyula utca 57 (no phone). M3 Lehel tér/night bus 6É. **Open** 24 hours daily. **No credit cards.**

Sport & Fitness

Hungary may have been declared unfit some years ago as far as football is concerned, but there's no shortage of opportunites to get your kit off, don a silly hat and do the strand.

There may be little world-class professional sport to watch in Hungary, but sport is still cheap entertainment and there are plenty of leisure activities. Horse-riding, swimming and tennis are popular at weekends and football is the main draw for spectators. Imported Western sports keep a few expats amused and natives bemused, but golf is still too expensive to be popular. The biggest event is the Grand Prix, held in August. For regular details throughout the year, consult the Hungarian daily *Nemzeti Sport* – you should be able to make out the times and venues of events.

Note: some sports clubs, particularly those catering mainly to wealthy foreigners, peg their prices to the Deutschmark.

Major Stadia

Népstadion
XIV. Istvánmezei út 1-3 (251 1222). M2 Népstadion.
This is the national stadium, built by and for the people (*nép*), in 1953. Its capacity is 76,000, only filled when major rock bands come to town. A roof would allow it to host major international sporting events; until one arrives, its biggest attraction are the Stalinist statues outside.

Budapest Sportcsarnok
XIV. Stefánia út 2 (251 6359). M2 Népstadion.
With a capacity of 10,000, this is the major indoor venue for sports events.

Spectator Sports

Football

Of all the tragedies which have befallen Hungarian sport this century, the fate of football is the saddest. The national team, the Mighty Magyars, the first Continental side to beat England at Wembley (6-3 in 1953), are now the miserable minnows of world soccer and have not qualified for the finals of any major tournament for ten years. (*See also* **They Think It's All Over** *page 206.*)

Club football attracts average crowds of 5,000. The season runs from August to late November, then from March until June. The first division, NB1, comprises 16 teams, half from Budapest. Games generally take place on Saturday afternoons, with admission about Ft200. Facilities are poor, but unless two rival Budapest sides are

meeting (particularly **Ferencváros** and **Újpest**) there is little danger at matches. Ferencváros is the only club where alcohol is not available.

Note: If you're stuck for somewhere to watch a big local or satellite-televised match, you could do worse than try the **Kétballábas** restaurant (*see chapter* **Restaurants**).

Ferencváros
IX. Üllői út 129 (215 6025). M3 Népliget.
The people's team, 'Fradi', served no masters during the Communist era. This earned the club popular favour from which sprang a right-wing following in the early 1990s. The stadium, an all-seater 20,000, is modern and can boast a real atmosphere when full. Ferencváros won the double in 1995 and then qualified for the Champions' League. Don't wear lilac (Újpest) here.

Kispest-Honvéd
XIX. Újtemető utca 1-3 (282 9789). M3 Határ út then tram 42 for six stops.
The former army side that supplied nine of the famous national side of the 1950s is a fairly modest one now. Kispest-Honvéd has won seven titles over the last decade but has met with little international success despite some financial interest from Belgian shareholders. The famous former Honvéd star, Ferenc Puskás, has an executive role propping up the club bar. The stadium, the Bozsik, holds 15,000 people, 6,000 seated. Recent investment has been limited to a members-only bar, the Bozsik's best facility. The fiercer fan element, the Kispest Sexy Hamburgers, stand behind the goal opposite the scoreboard. Seated section covered.

Újpest
IV. Megyeri út 13 (169 7333/169 2570). M3 Újpest Központ then bus 104 or 104A for four stops.
The Lilacs can boast the most passionate, if not the most numerous, support. This former police team, which as Újpest Dózsa lost to Newcastle in the 1969 Fairs' Cup final, has the biggest club ground in Budapest, holding 32,000 fans, 8,000 seated, uncovered. There is a pleasant bar/restaurant. Don't wear green (Ferencváros) here.

Horse Racing

Going to the races is a convivial and cheap way to spend the afternoon. Budapest has two courses, the flat (*galopp*) and trotting (*ügető*). Both courses are appealingly dilapidated and well supplied with bars. **Kincsem** has a restaurant.

The betting system is now computerised. Because of the heavy taxes, most punters avoid going for a win (*tét*) or place (*hely*) and prefer the *befutó*, a bet on horses to come in first and second or first and third. The *hármas* is 1, 2, 3, and the boxed *befutó* gives the option of any order. On

Gyms and fitness centres do good business in Budapest – see **Activities: Health & Fitness.**

course, bets must be read over at any of the dozens of windows under the main stand, the punter giving the type of bet, the stake, and the horse number(s). The odds, displayed on TV screens nearby, give expected returns on a Ft10 stake, the minimum bet. The numbers 3-25 means that horse 3 winning will give you Ft25 for your 10 wagered, or, in British terminology, 5/2.

Flat Racing
Kincsem Park *X. Albertirsai út 2 (263 7858). M2 Pillangó utca.* **Open** *Apr-Nov from 2pm Thur, Sun.* **Admission** Ft100.

Trotting
Ügetőpálya *VIII. Kerepesi út 9-11 (134 2958). Bus 95.* **Open** *all year from 3pm Sat; from 5pm Wed.* **Admission** Ft100.

Motor Racing

The Hungarian Grand Prix or *Hungaroring* is the biggest event in the sporting calendar. It was re-introduced in 1986 after 50 years but nearly winked back out of existence in 1995. Only last-minute talks at government level saved this traditional lossmaker. Its future still remains in doubt.

Hungaroring
20km E of Budapest off M3 motorway at Mogyoród (06 28 330 040). **Information** *Formula 1 Kft, V. Apáczai Csere János utca 11 (118 7610). M1, M2 or M3 to Deák tér.* **Open** *8am-6pm daily one month before the event.* **Date** *second Sunday in August.* **Admission** *on race day* Ft2,500, Ft4,500 standing; Ft8,000, Ft19,000 sitting.

Swimming

Komjádi Béla Sportuszoda
III. Árpád Béla fejedelem útja 8 (212 2750). Bus 6, 60, 86.
Hungary's national swimming stadium, named after the coach who, in 1932, led Hungary to its first Olympic gold in water polo. Expect a full house for top water polo matches and international swimming galas.

Activities

Cycling

Cycling is illegal on motorways and major roads, and, considering the standard of driving in Budapest, inadvisable during rush hour. Bikes can be taken on certain trains, normally the first or last carriage, but not on trams or the metro. The bike path alongside the road to Szentendre from town makes for a pleasant afternoon's ride. Margaret Island has two stalls by the roundabout near Margaret Bridge, generally open from 8am-dusk, where you can rent bikes for use in town.

The Friends of City Cycling Group
III. Miklós tér 1 (111 7855). Tram 1, Bus 6, 86.
Produces a *Map for Budapest Cyclists*, showing bike lanes, riding conditions and service shops.

Hungarian Camping & Caravan Club
VIII. Kálvin tér 9, First Floor (218 5259). M3 Kálvin tér.
Can provide information if required.

Hungarian Cycling Association

XIV. Szabó József utca 3 (252 0879). Bus 7, 78.
The Millenáris cycle track here is the only one in Hungary.

IBUSZ Leisure Department

V. Ferenciek tere 10, III/5 (118 2967). M3 Ferenciek tere. **Open** 8.30am-3.30pm Mon-Thur; 8am-2.30pm Fri. **No credit cards.**
IBUSZ can arrange cycling trips through the Danube Bend, in the Puszta and across southern Hungary for an average DM1,750. This covers two weeks' half-board for a double room and bike hire.

National Rail Office (MÁV)

VI. Andrássy út 35 (322 8275). M1 to Opera. **Open** 9am-6pm Mon-Fri.
The National Rail Office (MÁV) can provide a list of cycle-friendly stations and the surcharges per kilometre for cycling tickets (*kerékpárjegy*).

Schwinn-Csepel

VI. Hegedű utca 6 (142 4620). M1 Oktogon. **Open** 10am-6pm Mon-Wed; 10am-7pm Thur; 10am-6pm Fri; 10am-1pm Sat. **No credit cards.**
A bike shop with a service and repair department.

Golf

The bourgeois sport of golf was banned in Hungary in 1952 and prices at courses recently opened continue to keep the game inaccessible to most Hungarians. There is no course in Budapest and the nearest is 40km away at Kisoroszi.

Budapest Golfpark & Country Club

40km north of Budapest, along route 11 past Szentendre to Kisoroszi (06 60 321 673). **Office** *V. Bécsi utca 5 (117 6025).* **Open** *Mar-15 Nov* 8am-8pm daily. **Fee** Ft3,000 per round Mon-Fri; Ft3,500 per round Sat, Sun. **Club rental** Ft1,000; *carts* Ft300. **Membership** DM1,600 per year.

Hencse National Golf & Country Club

175km south-west of Budapest at Hencse, Kossuth Lajos utca 3 (82 351 209/fax 82 351 444). **Open** 7am-dusk daily. **Fee** *day card* DM50 Mon-Fri; DM66 Sat, Sun.
Set in the splendid surroundings of a National Park. Rooms cost DM100 for a single, DM125 double, with negotiable group fees.

Golf Range

Petneházy Club Hotel

II. Feketefej utca 2/4 (06 30 441 185). Tram 56 from Moszkva tér, then bus 63. **Open** 10am-8pm daily; *summer* 10am-9.30pm daily. **Fee** Ft300 per bucket of 36 balls, plus Ft150 for each club hired.

Health & Fitness

Hungarians make an effort about their appearance, despite all the fatty, sugary food. Gyms and fitness centres are usually filled from 7am until after dark. For information on aerobics contact the **Hungarian Aerobics Federation** *V. Széchenyi utca 8 (112 5699).*

A number of Budapest hotels have facilities available to non-guests:

Forum Hotel

V. Apáczai Csere János utca 12-14 (117 8088). M1 Vörösmarty tér/tram 2. **Open** *for non-guests* 7am-9pm daily. **Rates** Ft15,000 for three months' use; Ft600 per session in the swimming pool; Ft1,000 with sauna. **Credit** AmEx, DC, JCB, MC, V.

Kempinski Hotel

V. Erzsébet tér 7-8 (266 1000). M1, M2, M3 Deák tér. **Open** for non-guests 7am-10pm daily. **Rates** *single membership* Ft15,000 per month; *double membership* Ft25,000.
Entry is with a membership card which can be paid for with all major credit cards. There's a reduced rate of Ft6,000 per month if you use only the facilities 10am-5pm Mon-Fri.

Thermal Hotel Aquincum

III. Árpád fejedelem útja 94 (250 3360). HÉV to Árpád híd. **Open** *for non-guests* 7am-9pm daily. **Rates** Ft450 per hour before 10am; Ft950 per hour 10am-9pm; Ft8,000 per month for ten entries. **No credit cards.**

If the hotels don't measure up, you can try one of these cheaper centres:

Almássy tér Recreation Center

VII. Almássy tér 6 (267 8709). M2 Blaha Lujza tér/tram 4, 6. **Open** *swimming pool* 6.30am-9.30pm. **Admission** Ft120; ten sessions Ft1,000. Calanetics 9am-10pm Tue, Thur, Ft200 per session. **No credit cards.**
Pleasant, cheap place for a swim. Modest fitness facilities.

Andi Kondi

V. Hold utca 29 (111 0740). M2 Kossuth Lajos tér or M3 Arany János utca. **Open** 7am-9pm Mon-Fri; 8am-2pm Sat, Sun. **Rates** Ft300 per session; Ft2,000 ten sessions; Ft3,400 20 sessions. **No credit cards.**
One of the first of modern fitness centres in Budapest with over 40 machines. There are also various types of combined ticket for the solarium and aerobics classes. Facilities good, but a little cramped.

Astoria Fitness Center

V. Károly körút 4 (117 0452). M2 to Astoria. **Open** 7am-11pm Mon-Fri; 9am-9pm Sat, Sun. **Rates** Ft500 per session; Ft1,600 for four sessions; Ft2,400 for eight sessions; Ft3,400 for 12 sessions; Ft4,500 for 16 sessions. **No credit cards.**
The two solariums cost Ft600 per session; a 30-minute massage is Ft650. The Astoria 'techno gym' has a work-out for even the smallest of muscles.

Club Sziget

XIII. Margitsziget (112 9472). Bus 26. **Open** 7am-10pm Mon-Fri; 8am-6pm Sat, Sun. **Rates** Ft250 per session; Ft2,200 for ten sessions. **No credit cards.**
Cheapest fitness centre in town, with all the usual facilities.

Every Body Training Club

VI. Eötvös utca 12 (268 1450, ext 146). M1 Oktogon/ tram 4, 6. **Open** 7am-11pm Mon-Fri; 8am-5pm Sat, Sun. **Rates** Ft550 per day; Ft2,200 for five sessions; Ft4,000 for a month's use. **No credit cards.**
Centre run under the guidance of Ferenc Tóth, former world body-building champion, who can offer his professional advice. A sauna and Jacuzzi are also available. Regular aerobics classes are held.

Riding

Horsemanship is generally very popular with Magyars, no doubt harking back to the days when they galloped in here from Asia. There is ample opportunity for horse riding throughout the country, especially in the Puszta.

IBUSZ Leisure Department
V. Ferenciek tere 10, III/5 (118 2967). M3 Ferenciek tere. **Open** 8.30am-3.30pm Mon-Thur; 8am-2.30pm Fri.
Ibusz organises regular riding tours in the Puszta, the Danube Bend and Transdanubia. Groups are accompanied by a professional riding master and a multi-lingual guide. Cost for riding and full-board accommodation over ten days ranges from DM1,500-DM2,000, with single-room supplements and weekend rates of about DM600.

There are also various combinations of driving tours and dressage courses:

National Riding School
VIII. Kerepesi út 7 (113 5210). M2 Keleti pályaudavar. **Open** 8am-11am Mon-Sat; 2-5pm Sun.
Lessons cost Ft700 for a 45-minute session for children, Ft450 for Hungarian and Ft700 for foreign adults. English-language lessons are in the morning. Ten lessons are Ft2,850 for Hungarian children, Ft4,750 for foreign children, Ft3,450 for Hungarian adults and Ft4,750 for foreigners.

Petneházy Club Hotel
II. Feketefej utca 2-4 (176 5992). Tram 56 from Moszkva tér then bus 63. **Open** 9am-noon Tue-Fri; 2-5pm Sat; 9am-1pm Sun.
The club is 10km from town. Using the outdoor ring costs Ft700 per hour. Riding in the forest with a guide costs Ft1,200 per hour. Lessons at all levels are Ft500 per hour for children, Ft400 for adults. English-language instruction is scheduled at 4pm and at weekends. Staying at the Petneházy costs DM195 for two in high season, DM165 in low season, with 'American breakfast' and use of the swimming pool and sauna included.

Squash

City Squash Club
II. Marczibányi tér 13 (212 3110). Tram 4, 6. **Open** 7am-midnight daily.
There are four courts, on hire to non-members for Ft750 per person per hour (Ft1,050 per hour 5-10pm Mon-Fri). Racquets cost Ft150 per session. Light-coloured soles must be worn.

Hotel Marriott
V. Apáczai Csere János utca 4 (266 7000). M1 Vörörsmarty tér/tram 2. **Open** 7am-10pm Mon-Fri, 10am-8pm Sat-Sun.
There's only one court, costing Ft1,800 per hour. Racquet hire Ft300.

TSA Eurofit
I. Pálya utca 9 (156 9530). Bus 2, 78, 105. **Open** 7am-11pm daily. **No credit cards.**
There are two courts, on hire to non-members for Ft1,100 per hour until 4pm and Ft1,800 from 4-11pm. Racquets can be hired for Ft200 per session.

Swimming

Hungary has enjoyed remarkable success in competitive swimming. Alfréd Hajós won gold medals at the first modern Olympics in 1896, then built the pool on Margaret Island where generations of champions trained. In summer, open-air pools are popular. Certain pools and 'strands' (pools with an area where you can lie around in the sun) require swimming hats to be worn by both sexes. Day tickets, except at the **Gellért**, cost approximately Ft200 and books of 25 tickets cost around Ft3,000.

Gellért
XI. Kelenhegyi út 4-6 (185 3555). Tram 18, 19, 47, 49. **Open** 6am-7pm Mon-Sat; 6am-4pm Sun. **Rates** Ft600 day ticket; Ft11,900 for 25 days.
Grand, if expensive, setting for knocking out a few lengths. Warm indoor pool, relaxing outdoor pool, wave pool with a wave machine every hour, children's pool, thermal pool and sauna. Gay afternoons in the thermal pool on Wednesdays and Sundays.

Hajós Alfréd Nemzeti Sportuszoda
XIII. Margaret Island (111 4046). Tram 4, 6 then bus 26. **Open** 6am-5pm Mon-Fri; 6am-6pm Sat, Sun. **Rates** Ft120 day ticket.
The complex is named after its architect, who won Hungary's first Olympic gold medals for swimming and appeared in the first Hungarian national football team. Unfortunately, public use of the three pools – two outdoor, one indoor – is often limited by training or competitions. Sunbathing terrace and restaurant.

Lukács
II. Frankel Leó utca 25-29 (212 4088). Tram 17. **Open** 6am-7pm daily. Ft170 day ticket.
Nineteenth-century bath house with two swimming pools, four thermal pools, a spa, a Finnish sauna, a mud bath and physiotherapy. Caters for an older set.

Széchenyi Fürdő
Városliget, XIV. Állatkerti körút 11 (121 0310). M1 Széchenyi Fürdő. **Open** 6am-7pm daily; *winter* 6am-5pm Mon-Sat, 6am-4pm Sun. **Rates** Ft170 day ticket.
The hottest thermal pools in Budapest. The Széchenyi, housed in an elegant neo-Baroque building in City Park, really comes into its own in winter. Hardy folk trek over the ice from the thermal section to spend an afternoon playing chess in the outdoor pool under clouds of steam. A host of treatments also available.

Thermal Hotel Aquincum
III. Árpád fejedelem útja 94 (250 3360). HÉV Árpád híd. **Open** *to non guests* 7am-9pm daily. **Rates** *7-10am Mon-Fri* Ft450; *10am-9pm Mon-Fri* Ft950; *Sat, Sun* Ft1,200.
A boon for guests, but expensive otherwise. Three pools, sauna and solarium.

Thermal Hotel Helia
XIII. Kárpát utca 62-64 (270 3277). Trolleybus 79. **Open** *to non-guests* 7am-8pm daily. **Rates** *7am-3pm* Ft800; *3-10pm* Ft1,200.
Thermal waters transported from Margaret Island by tube. A wide range of thermal treatments on offer. Four pools, two thermal pools, sauna, underwater massage services.

Thermal Hotel Margitsziget
XIII. Margaret Island (111 1000). Tram 4, 6 then bus 26. **Open** *to non-guests* 7am-7pm daily. **Rates** Ft1,200 day ticket.
Built on the thermal springs of an old spa, this Margaret Island complex has three thermal pools – at 33, 35 and 39 degrees – two swimming pools, two single-sex saunas, a 28 degree swimming pool and a sunbathing terrace.

Strands

Doing the strand is an essential part of the Budapest summer. This involves posing by the open-air swimming pool and dealing with the occasional beer, swim and *lángos*. There are 12 strands

They Think It's All Over

Once, and once only, Hungary shook the sporting world. On 25 November 1953 its football team beat England at Wembley in a friendly match. Moreover, the 6-3 thrashing of a nation previously unbeaten by Continental opposition on its home turf represented a revolution in world football. It was the style with which Magyar brain overcame English brawn that opened people's eyes to a newer, modern game. Star of the show was Ferenc Puskás. His dragback which fooled English captain Billy Wright is one of the great moments in football history, a gorgeous split second of skill and wit.

Thanks to intelligent coaching and a rare crop of talented players who played regularly for the same club team, Hungary had toured Europe for three years without defeat. The game with England was billed as the match of the century, the clash of two styles. That afternoon in Budapest the streets were empty. Hungarian families gathered around radio sets, just like their English counterparts had clustered before TV sets for the coronation six months earlier. For 90 minutes the world stopped. After two world wars, Trianon and hard-line Communism, victory saw the biggest national celebration since the Millennium of 1896.

The players came home as heroes. After the 1956 Uprising, half the team, including Puskás, stayed abroad as refugees. The team broke up and Hungarian football has never touched such dizzy heights again. Puskás found further fame and fortune with Real Madrid. After managing teams on four continents, he came back in 1981 and can still be seen propping up the bar at Kispest-Honvéd games. Thirty-nine years later, he and other veterans of the match still have an annual get-together every 25 November.

In the smoky 6-3 borozó at IX. Lónyay utca 62, a wine bar themed in memory of the great victory, you'll find large sepia pictures of the 1953 match. In one shot, a group of Hungarians runs away laughing from a recently filled English net. Staring on in disbelief is England full-back Alf Ramsey. He was to get his revenge on the world in 1966, managing an English national side that won the World Cup without a trace of style or flair.

in Budapest. Some visitors stroll topless, while others go naked in certain sections of the Csillaghegyi Strand.

Csillaghegyi Strand

III. Pusztakúti út 3 (250 1533). HÉV Csillaghegy. **Open** *1 May-15 Sept, swimming pool open all year* 7am-7pm daily. **Rates** Ft150 day ticket.
There are four pools in a picturesque setting, with a combined capacity of 3,000. Nude sunbathing is practised on the southern slope.

Dagály

XIII. Népfürdő utca 36 (120 2203). M3 Lehel tér then bus 133. **Open** 6am-8pm daily. **Rates** Ft170 day ticket.
There are 12 pools, with a capacity of 12,000. Also a sauna and keep-fit rooms.

Palatinus

XIII. Margaret Island (112 3069). Tram 4, 6 then bus 26. **Open** *1 May-15 Sept* 8am-6pm daily. **Rates** Ft170 day ticket.
There are seven pools, including a thermal round pool, two children's pools and a teaching pool, plus slides and wave machines. Capacity of 10,000 and on a hot Saturday afternoon in July the Palatinus feels as if it is genuinely standing-room only. Fenced area for ball games and teenage kicks.

Római

III. Rozgonyi Piroska utca 2 (188 9740). HÉV Rómaifürdő. **Open** *1 May 15 Sept* 8am-7pm daily. **Rates** Ft170 day ticket.
Three pools and a water chute. Originally enjoyed by off-duty Roman centurions.

Tennis

There are more than 140 tennis clubs across the country, most with clay courts, including 30 in Budapest. Clubs charge about Ft500 per hour to hire a court, and some offer coaching lessons. Hotels also rent out courts to non-guests. The following is a selection from different areas of town.

Hungarian Tennis Association

XIV. Dózsa György út 1-3 (252 6687). M2 Népstadion.
The Association holds a full list of clubs and courts.

MTK

I. Aladár utca 1-3 (156 8765). Bus 78. **Open** 6am-6pm daily. **Rates** Ft400 per hour. 13 courts.

Spartacus-Hunor

I. Attila út 2 (212 3766). Bus 5, 78. **Open** 7am-8pm daily. **Rates** Ft400 per hour; Ft450 Sat, Sun. Nine courts.

Vasas SC

II. Pasaréti utca 11-13 (156 6537). Bus 5. **Open** 2-9pm Sat, Sun. **Rates** Ft500 per hour. Six courts.

Római Teniszakadémia

III. Királyok útja 105 (160 8616). Bus 34. **Open** 6am-11pm daily. **Rates** Ft700 per hour; Ft800 with floodlights. Eight courts.

Építők TC

X. Népliget, Építők sporttelep (263 0279). M3 Népliget. **Open** 7am-8pm daily. **Rates** Ft350 per hour. 12 courts.

BHSE

XIII. Margaret Island (112 9472). Bus 26 from Nyugati Station. **Open** 7am-9pm daily. **Rates** Ft400 per hour Mon-Fri; Ft500 per hour Sat, Sun. Eight courts.

Water Sports

There are plenty of opportunities to indulge in water sports in landlocked Hungary, some within easy reach of the capital.

Motorboats are banned on **Lake Balaton** but all sorts of pedal-powered rowboats can be rented. Tourinform at V. Sütő utca 2 (117 9800), open 8am-8pm daily, stocks the booklet *Water Tours in Hungary*. The Foundation for Family Sports, 2023 Dunabogdány, Petőfi utca 1 (26-391 071) arranges half-day, one- and two-day motorboat, canoeing and kayaking programmes from its base 30km outside Budapest.

Hotel Lidó

III. Nánási út 67 (250 4549/212-2827). Bus 34. **Open** 8am-6pm daily. **Rates** *kayaks* Ft400 per person, Ft600 two people; Ft800 four people. *Canoes* Ft600 a day for two people.
Modest hotel on the Danube which offers one-star bed and breakfast for Ft1,200 per person. Kayak and canoe courses available on request.

Hotel River Club

XIII. Népszigeti út 18 (221 4167). MS to Gyöngyösi utca, go down Meder utca and over the footbridge. **Open** *mid Mar-Oct* 7.30am-10pm daily.
The club on Népsziget in the Danube hires kayaks (Ft100 per hour per person), canoes (Ft100 per hour per person), water skis (Ft5,500 per hour) and jet skis (Ft5,000 per hour). Modest rooms available upstairs at Ft 1,400 per person, bar and disco downstairs with occasional summer barbecues. Professional coaching available on the Danube.

*There are 30 **tennis** clubs in Budapest.*

Theatre & Dance

It may not make much of a song and dance about it, but Budapest does have a small and dedicated stage set.

Since the Change of 1989, theatre and dance have felt pinched but are lucky to have avoided closings, unlike in neighbouring Slovakia and Poland. The scene is stagnant, however, and competition is fierce for the ever-shrinking subsidies dispensed by the Ministry of Culture. Yet despite bad times, alternative theatres and festivals keep popping up, never for long, but long enough to manifest that Hungarian creativity in dance and theatre depends on more than just money.

Curtains usually rise in Hungarian theatres at 7pm or 7.30pm. If not open all day, Budapest box offices begin selling tickets an hour prior to curtain. All ticket payment must be in forint, and prices range from Ft150 up to Ft2,000, with the average hovering around Ft450. Discounts are available for students with proper ID. Wheelchair access and hearing systems generally are unavailable, even in the State Opera House. Often there are no programmes and the coatcheck is usually mandatory, to the point of confrontations with stroppy theatre ushers.

Unless otherwise indicated, credit cards are not accepted at venues and agencies listed.

Ticket Agencies

Some English is usually spoken. If not, ask around. Transactions are in cash, and only in forints.

Central Theatre Booking Office
VI. Andrássy út 18 (112 0000/7/8/9). M1 Opera. **Open** 9am-1pm, 1.45-5.45pm Mon-Fri.
Tickets for all performance arts can be purchased here. **Branch:** II. Moszkva tér 3 (135 9136).

Music Mix-33 Ticket Service
V. Váci utca 33 (138 2237/117 7736). M3 Ferenciek tere. **Open** 10am-6pm Mon-Fri; 10am-2pm Sat.
Tickets for dance, theatre, also rock and classical music concerts. You can also buy tickets for events abroad.

Dance & Theatre Listings

Nézőpont
Monthly guide priced Ft40 from most ticket bureaus.

Pesti Műsor
This weekly magazine, in Hungarian, covers everything in the country and is the most accurate guide, for Ft49.

English-language newspapers
The *Budapest Sun* and *Budapest Week* each run incomplete weekly listings, which are not always accurate.

Theatre

The Hungarian theatre has much in common with its Western counterparts: the Stanislavsky-based acting method, similar theatre architecture, an international roster of familiar dramas and shrinking budgets. Ticket prices are climbing beyond the reach of formerly enthusiastic Budapest theatre-goers who now tend to stay at home with the television. But those who venture into the theatre can often still find excellence.

With its two opera houses and more than 30 theatres, Budapest truly is a performing arts capital. Yet there are few genuine new trends in theatre and lack of money and public indifference mean that no real alternative scene exists. In mainstream theatres it is usual to witness fine acting and be dazzled by stunning costume and scenic designs. Chekhov and Shakespeare are beloved by Hungarians. To hear Magyar spoken at its most eloquent, watch a familiar play by these dramatists.

Theatres

Katona József Színház
V. Petőfi S utca 6 (118 6599). M3 Ferenciek tere. **Open** box office 2-7pm daily
Long considered the best Hungarian theatre and the most travelled globally, this company of players excels in the classics. Their productions of Chekhov's *Three Sisters* and Jarry's *Ubu Roi* are outstanding.

Madách Theatre
VII. Erzsébet körút 29-33 (322 0677/322 2015). Tram 4, 6. **Open** box office 1-6pm Mon-Sat.
The chief rival of the Vígszínház produces Lloyd Webber blockbusters but their best production is the Hungarian rock opera, *Story of Mary* (Mária Evangéliuma). An excellent company that concentrates on big productions.

Municipal Operetta Theatre
Fővárosi Operett Színház
VI. Nagymező utca 17 (269 3870). M1 Oktogon. **Open** box office 9am-7pm daily.
Colourful productions of Hungarian operettas by composers such as Franz Lehár, Imre Kálmán and Pál Ábrahám, as well as the international favourite, Offenbach. Catch the very best Hungarian operetta – Kálmán's *The Csárdás Princess*. The Municipal Operetta Theatre is a beautiful late Habsburg venue, scheduled for restoration.

National Theatre
Nemzeti Színház
VII. Hevesi Sándor tér 4 (322 2879/342 6175). Tram 4, 6. **Open** box office 10am-6pm Mon-Fri; 1 hour before curtain Sat, Sun.
For over 200 years the National, housed since the 1960s in

Vígszínház – *Budapest's biggest theatre.*

an ugly socialist-realist building which replaced the Habsburg-era structure formerly on Blaha Lujza tér, has been producing both Hungarian and international dramas and musicals. Founded for nationalist reasons to promote the Hungarian language at a time when all other theatres performed in German, nowadays the National has a reputation for conservative programming and mediocre performances.

Pesti Színház
V. Váci utca 9 (266 5245). M1, M2, M3 Deák tér. **Open** *box office* 11am-7pm Mon-Fri; 1 hour before curtain Sat, public holidays.
The energetic sister theatre of the **Vígszínház** (it's the same company at a smaller venue) runs classics by Chekhov, Gogol, Miller and Shakespeare. Their production of Gogol's *Month in the Country* is particularly touching, warm, funny and well-designed.

Rock Theatre
Blue tent next to Nyugati Station. Box office: XI. Nagymező utca 19 (111 6405). M3 Nyugati. **Open** *box office* 2-7pm daily.
This company belts out the best in the musical tradition of the West End and Broadway, such as *Miss Saigon* and *Evita*. Productions are often in both Hungarian and English versions. The high-tech tent is just a temporary measure to house companies whose venues are being restored. In June 1996 the Rock Theatre company will move to the Művész színház (VI. Nagymező utca 22-24) and the Madách will shuffle in here.

Vígszínház
Comedy Theatre
XIII. Szent István körút 14 (111 1650). M3 Nyugati tér. **Open** *box office* 10am-1pm, 2-7pm, Mon-Fri; 1 hour before hour curtain Sat, Sun.
This Habsburg Empire jewel, Budapest's biggest theatre, is glittering again after recent renovation and houses one of central Europe's most dynamic acting companies, particu-

larly suited to big musicals such as *West Side Story*. Their co-production (with the Theatre du Campagnol de Paris) of *Le Bal*, from the 1982 French film of the same name, a show without dialogue, displays all their considerable skills.

Festivals

Further information can be had from either the Central Theatre Booking Office or the National Philharmonic Ticket Office (*see chapter* **Music: Classical & Opera**).

Csepürágó Festival, in the first week of June, is an all-day fest performed on Castle Hill. Then from 10-18 June, actors, singers and mimes perform in squares and on street corners. Hungary's most prominent theatre artists, as well the newest and rawest, all turn out for this.

Budapest Spring Festival
Box Office: V. Bárczy István utca 1-3 (266 4051/fax 118 9570). M1, M2, M3 Deák tér. **Open** *Feb-Apr* 10am-6pm Mon-Fri.
Central Office, Interart Festival Center, V. Vörösmarty tér 1 (117 9838/fax 117 9910/118 9943). M1 Vörösmarty tér. **Open** 10am-4pm Mon-Fri.
Held each March and April, and primarily a classical music event, this also features many local and international guest theatres and dance companies.

Alternative Theatre Festival
Alternativ Színházi Festivál
Contact: Szkéné Színház, XI. Műegyetem rakpart 3 (463 2451/fax 463 2450).
Held every April, this 12-day festival in Budapest is organised by the Association of Alternative Theatres. Established in 1994 by ten local companies, without government or corporate sponsorship. The Festival offers theatre and contemporary dance.

International Meeting of Moving Theatres
IMMT: Nemzetközi Mozgászinházi Találkozó
Contact: Szkéné Színház, XI. Műegyetem rakpart 3 (463 2451/fax 463 2450).
Biannual festival since 1978 featuring dance and theatre, a feature of Budapest Autumn Weeks (first week every Oct).

Dance

Dance in Hungary was always an expression of its folk culture. A century ago, ballet began its life quietly in the State Opera House. And only recently has Budapest seen an explosion of modern dance, drawing either from folk or international sources. Nowadays, Budapest offers a small but varied array of dance styles.

Hungary's lively and colourful folk culture is easily accessed through dance and music. During the year they are performed in the more touristy venues as well as in the authentic village-style táncház (Dance House) where newcomers can join in and learn the steps during the first hour. Later on the better dancers take to the floor and the evening can stretch well past midnight as everyone works themselves into a folk dance frenzy. A great way to meet Hungarians and their culture (*see also chapter* **Folklore**).

If you just want to watch fine folk dancing from the safety of a theatre seat, you've two very good choices: the Hungarian State Folk Ensemble (Magyar Állami Népi Együttes – MÁNE) or the Budapest Dance Ensemble (Budapest Táncegyüttes – BT). **Táncfórum** can provide performance scheduling information.

Apart from at the Hungarian National Ballet, classical dance can be seen in two annual festivals: Inter-ballet and Summer Opera-Ballet Festival. The Inter-ballet is part of the annual Budapest Spring Festival and features groups from around Hungary known for their modern works. The summer offers both local and second-string international guests.

The modern dance scene benefits from a constant flow of international companies aided by sponsors from the UK, France and Germany. Yet the scene suffers from a dearth of good local companies and slim sponsorship. There are, however, some interesting ensembles. Yvette Bozsik & Company is the current darling of the moderns. This former HNB ballerina has adroitly swung sponsorship her way and presents half a dozen programmes of modern choreography throughout the year. Tranz Danz, a small ensemble, presents modern works in collaboration with some of Hungary's best musicians, including jazz giant Mihály Dresch. And choreographer Gerzson Péter Kovács insists that he incorporates táncház motifs in his work. No dancing, uniformed soldiers are to be found in the Army Dance Theatre (Honvéd Táncszínház). Yet they are highly regarded for their modern works and do perform often.

None of these groups have theatres of their own. Táncfórum can, however, provide information about performances.

Information

Contemporary Dance Theatre Society

Kortárs Táncszínházi Egyesület
XI. Kőrösy József utca 17 (tel/fax 166 4776). Tram 4, 6, 18, 19, 47, 49. **Open** 4-7pm Tue-Thur. Contact Adrienn Szabó.
Publishes the only monthly bulletin concerning the contemporary dance scene; complete performance schedules and information on classes. Free from the above address. In Hungarian, but the schedule is easy to understand.

Szkéné Theatre

Műszaki Egyetem, XI. Műegyetem rakpart 3-9 (463 3741). Tram 18, 19, 47, 49. **Open** 9am-4pm Mon-Thur; 9am-2.30pm Fri; 1 hour before performance Sat, Sun.
A venue that also provides wider information about contemporary dance and alternative theatre. They also sponsor the International Modern Movement Theatre Festival (*see above*) at which obscure, talented dance groups collect from all over Europe to expose themselves in this tiny black box.

Táncfórum

I. Corvin tér 8 (201 4407). M2 Batthyány tér. **Open** 9am-3pm Mon-Fri.
Can provide dance performance information regarding Tranz Danz, Yvette Bozsik, Army and other companies.

Venues & Offices

Budapest Dance Ensemble

Budapest Táncegyüttes (BT)
FMH (Folklór Centrum), XI. Fehérvári út 47 (181 1360). Tram 47. **Open** box office 8am-8pm Mon-Fri.
Socialist-built cultural centre. Folk dancing and music of the Magyars and their neighbours. Performances are expensive, though, at around Ft1,000 a ticket.

Central European Dance Theatre

Közép-Európa Táncszínház
Budapesti Kamaraszínház, I. Színház utca 1-3 (175 8011 ext 125). M2 Moszkva tér then Várbusz.
VI. Anker köz 2 (342 2123). M1, M2, M3 Deák tér/tram 47, 49.
Open *box office* 9am-6pm Mon-Fri; 1 hour before performance Sat, Sun.
Budapest's most interesting dance ensemble usually works at the National Theatre, with tickets and information available from the addresses above. Its 20 members move through strange pieces featuring bizarre music, costumes and sets. Their rendition of Bulgakov's *The Master and Margarita* is stunning, blending Bulgakov's Moscow with Hungary's own brand of Communism.

Hungarian National Ballet

Magyar Nemzeti Balett
Magyar Állami Operaház, VI. Andrássy út 22 (153 0170). M1 Opera. **Open** box office 11am-7pm Tue-Sat; 10am-1pm, 4-7pm, Sun when there is a performance.
Erkel Színház, VIII. Köztársaság tér (133 0540). M2 Keleti pu. **Open** 11am-7pm Tue-Sat; 10am-1pm, 4-7pm, Sun when there is a performance.
Now in its 110th season, the Hungarian National Ballet relies on Russian classical ballet technique. Its repertoire of 49 ballets reflects this school and the 127 dancers don't disappoint, as many were trained in Kiev, Moscow or St Petersburg. However, the repertoire is weak on modern pieces, something this young company need to focus on. They perform in the splendid State Opera House and its ugly sister, the Erkel Theatre.

Hungarian State Folk Ensemble

Magyar Állami Népi Együttes
I. Corvin tér 8 (201 4407). M2 Batthyány tér. **Open** box office 9am-3pm Mon-Fri.
The Hungarian State Folk Ensemble uses the same office and venue as **Táncfórum**. This excellent company (which also tours internationally) rivals the Budapest Dance Ensemble in their authentic presentations of folk dancing and music from Hungary and the surrounding region. It's also pretty expensive at around Ft1,000 a ticket.

Inter-ballet Festival

Budapest Spring Festival Offices, V. Bárczy I. utca 1-3 (266 4051). M1, M2, M3 Deák tér. **Open** Feb-Apr 10am-6pm Mon-Fri.
Information about dance performance, as well as all other aspects of the festival.

Petőfi Csarnok

Városliget, Zichy Mihály út 14 (251 7266). M1 Széchenyi Fürdő. **Open** 9am-10pm Mon-Fri.
Call them (some English spoken) to ask about the many contemporary dance performances staged here.

Summer Opera-Ballet Festival

VIP-Arts Management, Magyar Állami Operaház, VI. Andrássy út 22 (153 0170). M1 Opera. **Open** box office 11am-7pm Tue-Sat; 10am-1pm, 4-7pm Sun when there is a performance.
The Summer Opera-Ballet Festival presents second-string international ballet dancers and the most expensive shows

Music Mix-33 Ticket Service *on Váci utca – dance, theatre, rock and classical concerts.*

in town, ranging from Ft1,050 to Ft3,300. It represents your only chance to see ballet in August. The same organisation also stages a costumed ball at the Opera House every New Year's Eve.

Táncház Venues

Staff at these socialist-built cultural centres, venues for a variety of community programmes, are unlikely to speak much English, but you can always try to find a helpful student. Most programmes are usually listed in *Pesti Műsor*. (*See also chapter* **Folklore**.)

Almássy téri Szabadidő Központ
VII. Almássy tér 6 (342 0387). Tram 4, 6. **Open** *box office* 8pm-8pm daily.

FMH (Folklór Centrum)
XI. Fehérvári út 47 (181 1360). Tram 47. **Open** *box office* 8.30am-8pm daily.

Marczibányi téri Művelődési Ház
II. Marczibányi tér 5a (212 5789). Tram 4, 6. **Open** *box office* 9am-8pm daily.

Classes & Information

Classes

Flash
V. József Attila utca 18 (137 1254/06 20 354 147). M1, M2, M3 Deák tér. **Open** classes at 4pm, 6pm, 8pm Mon-Fri.
Modern jazz ballet and dance, American jazz and stretching. For children over ten and adults.

Aranytíz
VI. Arany János utca 10 (111 6287). M3 Arany János utca. **Open** 2.30pm-4pm, 5.30-7pm Mon, Wed; 2-5.30pm Fri.
Jazz for beginners and advanced.

Summer Courses

IDMC
International Dance & Movement Centre
Egyetem, XI. Műegyetem rakpart 3-9 (463 3741). **Open** 9am-4pm Mon-Thur; 9am-2.30pm Fri.
Jazz, flamenco, tap, choreography classes and more, a two-week seminar, held in first half of August, since 1984. Quite popular programme.

International Summer Course of Dance
Hungarian Dance Academy, VI. Andrássy út 25 (267 8649/fax 268 0828). M1 Opera. **Open** 8am-4pm Mon-Thur; 8am-1.30pm Fri.
The training school of the Hungarian National Ballet, which offers a summer course every August. No audition necessary though previous ballet study advised. Classic ballet is taught according to the Vaganova Method. Minimum age is 14. Application deadline is 31 May. Programme includes classical ballet, jazz, modern and Hungarian folk dance. Prices for 1995 were $540 plus $15 registration fee. Classes may also be observed for $10 per day per subject.

Dance Supplies

Note that dance supplies are limited in selection and size and prices are high, so try to bring what you can from home.

Balerina
V. Irányi utca 12 (137 2544). M3 Ferenciek tere. **Open** 10am-6pm Mon-Fri; 10am-1pm Sat.
Dance clothes and shoes for men and women.

Max Muscle Aerobic Body Wear
V. Haris köz 3 (138 2008). M3 Ferenciek tere. **Open** 10am-6pm Mon-Fri; 10am-1.30pm Sat.
Specialises in Capezio clothing, but also supplies regular work-out gear.

Passé
V. Váci utca 67 (118 7368). M3 Ferenciek tere. **Open** 10am-5.30pm Mon-Fri; 10am-12.30pm Sat.
Budapest's best selection of dance wear for both sexes.

In Focus

Business

Cheques and credit cards may still be thin on the ground in Budapest, but business opportunities are there for the taking – if you can live with the local aversion to contracts.

McDonald's, Burger King, Dunkin' Donuts. Wherever you go in Budapest, you are never far from these trailblazers of American capitalism. At the most recent estimate, Hungary has received nearly $10 billion of the $20 billion invested in eastern Europe since 1990. General Electric bought Tungsram, the electric lightbulb manufacturer in 1990, while Ford, General Motors and Honda have set up greenfield sites. Western companies have been looking to the cheap but highly educated workforce in eastern Europe to take over labour-intensive operations. Hungary, which was the first in the region to implement legislative changes, benefited most.

But Hungary, as one headline had it, is the 'hare that became a tortoise'. There have been problems with privatisation, particularly with agriculture, public utilities and banking. Unemployment has risen as companies restructure, increasing an already heavy welfare burden and extending Hungary's foreign debt – already the highest *per capita* in eastern Europe. All this has helped slow down the transition and lowered Hungary's attractiveness for foreign investors. Hungary is now being left behind by the Czech Republic and Poland. Since March 1995 the government has embarked on austerity measures to boost exports, curb imports and cut public spending.

Any businessman will moan that social security costs, which add 50 per cent on top of wages, are the main drawback of setting up in Hungary. A buoyant shadow economy, which avoids direct

and indirect taxes, has kept Hungary afloat while all the macro-economic indicators spell disaster. The government estimates the black economy produces about 30 per cent of GDP and has set up a task force to bring the black economy into line.

After years of pitting wits against the Communist authorities it is not perhaps surprising that Hungarian business morals are questionable at times. Bribes to police or customs are common, while bank managers have been known to agree to loans if they receive a percentage of the interest. Many western businessmen have fallen foul of the Hungarian disregard for a contract, whether written or verbal. Seeking recourse in the legal process takes a minimum of two years, and unscrupulous Hungarians will assume that anyone intending legal action will give up in the end.

Work habits in Budapest can be frustrating. Shops or offices claiming to be open 24 hours a day can be closed when you go to visit. Most workers shoot off at 4pm in the afternoons, often to go to their second job, the one that is not taxed and pays better. Forget Friday afternoons. Between the end of June and late August finding a decision-maker in any company proves well nigh impossible.

If you're visiting on a business trip, bring plenty of cards with you. These are produced and distributed at every conceivable opportunity.

Note: Rt – similar to PLC; Kft – limited company.

Stock Exchange

In the Habsburg days the Budapest Stock Exchange was the third biggest in Europe by capitalisation. After a 40-year interlude, the Budapest Stock Exchange re-opened in June 1990, the first *bourse* to recommence in the former Communist countries. Progress has been slow, with only 40 companies listed – fewer than the number of brokerages operating. Government securities still account for the overwhelming majority of transactions. Foreign institutional investors account for well over half the equity turnover.

Budapest Stock Exchange

V. Deák Ferenc utca 5 (117 5226/fax 118 1737). M1 Vörösmarty tér/tram 2, 2A. **Open** 10.30am-1pm Mon-Fri. Visitors can watch trading through the glass walls. If you want to organise a tour, ring Katalin Jakab (266 5677/118 4762).

Budapest Commodity Exchange

XIII. Róbert Károly körút 61-65 (269 8571/fax 269 8575). Tram 1, 12, 14. **Open** 10-11.30am Tue, Thur. Visitors are welcome to see the Exchange in action. Officials recommend 10.30-10.45am as the best time.

Banks

In 1988, the National Bank of Hungary (NBH) was split up into three large commercial banks – Magyar Hitel Bank, Budapest Bank and K&H

Bank – which all had bad loans to large state enterprises. Overstaffed and with outdated technology, these banks have made heavy losses.

New joint venture banks opened in Budapest to service international clients that had also moved here. They brought the newest banking technology and could access international capital markets to find cheaper financing. Most of these banks have grown significantly. Smaller banks have tried to move into niches such as private banking and credit cards but analysts expect them to merge with larger banks.

Bank transfers are now speedier since the giro system came into operation at the end of 1994. Cheques are still rare and credit cards are only just gaining widespread acceptance.

The following are the head offices for the major banks in Budapest.

Budapest Bank

V. Alkotmány utca 3 (269 2333/fax 269 2417). M2 Kossuth Lajos tér/tram 2, 2A. **Open** 8am-1pm Mon-Thur; 2-5pm Mon and Thur; 8-11am Fri.

Central-European International Bank (CIB)

Közép-Európai Nemzetközi Bank
II Medve utca 4/14 (212 1330/fax 212 4200). M2 Batthyány tér. **Open** 9am-12.30pm Mon-Thur; 9-11.30am Fri.

Citibank Budapest

V Váci utca 19-21 (138 2666/118 9694). M1 Vörösmarty tér, M3 Ferenciek tere. **Open** 8.30am-5pm Mon-Fri.

Creditanstalt

V. Akadémia utca 17 (269 0812/fax 153 4959). M2 Kossuth Lajos tér/tram 2, 2A. **Open** 9am-3pm Mon-Thur; 9am-1pm Fri.

Hungarian Foreign Trade Bank

Magyar Külkereskedelmi Bank Rt
V. Szent István tér 11 (269 0922/fax 269 0959). M1 Bajcsy-Zsilinszky, M3 Arany János utca. **Open** 8am-4pm Mon-Thur; 8am-1pm Fri.

Hungarian Credit Bank

Magyar Hitel Bank
V. Szabadság tér 5-6 (269 2122/fax 269 2245). M2 Kossuth Lajos tér. **Open** 8am-4pm Mon-Fri.

Internationale Nederlanden Bank

VI. Andrássy út 9 (268 0140/fax 269 6447). M1 Bajcsy-Zsilinszky. **Open** 9am-3pm Mon-Fri.

National Commercial & Credit Bank

Országos Kereskedelmi & Hitel Bank (K&H)
V. Arany János utca 24 (112 5200/fax 111 3845). M3 Arany János utca. **Open** 8am-1pm Mon-Fri.

OTP Bank

V. Nádor utca 16 (153 1444/fax 112 6858). Bus 15, 105. **Open** 8am-4.30pm Mon-Thur; 8am-2pm Fri.

Postabank

V. József Nádor tér 1 (118 0855/fax 117 1369). M1 Vörösmarty tér. **Open** 8am-6pm Mon, Thur; 8am-1.30pm Tue, Wed, Fri.

http://www.timeout.co.uk

Government Organisations

Hungarian Investment & Trade Development Agency
V. Dorottya utca 4 (266 7034/fax 118 3732). M1 Vörösmarty tér/tram 2, 2A. **Open** 9am-3pm Mon-Thur; 9am-noon Fri.
The ITD is a good first point of contact for businessmen. They have a useful library and plenty of information.

State Privatisation & Holding Company
Állami Privatizáció és Vagyonkezelő Rt
XIII. Pozsonyi út 56 (269 8600/fax 149 5745). Trolleybus 76, 79. **Open** 8am-4pm Mon-Fri.
The organisation responsible for selling state-owned assets, including utility companies.

Embassies & Agencies

American Embassy (Commercial Department)
VI. Bajza utca 31 (322 9015/fax 342 2529). M1 Bajza utca. **Open** 8.30am-4.30pm Mon-Fri; 8.30am-noon Wed.

The Madách Trade Centre.

Amercian Chamber of Commerce
VI. Dózsa György út 84A, Room 222 (269 6016/fax 342 7518). Bus 20, 30/trolleybus 75, 79. **Open** 8.30am-5pm Mon-Fri.
Consultations by appointment only.

British Embassy (Commercial Section)
V. Harmincad utca 6 (266 2888/fax 266 0907). M1 Vörörsmarty tér/bus 2, 15, 15A/Tram 2, 2A. **Open** 9am-1pm, 2-5pm, Mon-Fri.

British Chamber of Commerce
I. Iskola utca 37, First Floor, Flat 4 (201 9142/fax 201 9142). M2 Batthyány tér. **Open** 9am-noon, 2-5pm, Mon-Fri.
Consultations by appointment only.

Business Services

Accountants & Consultants

All the 'Big Six' are in Budapest and have been for a number of years. The office hours given are official but you can often reach someone much later.

Arthur Andersen
East-West Centre, VIII. Rákóczi út 1-3 (266 9744/fax 266 9661). M2 Astoria/bus 1, 7, 7A, 9, 78/tram 47, 49. **Open** 8.30am-5.30pm Mon-Fri.

Coopers & Lybrand
II. Lövőház utca 30 (212 4720/fax 156 4895). M2 Moszkva tér/tram 4, 6. **Open** 8.30am-5.30pm Mon-Fri.

Deloitte & Touche
V. Vármegye utca 3-5 (267 2062/fax 267 4182). M3 Ferenciek tere/bus 15, 15A. **Open** 8.30am-5.30pm Mon-Fri.

Ernst & Young
XIV. Hermina út 17 (252 8231/fax 252 8778). Bus 55/trolleybus 72, 74. **Open** 8.30am-5.30pm Mon-Fri.

KPMG Reviconsult
XII. Muros utca 19 21 (202 2299/fax 202 4405). M2 Moszkva tér. **Open** 8.15am-5pm Mon-Fri.

Price Waterhouse
VII. Rumbach Sebestyén utca 21 (269 6910/fax 269 6936). M1, M2, M3 Deák Ferenc tér. **Open** 8.30am-7pm Mon-Fri.

Conference Facilities

As well as the places below, most of the major hotels also host conferences.

Budapest Convention Centre
Budapest Kongresszusi Központ
XI. Jagelló út 1-3 (166 9625/fax 185 2127). Tram 61/bus 8, 8A, 12, 112, 139. **Open** 9am-5pm Mon-Fri.

European Serviced Offices (ESO)
VI. Révay utca 10 (269 1100/fax 269 1030). M1 Bajcsy-Zsilinszky út. **Open** 8am-7pm Mon-Fri.
As well as conference facilities, ESO lets out office suites on short-term leases and offers multilingual secretarial services.

Regus Business Centre
Emke Building, VII. Rákóczi út 42 (267 9111/fax 267 9100). M2 Blaha Lujza tér/tram 4, 6. **Open** 8am-6pm Mon-Fri.
Offices can also be leased on short-term contracts with multilingual secretarial services.

Couriers

These companies will pick-up packages. Sending a document to the UK or US costs Ft3,500-Ft5,000.

DHL Hungary
VIII. Rákóczi út 1-3 (266 5555, Fax 266 2504). M2 Astoria/tram 47, 49. **Open** 8am-6pm Mon-Fri. **Credit** AmEx, MC, V, DC, JCB

TNT Express Hungary
VII. Nagy Diófa 7 (269 6464). M2 Blaha Lujza tér/tram 4, 6. **Open** 8am-6pm Mon-Fri. **No credit cards.**

Commercial Estate Agencies

Many of the international commercial property companies have set up in Budapest. This is one sector where domestic firms are still a long way from challenging international companies.

Office space has increased dramatically since 1990 with the construction of a number of western-quality office blocks. In mid-1995 top-quality office space cost DM40-DM45 per square metre per month. Rents are stated in Deutschmarks as a hedge against inflation. It is, in fact, illegal to charge rent in foreign currency. British firms dominate the commercial property scene so all the offices listed have English-speaking staff.

DTZ Hungary
VII. Rumbach Sebestyén utca 21 (269 6999/fax 269 6987). M1, M2, M3 Deák Ferenc tér/tram 47, 49. **Open** 8.30am-5pm Mon-Fri.

Healey and Baker
Emke Building, VII. Rákóczi út 42 (268 1288/fax 268 1288). M2 Blaha Lujza tér/tram 4, 6. **Open** 9am-5.30pm Mon-Fri.

Jones Lang Wootton
East-West Centre, VIII. Rákóczi út 1-3 (266 4981/fax 266 0142). M2 Astória/tram 47, 49. **Open** 9am-6pm Mon-Fri.

Richard Ellis
VI. Révay utca 10 (269 1020/fax 269 1030). M1 Bajcsy-Zsilinszky út. **Open** 9am-6pm Mon-Fri.

Lawyers

These firms have English-speaking lawyers.

Allen & Overy/Déry & Co
Madách Trade Centre, VII. Madách Imre út 14, Fifth Floor (268 1511/fax 268 1515). M1, M2, M3 Deák Ferenc tér/tram 47, 49. **Open** 8.30am-7pm Mon-Fri.

Baker & McKenzie
VI. Andrássy út 125 (251 5777/fax 342 0513). M1 Hősök tere. **Open** 8am-8pm Mon-Fri.

Clifford Chance/Köves és Társai
Madách Trade Centre, VII. Madách Imre út 14 (268 1600/fax 268 1610). M1, M2, M3 Deák Ferenc tér/tram 47, 49. **Open** 8am-8pm Mon-Fri.

McKenna and Co/Veróci, Őrmai és Társa

XII. Maros utca 22 (201 9199/fax 156 5391). M2 Moszkva tér/tram 4, 6, 18. **Open** 8am-5pm Mon-Fri.

Relocation Services

The following companies help deal with residence and work permits.

Business Umbrella
House of the Americas, V. Báthory utca 1 (111 5020/fax 111 5221). M2 Kossuth Lajos tér. **Open** 9am-5pm Mon-Fri.
Business Umbrella also arranges translation, interpreting and customs clearance.

Settlers Hungary
XII. Sashegyi út 18 (06 30 485 441/fax 165 1990). Bus 8, 8A. **Open** 8.30am-4.30pm Mon-Fri.
Settlers Hungary also helps with finding schools, registering cars and customs clearance.

Staff Hire Agencies

Inflation can cause rates to vary wildly.

Adia
VI. Bajcsy-Zsilinszky út 27 (269 1164/fax 269 3774). M3 Arany János utca. **Open** 9am-4pm Mon-Fri.

Select
XIII. Szent István körút 4, First Floor, No 2 (269 3944/fax 269 3945). M3 Nyugati/tram 4, 6. **Open** 9am-5pm Mon-Fri.
A proficient multilingual secretary charges Ft800-Ft1,200 per hour.

Online Services

The local dial-in number for Compuserve is 291 9999. To connect with America Online, Prodigy and eWorld you need to dial 269 7023. For Microsoft Network the number is 267 4636. Hungarian telecommunications remain pretty clunky – you'll probably need to insert a 'w' before the first digit – and the process of logging on requires the same persistence you'll need in any dealings with the telephone system.

The Menedzser, or 'Manager', chain, for the Budapest wannabe executive.

Children

From high chairs to chairlifts, pony-carts to puppet theatres, there's plenty in Budapest to keep the little ones amused.

Budapest has some excellent parks and playgrounds, zoos, puppet theatres, folk dance clubs and craft workshops for children to enjoy and learn from. There are also plenty of funny old vehicles to ride. Even on a fairly long stay, visitors will find more than enough child-orientated entertainment to keep everyone amused.

THE HUNGARIAN FAMILY

Hungarians love children. Don't be surprised if people, especially old ladies, stop to stroke and praise your child. Still, the Hungarian family is getting smaller. Young parents usually can't afford more than one or two kids and the housing problem is so serious that young families often live at the grandparents' house.

The Hungarian family is still fairly traditional in its approach to child-rearing. You don't see too many parents with small children in restaurants, or other 'grown-up' places, because children are supposed to stay at home with their mothers until they learn how to behave like little adults.

PRACTICALITIES

Under-12s may not travel in the front seats of cars, but seat belts and baby-seats are not compulsory in the back. Disposable nappies, baby food and other essential baby equipment are available all over the city.

DIFFICULTIES

Heavy traffic and air pollution mean that long weekday walks along busy downtown streets are not advisable. Instead try the Danube Korzó, the pedestrian streets around Váci utca, or one of the parks and playgrounds listed below.

If travelling with a young baby, you should know that only the narrowest pushchairs can get through the doors of all buses and trams. Access can also be a problem when shopping, except in a few new, spacious Western-style shops in the downtown area.

Alas, with the exception of fast-food joints, five-star hotels and the restaurants listed below, few Budapest eateries offer high chairs. You certainly won't find many separate children's menus.

ENTERTAINMENT

Check the listings in English-language weeklies, *Magyar Narancs* or *Pesti Műsor* or telephone Tourinform (117 9800).

Folk Dance Clubs

The folk music movement (*see chapter* **Folklore**) does not leave kids out of the fun. The following Dance Houses (*táncházak*) are for children. Venues may be closed in July and August.

Muzsikás táncház

at FMH Cultural Centre (Fővárosi Művelődési Ház)
XI. Fehérvári út 47 (181 1360). Tram 47. **Open** 5-6.30pm Tue, closed in summer. **Admission** Ft150; Ft100 children. **No credit cards.**
The best-known Hungarian folk music band offers a weekly *táncház* (Dance House) for youngsters: live folk music and the teaching of traditional dances, including folk tales and games in a playful atmosphere.

Kalamajka táncház

at Inner City Cultural and Youth Centre (Belvárosi Művelődési Ház)
V. Molnár utca 9 (117 5928). M3 Ferenciek tere. **Open** 5-6.30pm Sat. **Admission** Ft150; Ft100 children. **No credit cards.**
This children's *táncház*, which turns into a wild grown-up *táncház* at night, is right in the city centre. Songs, dances and folk tales are taught by talented folk singer Éva Fábián.

Budapest Puppet Theatre

Budapest Bábszínház
VI. Andrássy út 69 (342 2702, 321 5200). M1
Vörösmarty utca. **Shows** 3pm Mon-Thur; 10.30am, 4pm,
Fri-Sun. Closed in summer. **Admission** Ft100-Ft200. **No
credit cards.**
International fairy tales and Hungarian folk stories make up
the repertoire. Language is usually not a problem and the
shows are excellent and highly original. Book at weekends.

Kolibri Theatre

VI. Jókai tér 10 (112 0622/153 4633). M1 Oktogon.
Shows 10am daily; 3pm Fri-Sun. **Open** box office 2-6pm
daily. Closed in summer. **Admission** Ft150-Ft190. **No
credit cards.**
Small theatre that presents fairy tales.

Circus

XIV. Állatkerti körút 7 (343 9630). M1 Széchenyi fürdő.
Open 3pm, 7pm Mon-Sat; 10am, 3pm, 7pm Sun.
Admission Ft200-Ft350 Mon-Thur; Ft250-Ft400 Fri-
Sun. **No credit cards.**
A permanent building with shows all year round,
although inside it looks just like an old-fashioned travelling circus. There are international and Hungarian performances with acrobats, magicians, jugglers, clowns and
animals. Book in advance to avoid sitting next to the deaf-
ening orchestra.

Planetarium

People's Park (Népliget), south-west corner (265 0725).
M3 Népliget. **Open** 9.30am-3.30pm Mon-Fri; 9am-4pm
Sat, Sun. **Admission** Ft150. **No credit cards.**
Temporary exhibits as well as educational children's shows.
Popular with older kids.

Several Budapest cinemas show cartoons and children's films. Most, however, are dubbed, so language will be a problem unless it's a well-known
story. Check film listings in *Pesti Műsor* or *Magyar
Narancs* under *Gyerekeknek ajánlott filmek* (films
recommended for children) or look in the local
English-language papers. Most hotels and flats for
rent have satellite and/or cable TV, including the
Cartoon Network.

Museum of Transport

Közlekedési Múzeum
XIV. Városligeti krt 11 (343 0565). Trolleybus 72, 74 or
walk across City Park from M1 Széchenyi Fürdő. **Open**
10am-5pm Tue-Sun. **Admission** Ft60; free students,
children. **No credit cards.**
Life-size and model trains, cars and ships. You can climb the
steps of an old train engine and peek into the wagons, you
can also turn a ship's wheel, but that's it for hands-on stuff.

Museum of Aviation

Repüléstörténeti Múzeum
Petőfi Hall (Petőfi Csarnok), XIV. Zichy Mihály út 16
(343 0009). **Open** 10am-6pm Tue-Sun. **Admission**
Ft60; free students, children. **No credit cards.**
Small and life-size aeroplanes, helicopters and spaceships.

Amusing times at **Vidám Park**.

Military History Museum

Hadtörténeti Múzeum
I. Tóth Árpád sétány 40 (156 9522). M2 Moszkva tér
then Várbusz. **Open** 10am-5pm Tue-Sat; 10am-6pm Sun.
Admission Ft100; Ft50 children. **No credit cards.**
Uniforms and shining suits of armour, the history of war in
photographs and old cannons outside to climb on.

Underground Railway Museum

Földalatti Múzeum
Deák tér metro station. M1, M2, M3 Deák tér. **Open**
10am-6pm Tue-Sun. **Admission** Ft35 or one metro
ticket. **No credit cards.**
The old-fashioned 'little metro' (M1) can be fun in itself, but
checking out the even older carriages in this small museum
will also be interesting for most children.

Telephone Museum

Telefónia Múzeum
I. Úri utca 49 (212 2243). M2 Moszkva tér then Várbusz.
Open 10am-6pm Tue-Sun. **Admission** Ft30; Ft10
children. **No credit cards.**
A small museum where children can call each other, push
buttons, send faxes and try everything out.

Stamp Museum

Bélyeg Múzeum
VII. Hársfa utca 47 (342 3757). Tram 4, 6 Wesselényi
utca. **Open** 10am-6pm Tue-Sun. **Admission** Ft20; free
children. **No credit cards.**
Over 11 million stamps on 3,000 pull-out glass plates in one
big room. A must for philately fanatics.

Zoo

Állatkert
XIV. Városligeti körút 6-12 (268 1970). M1 Széchenyi
fürdő. **Open** summer 9am-7pm daily; winter 9am-4pm.
Admission weekends Ft200 adults; Ft100 children;
weekdays Ft150; Ft80 children; Ft80 disabled; free under-
2s. **No credit cards.**
You need two or three hours to see everything here. As well
as the usual lions and monkeys there are also aquaria, nice
art-deco buildings, pony-carts, a beautiful exotic bird house,
a small domestic animal petting corner and the only public
nappy-changing room in town. Most animals are kept in
small cages, especially in winter when they are kept inside,
so a summer visit is less disappointing.

Amusement Park

Vidám Park
XIV. Városligeti körút 14-16 (343 0996). M1 Széchenyi
Fürdő. **Open** summer 9.45am-8pm; winter 9.45am-sunset.

Admission Ft50; Ft20 under 14s; approx Ft60 a ride. **No credit cards.**

A big tacky old fun park with wooden roller coaster, big wheel, ancient merry-go-round, ridiculously unfrightening ghost trains and some newer, scarier rides. Next door there's a tiny children's fun fair (Kis Vidám Park) for toddlers and pre-schoolers.

Parks & Playgrounds

There are plenty of parks and playgrounds in Budapest, but the dreadful air pollution and safety standards make it advisable to stick to the following places.

Margaret Island

Margitsziget
Tram 4, 6 to Margaret Bridge or bus 26 from Nyugati station.
This Danube island is one huge recreational area with lots of green grass, enormous old trees, swimming pools, playgrounds and a small zoo with domestic animals. From the roundabout near the Margaret Bridge entrance you can rent bicycles, four-wheel pedalos and tiny electric cars for children. Horse-drawn carts and open-topped minibuses leave on round trips of the island every half hour. The best playground is near the Alfréd Hajós swimming pool on the southwest side. The island is also well-sprinkled with kiosks selling snacks, drinks and ice cream in summer.

City Park

Városliget
M1 Hősök tere.
Lots to do here apart from the Zoo, Amusement Park and Circus listed above. Heroes' Square (Hősök tere) is teen Budapest's favourite skate-boarding area. Behind it is a boating pond with ducks and swans, some of which turns into an ice-skating rink in winter. Beyond the lake is the Vajdahunyad Castle, which houses the Museum of Agriculture (Mezőgazdasagi Múzeum) with lots of stuffed animals and tools. Safety standards are low on the slides and wooden castles in the south corner. The playground between the zoo and the pond, however, is in good shape and has a

trampoline area where children can bounce up and down for Ft60 for five minutes. There are also ping-pong tables. For ball games you should check out the football fields, basketball and tennis courts behind Petőfi Csarnok on the east side of the park.

Óbuda Island

Óbudai/Hajógyári sziget
HÉV to Filatorigát, bus 142 or boat from Vigadó tér.
An island full of green areas and long slides just north of Árpád bridge (Árpád híd).

Károlyi Garden

Károlyi kert
M2 Astoria, M3 Kálvin tér. **Open** 8am-sunset daily.
Admission free. Dogs not allowed.
One of the few clean fenced-around playgrounds downtown. Sand box, slide, ride-on toys, two ball areas and no dogs.

József Nádor tér

M1, M2, M3 Deák tér. **Open** 7am-sunset daily.
Admission free. Dogs not allowed.
A great new playground with wooden castles, a ship with slides, swings, ride-on toys, a sandpit and a stream with tiny dams for watery experiments. Heavy traffic in the neighbourhood, though, especially on weekdays.

Train & Boat Rides

You can go up to the Buda hills for some fresh air on the cogwheel train that departs across the street from the Budapest Hotel (M2 Moszkva tér then two stops on trams 18 or 56). If you take it all the way up to Széchenyi hill (Széchenyi hegy), which takes about 25 minutes, you can also walk across the park to the Children's Train which is operated by children, except for the engine drivers. This does not run very often, so it's best to check the schedule when you get there and spend waiting time in the neighbouring playground (*see also chapter* **Getting Around**).

The Children's Train, where only the drivers are adult.

Chairlift

Libegő

M2 Moszkva tér then bus 158. **Open** *summer* 9am-5pm, *winter* 9.30am-4pm, daily. **Fare** Ft100; Ft 60 children.

This ski-lift-style ride goes to the top of János hill (Jánoshegy). The view is best on the way down.

Sikló

I. Clark Ádám tér. Tram 19. **Fare** Ft100; Ft60 children.

The renovated funicular (Sikló) goes from Clark Ádám tér up to the Castle District. It's a short ride, but the view is great and the carriages are cool.

Boat Trips

There are several possibilities for boat rides on the Danube. Cheapest is the ferry between the Pest end of Petőfi bridge and Pünkösdfürdő in the north end of the city which picks up and drops off at each of the bridges and at Vigadó tér. This is free for under-4s and about Ft150 for everyone else (*see chapter* **Getting Around**). A sightseeing cruise costs about Ft400-Ft500 (half price under-14s) and offers a bigger boat and a tour guide. Call Ibusz or Tourinform for details (*see chapter* **Essential Information**).

Hungarian parents tend to use grandmothers as baby-sitters (always enthusiastic and free). If you didn't bring granny with you, the agencies listed below offer the most reliable and best qualified child-minding services in town. You may also be able to arrange baby-sitting through your hotel.

Minerva Family Helping Service

Minerva Családsegítő Szolgálat

VIII. Szerdahelyi utca 10 (113 6365). Tram 28, 29. **Open** 24-hour answering machine. **No credit cards.**

English-, German-, French- and Spanish-speaking baby-sitters and full- or part-time nannies. Sitting is Ft250 an hour.

Ficuka Kid Center

Baby Hotel & Baby-sitter Service

V. Váci utca 11/B, First Floor (138 2836). M1, 2, 3 Deák tér. **Open** 9am-5pm daily. **Prices** Ft250 per hour. **No credit cards.**

Leave your kids here while you shop on Váci utca or call them for night-time baby-sitting.

Budapest has plenty of clothing and toy stores and children's sections in the bigger department stores. Here are some of the best places.

Pro-baby

V. Deák Ferenc utca 13 (117 2189). M1, M2, M3 Deák tér. **Open** 10am-6pm Mon-Fri; 10am-2pm Sat. **Credit** EC.

Expensive, but child- and parent-friendly store with a wide selection of toys, clothes and baby and toddler equipment.

Totyi & Tini

V. Bárczy István utca 3 (117 9429). M1, M2, M3 Deák tér. **Open** 10am-6pm Mon-Fri; 10am-1pm Sat. **Credit** AmEx, DCI, JCB, MC, V.

Hungarian-designed dress-up and play clothes at fair prices.

Gondolkodó Toy Store

VI. Király utca 25 (322 8884). M1 Opera. **Open** 10am-6pm Mon-Fri; 9am-1.30pm Sat. **No credit cards.**

Toys and games from the best chess software to beautiful wooden puzzles and local hero Rubik's latest inventions.

Burattino

IX. Ráday utca 47 (215 5621). **Open** 10am-6pm Mon-Fri; 10am-1pm Sat. **No credit cards.**

A great selection of wooden blocks, trains and puzzles.

Puppet Show

V. Párizsi utca 3 (118 8453). M3 Ferenciek tere. **Open** 10am-6pm Mon-Fri; 10am-1pm Sat. **No credit cards.**

A little shop in a courtyard with lots of cute animal puppets. Friendly staff demonstrate how to make them move.

Aside from fast-food places and five-star hotels, very few Hungarian restaurants offer high chairs. The following are the exceptions (even though you'll be lucky if there's more than one chair).

Marcello's

XI. Bartók Béla út 40 (166 6231). Tram 18, 19, 47, 49. **Open** noon-10pm Mon-Sat. **Average** Ft500. **No credit cards.**

A tiny pizzeria with a self-service salad bar and friendly staff. Call to reserve the high-chair.

Náncsi néni Restaurant

II. Ördögárok út 80 (176 5809). Bus 157. **Open** noon-11pm daily. **Average** Ft1,100. **Credit** AmEx, MC, V.

Hungarian cuisine at its best, with a great garden where you can dine under 100-year-old trees. One high-chair and a nice garden play area. Reserve the high chair with the table.

Bagolyvár Restaurant

XIV. Állatkerti út 2 (321 3550). M1 Hősök tere, trolleybus 72, 75, 79. **Open** noon-11pm daily. **Average** Ft1,500. **Credit** AmEx, DC, V.

A pleasant Hungarian restaurant with a play area in the garden and one high chair.

Tabáni Kakas Restaurant

I. Attila út 27 (175 7165). Tram 18. **Open** noon-midnight daily. **Average** Ft700. **Credit** AmEx, MC.

Great Hungarian and Jewish cuisine is doshed up in an old-fashioned atmosphere. Reserve a table and specify if you'd like a high chair.

In an emergency call 04 or 111 1666 and ask for someone who speaks English. With sick children you can also go to Heim Pál Children's Hospital 24 hours a day.

Heim Pál Gyermekkórház *VIII. Üllői út 86 (201 0720). M3 Nagyvárad tér.*

Magyar-British International Elementary School *XI. Kamaraerdei út 12-14 (209 1218). Bus 87.*

American International School of Budapest *XI. Kakukk utca 1/3 (175 8685). Bus 21.*

International Kindergarten & School *XII. Konkoly Thege utca 19B. (175 8258). Bus 21, 90.*

Gay & Lesbian

Budapest is hardly San Francisco, or Soho for that matter, but there is a small, quiet scene – just keep your head above water in the Turkish baths, you never know what's lurking.

Despite a Hungarian journalist, Károly Kertbeny Benkert, being the first person in the world to use the word 'homosexual' in journalism, homosexuality remained closeted in Hungary until after 1989. Since then, gays and lesbians have been slowly emerging. There is no homosexual history here, although there have long been the Turkish baths and some of the great Hungarian celebrities of this century have been gay, lesbian or bisexual: poet laureate József Attila, contemporary poet György Faludy, screen queen and chanteuse Katalin Karády, stage great Hilda Gobbi and noted authoress Erzsébet Galgóczy, to name a few.

'Homosexual', the word, was first penned by Benkert when he was working in Berlin in 1869. He published an open letter calling on the Prussian Interior Ministry to cease prosecuting homosexuals as criminals, but to treat them medically for their illness. The mindset of Hungarians hasn't changed much since.

The Stonewall Rebellion, its antecedents and victories, have bypassed Hungary. Sexually transmitted diseases have not, though the rate for HIV cases remains low. Gay-positive Parliamentary legislation has met with consistent opposition. Homosexuality was decriminalised in 1961 and the age of consent is 18. Nobody grows up gay in Hungary and the coming-out process is long and difficult. Despite its legality, homosexuality remains anathema to this family-orientated, often conservatively religious and fiscally oppressed society. Gay youths have very little privacy, most living at home. At best, homosexual acceptance is delayed; many come out late or not at all.

Lesbians remain virtually invisible in Hungarian society. In recent years, however, they have raised their profile on the club scene and in the women's organisation NaNE (*see chapter* **Women's Budapest**). There are as yet no lesbian clubs or bars, though **Angel** does have a dyke clientèle and lesbians also frequent Capella and Várlak.

The scene is small and quiet, consisting of seven bars/discos, a handful of sex shops, cruising areas and nude beaches, one monthly magazine, some gay-friendly cinemas and theatres and the Turkish baths. There is no gay neighbourhood but most of the bars/discos are within a kilometre of each other. Places are always opening up and closing down, nailed on technicalities by unsympathetic authorities or evicted by landlords.

Gay-bashing is not a widespread problem but caution should be exercised, especially by non-whites, upon entering the Népliget Park cruising area (it's busiest around the Planetarium); there have been attacks by skinheads.

The **Angel Private Club** – set to expand.

Advice & Information

Aids Hotline
AIDS telefonszolgálat
(166 9283). **Open** 9am-8pm Mon-Sat.

Blood-testing services
AIDS-segélyszolgálat
Budapest, XI. Karolina út 35B (166 9283). **Open** 5-8pm Mon, Wed, Thur; 9am-12.30pm Tue, Fri. Seven-day wait. Donations accepted.

NaNE Women's Association
IX. Vámház körút 7 (Hotline 216 1670 6-10pm daily/office 216 5900).

Mások
1461 Budapest, PO Box 388 (137 0327). **Price** Ft148.

Available in sex shops and bars/discos, this monthly 50-page magazine covers the scene, providing personal ads and information on health and bars/discos in English and German as well as Hungarian.

Eating Out

Club 93 Pizzeria
VIII. Vas utca 2 (no phone). M2 Astoria. **Open** 11am-midnight daily. **Average** Ft500. **No credit cards.**
This popular pizza joint is gay-owned and -staffed.

Amstel River Café
V. Párisi utca 6 (267 0285). M3 Ferenciek tere. **Open** 9am-11pm daily. **Average** Ft1,000. **No credit cards.**
Full menu and great beer on tap in pleasant interior plus pavement seating on a pedestrianised street. Mixed clientèle; gay staff.

Cyrano
V. Kristóf tér 7/8 (266 3096). M1, M2, M3 Deák tér. **Open** 11am-5pm, 6pm-midnight, daily. **Average** Ft1,700. **Credit** AmEx, DC, MC.
Gay-owned. Great menu of great Hungarian and international cuisine served under the chandelier used in Depardieu's *Cyrano de Bergerac*. Reservations recommended.

Café New York
VII. Erzsébet krt 9-11 (322 3849). M2 Blaha Lujza tér/tram 4, 6. **Open** 9am-11pm daily. **Average** Ft600. **Credit** AmEx, DC, MC, V.
A *grande dame* of a place which Cocteau would have liked for its decaying elegance. A large menu of Hungarian and international cuisine prepared by an inconsistent kitchen and served by able though snail-paced waiters.

Művész Café
VI. Andrássy út 29 (267 0689). M1 Opera. **Open** 9am-midnight daily. **No credit cards.**
A *belle epoque* jewel of a café, one of the few to survive this torn city. Tasty patisserie items and *cappuccini* served by uninterested waiters. Perfect location for the before/after opera/ballet crowd.

Várlak Pub – *the only gay anything in Buda.*

Bars & Discos

Action Bar
V. Magyar utca 42 (266 9148). M3 Kalvin tér. **Open** 9pm-4am daily. **Cover charge** Ft200. **No credit cards.**
Rude bar staff, porno videos, dark room, toilets, draught beer. Count your change. Popular.

Angel Private Club
VII. Szövetség utca 33 (no phone). **Open** 9pm-5am Thur-Sun. **Annual membership** Ft2,000. **Admission** Ft300 members; Ft500 non-members. **No credit cards.**
Budapest's most popular club in a large, new location. Downstairs there's a well-lit basement bar and black cave disco. Las Vegas meets Hellenic Greece in the lounge bar upstairs, where there's also a stage for drag shows (midnight Friday and Sunday) starring Csepi, the Hungarian Madonna. Sunday is 'dyke and straight night'. Management have the lease for the whole building and hope to expand it to include a small hotel, fitness centre and information service.

Café Capella
V. Belgrád rakpart 23 (118 6231). M2 Ferenciek tere/tram 2. **Open** 6pm-4am daily. **No cover charge. No credit cards.**

The Danube Cruise

Day or night the promenade in front of Budapest's five-star hotels – the Duna Korzó – is the main catwalk for locals and foreigners, hard currency whores and romantics seeking beardless students or ballet dancers. Begin your Danube cruise at the Vigadó tér (by the Marriott Hotel). The main gay stretch is between here and the statue of Petőfi Sándor near Elisabeth Bridge. It's most popular between happy hour and 9pm. It's also quite popular with the police for their favourite sport, passport checking, so beware. Very little of the trade is Hungarian; more commonly the client will be shelling out for a junior member of the Ukrainian mafia, a soldier gone AWOL from the war in Bosnia, or a Romanian medical student turning tricks for text books.

If the call of the wild attracts you, flee to the forests of the Germanus Gyula Park, just north of Margaret Bridge on the Buda side. Or beat the bushes in the woods of Népliget Park in south Pest. In either place you will find fewer prostitutes and more truck drivers, plus the occasional policeman who forgot why he was patrolling the park in the first place. Run if you see a flashlight – the Mounties are coming.

Fans of Esther Williams should visit the pools and baths of Budapest for water sports. Check out the showers and nude sunbathing deck at the Palatinus on Margaret Island and the Gellért Hotel Spa. Both are favourite locations for hardcurrency whores, so take lots of small bills; an hour will cost roughly Ft5,000, for whatever, anywhere in the city. In colder weather, cruising moves indoors to the baths and bars.

Large, airy, white-brick basement, lots of wrought iron and candle-lit table seating, two bars and a dance floor. Hasn't yet found its crowd but it's an excellent location.

Darling Bar
V. Szép utca 1 (no phone). M2 Astoria. **Open** 7pm-5am daily. **No cover charge. No credit cards.**
Small bar featuring draught beer, porno videos upstairs, trade and tourists.

Lokále Bar and Disco
VII. Kertész utca 31 (no phone). M2 Blaha Lujza tér/tram 4, 6. **Open** 10pm-4am Mon-Wed, Fri-Sun. **No credit cards.**
Trade, tourists and ugly drag queens make this a fun and sleazy place in the company of friends. Ft300 'minimum consumption'. Not worth turning up before 11pm.

Mystery Bar
V. Nagysándor J utca 3 (112 1436). M3 Arany János. **Open** 9pm-4am daily. **No credit cards.**
Small, friendly watering-hole popular with expats and tourists. Draught beer.

Várlak Pub
I. Ostrom utca 14 (118 7596). M2 Moszkva tér. **Open** 1pm-1am daily. **No credit cards.**
The only gay anything on the Buda side of town. Friendly pub serving draught beer and *cappuccino*. Sometimes live music, such as classical guitar. Bartender Mátyás is a well-known local drag queen and enjoyably bubbly character. Mixed crowd.

The Baths

Some advice: don't pay more than Ft200 per person, but do pay extra for massage and pedicures. Tip Ft20, once only. Store your things in your bathing cabin (it's double-locked; you have one key, the attendant has the other). Bathing suits are not *de rigueur* as a modesty apron is provided. You get only one towel at the end. Because of bodily emissions, it's not advisable to submerge your head in any of the pools. Soap and shampoo are available to buy. Note: ticket offices close one hour before baths.

Gellért Hotel Bath Spa
XI. Szent Gellért tér (185 3555). Tram 18, 19, 47, 49. **Open** 6.30am-7pm Mon-Sat; 6.30am-4pm Sun. **Admission** Ft600.
Proceed to the last door on the right, give in your receipt, collect towel, turn right, go upstairs or downstairs to dressing cabins. Dry sauna, steam bath, three pools of varying temperatures, and massage. Gorgeous Art Nouveau interior. Clientèle includes tourists, expats, hustlers.

Rudas
I. Döbrentei tér 9 (156 1322). Tram 18, 19/bus 7. **Open** 6am-7pm Mon-Fri; 6am-1pm Sat, Sun (closed Sun 15 June-31 Aug). **Admission** Ft200. **Men only.**
The most beautiful of the original Turkish baths. Cleanest water, too. Dry sauna, steam bath, six pools of varying temperatures and massage. Popular with athletes. Gays be wary as it is quite straight. The stained-glass, chinked dome is stunning and covers the largest pool.

Rác
I. Hadnagy utca 8-10 (156 1322). Tram 18, 19/bus 7. **Open** *men* 6.30am-7pm Tue, Thur, Sat; *women* 6.30am-7pm Mon, Wed, Fri. **Admission** Ft170.

Terribly gay, lots of steamy sex among the war veterans, hustlers and tourists. Dry sauna, steam bath, three pools of varying temperatures, massage and pedicure.

Király
I. Fő utca 84 (201 4392). Tram 4, 6. **Open** *men* 6.30am-7pm Mon, Wed, Fri; *women* 6.30am-7pm Tue, Thur, Sat. **Admission** Ft170.
The Király is the second nicest original Turkish bath in Budapest. It's also quite carnal, with the tourists, trade and elderly. Dry sauna, steam bath, three pools of varying temperatures and massage.

Lukács
II. Frankel Leó utca 25-27 (212 4088). Tram 4, 6. **Open** 6am-7pm daily. **Admission** Ft170.
Seek the 'Mud Bath' (*iszapfürdő*). Wild action at dusk. Filthy water. Afterwards, cruise the park between the Lukács and the Danube. Cruising continues in Germanus Gyula Park to the south.

Shopping

Condom-friendly sexual lubricants are generally not sold in Hungary. Condoms and other sex paraphernalia are available in the following stores:

Intim Center
V. Károly körút 14 (117 0918). M1, M2, M3 Deák tér/tram 47, 49. **Open** 9am-9pm Mon-Fri; 9am-6pm Sat, Sun.

Intim Lapüzlet és Videotéka
VII. Dob utca 17 (no phone). M2 Astoria/tram 47, 49. **Open** 10am-6pm Mon-Fri; 10am-4pm Sat.

Sport & Sunshine

Csillaghegyi (Árpád) Strand
III. Csillaghegy, Pusztakúti út 3 (250 1533). HÉV Csillaghegy. **Open** 7am-7pm daily. **Admission** Ft150.
Many pools plus nude sunbathing area located atop the hill. (five minutes from the HÉV suburban railway stop that departs from Margit Bridge HÉV station)

Dagály Strand
XIII. Népfürdő utca 36 (120 2203). Bus 133 from Lehel tér metro. **Open** 6am-6pm daily. **Admission** Ft170.
Twelve pools, water chutes, nude sunbathing on roof.

Palatinus Strand
Margit Isle (112 3069). Bus 26 from Nyugati Station. **Open** 7am-6pm daily. **Admission** Ft170.
Nude separate-sex sunbathing on roof. This is the most cruisey pool for tourists, expats, locals and hookers. During a police bust in summer 1994, 28 male hustlers were arrested in a single afternoon. Fun place.

Miscellaneous

Rainbow Association for Homosexual Rights
Szivárvány
1243 Budapest, PO Box 690.

Vándor Mások
1360 Budapest, PO Box 2.
The first recreational group for gays in Hungary offers monthly hikes in the countryside. Their calendar of walks is listed in *Mások*, or write for further information.

Students

Lots of schools for getting to grips with the galaxy's most difficult language, a few cheap places to eat meat and potatoes, and even one university where your diploma is worth more – in the outside world – than the paper on which it is printed.

Budapest University of Economic Sciences, *independent since 1948 – full Marx required.*

Budapest is home to 40 higher education institutions, including half of Hungary's universities. In 1990, the last year for which statistics are available, the number of students per capita was one of the lowest in Europe – Hungary beat only Albania and Romania. Since then, a score of new universities and institutes of higher vocational education (*főiskolák*, also called colleges) have opened.

To enrol at a state university, students must have a secondary school degree and pass written and oral entrance examinations. In economy, law, medicine and the arts, applicants greatly outnumber available places. It usually takes university students five years to complete their studies; those at colleges finish a year earlier. The academic year

has two terms; it begins in early September, and final exams are in May. Generally, the Hungarian system of higher education is less flexible than in the West, and its students poorer – even more so after recent government austerity measures introduced modest but unprecedented tuition fees.

Universities

Few of Budapest's university buildings were designed for higher education. The main building of ELTE once housed a Catholic monastery; the English department of the Humanities Faculty was a Communist Party training school; and the University of Economic Sciences used to be a

Customs Building – in the lobby sits a statue of Karl Marx, who formerly lent his name to the institution, and now watches over future businessmen.

Central European University (CEU)

V. Nádor utca 9 (327 5000/fax 111 6073). M2 Kossuth Lajos tér. **Open** 9am-5pm Mon-Thur; 9am-3pm Fri.
Founded in 1991 by George Soros, CEU offers postgraduate courses for students from central and eastern Europe and the former USSR. Departments include History, Legal Studies, and Political and Environmental Sciences.

Eötvös Loránd University

Eötvös Loránd Tudományos Egyetem (ELTE)
International Secretariat – V. Pesti Barnabás utca 1 (postal address 1364 Budapest, Pf 107) (267 0966 ext 171/fax 266 3521). M3 Ferenciek tere. **Open** 10am-noon, 1-3pm, Mon, Wed; 10am-noon Fri.
The largest and oldest Hungarian university, it was founded in 1635 in Nagyszombat (now Trnava, Slovakia), moved to Buda in 1777, and to Pest in 1784. Today there are 12,000 students at the Faculty of Humanities, Sciences, Law and the Institute of Sociology.

Budapest University of Economic Sciences

Budapesti Közgazdaságtudományi Egyetem (BKE)
International Studies Centre – IX. Fővám tér 8 (217 0608). Tram 2, 47, 49. **Open** 8am-4.30pm Mon-Thur; 8am-2pm Fri.
An independent institution since 1948, the BKE (known as the Közgáz – 'public gas' – a pun on the Hungarian for economics: *gazdaság*) has 4,000 students, and issues diplomas in Business Administration, International Economics and Business, and Social and Political Studies.

Budapest Technical University

Budapesti Műszaki Egyetem (BME)
International Student Centre – XI. Műegyetem rakpart 3 (463 1408/fax 463 2520). Bus 86. **Open** 9am-4pm Mon-Thur; 9am-2pm Fri.
Established in 1782, the BME now has over 9,000 students studying at seven faculties that include Architecture and Chemical, Electrical and Civil Engineering. The education is highly practical, and BME is among the few Hungarian institutions whose diplomas are accepted throughout the world.

Semmelweis University of Medicine

Semmelweis Orvostudományos Egyetem (SOTE)
English Secretariat – VIII. Üllői út 26 (210 0271). M3 Klinikák. **Open** 9am-3pm Mon-Thur; 9am-1pm Fri.
Over 200 years old, but only in its current form since 1955, when the faculties of Pharmacy and Dentistry were incorporated. Ignác Semmelweis, who discovered the cause of puerperal fever, was a professor here last century.

Learning Hungarian

Although Hungarian is one of the most difficult languages for foreigners to learn, it's useful to learn a little, since few Hungarians speak English.

Eötvös Loránd University, Faculty of Humanities

V. Pesti Barnabás utca 1 (267 0966). M3 Ferenciek tere. **Open** 9am-4pm Mon-Thur; 9am-2pm Fri.
ELTE organises a summer university for foreigners with Hungarian-language classes. During the academic year, a two-term Hungarian course is available. Participants are registered as regular students, and, if they study at a college in their home country, may use the credits they receive here.

ELTE also offers 20-week intensive Hungarian courses for $1,600. Survival evening courses cost Ft300 for 45 minutes.

Hungarian Language School

VI. Eötvös utca 25A (112-5899). M1 Oktogon/tram 4, 6. **Open** 9am-4pm Mon, Tue, Thur, Fri; 9am-7pm Wed.
Two-, three-, six- and 12-week courses throughout the year at different levels. A two-week survival course costs Ft2,800, a three-week intensive course is around Ft15,900.

Arany János Nyelviskola

VI. Csengery utca 68 (111 8870). M1 Oktogon/tram 4, 6. **Open** 10am-5.30pm Mon-Thur; 10am-3.30pm Fri.
One of the largest language schools, offering courses in most European tongues. A 45-minute Hungarian lesson costs Ft320; 30- and 60-lesson courses are available at Ft9,600 and Ft19,200. International student ID nets a 10 per cent discount.

Mensae

Most universities have one or more self-service restaurants that offer bargain menus at Ft150-Ft200, and slightly more expensive à la carte food. You only need student IDs for the bargain menus. Anyone can wander in and scoff the à la carte stuff.

Budapest University of Economic Sciences

IX. Fővám tér 8 (218 0977). Tram 2, 47, 49. **Open** 11.30am-2.30pm Mon-Fri.
Offers two three-course menus at Ft120-Ft150. If you prefer à la carte, expect to pay Ft300-Ft400 for a main course. Soup prices range from Ft50 to Ft100, and there's a salad bar, too.

Eötvös Lorand University

XIV. Ajtósi Dürer sor 19 (343 0148). Trolleybus 74, 75. **Open** 11.30am-2.30pm Mon-Fri.
The usual selection of dishes with an unusual system of catering. After the food is selected and paid for (Ft200 for an average meat-and-potato dish), you will get two receipts. One is to be handed over to a woman who appears after you are seated, the second to the waiter who actually brings the food. Service, unsurprisingly, may be sluggish.

University of Food Sciences & Horticulture

Kertészeti és Élelmiszeripari Egyetem
XI. Szüret utca 2-18 (185 0666). Tram 61. **Open** 11.30am-2.30pm Mon-Fri.
The usual fare but worth a visit for the arboretum (entered from Ménesi út) that surrounds it. Wander along the winding paths and discover plants from all parts of the world.

Budapest Technical University

Stoczek Building, XI. Stoczek utca 1-3 (463 3754). Bus 86. **Open** *bistro* 11am-7pm daily; *restaurant* 11am-3pm Mon-Fri.
The restaurant on the first floor offers the standard Hungarian meat-and-potato menu at average prices; the bistro upstairs features soups, burgers and pasta for around Ft100.

Bölcs Bagoly & Brooklyn Jazz Restaurant

V. Váci utca 3 (267 0966 ext 140). M3 Ferenciek tere. **Open** 11.30am-2.30pm Mon-Fri.
Central location and moderate prices are the advantages of Bölcs Bagoly (Wise Owl), which serves soups, meat, and pasta for under Ft200. In the basement, the somewhat inappropriately named Brooklyn Jazz Restaurant is cosier than the restaurant upstairs, despite horrible cardboard décor. The place changes to a jazz bar or discothèque between 9pm-4am on Fridays and Saturdays.

Women's Budapest

These sisters already did it for themselves under Communism and now they just wanna have fun.

The first thing that hits most newcomers to Budapest is the short-skirt shock. Hungarian women don't believe in covering anything up unless it's in danger of becoming frostbitten.

A rebellion against years of Communist suppression of individuality? No. It's a celebration of youth, sex appeal and body language. The women like being looked at, and the men like looking. Get used to it.

Besides, Hungarian women do deserve some fun, at last. For 40 years they were supposed be the tough, trousered, tractor-driving heroines of socialism. They never really bought the idea but they did get used to going out to work and most women still have employment of some sort. Unfortunately no one ever explained equality to Hungarian men so they carry on expecting the dinner on the table and the children fed and bedded.

Western clothes stores and pre-prepared meals have made life a little easier and a little more fun for those who can afford them. Twenty-five years ago you could only get one kind of perfume, 'Red Square'; now the high streets are packed with the latest Paris scents.

But 1989 really was just another cosmetic revolution as far as women are concerned. Men remain macho and the economic strain of the post-Communist transition has fallen largely on women. Most of the opportunities for making a fast buck and rising to the top in the post-Communist order have also fallen to men. There are fewer women in parliament now than there were pre-1989. And there is twice as much pornography. The biggest legacy of the Communists' campaign to promote women is that feminism has become *the* F-word. Utter it at your peril.

A few women's rights groups have sprouted but they have enjoyed a narrow response from a small section of the population. Most feminist campaigning is instigated by Western women's groups coming to convert their oppressed sisters in the East. However, the oppressed Eastern sisters are generally too busy finding themselves husbands, changing nappies and stirring pots of *gulyás*.

The lack of a women's movement means there are none of those trendy women-only cafés, galleries or clubs that you'll find in other European capitals. Women's organisations are only just beginning to establish domestic violence hotlines, and support groups (*see below*).

On the plus side, men here are generally courteous and, although they may treat you with a fair dose of machismo, seldom adopt the hands-on approach common in some other countries. There is a comforting sense of security on the streets of Budapest. Pickpockets are common; physical harrassment and violent attacks are not. Aside from one or two dark and dismal parts of town, women can walk safely on their own at night and enjoy an independence rapidly being eroded in other cities.

*Party time at the **Feminist Network**.*

Contacts

Ariadne Gaia Foundation
Ariadne Gaia Alapítvány
V. Szép utca 3 III/1 (117 4779). M3 Ferenciek tere.
Contact Magda Rohánszky.
Offers courses on women's assertiveness, counselling training, group therapy and counselling, in English if required.

Feminist Network

A Feminista Hálózat
Budapest 1399, PO Box 701, 1092. Contact Judit
Acsády.
The first real grass-roots campaign group for women, the
Network organises meetings, training and campaigning ses-
sions and publishes a quarterly magazine, *Nőszemély* (*The
Female Person*), – which includes essays and articles on
women's social and political situation in Hungary today.

Women United Against Violence

NaNE – Nők a Nőkért Együtt az Erőszak Ellen
IX. Vámház körút 7. M3 Kálvin tér/tram 47, 49.
Postal address: Pf 660, 1462 Budapest (216
5900/helpline 216 1670). **Open** *office* 9am-5pm, *helpline*
6-10pm, daily. Contact Ildikó Szineg
Rape and domestic violence are low-profile issues in Hungary. There is no law against marital rape and little sympathy for rape victims. This telephone helpline was set up
in 1993 to give support and information to battered and
raped women and children, to campaign for changes in law
and policy, and to challenge social attitudes to violence.

Association of Hungarian Women

Magyar Nők Szövetsége
VI. Andrássy út 124 (131 9734/fax 112 5071). M1
Hősök tere. **Open** 10am-3pm Mon-Fri. President Judit
Thorma.
Now independent, the original Communist-era women's
association has survived to fight another day.
Understandably, they're not particularly radical – they have
seen it all before. It has 40 member organisations, 500 indi-
vidual members and aims 'to work for the equal opportuni-
ty of women and participation in social and political life'.

Union of Women Entrepreneurs

Vállalkozó Nők Egyesülete
VI. Andrássy út 124 (131 9734/fax 112 5071). M1
Hősök tere. **Open** 10am-3pm Mon-Fri.
Set up with a gift of money from an American women's
group, this sounds more impressive than it actually is, and
gives legal and professional advice to around 300 members.

Association of Gypsy Mothers

Magyarországi Cigány Anyák Érdekszövetsége
VII. Király utca 75 I/2 (121 6359). Tram 4, 6. **Open** 24
hours daily.
The triple burden of sexual and racial discrimination and
poverty has led Hungary's Roma women to club together.
Still the organisation only has a few members.

Roma Women in Public Life

Roma Nők a Közéletben
Budapest 1462, PO Box 660 (111 7594). Contact Blanca
Kozma.
One of the newest organisations, this second Gypsy women's

At work at **Women United Against Violence.**

organisation is the project of a Gypsy politician, Blanca
Kozma, who is president of one of the Roma-elected parliaments in Budapest. The idea is to get Roma women more
involved in decision-making within the Gypsy community
and to encourage them to establish real political representation. Membership is mushrooming.

MONA Hungarian Women's Foundation

Magyarországi Női Alapítvány
XIII. Tátra utca 30B (270 1311/fax 120 1115). Tram 4,
6. **Open** 9am-5pm Mon-Fri. Contact Mária Neményi or
Gabi Szilárd.
Since 1992 MONA has been doing its best to draw together
women from various campaign organisations and interest
groups. They launched themselves with a round table on
why there is no strong women's movement in Hungary and
since then have held meetings for women mayors, women
journalists and women in business. If you want to get a perspective on the women's movement in Hungary, then MONA
is the place to start.

Ombudswoman

Ombudsnő
VIII. Muzeum körút 4C (266 9833 ext 2308). M2
Astoria/tram 47, 49. **Open** 2-6pm Thur.
The Ombudswoman programme provides a Women's
Information and Resource Centre which puts women in touch
with psychiatrists, lawyers and social workers. There's also
an information hotline and a recently established media
group. A ground-breaking interdisciplinary Gender Studies
Centre, including a library, is now in its nascent stages.

Lesbian Budapest

If being a feminist is tough in Budapest, being
a lesbian is even harder. Practically the only
time gay women get a mention at all is in
adverts for 'lesbian sex shows' in the city centre. Lesbianism is still kept swept firmly under
the carpet. And despite a growing number of
clubs for gay men in Budapest there is still
very little on offer for lesbians. One club, The
Angel, has a mixed gay and lesbian evening
on Sundays. The Várlak and Capella bars are
also mixed. (*See chapter* **Gay & Lesbian**.)

Excitement awaits a few hours away

Trips Out of Town

Getting Started

There are trains, buses and jetfoils – or there's always Halál út, the Death Road to Vienna.

Budapest contains 20 per cent of Hungary's population. No other town is a tenth of its size. Away from the capital and the major tourist destinations of the Balaton, you'll find a different world: sleepy, backward, friendly. Trips out of town can be like stepping back in time.

Hungary is a small country. By bus, rail or car, two or three hours is the longest it'll take to get just about anywhere. At a more leisurely pace, boats serve destinations along the Danube. Hitching is popular among young Hungarians, especially around the Balaton in summer, but unless you're suddenly stranded or on an absurdly tight budget, it's not worth the bother. Trains and buses are frequent, reliable and very cheap.

Driving on Hungary's single-carriageway road system can be hazardous and hair-raising (*see chapter* **Getting Around**). New motorways are either being planned or under construction.

The better hotels will be able to help you with information and transport bookings. For more information about travel outside Budapest, try:

Ibusz

V. Petőfi tér 3 (118 5707). M3 Ferenciek tere. **Open** 24 hours daily. **Credit** V.
The national tourist agency has branches all over Hungary and can book accommodation, organise tours and train travel and provide information.

Tourinform

V. Sütő utca 2 (117 9800). M1, M2, M3 Deák tér/tram 47, 49. **Open** *2 Mar-14 Nov* 8am-8pm daily; *15 Nov-1 Mar* 8am-3pm Sat, Sun.
The helpful, multilingual staff can dispense lots of information about destinations outside Budapest.

By Bus

Buses are cheap and reasonably comfortable. Prices are per kilometre, with no discount for returns, except for Vienna. Prices listed below are for one-way tickets, which can be bought in advance or on the coach. There are three main bus terminals:

Erzsébet tér

V. Erzsébet tér (117 2138/117 2966/int 117 2562). M1, M2, M3 Deák tér/tram 47, 49. **Open** 6am-9pm daily.
International destinations, south and west Hungary.

Népstadion

XIV. Népstadion (252 4496). M2 Népstadion. **Open** 6am-8pm daily.
Serves the north and east

Árpád híd

XIII. Árpád híd (117 2318/117 2966). M3 Árpád híd.
Destinations north along the Danube

To **Balatonfüred** (132km): *Erzsébet tér.* Journey time about two hours 30 minutes. Ft554. Three buses daily 6.30am-4.40pm. Last return 4.20pm.
To **Eger** (128km): *Népstadion.* Journey time about 2 hours. Price Ft554. 14 buses daily 6.15am-8.45pm. Last return 6.45pm.
To **Esztergom** (66km): *Árpád híd.* Journey time about one hour 15 minutes. Price Ft196. Frequent buses 6am-10.50pm. Last return 9.25pm.
To **Keszthely** (190km): *Erzsébet tér.* Journey time about three hours 40 minutes. Price Ft799. Two buses daily 6.30am-3.40pm, two extra Sat, Sun. Last return 4.30pm.
To **Pécs** (198km): *Erzsébet tér.* Journey time about 4 hours. Price Ft849. Five buses daily 6am-4.20pm. Last return 4.30pm.
To **Siófok** (106km): *Erzsébet tér.* Journey time about two hours 15 minutes. Price Ft512. Six buses daily 6.30am-4.40pm. Last return 6.15pm.
To **Sopron** (210km): *Erzsébet tér.* Journey time about four hours. Price Ft813. Four buses daily 6.30am-4pm, two extra Mon-Fri. Last return 2.15pm.
To **Szentendre** (20km) *Árpád híd.* Journey time about 30 minutes. Price Ft84. Frequent buses 7am-10pm. Last return 7.20pm.
To **Vienna** (Bécs) (265km): *Erzsébet tér.* Journey time about 4 hours 45 minutes. Price single Ft2,450, return Ft3,450. Three buses daily 7am-5pm. Last return 7pm.
To **Visegrád** (43km): *Árpád híd.* Journey time about one hour 10 minutes. Price Ft172. Frequent buses 7.30am-8.30pm. Last return 8.25pm.

By Train

Trains are cheap and relatively reliable. Avoid személy trains, which stop at all stations. Gyors are so-called fast trains. InterCity trains are the speediest and most comfortable, equipped with buffet cars and air-conditioning that sometimes works.

Tickets are priced by the kilometre with no discount for returns. For InterCity trains you have to reserve a seat for Ft160. At rush hours arrive about half an hour before the train is due to leave, as there will be queues at station ticket offices. You can also buy tickets from the conductor on the train, though you may have to fork out a small fine.

No one speaks English at stations. Yellow departure timetables are posted at all of them. At

*Although hitching is possible in Hungary, it's not worth the bother because **train travel** is so cheap by Western standards.*

ticket offices it's easiest just to write what you want on a piece of paper: destination, number of tickets, and the time of the train you want.

Oda-vissza means return. An R in the timetable means that you have to reserve a seat. International student cards are not valid but you can get a 33 per cent discount if you are under 26 or look like it (ask for *harminchárom százalék*).

The three main stations are Keleti, Nyugati and Déli, all of which are on underground lines. There is no real logic as to which train goes from which station so always make sure you check.

MÁV Information

VI Andrássy út 35 (322 7860). M1 Opera. **Open** 9am-6pm. **No credit cards.**
You can buy train tickets here, they have all necessary information, and there's usually someone who speaks English. Phone line manned until 8pm.

To **Balatonfüred**: *Déli.* Journey time about two hours 20 minutes. Price Ft504. Six trains daily 6.25am-5.20pm. Last return 5.20pm.
To **Eger**: *Keleti.* Journey time about two hours. Price Ft504. Four trains daily 7.05am-7.20pm. Last return 8.36pm.
To **Esztergom**: *Nyugati.* Journey time about 90 minutes. Price Ft192. Ten trains daily 6.35am-10.20pm. Last return 6.55pm.
To **Pécs**: *Déli.* Journey time about two hours 30 minutes. Price Ft840 plus Ft160 reservation. Four InterCity trains daily 7.30am-7.30pm. Last InterCity return 6.10pm.
To **Keszthely**: *Déli.* Journey time about three hours 15 minutes. Price Ft720. Five trains daily 7.10am-5.10pm. Last return 6.20pm. Make sure you're sitting in the right carriage as the train sometimes splits.
To **Siófok**: *Déli.* Journey time about 90 minutes. Price Ft432. Six trains daily 7.10am-9.10pm. Last return 8.15pm.
To **Sopron**: *Keleti.* Journey time about three hours. Price Ft780 plus Ft160 reservation. Three InterCity trains daily 7.20am-5.25pm. Last InterCity return 6.36pm.
To **Szentendre**: *HÉV Batthyány tér.* Journey time 40 minutes. Price Ft89. Trains every 10-15 minutes 3.50am-11.40pm. Last return 11.30pm.
To **Vienna**: *Keleti/Déli.* Journey time about three hours 30 minutes. Price one way Ft4,000 payable in hard currency or in forints if you have exchange receipts. Eight trains daily 6am-9.25pm. Last return 7.05pm.

By Car

Most roads in Hungary are single carriageway and everybody seems to be in a hurry. You'll see some pretty hair-raising manoeuvres. The 1996 completion of the Budapest-Vienna motorway does however mean that you'll miss the delights of the Győr-Hegyeshalom stretch, fondly nicknamed Halál út – Death Road.

Getting out of Budapest is easy and routes are well signposted. From Buda follow M1 signs for Vienna and Sopron, M7 for destinations at the Balaton, and the single carriageway E73 for Pécs. From Pest follow M3/E71 signs for Eger. From Árpád híd take the 10 for Esztergom and the 11 for Szentendre and Visegrád, following the west bank of the Danube.

There are often lengthy queues on the M1 at the Hungarian-Austrian border. At weekends and high season you might have to wait an hour or so.

By Boat

In summer, leisurely boats and nippy jetfoils cruise up the Danube to Szentendre, Visegrád and Esztergom. Jetfoils will also whisk you onwards to Vienna via Bratislava. Although it's interesting to arrive in a new country by river, the jetfoil to Vienna has no real deck area to catch the view, and not much of a view anyway after you've passed the Danube Bend. There's an expensive bar on board, but only the most rudimentary selection of sandwiches and cold cuts if you get hungry on the six-hour journey. Take a picnic and a good book.

All boats to and from Esztergom stop at Visegrád. Most Szentendre boats continue to Visegrád, making a total of five boats to Visegrád every day. It's easy to visit Visegrád plus either Esztergom or Szentendre in a day-trip. Taking in all three by boat on one day is theoretically possible but pushing it. Some Japanese seem to manage it, though.

Boats run daily from 1 April-23 September. Esztergom jetfoils run from 26 May-3 September on Saturdays and holidays, and also on Fridays between 30 June-3 September. Vienna jetfoils run daily from 8 April-29 October and are priced in Austrian schillings, though any hard currency should be acceptable. Get those ones in advance. Tickets for other boats can be bought on board or in advance at major hotels or the MAHART Tours booking office on Belgrad rakpart.

Boat to **Szentendre** and **Visegrád**: *Vigadó tér terminal (118 1223).* Journey time to Szentendre about one hour 40 minutes; to Visegrád about three hours. Price to Szentendre Ft260; to Visegrád Ft290. Three boats daily 7.30am-2pm (on the 2pm change at Szentendre for Visegrád). Last return from Szentendre 7.40pm; from Visegrád 6.30pm.
Boat to **Visegrád** and **Esztergom**: *Vigadó tér terminal (118 1223).* Journey time to Visegrád about three hours 20 minutes; to Esztergom about five hours 20 minutes. Price to Visegrád Ft290; to Esztergom Ft320. Three boats daily 7.45am-2pm. Last return from Visegrád 6.30pm; from Esztergom 5pm.
Jetfoil to **Esztergom**: *Vigadó tér terminal (118 1223).* Journey time one hour 10 minutes. Price Ft600. One jetfoil at 9.20am Saturdays and holidays, 26 May-3 Sept, and also on Fridays between 30 June-3 Sept. Return 4.30pm.
Jetfoil to **Visegrád**: *Vigadó tér terminal (118 1223).* Journey time 50 minutes. Price Ft600. One jetfoil at 9am on Saturdays and holidays, 26 May-3 Sept, and also on Fridays between 30 June-3 Sept. Return 4.40pm.
Jetfoil to **Vienna**: *International terminal, V. Belgrád rakpart (between Elizabeth and Szabadság Bridges) (118 1743).* Journey time about six hours. Price ATS750 one-way, ATS1,100 return. Discounts for students; children under 6 free, 6-15 half-fare. One jetfoil at 9am April-May, Sept-Oct. Two boats daily at 7.40am and 2pm June-Aug. Return 9am April-May, Sept-Oct, 8am and 2.50pm June-Aug. Arrive one hour prior to departure for check-in and passport control.

The Danube Bend

A couple of day-trips will allow you to explore this beautiful stretch of the river at your leisure – alternatively squeeze Visegrád, Esztergom and Szentendre all into one day.

The Danube Bend, 40 kilometres north of Budapest, is spectacular and beautiful: certainly the most scenic stretch on the river's 3,000-km course from the Black Forest to the Black Sea. Here the Danube widens and turns sharply south into a narrow valley between the Börzsöny and Pilis Hills before flowing onwards to Budapest.

The two main settlements on the west bank, Visegrád and Esztergom, were respectively a Hungarian medieval capital and royal seat. Both are easily accessible as day-trips by train, bus or regular summer boats from Budapest (*see chapter* **Getting Started**). Visegrád's hill-top citadel, the ruins of a thirteenth-century palace, is breathtaking. Esztergom, centre of Hungarian Catholicism, is dominated by the nation's largest cathedral.

Although both places can be fitted into one day, most visitors also aim for Szentendre, a quaint former Serbian village and artists' colony. Taking in all three will be stretching a day to its limits, so a couple of hotels in Esztergom, terminus for the Danube Bend ferry service, have been included.

Szentendre

If the visitor to Budapest takes only one day trip, invariably it will be to Szentendre, a settlement of 20,000 people 20 kilometres from the city.

Without a solid grasp of history, however, many will leave disappointed. After the pleasant 40-minute suburban train journey alongside the Danube, Szentendre looks like the classic tourist trap: pony carriages, tacky shops, naff galleries and, most of all, tourists. The trick is to take Szentendre for what it really is, or was before the tourist industry grew up around it: an eighteenth-century Serbian settlement. Treat yourself to a Sunday there. Follow the smell of the incense wafting out from the Serbian churches. It's a rare atmosphere untarnished by tack.

A wave of Serbian refugees moved here after the Turks won the Battle of Kosovo in 1389, building many small wooden churches. The Turks then invaded Hungary. Although Szentendre was liberated in 1686, the Turkish recapture of Belgrade four years later caused a second flood of Serbian refugees. They enjoyed religious freedom under Habsburg rule and traded in leather and wine. Szentendre prospered and the Serbs rebuilt their churches, this time from stone. Although with western Baroque exteriors, the interiors preserve Orthodox traditions. All places of sanctuary had to face east, irrespective of dimension or streetscape. The resulting disjointed lay-out gives Szentendre its distinct Balkan atmosphere.

The first church the visitor comes to is the Pozarevacka, in Vuk Karadzics tér. For a Ft30 entrance, an old lady will put Slavonic church music on the cranky reel-to-reel. The candlelight and Szentendre's oldest icon screen do the rest. You can still smell the incense in the Balkan Adria café opposite. In the main square, Fő tér, Blagovestenska Church provides a heady mix of deep music, incense and a huge, glorious iconostasis. The most stunning is the Belgrade Cathedral, seat of the Serbian Orthodox Bishop, with its entrance in Pátriäka utca. This is only open for Sunday services, but these offer a moving experience. On the same grounds is a museum of Serbian Church Art, worth Ft30 for the bishop's garments and icons, but don't expect any decent documentation.

In 1774 a royal decree demanded the Serbs take an oath of allegiance to Hungary or be otherwise forbidden to trade. This killed Szentendre as a trading centre. A series of floods and epidemics did the rest. Most Serbs moved on.

When a group of artists discovered Szentendre in the 1920s, they found a living museum of Serbian houses and churches. Encouraged to stay, they formed an artists' colony. The Barcsay Collection, Dumtsa Jenő utca 10, contains the abstract works of one of the colony's founders. Later generations set up dozens of galleries, with varying degrees of artistic success (*see chapter* **Art Galleries**). The alternative set who formed the underground music and art group Bizottság (*see chapter* **Music: Rock, Roots & Jazz**) still remain; check out the weird statues in ef Zámbó's garden, in Bartók Béla utca.

Musical activity is otherwise focused on the Dalmát Pince, Malom utca 5, a cellar ideal for regular live jazz gigs.

Bars are either trendy (the Art Café in Fő tér) or rip-off (the Régimódi diagonally opposite). The Montenegro in Kossuth Lajos utca is just right: full of local characters and fake leopardskin furniture. For lunch try La Paella, a Spanish restaurant on a boat moored near the ferry terminal, run by a family from Uruguay.

Tourism took a strange turn in the 1960s, when the government decided to site the huge Open-air Ethnographical Museum (Skanzen) a short bus journey from Szentendre. Still being constructed 20 years after its opening, its aim is to show village life over three centuries from ten designated regions of Hungary. So far only three areas are complete. The museum is closed in winter.

Tourinform

Dumtsa Jenő utca 22 (26 317 965). **Open** *May-Sept* 8am-5pm Mon-Fri; 10am-2pm Sat, Sun. *Oct-April* 8.30am-4.30pm Mon-Fri.
Helpful and English-speaking.

Visegrád

Despite the spectacular mountain-top Citadel overlooking the most beautiful stretch of the Danube, the village below is small and sleepy with only the ruins of the lower Palace to make it worth a visit.

The Citadel and Palace were built in the thirteenth and fourteenth centuries. The latter was the setting for the Visegrád Congress of 1335, when the kings of Hungary, Czechoslovakia and Poland quaffed 10,000 litres of wine while discussing trade strategy. In a similar but more sober event 656 years later, the Visegrád Group of Hungary, Poland, the Czech Republic and Slovakia planned gradually to remove trade restrictions by 2001.

King Mátyás Corvinus overhauled Visegrád Palace in splendid Renaissance style. All this fell into ruin after the Turkish invasion and mud slides buried the Palace. It wasn't until bits of it were discovered in 1934 excavations that people believed there had ever been anything there in the first place. What you'll see today is mostly ruins. There are modern replicas of the Lion Fountain and the Hercules Fountain, but otherwise your imagination will have to do the rest. Some original pieces uncovered during excavations can be found at the Mátyás Museum, in the Salamon Tower halfway up the hill to the Citadel.

There are three ways up to the Citadel: a strenuous walk up the stony Path of Calvary (25 literally breathtaking minutes); one of the thrice daily buses from the village (ten minutes); or a taxi (Ft750 – phone 328 202) or car up Panoráma út. You won't be disappointed. The exhibitions are naff and boring, but the view from the Citadel walls is magnificent.

Once back to earth, we'd recommend a beer in the eighteenth-century Baroque former royal hunting lodge, now a tennis club at Fő utca 41. For lunch, the Fekete Holló, Rév utca 12, with its open fire, can rustle up chicken or trout with all the trimmings for Ft1,000.

Probably the best way to see Visegrád is from the bank opposite. Take the hourly ferry across to Nagymaros, and splash around at the only spot on the river where it's possible to swim.

Visegrád Tours

Rév utca 15 (26 398 160). **Open** 9am-6pm daily.
They're a bit sullen here, but it's the only information office in town.

Esztergom

Although Esztergom is Hungary's most sacred city, home of the Archbishop and the nation's biggest church, it has a real-life edge that makes it worth a night's stopover. Not all of its 30,000 inhabitants are pious; there's a huge Suzuki car factory on the outskirts and in town a string of rundown bars full of drunken fishermen.

It is the past that brings visitors here, however. Esztergom was Hungary's first real capital. The nation's first Christian king, Szent István, was crowned here on Christmas Day 1000. He built a royal palace, unearthed in 1934, parts of which can be seen in the Castle Museum south of the Cathedral.

For nearly three centuries Esztergom was the royal seat until the Mongol invasion all but destroyed the city. It suffered more damage under the Turks, but was gradually rebuilt in Baroque style during the eighteenth and nineteenth centuries. Most of what's worth seeing was constructed then, in the riverside area of Víziváros: the Víziváros Parish Church on Mindszenty tere; the Christian Museum on Berényi Zsigmond utca and the Balassi Bálint Museum in Pázmány Péter utca.

It's the Cathedral that dominates, though. What strikes most is the size of the thing. When the Catholic Church moved its base back to Esztergom in 1820, Archbishop Sándor Rudnay wanted a vast monument on the ruins of a twelfth-century church destroyed by the Turks. It took 40-odd years and three architects and fairly bleak it is too. Main bright spot is the Bakócz Chapel by the south entrance, built in red marble by Florentine craftsmen, dismantled into 1,600 pieces during the Turkish era and reassembled in 1823.

On the north side, the Treasury holds a collection of golden treasures rescued from the medieval church. The crypt contains the tomb of Cardinal Mindszenty, who was tortured by the Communists in 1948 and then holed up in the American Embassy for 15 years.

It took 40 years and three architects to create the enormous Cathedral at **Esztergom**.

In town you'll find a dozen or so reasonable restaurants; the Csülök Csárda, Batthyány utca 9, is as good as any. The delapidated Hotel Fürdő, Bajcsy-Zsilinszky utca 14 (311 688), can provide a cheapish double room and some old thermal baths. The Hotel Esztergom, Nagy Duna sétány (312 883), is a more expensive modern job with a river terrace and sports centre.

For the best view of Castle Hill and the city, walk up St Thomas Hill to the east. Although all you'll see there now is a modest nineteenth-century chapel – the original was destroyed by the Turks – this was the site of a religious chapter named after Thomas à Becket. It was founded by French princess Margaret Capet whose father-in-law, King Henry II of England, was implicated in Becket's murder – appropriate for a town that is essentially the Magyar Canterbury.

GranTours
Széchenyi tér 25 (33 313 756). **Open** 8am-4pm Mon-Fri; 8am-noon Sat.
Efficient and English-speaking.

The Balaton

What is 77 kilometres long, shallow throughout and the only place you're likely to catch a fogas? Lake Balaton – the former Eastern Bloc's favourite holiday resort.

Hungary is a land-locked country, which perhaps explains why locals get so hyperbolic about the Balaton, largest lake in western and central Europe. Take these words from turn-of-the-century writer Károly Eötvös, often quoted in Communist-era guide books:

'Lake Balaton is fantasy and poetry, history and tradition, a volume of bitter-sweet tales, the age-old home of wild Hungarians; it is both the pride of our past and a brilliant hope for our future.'

But while Hungarians experience the Balaton from the comfort and seclusion of weekend cottages, for the foreign tourist it's a different story: high-rise hotels and concrete beaches, white plastic chairs and advertising umbrellas, a string of over-priced resorts, the breeding-ground of wild mosquitoes. Though there are some beautiful spots on and around the lake, particularly along the north shore, a trip to the Balaton is first and foremost an excursion into deepest naff – which doesn't mean to say that it can't be a lot of fun.

Wild Hungarians may still be found in the bars and discos of Balatonfüred or Siófok, but this area was also an age-old home for all sorts of other folk, even before the lake formed around 20-22,000 years ago. Between then and the arrival of the Magyars in the late ninth century, there were Celts, Romans, Huns, Lombards, Avars, Franks and Slavs, whose word for swamp, *blatna*, probably gave the shallow lake its name. The Magyars brought fishing, agriculture, livestock-breeding and built a lot of churches before the Mongols came and trashed the place in 1242. The Turks later occupied the south shore and scuffled with Austrians along the other side throughout the sixteenth and seventeenth centuries. Once they were driven out, the Habsburgs came along and blew up any remaining Hungarian castles.

Most of the interesting sights, therefore, date from the eighteenth century, when agriculture and viticulture began to flourish and Hungarian land-owners brought in Slav, German and Croat peasants to work their estates. It was a time of Baroque building and decoration, the best remaining examples of which are the Abbey Church in Tihany and the huge Festetics Mansion in Keszthely. Wine is still produced in large quantities, particularly in the area around Badacsony – full of small cellars

where you can taste the wares and buy by the five-litre plastic container.

Although Balatonfüred was declared a spa in 1785, it wasn't until the nineteenth century that bathing and the therapeutic properties of the area's thermal springs began to draw the wealthy in large numbers. In 1836 Baron Miklós Wesselényi, leading reformer of the period, was the first to swim from Tihany to Balatonfüred. Lajos Kossuth suggested steamships, and Count István Széchenyi rustled some up. Passenger boat services still link many major resorts, although the ferry from the southern tip of the Tihany peninsula to Szántód – a ten-minute journey spanning the lake's narrowest point – is the only one that takes cars.

The southern shore – these days one 80-kilometre stretch of tacky resort after tacky resort – was developed after the opening of the railway in 1861, which runs along the lake en route from Budapest to Zagreb. The line along the hillier and marginally more tasteful north shore wasn't completed until 1910. Even so, the Balaton didn't become a playground for anyone but the well-to-do until after World War II, when the Communists reconstructed the area with an eye to mass recreation. You'll still see a category of lodging called an *üdülő*. Once holiday homes for the workers of particular factories or trade unions, many *üdülők* are now privatised.

Before the fall of the Wall, Hungary was one of the few places where East Germans could travel and the Balaton became the place where West Germans would meet up with their poor relations. Tourism is still heavily geared towards the needs of Germans and Austrians – as testified by all the bar bands playing oom-pah-pah music – and a smattering of Deutsch will be more useful than English in these parts. Though a trip to the Balaton is hardly getting away from it all, you'll at least be going somewhere not often frequented by Brits – which also makes for some entertaining English on restaurant menus, such as 'Propositions of the chef: Sailor Dish (for two persons)' or 'In the over preparing paste'.

*Taking it easy on one of the public beaches at **Siófok**, sin city and largest resort on the Balaton.*

*The Abbey Church at **Tihany** – one of Hungary's most important Baroque monuments.*

The lake itself is weird. A 77-kilometre-long rectangle, 14 kilometres at its widest, it covers an area of about 600 square kilometres but is shallow throughout. Lake Geneva contains 20 times as much water. At its deepest (the so-called 'Tihany Well' off the tip of the peninsula that almost chops the lake in half), the Balaton reaches only 12-13 metres. At Siófok and other south shore resorts you can paddle out 500-1,000 metres before the water gets up to your waist, which does mean it's very safe for children.

But it's not ideal swimming water. It's silty and milkily opaque and feels oily on the skin. The shallowness also means it warms up quickly, and isn't the most refreshing splash on a brain-baking July afternoon. It does, however, freeze well in the winter, and is apparently good for ice-skating, but if you visit before May or after October (high season is July and August), you won't find very much open even in the larger towns.

Motor boats are strictly no go here but there's sailing and windsurfing on the lake. Fishing, too. The Balaton is home to around 40 varieties of fish – including fogas, the Hungarian pike-perch, which is unique to the lake and a suitable accompaniment for one of the many drinkable local wines. It also teems with eels, literally tons of which die off each summer (partly because of chemical pollution) and have to be removed.

There are also too many mosquitoes. Once the government sprayed both the lake and the Danube to curb the bug population. Now this job has supposedly devolved to local councils, who say they can't afford it. The result is so many mosquitoes that you can't go out at night without lathering yourself in an assortment of repellents. Thousands cluster around the bright lights of every resort and, walking by the lake in the dark, you'll feel dozens of insects bounce off your face at every step.

Another downer is the pegging of prices to the Deutschmark, which means the Balaton is getting expensive for everyone except the Germans. Affordable hotels do exist, but you pay a lot for what you get. Fine dining is hard to find, as is anything cheap and cheerful apart from the occasional pizza. Moderately expensive Hungarian restaurants serving up standard meat and vegetable dishes are the order of the day. Vegetarians will find little.

Nevertheless, the Balaton can make for a fun trip out of town. Most destinations can be reached by train in two or three hours. Siófok and other resorts at the western end of the lake are doable in a day. Perhaps the most agreeable method is to take a long weekend circumnavigating the lake, stopping here and there for a swim or a beer, and driving up into the hills behind the northern shore. Here you've got rolling countryside, quiet villages, the occasional ostrich farm and roadsides decked with wild flowers. From the oddly-shaped volcanic hills above Badacsony (the Kisfaludy Ház restaurant, although somewhat tackily folkloric in theme, has a beautiful terrace), the view across vineyards and the milky green waters of the lake, ploughed by a steamship or two and fading into a distant heat haze, is pretty enough to touch a chord in even the most cynical of travellers.

Balatonfüred

The north shore's major resort is also the Balaton's oldest and has long been famed for the curative properties of its waters. The State Hospital of Cardiology and the Sanitorium dominate the Baroque and these days somewhat delapidated Gyógy tér at the old town centre. In the middle of the square the Kossuth Well dispenses warm mineral-rich water, which is the closest you'll get to the thermal springs without checking into the hospital.

There also used to be a theatre here, built in the mid-nineteenth century when Balatonfüred was a major hangout for nationalist writers, artists and politicians. 'Patriotism towards our nationality' read the banner outside, and the theatre was intended to encourage Hungarian writing and acting at a time when German was still more widely spoken. Ironic, then, that tourism has reinstated German as the region's lingua franca.

There is a busy harbour with a pier, a shipyard, promenade, six major beaches and an assortment of not terribly inspiring things to see. Popular romantic writer Mór Jókai cranked out many of his 200 novels here, and his summer villa (at the corner of Jókai Mór utca and Honvéd utca) is now a memorial museum. Across the road is the neoclassical Kerék templom (Round Church), built in 1846. The Lóczy Cave (*barlang*), off Öreghegy utca on the northern outskirts of town, is the largest hole in the ground hereabouts.

The new Hotel Flamingo at Széchenyi utca 16 (87 340 392) is par for the tacky course, but has a private beach and rooms with balconies more or less overlooking the lake. Modest but comfortable is Hotel Thetis on Vörösmarty utca 7 (87 341 606).

Perhaps because of the many oldsters coming to take the waters, Balatonfüred is a calm and almost genteel place, although there is life after dark. The Fregatt Pub on Blaha Lujza utca is a good spot for an early evening beer. After dinner at one of the many restaurants along Tagore sétány and up Jókai Mór utca, the Wagner Club and Galéria offer pop techno, go-go dancers and teenagers on the dance floor moving just as if they were carefully kicking pennies, foot to foot.

From the end of the pier, with the lights of Siófok in the distance and the Tihany peninsula looming darkly to the west, the lake looks lovely by moonlight.

Balatontourist Balatonfüred
Blaha Lujza utca 5 (87 342 823). **Open** *June-Sept* 8.30am-6.30pm Mon-Sat; 8.30am-noon Sun. *Oct-May* 8.30am-4pm Mon-Fri; 8.30am-noon Sat.

Tihany

Declared a national park in 1952, the Tihany Peninsula is one of the quietest and most unspoilt places in the Balaton region – though even in this picturesque, historic spot, summer means the blooming of Coke and Lucky Strike umbrellas.

The 12 square kilometres of the peninsula jut 5km into the lake, almost cutting it in half. Tihany village lies by the Inner Lake, separate from the Balaton and 25m higher. On the hill above stands the twin-spired Abbey Church, completed in 1754. This is one of Hungary's most important Baroque monuments, and not just because of its outstanding wood-carvings – though there are certainly plenty of those. King Andrew I's 1055 deed of foundation for the church originally on this site was the first written document to contain any Hungarian – a few score place names in a mainly Latin text. (It resides at the Pannonhalma Abbey near Győr.)

The Abbey museum in the former monastery next door has exhibits about Lake Balaton and a small collection of Roman statues in an enjoyably cool cellar. If you get tired of the splendid views across the lake, nearby there are also museums devoted to folklore, fishing and pottery.

There isn't that much else to see and do in Tihany, however. The Kakas, in a rambling old house below the Erika hotel, is an agreeable spot for lunch or dinner and, unusually, open all year round. Places to stay are limited, although the Hotel Park by the lake on Fürdőtelepi utca (87 348 611), formerly a Habsburg summer mansion, offers a modicum of elegance and its own private beach. Go for rooms 15, 16 or 17 (the expensive ones with grand balconies), and just say no if they try to stick you in the ugly 1970s annex on the same grounds. Otherwise private rooms in Tihany village can be arranged through Balatontourist.

Do the Strand

A strand is what Hungarians call a spot to go bathing. In Budapest the term is used for open-air pools that also have space for sunbathing. In the Balaton, they're concrete beaches with a bit of grass to lie out on. You'll find strands everywhere.

Entrance is about Ft100. Once inside you will find stalls selling ice cream, sausages, corn on the cob, lángos, cheap jewellery, cassettes, waffles, postcards, Mickey Mouse towels and rubber rings. There'll be a ladder to climb down into the water, and a line of red buoys to stop you swimming out very far. Trees provide a bit of shade. You also get the chance to rent a pedalo and the experience of rubbing shoulders (in high season, almost literally) with a horde of German tourists. There is also usually a water slide that will usually be closed.

We'd recommend staying in Balatonfüred, just 11 kilometres distant, and doing Tihany as a side-trip or stopover on the way to the next town.

Balatontourist Tihany

Kossuth utca 20 (87 348 519). **Open** *June-Sept* 8.30am-6.30pm Mon-Sat; 8.30am-noon Sun. *Oct-May* 8.30am-4pm Mon-Fri; 8.30am-noon Sat.

Keszthely

The only town on the Balaton that isn't totally dependent on tourism, Keszthely has a mellow feel quite different from other lakeside resorts. The two busy strands seem to swallow up all the tourists, while the agricultural university means a bit of life off-season as well as some variety at night.

Main tourist attraction is the Festetics Palace, a 100-room Baroque pile in pleasant grounds at the north end of the town centre. The Festetics family owned this whole area and Count György (1755-1819) was the epitome of an enlightened aristocrat. He not only constructed the palace but also built ships, hosted a salon of leading Hungarian literary lights, and founded both the Helikon library – now in the southern part of the mansion and containing more than 80,000 volumes – and the original agricultural college, these days the Georgikon Museum at Bercsényi utca 67.

The Gothic Parish Church on Fő tér has a longer history than most Balaton buildings. Originally built in the 1380s, it was fortified in 1550 in the face of the Ottoman advance. Though the rest of the town was sacked, it managed to hold out against the Turks. In 1747 the church was rebuilt in the Baroque style.

The Hotel Bacchus at Erzsébet királyné utca 18 (83 314 096) is a small and friendly modern hotel, ideally located halfway between the town centre and the strand, with a terrace restaurant that's one of the best in town. If you'd prefer a place by the lake try the Béta Hotel Hullám at Balatonpart 1 (83 315 950), a 1930s joint with airy, high-ceilinged rooms.

There are many bars and restaurants on and around Kossuth Lajos utca, the main street. The Donatello Pizzéria at Balaton utca 1 (83 315 989) is an acceptable Italian restaurant. There's a beautiful garden out the back with fishpond, fountain and rockery, and one feature all too rare in this part of the world: staff who try hard.

Keszthely is an excellent base for venturing up the lake towards Badacsony with its wine cellars and volcanic hills or the cute little village of Szigliget with its fourteenth-century castle ruins. Hévíz, eight kilometres inland, has the largest thermal lake in Europe. Bathing is possible all year round (in winter the lake steams dramatically). The slightly radioactive water is covered in lilies and is recommended for the treatment of locomotive disorders and nervous ailments.

Tourinform

Kossuth Lajos utca 28 (83 314 144). **Open** *June-Sept* 9am-5pm Mon-Fri; 9am-1pm Sat, Sun. *Oct-May* 8am-4pm Mon-Fri; 9am-1pm Sat.

Right across the street there's also a branch of Ibusz and a similar concern called Keszthely Tourist.

Siófok

Siófok is Balaton's sin city: big, loud, brash and packed in high season. Although it's the lake's largest resort – Greater Siófok stretches for 15 kilometres along the shore – there really isn't much in the way of sightseeing. Here hedonism reigns. By day people do the strand. Nights are devoted to drinking, dining, dancing and sex.

The Petőfi sétány strip runs for about two kilometres between the harbour, where the Sió canal meets the lake, and the four big Communist-built hotels – the Pannonia, Balaton, Hungaria and Lido. Ugly concrete blocks, their classy old neon signs nevertheless look great at sunset. In between are bars with oom-pah-pah bands, amusement arcades, western-style steakhouses, topless places, virtual-reality rides, parked cars blasting pop techno, naff T-shirt stalls and an endless procession of Hungarian, German and Austrian tourists.

One joint on the strip, the Wart Hog Rider's Base, is a heavy metal disco done out army surplus style – sandbag sofas, sawn-off oil drum tables, bar staff in camouflage and the Balaton's flabbiest go-go dancers. The Roxy at Szabadság tér 4 is a decent brasserie where the drinks are well-made. Flört at Sió utca 4 is probably Hungary's best nightclub: two dance floors (one techno, one tacky), some occasionally excellent DJs, a succession of bars on different levels of the barn-like main room, and a roof terrace overlooking the Sió Canal. In summer young Budapesters sometimes drive down for the night just to come and dance here.

There are restaurants everywhere, rather too many of them catering to German tastes. The Pizza Bella at Szabadság tér 1 (84 310 826) serves up average Italian eats. On the strip there are all sorts of food stalls, including a Thai place. The Diana Hotel at Szent László utca 41/43 (84 313 630), one of the best in town, also has a restaurant that, if you're going to try it anywhere, is the place to eat fogas. The Janus at Fő utca 93-85 (84 312 546) is another good new hotel, though pricey – but you'll not find very many bargains in this town. On the strip and a little cheaper, the Hotel Napfény by the harbour at Mártírok utca 8 (84 311 408) at least has good big rooms with balconies.

Tourinform

Fő tér 41 (84 310 117). **Open** *June-Sept* 8am-8pm daily. *Oct-May* 9am-4pm Mon-Fri; 9am-1pm Sat.

In summer there's a also a small Tourinform office in the water tower on Szabadság tér. All the other tourist agencies have offices nearby.

Over-nighters

Eger, Pécs and Sopron form a triangle with Budapest at its heart – all three are good for an overnight stay.

Eger

A sweet little town, 128 kilometres east of Budapest at the foot of the Bükk Hills, Eger is famous for three things: its fine Baroque buildings; a siege at which locals repelled the Turkish army; and Bull's Blood, the heavy red wine known in Hungarian as Egri Bikavér.

It's a playful sort of place. Children play Pooh sticks on bridges over the Eger stream. In summer half the population seems to be on inline skates: gangs of schoolchildren cling to the backs of buses for an illicit tow up Kossuth Lajos utca; whole families skate across pedestrianised Dobó tér.

They take their history seriously, though. The siege of Eger, in which a force of local defenders held the Castle against a much larger Ottoman army, is one of Hungary's few famous victories. The Turks came back and finished the job 44 years later, but the earlier siege of Eger was fixed in the nation's imagination by Géza Gárdonyi's 1901 adventure novel *Egri csillagok* (published in English as *Eclipse of the Crescent Moon*), required reading for every Hungarian schoolkid.

The Castle was later dynamited by the Habsburgs in 1702. What remains is big but pretty dull, although a walk along what's left of the battlements affords a fine view over Eger's Baroque and remarkably flatblock-free skyscape. The one remaining Turkish minaret (the corner of Knézich utca and Markó Ferenc utca) also has a great view, although it's a long climb to get to it.

Eger's Baroque buildings are splendid, most notably the 1771 Minorite church, centrepiece of Dobó tér. There are more listed buildings in this town than anywhere else in Hungary bar Budapest and Sopron. The Bazilika on Eszterházy tér is an imposing neo-classical monolith crowned with crucifix-brandishing statues of Faith, Hope and Charity. There are also many curious buildings along Széchenyi utca and Kossuth Lajos utca.

Small and with a mostly pedestrianised centre, Eger is ideal for strolling. There are some wonderful old shops, including a beautiful bookbinder's on Szent János utca. One could easily do Eger in a day, but it's a relaxing and rewarding overnighter. The Senátorház hotel at Dobó tér 11 (36 320 466) is comfortable and ideally situated. The Minaret Hotel (right beside the actual Minaret) at Knézich Károly utca 4 (36 410 020) is cheaper.

Local wines are most entertainingly sampled just out of town at Szépasszony-völgy, the Valley of Beautiful Women, a horseshoe-shaped area of dozens of wine cellars, many with tables outside. Wine is cheap enough to allow a level of consumption that would diminish anyone's standards of feminine pulchritude (hence the name), Gypsy fiddlers entertain drinkers, and parties come to eat, dance and make excessively merry. Afternoon is best, as places start closing by early evening. The Valley bustles most during the two-week harvest festival in September. It's a ten-minute walk or a cab ride. (You'll almost certainly have to walk back.)

The Star of Eger

Unhappy the land that has need of heroes. Hungarians are so short of them they've made a hero of author Géza Gárdonyi simply for creating a few cardboard fictional heroes of his own. His *Egri csillagok* (*Stars of Eger* – published in English as *Eclipse of the Crescent Moon*) is a 1901 adventure tale about the 1552 Siege of Eger – one of the only battles the Hungarians ever won. This has earnt Gárdonyi his own statue within the Castle walls, where there's also a Panoptikum featuring waxworks of his characters. On Gárdonyi utca, there's a Gárdonyi Géza Memorial Museum, where his house has been preserved. Copies of the novel are piled up in every Eger bookshop, on sale at every postcard stall and in English and German translation. Pity it's such a poor novel – episodic, uneven and full of characters that don't develop – especially as this boys'-own account seems to have displaced the actual history.

A statue of commander István Dobó and his pals routing Turkish invaders stands in Eger's Dobó tér. There's also a statue of Gárdonyi on XI. Bartók Béla út in Budapest.

*The Castle at **Eger** as seen from the town's one remaining Turkish minaret – a long climb but worth it for the view.*

For lunch try the Gyros Greek restaurant at Széchenyi utca 10. It's inconsistent but they seem to do their best. For dinner we'd recommend the Talizmán at Kossuth Lajos utca 19, a laid-back and inexpensive cellar restaurant offering everything from Hungarian standards to low-calorie and vegetarian dishes.

After dinner take a stroll by the Eger stream, listen to the croak of the occasional frog, and eye the plaque of Esperanto inventor Zamenhof on Eszperantó sétány.

Tourinform

Dobó tér 2 (36 321 807). **Open** 9am-6pm Mon-Fri; 10am-6pm Sat, Sun.
Friendly and helpful, but not always an English-speaker in evidence.

Eger Tourist

Bajcsy-Zsilinszky utca 9 (36 411 724). **Open** *May-Sept* 8.30am-7.30pm Mon-Fri; 9am-1pm Sat. **No credit cards**. Can help you find accommodation.

Pécs

Spread out on the southern slopes of the Mecsek Hills, down near the ex-Yugoslavian border, Hungary's fourth-largest city has a warm and sheltered climate, enough fig trees and Turkish monuments to lend it a vaguely eastern air, a curious collection of architecture and a clutch of interesting art museums. It's a peaceful place by day, especially in summer, when it acquires a distinctly lazy feel. At night there are plenty of bars, cafés and restaurants – a reflection of both the town's large student population and its lively trade in conferences and festivals. If you're only going to make one foray out of Budapest, Pécs must be the main contender.

Romans settled here and called their town Sopianae – a name that survives as a Hungarian cigarette brand. Assorted tribes asserted squatting rights before the Magyars set up shop at the end of the ninth century. The town prospered on the trade route between Byzantium and Regensburg, King Stephen established the Pécs diocese in 1009, and Hungary's first university was founded here in 1367.

And then came the Turks in 1543, pushing the locals outside the walls that still define the city centre, and flattening the rest of the place. Thus, as in the rest of Hungary, little pre-Turkish stuff survives. But after staying here 143 years, the Turks did leave a couple of mementoes – the most significant Turkish monuments remaining anywhere in the country.

On Széchenyi tér stands the former mosque of Pasha Ghazi Kassim, built from the stones of the gothic church that formerly occupied this site, and later converted back into a church by the Jesuits. These days it's the Belvárosi Plébániatemplom (Inner City Parish Church), but, domed and angled towards Mecca at variance with the square's

north-south orientation, still lends an eastern feel to the city's main intersection. The minaret was demolished in 1753.

The mosque of Pasha Hassan Jokovali, complete with minaret, is at Rákóczi utca 2. The most intact Turkish structure in Hungary, this was also converted into a church but later reconstructed as a mosque. The entrance hall houses a small and not terribly interesting exhibit of Ottoman finds.

After the Turks, Pécs was slow to revive. Coalmining spurred prosperity in the nineteenth century. Since World War II there has been uranium-mining and, lately, a thriving black market trade with nearby Serbia. Waves of prosperity are clear in the architecture: the forms of the Baroque and art nouveau buildings in the old centre are echoed in the 1970s shopping centres and office blocks down the slope.

Pécs is built around two main squares: the aforementioned Széchenyi tér and Dóm tér, at which stands the four-towered, mostly neo-Romanesque Basilica of St Peter. Below this is Szent István tér,

Csontváry

Do Csontváry's canvases hold your eye because they're huge and intricate? Or do you keep glancing around the detail because they're poorly constructed? Are his colours lush and astonishing? Or lurid and appalling?

People either love or hate Csontváry, born Tivadar Kosztka in 1853 and a pharmacist until he had a vision at the age of 37. His canvases are certainly unique, with themes that range from Bible stories to Serbian power stations. They're also enormous. His extraordinary Baalbek, part of the collection at Pécs' Csontváry Múzeum (Janus Pannonius utca 11) is 300 square metres of luminous Middle Eastern landscape. Picasso is said to have admired them, asking to be left alone in the room for an hour when a Csontváry exhibition went to Paris in the 1940s.

In a way Csontváry is Hungary's Van Gogh: born in the same year and equally unappreciated in his lifetime, he starved to death in 1919 in his studio on Budapest's Bartók Béla út. When his belongings were being auctioned off, a few of his works were saved at the last minute by a young architect called Gerlóczy. He outbid a team of drovers, who wanted them as tarpaulins for their carts. Outside the Csontváry Múzeum, such other canvases as survived this fate now hang in Budapest's National Gallery (*see chapter* **Museums**).

with Roman ruins and a small park with cafés and a weekend market.

Káptalan utca runs east off Dóm tér. Pécs teems with art museums and many are to be found up here. Those dedicated to Csontváry (nearby is Janus Pannonius utca 11 – *see* **Csontváry** *page xx*) and Hungarian op-artist Victor Vasarely (Káptalan utca 3) are the most interesting. Zsolnay tile, that coloured stuff you see on top of Budapest's more extravagant Dual Monarchy buildings (and in Pécs on top of new buildings too), is made in this town, but the Zsolnay Ceramics Exhibit over the road from the Vasarely museum isn't too interesting: mostly vases in glass cases.

The Santa Maria, at Klimó György utca 12, with an inexplicably nautical interior built into the old city walls, is a good spot for dinner. Otherwise Király utca, the pedestrian street off Széchenyi tér, bustles at night with bars, cafés and restaurants. You'll probably want to look at the neo-Renaissance Pécs National Theatre, which is just down here. You might also inspect the interior of the István Pince wine cellar at Kazinczy utca 1 – a fine old example of the borozó genre.

Pécs' best hotel, the Art Nouveau and genuinely elegant Palatinus, is down here at Király utca 5 (72 233 022). The friendly Hotel Főnix at Hunyadi út 2 (72 311 680), just off the north of Széchenyi tér, is much cheaper and just as central.

At weekends, on the outskirts of town, Pécs has one of Hungary's largest flea markets. Catch bus 3 or 50 from the station, or else hail a cab and ask for the Nagyvásár. You'll find acres and acres of junk at the end of the ten-minute ride.

Tourinform

Széchenyi tér 9 (72 212 632). **Open** 9am-5pm Mon-Fri; 10am-3pm Sat. **No credit cards.**
Can provide information and help with accommodation.

Sopron

Sopron is way up in the north-west of Hungary, in a little Magyar nodule that extrudes into Austria. The location has had two effects on this fascinating small, old town. The first is that it escaped devastation by both Mongols and Turks and has managed to retain a medieval feel you won't find anywhere else in Hungary outside Budapest's Castle District. The second is that Austrians flood over the border to go shopping on the cheap.

The Várkerület, which encircles the Old Town, bustles with tiny shops selling bargain booze and cigarettes, budget salamis and household gadgets. Opticians proliferate. There are dentists, hairdressers and beauticians everywhere. Just about every business doubles as a money-changer.

Stepping from all this through one of the entrances into the Old Town is like cracking open a stone to find an extraordinary crystal formation within. Here cobbled, medieval-patterned streets

are relaxed and traffic-free. Practically every building is listed: medieval dwellings rub gables with Gothic churches and Baroque monuments. Commerce continues, but quietly, in discreet boutiques and jewellery shops nestling by small museums.

The Firewatch Tower, symbol of Sopron, sums up the town's history and offers a view that takes it all in. It's built on Roman foundations, with a twelfth-century base, a sixteenth-century column and balcony, a seventeenth-century spire, and a 'Fidelity Gate' installed in 1922 to mark the town's decision (they voted on it) to remain part of Hungary after Trianon. From the top you can see the streets and walls of the Old Town, following the lines of the previous Roman settlement, and the vine-covered hills beyond the outskirts.

Though there's plenty to look at it in the daytime – the various old houses and museums around Fő tér and the Medieval Synagogue at Új utca 22 are particularly interesting – it's at night, after the day-trippers have all gone, when Sopron is at its most atmospheric. Wandering the medieval streets, quiet except for the chatter and clatter from restaurants and wine cellars, only a rare parked car intrudes between you and the illusion that you have stepped back several centuries.

For breakfast or coffee try the restored 1920s Várkapu coffeehouse at Hátsókapu utca 3. For lunch the restaurants Gambrinus (inexpensive Hungarian standards) and Corvinus (reasonable pizzas) both have tables outside on Fő tér, centrepiece of the town. The baroque Gangel restaurant at Várkerület 25 is probably the most handsome spot for dinner. Strangely, the John Bull pub at Széchenyi tér 12 isn't bad either – and despite a menu with shepherd's pie and trifle, none of the staff speak English. The Mekong at Deák tér 46 offers some Vietnamese variety.

The Palatinus Hotel at Új utca 23 (99 311 395) is ugly and has small, dark rooms but is right in the middle of the Old Town. The Pannonia at Várkerület 75 (99 312 180) is roomier but more expensive. Cheap rooms can be found at the nameless pension at Damjanich utca 9 behind the bus station.

Although most of the sights are in the Old Town, even the determinedly profit-seeking Várkerület contains some curiosities. Inspect the 1623 pharmacy at number 29, or the ancient Goger opticians opposite.

Locomotiv Tourist

Új utca 1 (99 311 111). **Open** *Sept-April* 9am-5pm Mon-Fri; 9am-1pm Sat. *June-Aug* 9am-5pm Sat.
Sopron station, Állomás utca 2 (99 311 422). **Open** 6am-5pm daily.
Friendly and helpful, with some English speakers on staff. The Új utca branch is above some Roman ruins, now the Forum Museum, which they'll show you around.

Express

Mátyás király út 7 (99 312 024). **Open** 8am-3.30pm Mon-Fri.
Can assist in finding accommodation.

Vienna

Only six hours up the Danube by jetfoil, Budapest's sister city still rings with the echoes of its dynastic past.

Vienna is still often thought of as Budapest's 'sister city'. A big sister, certainly – and for most of history an extremely bossy sister too (though once it got tired of having its pigtails pulled, Budapest did learn how to fuss and scratch and get its own way sometimes).

Close but competitive in the Dual Monarchy days, the Danubian siblings long ago went their separate ways. You can still see they're related, though. Budapest and Vienna share Habsburg-era similarities but are distinguished by some very stark postwar contrasts – a mix that makes a visit to the Austrian capital a particularly rewarding side-trip. Where Budapest has been run-down by decades of Communism, Vienna has actually benefited from being on the frontline of western capitalism. Where Budapest is poor, self-conscious and shabby, Vienna is prosperous, smug and almost disconcertingly clean.

Budapest is very much a national capital, its whole nineteenth-century shape designed around a monumental celebration of Hungarian identity. Vienna, on the other hand, seems less the capital of Austria than a combination of the dynastic city-state it once was, and the present-day world city that is headquarters for so many international institutions. Long a cosmopolitan melting-pot, today registered foreigners count for more than one in ten of its 1.5 million inhabitants.

In Budapest the Danube dictates the whole feel of the city; in Vienna you'd hardly notice it was there. Arriving by jetfoil (*see chapter* **Getting Started**) you're dumped at a modern ferry terminal on the Danube Relief Channel, with nothing to see but a few cranes, dredgers and United Nations buildings, so far out of town that it can be hard even to find a taxi. Arriving any other way, you might not see the Danube at all, unless from the top of the big wheel in the Prater – a landmark still much the same as it was in Harry Lime's day, except with safer doors.

But prices are the first thing that hit home. A Wiener melange in a famous Viennese coffee house such as Sacher or Demel costs four or five times as much as a similar cup in Budapest's Művész. But at least Vienna can still afford its coffee houses and a couple of dozen old places are still pretty much intact and alive. Sacher is crap, mind you. Demel, on the other hand, at Kohlmarkt 14, is a trip: dauntingly Baroque, with waitresses who

speak an absurd formal German no one uses anywhere else, and just about the most chocolatey chocolate cake in the world. At Central, on Herrengasse, where Trotsky once sat sipping coffee and planning the Russian Revolution, sits a dummy of poet Peter Altenberg, who in life more or less lived in the place.

While Budapest's ancient centre is now perched out of the way up on Castle Hill, the medieval heart of Vienna is still the city centre today. You could spend a couple of days exploring without ever having to step beyond the Ringstrasse – the circular avenue which follows the line of the old city walls. From the pedestrianised Stephansplatz, where St Stephen's Cathedral provides Vienna with its centrepiece, history radiates in concentric circles. In the medieval streets around the square and off bustly Kartner Strasse, you'll find backstreet palaces, small churches, atmospheric old squares and alleys, and any number of houses where Mozart once lived.

The area between the Cathedral and the Danube, on and around Rotenturmstrasse, is known as the Bermuda Dreiecke (Bermuda Triangle). This is the main nightlife area, where the visitor can disappear into one of dozens of late-night bars.

The next band of history, over in the south-west corner of the Innere Stadt, is dominated by the 59-acre Hofburg complex: a sprawl of palaces and parks, statues and fountains, Baroque squares and still-functioning imperial stables. This was the seat of the Habsburgs (among all the treasures and monarchical glitz you can still view the spartan iron bed that nightly reinforced Emperor Franz Joseph's sense of imperial duty) and the sense of power and wealth, concentrated here for centuries, is still quite palpable.

The Ringstrasse (serviced, like Budapest's Nagykörút, by trams) runs in a polygonal horse-shoe shape, beginning and ending at the Danube Canal. This was the line of the old city walls. Vienna has always been a border town, and the defences were knocked about and reinforced time and again throughout history (it was here that the Ottoman advance into Europe was halted in 1683) before Franz Joseph began demolishing them for good in 1857. Along the Ring, punctuated by gardens, are all the monumental public buildings of late Imperial Vienna: the ugly Opera House, the Natural History and Art History Museums (on a

Vienna's *Scloss Schoenbrunn – one of many good reasons to make the trip from Budapest.*

rainy day, check out the Breughels), the Parliament, City Hall, University and Burg Theater. It's all pretty dry stuff, in weighty neo-Gothic and neo-Renaissance styles.

It was in reaction to the pretentiousness of this façade that architect Alfred Loos designed his 'house without eyebrows' – utterly without ornamentation of illusions of past grandeur – which stands cheekily on the Michaeler Platz, opposite the gate into the Hofburg. (Griensteidl, on the ground floor, is a reasonable spot for lunch.)

For more of a taste of turn-of-the-century Vienna, move beyond the Ring to the next concentric circle. At Friedrichstrasse 12 stands the gilt-domed Sezession – home for Gustav Klimt, Otto Wagner and the 17 others who 'seceded' from the Viennese art establishment to found the local version of Art Nouveau. Northwards on the same radius you can visit the Sigmund Freud Museum at Berggasse 19, where the psychoanalyst's working rooms are now a public exhibit.

Beyond this outer ring lie the suburbs and working-class estates, breeding-ground of unrest and revolution in the city that Karl Kraus, on the eve of World War I, dubbed the 'proving-ground for world destruction'. The bureaucratic towers of UNO City, headquarters for the International Atomic Energy Authority, the United Nations Industrial Development Organisation and an assortment of other UN organisations, are the principal monuments to Austria's postwar neutrality.

Contemporary Vienna, removed from the centre-stage of history, is a relaxed and sleepily prosperous place where nothing very much happens any more. You can find just about anything you want in the shops and also eat very well. (After heavy Hungarian food, Neue Wiener Kuche is a light and pleasant shock to the system.) You'll mostly have to pay well for the privilege, though the Naschmarkt (just south-west of the Sezession) offers a centrally located Saturday morning flea market and daily stalls serving every kind of food you can imagine, from Japanese seafood to (presumably) Hungarian 'Hussar Sausages'. Vienna is full of shops selling pricey executive toys, designer fountain pens and improbable furniture, but secondhand book and music stores are dotted all over too.

Accommodation is expensive. If you want to splash out and get a true taste of *mitteleuropäisch* elegance, try the Bristol at Kärtner Ring 1 (00 43 1 515 160) or the Sacher round the corner at Philharmonikerstrasse 4 (00 43 1 514 56). There's no particularly good area for finding cheap hotels, but the Vienna Tourist Office will be able to help.

It's possible to get to Vienna and back in a day, but scarcely worth the bother. An overnighter makes more sense, but we'd recommend two nights as the ideal short stay. Just expect to spend about as much in 48 hours as you would in a week in Budapest.

Vienna Tourist Office

1010. Kärtner Straße 38 (00 43 1 513 8892).
West Station (00 43 1 892 3392).
Open 9am-7pm daily.
English-speaking and extremely helpful at both branches, the West station staff can help you find accommodation.

Further Abroad

Discover that the whole central European thing is not a myth by visiting the Balkans and points east.

Budapest is a very good staging post for an assortment of uncommon destinations. War and instability have made travel difficult in parts of former Yugoslavia. UK citizens require visas for Romania, Serbia and the Ukraine, but not for Croatia, Slovakia or Slovenia. Citizens of other countries should check with their embassies.

Croatia

Zagreb is about six hours by train from Budapest. Apart from one bombing in May 1995, the capital has seen no fighting since 1991, although the visitor will have to cope with the nationalist mood of the inhabitants. It's an attractive town and, even at war, quite a friendly and relaxing one, too. Bars and clubs are surprisingly good (check the streets that run off the north-west corner of the main square) but restaurants, apart from poor pizza joints, are scarce and expensive. Hotels are pricey.

Throughout the summer, an overnight train runs from Budapest to the port of Rijeka. Tourism has been reviving on the Istrian peninsula. Opatja, north of Rijeka, is like the Austro-Hungarian riviera. Pula, a three-hour bus ride away, is an attractive Roman port with a coliseum. There are boats to destinations down the coast. War allowing, Dubrovnik, despite having been heavily bombed in 1991, is still an especially beautiful town.

Romania

In Transylvanian Romania, you still see horses and carts sharing roadspace with oil tankers, and in parts some folk customs have remained largely unchanged for centuries.

In the cities, hotel prices are pegged five times higher for foreigners than for locals. Food and service are appalling and outside hotel bars and discos there is a lack of anything resembling nightlife. The people, though poor, are friendly enough. A visit to Romania, even five years after Ceausescu, is still a shock to the system. Visiting some rural areas is like travelling back in time to fourteenth-century Switzerland. Don't expect modern creature comforts, and if intending to stay in the country, remember to pack some flea powder.

Most Romanian cities are easily accessible from Budapest by rail, but expect some uncomfortable train journeys.

Serbia

It is possible to have a good time in Belgrade, but not so good it's worth the hassle to get there: up to three days' queuing to get a visa, insanely rigorous border controls and an attitude of hostility to foreigners from NATO countries. Food and drink can be found, but are expensive unless you change money on the black market. Student clubs offer nightlife, otherwise most places seem to be run by gangsters, with weapons' checks at the door.

Slovakia

Bratislava is only three hours from Budapest by train and can also be reached by jetfoil up the Danube (*see chapter* **Getting Started**). It's a small, sleepy capital, with countless flatblocks encircling a centre that has a collection of bizarre architecture, including a big, ugly castle and a bridge like something out of a science fiction movie. Wine cellars abound and the beer is good and cheap. The Tatras, on the border with Poland, are like a mini-Alps with possibly the cheapest skiing in Europe. Tatranska Lomnica is the most distinguished resort.

Slovenia

Virtually uninvolved in the war, this small former Yugoslav state, with Alps and a short Adriatic coastline within 40 minutes of each other, is like a half-price Austria. Lake Bled, surrounded by woodland and mountains, is a popular destination, but the capital, Ljubljana, is the main attraction (seven hours from Budapest by rail). A long-established radical art scene – this is the home of NSK (Neue Slowenische Kunst) a multi-headed arts organisation centred on the group Laibach – is reflected in some interesting nightlife options.

Ukraine

Poor and in places irradiated, with highwaymen who rob buses (and even give you a receipt you can show the next band of highwaymen), a trip to the Ukraine really is a journey into the Wild East. Visas are issued only to people who have a letter of invitation from an official organisation. Kiev is beautiful, though.

Survival

Survival

You should survive in Budapest – but you might have to queue first.

Bureaucracy/Living/Working

Gone are the days when the mystique of the West meant a foreigner could simply walk into any job. Teaching is still a sure bet and although some form of qualification is becoming a requirement in many schools, the lack of one does not usually prove to be an insurmountable obstacle. There is also a big market for private lessons.

If you do want to work you are legally required to have a work permit and a residence permit, but many don't bother, as obtaining them involves endless hassles with Hungarian bureaucracy. To make matters worse, the system seems to change every year.

As the system stands, the first step is to obtain a work permit. Only your local employer can do this for you. They will need from you a medical certificate which can be issued by most doctors or obtained from Orvosi Rendelő on Budafoki út for the sum of Ft3,200. They also need your degree or certificate of relevant qualifications, along with an official translation of same. This can be had from Országos Fordító Iroda on Bajza utca for Ft1,000.

Once you have your work permit, getting a residence permit should be no problem apart from a lot of queuing and red tape. Go to the KEOKH office on Városligeti fasor. Take a Hungarian speaker with you. On the wall is a list of the

documents you'll need. This drill may change, but at the moment you have to have: an application form (*kérelem tartózkodási engedély kiállítására*) and residency registration form (*szálláshelybejelentő lap külföldiek részére*) both available there; a copy of your rental agreement or an affidavit saying that the landlord is letting you stay rent-free; a valid passport; two passport photos; Ft3,000 in official stamps obtainable there; an employer's certification of employment; a copy of your work permit; and another medical certificate obtainable from Állami Népegészségügyi és Tiszti Orvosi Szolgálat on Váci út. Expect to queue a lot, especially the first time around. The process usually takes more than one visit and requirements change frequently, so check before setting out.

Additional information is available from the foreign Chambers of Commerce and the British Embassy. The US Chamber of Commerce and Arthur Andersen have produced a free booklet to help you through this process, and Settlers Hungary will take care of the whole business for a price.

Orvosi Rendelő
XI. Budafoki út 111-113 (203 0091). Bus 3, 10, 10A, 83, 110. **Open** 8am-noon Mon-Fri.

KEOKH
VI. Városligeti fasor 46/48 (118 0800). M1 Hősök tere. **Open** 8.30am-6pm Tue; 8.30am-1pm Wed; 10am-6pm Thur; 8.30am-noon Fri.

Állami Népegészségügyi és Tiszti Orvosi Szolgálat
XIII. Váci út 174 (129 0490). M3 Újpest Városkapu. **Open** 8am-noon Mon-Fri; 1-3pm Mon-Thur.

US Chamber of Commerce
VI. Dózsa György út 84A, Room 222 (269 6016). M1 Hősök tere/bus 20, 30. **Open** 8.30am-5pm Mon-Fri.

Országos Fordító Iroda
VI. Bajza utca 52 (269 5730). M1 Bajza utca. **Open** 9am-6pm Mon-Thur; 8.30am-12.30pm Fri.

Settlers Hungary
XII. Sashegyi út 18 (165 1990). Tram 59. **Open** 8am-5pm Mon-Fri. **No credit cards.**
This agency will help you sort out your work permit for Ft25,000 and organise your resident's permit for Ft40,000.

Legal Help

If in need of legal assistance contact your embassy who will provide you with a list of English-speaking lawyers. (*See also chapter* **Business**.)

Useful Numbers

Inland operator (24 hours): **01**
International operator (24 hours): **09** (English spoken)
Police: **07**
Fire/emergency: **05**
Ambulance: **04** or (for English) **111 1666**
Inland directory enquiries: in Budapest **117 0170**; outside Budapest **267 3333**
International directory enquiries: **267 5555** (English spoken)
Sending telegrams (charged to your phone bill): **02** (English spoken)
Wake-up service: **266 4422**
Exact time: **08**

You can either do this or take your letters to the **Post Office** and let them do it for you.

Communications

Post

The postal service in Hungary is efficient despite employing some of the stroppiest staff in the business. Letters from the UK generally take about four days to arrive. Post boxes are square red things sporting post horn and envelope symbols. These are relatively rare, though, and it's more usual to take your letters to the post office where the person behind the desk will put the stamp on and post it for you. Expect to queue a bit, especially at Christmas.

Most post offices are open from 8am-7pm. There are no late-night post offices.

Postal Rates & Post Boxes

Letters weighing up to 30g cost Ft12 within Budapest and Ft22 to the rest of Hungary. A letter up to 20g to neighbouring countries (those literally bordering on Hungary) costs Ft22. A letter to anywhere else in the world costs Ft60 up to 20g, Ft120 up to 100g. To send them airmail (*légiposta*) is an extra Ft7. Postcards to neighbouring countries are Ft14 and Ft40 elsewhere.

To send something registered (*ajánlott*) is an extra Ft38 and express an extra Ft40.

PO boxes are obtainable at most post offices for a fee of Ft1,200 a year. Poste Restante letters will go to the office at Nyugati Station.

For courier services and express mail *see chapters* **Business** *and* **Shopping**.

American Express

Card-holders or clients with American Express traveller's cheques can use their mail service. Letters should be addressed to: American Express Travel Service, Client Mail, Deák Ferenc utca 10, 1052 Budapest (266 8680). M1, M2, M3 Deák tér.

Sending Packages

There is a complicated system for packages depending what, when and how you are sending it. Try to keep the package small, under 2kg. This will ensure the cheapest rate: Ft240 up to 500g, Ft720 up to 2kg. Packages should also be done up with string and you will also need a blue customs declaration form (*vámáru-nyilatkozat*) from the post office. Also try to keep the value to a minimum, as sending anything worth over Ft10,000 is so complicated it's hardly worth the bother. Special boxes can be purchased at the post office. Most post offices can also supply a booklet in English detailing postal charges. (*See also chapter* **Shopping**.)

Telephones

In dealing with the Hungarian phone system, let patience be your watchword. Things are improving, as new digital exchanges are built, but there are still people who've been on the waiting list for a phone since the 1960s. Don't be surprised if you get cut off in the middle of a conversation and remember that an engaged tone doesn't always mean what it seems. If at first you don't succeed, dial, dial and dial again.

Public Phones

Most of these have been modernised. Some take Ft5, Ft10 or Ft20 coins. Others are card phones, your best bet if phoning abroad or making a lot of local calls. Cards cost Ft500 for 50 units or Ft1,100 for 120 units and come in multi-coloured designs which are now collectable. Kids may buttonhole you outside the phone box and ask for used cards. Cards can be bought at post offices, newsagents, small tobacco shops and from the men with trays like cinema ice-cream sellers who ply their trade at stations (though be careful, especially at Nyugati, as some of these guys are selling used ones for collectors). Cards will also be on sale at most metro stops.

Making Calls

To make an international call dial 00, wait for the second purring dial tone, then dial the country code and number. Australia 61, Austria 43, Canada 1, France 33, Germany 49, Ireland 353, New Zealand 64, UK 44, USA 1.

To call other places in Hungary from Budapest or to call Budapest from the rest of the country you have to dial 06 first, wait for the second tone, and then follow with code and number. You also have to dial 06 before calling mobile phones. These are common due to the unavailability of domestic lines and general unreliability of the phone system.

To call Hungary from abroad dial 36 and then 1 for Budapest.

International rates are the same at any time of the day or night. There are no cheap hours.

Faxes

Some post offices have a fax service but this involves a lot of waiting around. Major hotels also have fax services. Otherwise try the phone, fax and telex centre at:

MATÁV
V. Petőfi Sándor utca 17 (117 5500). M3 Ferenciek tere. **Open** 8am-8pm Mon-Fri; 9am-3pm Sat, Sun. **No credit cards**.

Mobile Phones & Pagers

If you need a phone but your apartment doesn't have one, mobile phones or pagers are the best bet. The digital GSM system is fully established here and reliable, although costly: a phone and connection card will set you back around Ft150,000. To buy the connection card you either need a resident's permit (*see above*) or must get it through the company you work for. For more details, try the two GSM companies which operate in Hungary.

Westel
V. Petőfi Sándor utca 12 (266 5723). M3 Ferenciek tere. **Open** 9am-8pm Mon-Fri; 9am-5pm Sat, Sun. **Credit** AmEx, JCB, MC, V.

Pannon GSM
XIII. Váci út 37 (270 4130). M3 Dózsa György út. **Open** 9am-7pm Mon-Fri; 9am-2pm Sat. **No credit cards**.

There are two pager companies both of which have English services. A pager will cost in the region of Ft50,000.

Eurohívó
XIII. Váci út 37 (270 4160). M3 Dózsa György út. **Open** 8am-6.30pm Mon-Fri; 8.30am-1.30pm Sat. **No credit cards**.

Operator Hungária
Dózsa György út 84-86 (267 9911). M1 Hősök tere/trolleybus 75, 79. **Open** 9am-3.30pm Mon-Fri. **No credit cards**.

Disabled Travellers

Despite being home to the world famous Pető Institute, which treats children with cerebral palsy, Budapest does not have much access for the disabled. Public transport is basically inaccessible, as are most buildings. There are, however, some possibilities. The airport minibus is accessible. There is a special BKV bus, use of which can be arranged through MEOSZ, who also have their own minibus and can provide a helper. The Museum of Fine Arts (*see chapter* **Museums**) is also now apparently accessible after recent renovation. There are a limited number of trips available such as Balaton by train once a week. For more details phone:

Hungarian Disabled Association
MEOSZ
III. San Marco utca 76 (188 2388). Tram 1. **Open** 8am-4pm Mon-Fri.

Left Luggage

Twenty-four-hour left-luggage facilities are available at Nyugati and Keleti stations: Ft80 or Ft160 for large items. Prices run from midnight to midnight. Lockers do exist at all three main stations but are rarely available. These cost Ft60. There are also facilities at Erzsébet tér bus terminal, open 6am-7pm Mon-Thur; 6am-9pm Fri; 6am-6pm Sat, Sun. Price Ft60 per item.

Driving in Budapest

Budapest has all the traffic problems of most modern European cities with a few extra ones thrown in for good measure. Hungarian driving is not good. Hungarians have constant urges to overtake in the most impossible places, they lack concentration and jump traffic lights. There are a lot of accidents, mostly cars going into the backs of other cars. Many vehicles are of poor quality. Roads are even worse. Cobbled streets abound, designed to tax even the sturdiest suspension. There has been a huge influx of Western cars in recent years, slowly replacing the toy-like Trabants and other two-strokes. This has increased traffic levels and daytime parking problems. Talk of restricting traffic in certain areas has not amounted to much.

There was a time when a Western car would almost certainly get stolen and taken somewhere in the former Soviet Union. This trade has diminished but it is wise to take precautions. Keep cars locked and fitted with an alarm if possible. Take the radio out and do not leave anything visible inside. If you cannot find your car where you left it, it does not necessarily mean it has been stolen. It may have been towed for illegal parking. If so, go to the nearest police station. In the centre this is at V. Szalay utca 11-13 near the Parliament.

● Seatbelts must be worn at all times.

● Always carry your passport, driving licence (not necessarily an international one – UK and US ones are generally accepted), vehicle registration document, evidence of motor insurance (green card insurance is not compulsory for those insured in the UK although it is in many neighbouring countries such as Romania and Slovenia), and *zöldkártya* (exhaust emissions certificate) for cars registered in Hungary.

● Do not leave anything of value in the car, especially car documents.

● Headlights are compulsory by day when driving outside town, although not on motorways.

● Priority is from the right unless you are on a priority road, signified by a yellow diamond on a white background. Whatever the case, drive with caution on one-way roads.

● Watch out for other drivers. They may not be watching out for you.

● Watch out for trams, particularly in places where passengers alight in the middle of the road (this takes a bit of getting used to for people from non-tram towns).

● Watch out for drunks, and people walking on country roads at night, and bicycles without lights or markings.

● The speed limit on motorways is 120 kph, on highways (signified by a white car on a blue background) 90 kph, on all other roads 80 kph unless otherwise indicated, and 50 kph in built-up areas. Speed traps abound, with spot fines that vary greatly, especially for foreigners. These are sometimes negotiable.

● The alcohol limit for driving is basically zero (0.08 per cent) and there are many spot checks, especially at night, with severe penalties for the guilty. Take a taxi if drinking.

Breakdowns

A 24-hour breakdown service is provided by the Magyar Autóklub. They have reciprocal agreements with many European associations, so check before you come. English and German are usually spoken, but if not they will ask you for the model (*típus*), colour (*szín*) and the number plate (*rendszám*) of the vehicle and also the location. Assistance is usually fairly rapid.

Magyar Autóklub
(212 3952). **Open** 24 hours daily. **No credit cards** but will accept a credit letter from affiliated organisations.

There are also these private breakdown services:

Hungária
(189 1203). **Open** 24 hours daily. **No credit cards**.

Budasegély
(269 7062/269 7218). **Open** 8am-7pm daily. **No credit cards**.

Start
(276 8302). **Open** 24 hours daily. **No credit cards**.

Parking

Parking is not easy any more and towing and wheel clamping are in force. Most town parking is on the pavements – just copy everybody else. Certain areas have parking meters which, during working hours, cost Ft80 an hour in the centre for a maximum of two hours, and somewhat less in other districts. Certain central areas are controlled by parking attendants – V. Március 15 tér, or under the Nyugati Station flyover, for example, where prices are Ft60-Ft80 an hour. There is one multi-storey car park on V. Bárczy István utca 2 just off Petőfi Sándor utca, costing Ft100 an hour.

Petrol

Hundreds of filling stations have sprung up during the last few years, most of which are open 24 hours daily and sell all types of fuel. Unleaded is *ólommentes*. Stay away from any fuel marked with a K as this is for lawnmowers and Trabants.

Most stations are self-service but some still have attendants, to whom people generally give a modest tip. Nearly all transactions are in cash.

Car Service Agents

BMW
XIII. Kassák Lajos utca 75 (140 7640). M3 Árpád híd. **Open** 9am-6pm Mon-Fri. **No credit cards**.

Citroen
IX. Könyves Kálmán körút 26 (216 7100). M3 Nagyvárad tér. **Open** 8am-5pm Mon-Fri. **No credit cards**.

Fiat
VIII. Kálvária utca 9 (134 4531). **Open** 8am-5pm Mon-Thur; 8am-3pm Fri. **No credit cards**.

Ford
XIII. Váci út 84 (270 3433). M3 Dózsa György út. **Open** 6am-10pm Mon-Fri. **Credit** AmEx, DIC, JCB, MC, V.

Honda
XI. Fehérvári út 130 (186 97 63). Tram 18, 47. **Open** 7am-6pm Mon-Thur; 7am-5pm Fri. **No credit cards**.

Mercedes Benz
XIII. Kárpát utca 21 (129 9990). Trolleybus 79. **Open**
7am-8pm Mon-Fri. **No credit cards.**

Opel
XIV. Mexikói út 15/19 (251 8555). M2 Népstadion.
Open 6am-6pm Mon-Fri. **No credit cards.**

Peugeot
XIII. Mohács utca 19A (270 3045). Tram 1, 12, 14.
Open 7.30am-6pm Mon-Fri. **No credit cards.**

Renault
XI. Budaörsi út 121 (186 9513). Bus 40. **Open** 7am-5pm
Mon-Fri. **No credit cards.**

VW/Audi
III. Mozaik utca 1/3 (250 0222/250 0247).
HÉV Filatorigát. **Open** 6am-10pm Mon-Fri. **No**
credit cards.

Embassies & Consulates

For a full list of embassies look in the phone book
or yellow pages under *Külképviseletek.*

American Embassy
V. Szabadság tér 12 (267 4400/after hours 153 0566).
M3 Arany János utca. **Open** 8.30am-11am Mon-Fri.

Australian Embassy
XII. Királyhágó tér 8/9 (201 8899). M2 Déli. **Open** 9am-
noon Mon-Fri.

British Embassy
V. Harmincad utca 6 (266 2888). M1, M2, M3 Deák tér.
Open 9.30am-noon, 2.30-4pm, Mon-Fri.

Canadian Embassy
XII Budakeszi út 32 (275 1200). Bus 22. **Open** 9am-
11am Mon-Fri.

New Zealand Consulate
I. Attila út 125 (175 3245). M2 Déli. **Open** 9am-noon
Mon, Wed; 1-4pm Tue, Thur.

Health

Despite severe cutbacks and restrictions, the
Hungarian health service is still considered one of
the best in eastern Europe. The service provided
is adequate, although a lot of queuing is involved.
Most doctors speak English. Emergency care
is provided free to citizens of the UK, Finland,
Norway, Sweden and former Socialist countries,
although it is probably wise to have medical insurance. Those living here should get a TB (social
security) card through their company, to obtain
free state health treatment, and register with a
local GP. Private clinics now offer the opportunity
to avoid the queues.

Emergencies/Hospitals

In an emergency the best thing to do is to go to the
casualty department of any hospital. Take along
a Hungarian speaker and always carry some form
of identification.

Ambulances

The normal emergency number is 04. Or call 111
1666 where they speak English and German.

Private Clinics

IMS
XIII. Váci út 202 (129 8423/149 9349). M3 Újpest
Városkapu. **Open** 8am-8pm Mon-Fri. **Credit** AmEx, MC.
A 24-hour emergency service is available on 250 3829, but
this service does not accept credit cards.

Professional Orvosi Kft
V. Múzeum körút 35, Third Floor, no 6 (117 0631). M3
Kálvin tér. **Open** 4pm-8pm Mon; 8am-noon Tue, Thur;
8am-noon, 4-8pm, Wed. **No credit cards.**

SOS Emergency Medical Service
VIII. Kerepesi út 15 (118 8288/24-hour 118 8212). M2
Keleti. **Open** 24 hours daily. **Credit** AmEx, MC.

R Klinika
II. Felsőzöldmáli út 13 (250 3488/250 3489/250 3490).
Bus 29. **Open** 8am-6pm daily, 24 hours in emergencies.
Credit AmEx, JCB, MC, V.

Pharmacies

Pharmacies (*patika* or *gyógyszertár*) are marked
by a green cross outside. Opening hours are gen-
erally 8am-6pm or 8am-8pm Mon-Fri, with some
also open on Saturday mornings. The following
pharmacies are open 24 hours:
I. Széna tér 1 (202 1816).
II. Frankel Leó utca 22 (212 4406).
VI. Teréz körút 41 (111 4439).
VII. Rákóczi út 39 (114 3694).
IX. Üllői út 121 (215 3800).
XII. Alkotás utca 1B (155 4691).

Dentists

Although there is state dental care, most people
go private if they can. Prices are fairly reasonable
compared to the West, as evidenced by the number of Austrians flocking over the border to have
their molars scrutinised. Here is a selection of
dental clinics:

Dental Co-op
XII. Zugligeti út 60 (176 3600). Bus 22. **Open** 9am-6pm
Mon-Fri; 1-6pm Thur. **Credit** AmEx, MC, V.

Budapest **dentists** *charge reasonable prices.*

Super Dent

XIII. Dózsa György út 65 (129 0200 ext 180). *M3 Dózsa György*. **Open** 8am-2pm Mon, Wed, Fri; Tue,Thur 8am-7pm. **Credit** AmEx.

SOS Dental Clinic

VI. Király utca 14 (322 0602/322 7010). *M1, M2, M3 Deák tér/tram 47, 49*. **Open** 24 hours daily. **Credit** AmEx, DC, JCB, MC, V.

Chiropractor

Dr Jack Conway

XI. Györök utca 2 (185 2515). *Tram 19, 49*. **Open** 8am-noon, 1.30-4pm, Mon, Thur; 8am-noon Tue, Wed, Fri. **No credit cards**.

Poison Control Centres

Erzsébet Kórház

VII. Alsóerdősor utca 7 (322 3450). *M2 Blaha Lujza tér*.

Heim Pál Kórház

XI. Üllői út 86 (210 0720/269 9398). *M3 Nagyvárad tér*. For children only.

AIDS & Sexually Transmitted Diseases

AIDS remains at a relatively low level in Hungary, although this may increase with the influx of foreigners and high promiscuity.

24-hour AIDS hotline

(138 2419 6am-4pm/138 4555 4pm-6am).

Skin & Genital Clinic

Bőr és Nemikórtani Klinika
VIII. Mária utca 41 (210 0310). *M3 Ferenc körút*. **Open** 8am-4pm Mon-Fri.

This is the place to go if you have STD problems. An AIDS test here costs Ft4,000.

Anonymous AIDS Advisory Service

Anonim AIDS Tanácsadó Szolgálat
XI. Karolina út 35B (166 9283). *Tram 61*. **Open** *hotline* 9am-8pm Mon-Sat; *in person* 5-8pm Mon, Wed, Thur; 9am-12.30pm Tue, Fri.
Free anonymous AIDS tests available.

Drug Ambulance

(129 1209).

Alcoholics Anonymous

VII. Kertész utca 28, First Floor (168 5426). *M2 Blaha Lujza tér*.
Meetings in English on Tuesdays at 5.30pm and Fridays at 6.30pm. Call László at the above number for details.

Domestic Violence

NaNE Women's Association

IX. Vámház körút 7 (216 5900/6-10pm daily 216 1670). *M3 Kálvin tér*. **Open** 9am-6pm Mon-Fri.
Offers support and information to battered and raped women and children. (*See also chapter* **Women**.)

Veterinarians

Budapest Állatkórház

XIII. Lehel út 43/47 (270 0361/270 1166). *M3 Árpád híd/tram 1*. **Open** 24 hours daily.

Contraception & Abortion

Condoms are available at chemists, Azúr shops and many supermarkets.

Abortion is legal and widely used, although not as widely as under Communism, when contraception was not easily available. For abortions you should refer to a local doctor or gynaecologist.

Unless they don't like the look of your face, you're unlikely to meet the Budapest **Police**.

Alternative Medicine

Alternative medicine is very much in its infancy in Hungary, with much talk of wonder cures but as yet little organisation or substance.

Eurosana Homeopathy
XII Eötvös utca 41 (175 6211). Bus red 21. **Open** 10am-4pm Mon-Fri.

Lost Property

If you lose something, you can enquire at the police station in the area where you thought you lost it, but don't hold out much hope. Take along a Hungarian speaker, especially if you need a statement for insurance purposes. Hungarian police are not renowned for their language skills.

At Ferihegy Airport phone 157 9123. For anything left on trains, go to the station you arrived at and be persistent but pleasant; it has been known to get results. For taxis, phone the company you rode with. Főtaxi claims to hold on to items left in their vehicles for five years.

BKV Lost Property Office
Talált Tárgyak Osztálya
VII. Akácfa utca 18 (322 6613). M2 Blaha Lujza tér. **Open** 7.30am-3pm Mon-Thur; 7.30am-7pm Wed; 7.30am-2pm Fri.

Police & Security

The stupidity of Budapest police is the subject of many Hungarian jokes. You will have little contact with them unless you have something stolen or commit a crime. The police can stop anyone and ask for identification but this is unlikely unless they think you look like an illegal immigrant. If robbed or you lose something, report it to the police station in the district where the incident took place. Take a Hungarian speaker with you.

Lost Passports

Report the loss immediately to the local police station and then also to your consulate who will issue you with an emergency passport. You will not be allowed to leave the country without it.

Public Toilets

There are public toilets at various locations for which you will have to pay a small fee to an attendant. Easier by far is just to pop into a bar or café, although here too you often pay. Ft20 is normal.

Religious Services

International Church of Budapest
III. Kiskorona utca 7 (176 4518). M3 Árpád híd.
Multi-denominational worship in English and children's ministry on Sundays at 10.30am.

International Baptist Church
Móricz Zsigmond Gimnázium, II. Törökvész út 48-54 (Pastor Bob Zbinden 250 3932). Bus 11.
Services on Sundays from 10.30am.

Jézus Szíve Templom
VIII. Mária utca 25 (118 3479). M3 Ferenc körút.
Catholic mass in English on Saturdays at 5pm.

Anglican Services

St Columbia Church of Scotland, Presbyterian and St Margaret's Anglican/Episcopal Chaplancy
VI. Vörösmarty utca 51 (no phone). M1 Vörösmarty utca.
Anglican eucharist on first and third Sundays at 11am. Anglican Holy Communion second, fouth and fifth Sundays of the month at 9am. Presbyterian services second and fourth Sundays at 11am. Joint Presbyterian/Anglican service fifth Sundays at 11am. Sunday school at 11am Sept-May.

Jewish Services

Central Synagogue
VII. Dohány utca 2 (no phone). M2 Astoria/tram 47, 49.
Services take place at 9am Saturday; 6pm Sunday-Friday.

Jewish Community Centre
VII. Síp utca 12 (342 1335). M2 Astoria/tram 47, 49. **Open** 8am-noon Mon-Fri.
Summer services in Hebrew.

Libraries

There are three English-language libraries.

The American Library
VII. Bajza utca 31 (342 4122/322 8600). M1 Bajza utca. **Open** 11am-4.45pm Mon, Wed-Fri; 11am-6.45pm Tue.
Membership free to anyone over 16.

The British Council Library
VI. Benczúr utca 26 (321 4039). M1 Bajza utca. **Open** 11am-6pm Mon-Thur; 11am-5pm Fri.
Excellent magazine and periodicals section and English-teaching section, also a huge video library. Membership open to anyone over 16 for a one-off fee of Ft500.

The National Foreign Language Library
V. Molnár utca 11 (118 3188/118 3688). M3 Ferenciek tere. **Open** 9am-8pm Mon, Tue, Thur, Fri; noon-8pm Wed.
Only foreigners with residence permits and a passport may check out books here. Good periodicals section; helpful staff.

Foreign Media

There are three English-language weekly newspapers: *Budapest Week*, *Budapest Sun* (both with listings and entertainment guides) and *Budapest Business Journal*. Most newspaper kiosks and hotel lobbies will have foreign newspapers either same day or one day old. Bestsellers bookshop carries many newspapers and magazines as well as a large stock of books in English. (*See also* chapters **Media** *and* **Shopping**.)

Further Reading

Books from Corvina, City Hall and other Hungarian publishers are unlikely to be readily available in the UK or US. In Budapest you'll find them in good general Hungarian bookshops as well as in those that specialise in English publications.

History

Bender, Thomas & Schorske, Carl *Budapest & New York: Studies in Metropolitan Transformation 1870-1930*
Patchy compilation of academic essays.
Buza, Péter *Bridges of the Danube* (City Hall)
Everything you ever wanted to know about Budapest's famous bridges, with occasional absurd asides.
Crankshaw, Edward *The Fall of the House of Habsburg* (Papermac)
Solid, anti-Hungarian account of the Habsburg monarchy.
Garton Ash, Timothy *We the People: The Revolution of 1989 Witnessed in Warsaw, Budapest, Berlin and Prague* (Granta, 1990)
Instant history by on-the-spot Oxford academic.
Lázár, István *Hungary: A Brief History* (Corvina)
This 'colourful essay presenting the story of the Hungarians as one person sees it' is mostly a load of bollocks.
Lukács, John *Budapest 1900* (Weidenfeld)
Readable and erudite literary and historical snapshot of Budapest at its height. Probably the best book about the city's history and culture currently in print.
Taylor, AJP *The Habsburg Monarchy 1809-1918* (Penguin)
Terse history of the closing Habsburg era.

Biography, Memoir & Travel

Brook, Stephen *The Double Eagle: Vienna, Budapest & Prague* (Hamish Hamilton)
Fussy but entertainingly detailed travelogue of the Habsburg capitals in the early '80s.
Fermor, Patrick Leigh *Between the Woods and the Water/A Time of Gifts* (Penguin)
In the 1930s Fermor took a bike through Hungary. These picaresque and evocative memoirs are the result.
Magris, Claudio *Danube*
A literary travelogue down central Europe's main waterway.
Pressburger, Giorgio & Nicola *Homage to the Eighth District* (Readers International)
Authentic and touching street-level recollections of Budapest Jewish society before and during World War II.
Rimmer, Dave *Once Upon a Time in the East* (4th Estate)
Communism from ground level – mad, stoned travelogue of lamentable behaviour in assorted east European revolutions.
Szep, Ernő *The Smell of Humans*
Survivor's short, stark memoir of the Hungarian Holocaust.

Fiction

Ady, Endre *Neighbours of the Night: Selected Short Stories* (Corvina)
Prose pieces from the poet featured on the Ft500 note. Somewhat stiffly rendered in English, but at least they translate, unlike his gloomy but stirring poetry.
Alexander, Lynne *Safe Houses* (Penguin)
Brilliant, disturbing novel of Hungarian emigrés in New York.

Esterházy, Péter *A Little Hungarian Pornography* (Corvina/Quartet)/*Helping Verbs of the Heart* (Corvina)/*The Glance of Countess Hahn-Hahn* (Weidenfeld & Nicholson)
One of Hungary's most popular contemporary writers, Esterházy's postmodern style represents a break with tradition.
Fischer, Tibor *Under the Frog* (Penguin)
Seriously funny and impeccably researched romp through Hungarian basketball and the 1956 revolution.
Gárdonyi, Géza *Eclipse of the Crescent Moon* (Corvina)
Boy's-own adventure about the 1552 Turkish siege of Eger.
Göncz, Árpád *Homecoming & Other Stories* (Corvina)
Dry short stories from Hungary's popular President, playwright and translator of Hemingway and Faulkner.
Konrád, George *The Case Worker/The Loser* (Penguin)
Dark, depressing stuff by Communist Hungary's most prominent dissident.
Kosztolányi, Dezső *Skylark* (Chatto)/*Anna Édes* (Corvina)/*Darker Muses, The Poet Nero* (Corvina)
Kosztolányi, who wrote these novels in the 1920s, was probably the best Hungarian prose writer this century.
Örkény, István *One Minute Stories* (Corvina)
Vignettes of contemporary Budapest: absurd, ironic, often hilarious and all extremely short.
The Kiss: Twentieth-century Hungarian Short Stories
From Ady to Eszterházy: 31 short stories add up to a good sampler of modern Magyar lit.

Children

Molnar, Ferenc *The Paul Street Boys* (Corvina)
Turn-of-the-century juvenile classic of boys' gang warfare over a derelict District VIII building site.
Dent, Bob *Budapest for Children* (City Hall)
Suggestions for how to keep the little blighters entertained.

Architecture

Gerle, János *The Turn of the Century* (City Hall)
Walking tours round the most interesting architecture.

Language

Payne, Jerry *Colloquial Hungarian* (Routledge)
More enjoyable and entertaining than most language books.
Hungarian-English English-Hungarian Tourist's Dictionary (Akadémiai Kiadó)
Cheap, readily available and pocket-sized.

Miscellaneous

Bodor, Ferenc *Coffee Houses* (City Hall)
Utterly brilliant vignettes of Budapest coffee culture
Ernyey, Gyula *Made in Hungary: The Best of 150 Years in Industrial Design* (Rubik Innovation Foundation)
Entertaining coffee table compendium of Hungarian innovation, including the Biro, Unicum bottle and Rubik's Cube.
Gundel, Károly *Gundel's Hungarian Cookbook* (Corvina)
The best of Hungarian recipe books, by the man who more or less invented Hungarian cuisine.
Lang, George *The Cuisine of Hungary* (Bonanza)
Detailed study of the development of Magyar cuisine.
Art and Society in the Age of Stalin (Corvina)
Interesting collection of essays on socialist realism.

Index

Budapest Guide
Advertisers Index
Please refer to the relevant sections for addresses/telephone numbers

You can get there from here.

Calling around the world is easy. Really. Just dial the AT&T access number of the country you're calling from. An AT&T Operator or English-language voice prompt will help connect you to the States and over 75 countries quickly and easily. It's that simple. With easy billing to either your AT&T Card or U.S. Local Telephone Company calling card, or by calling collect.* So when someone tells you you can't get there from here, pick up the phone and call 'em on it.

Call with AT&T.

00•-800-01111* *

AT&T

* Applies only to AT&T
USADirect®, Service calls.
* Await second dial tone
* * Public phones require
coin or card

Maps

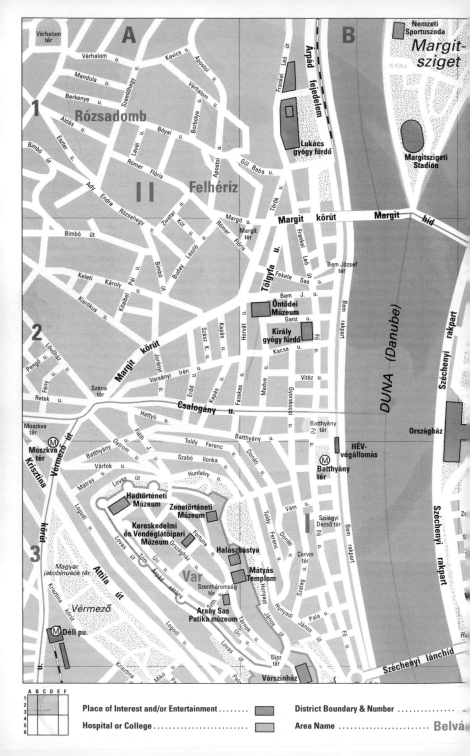

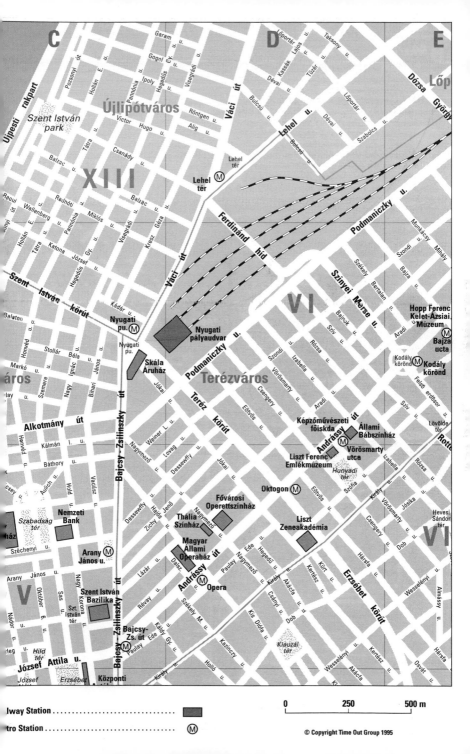

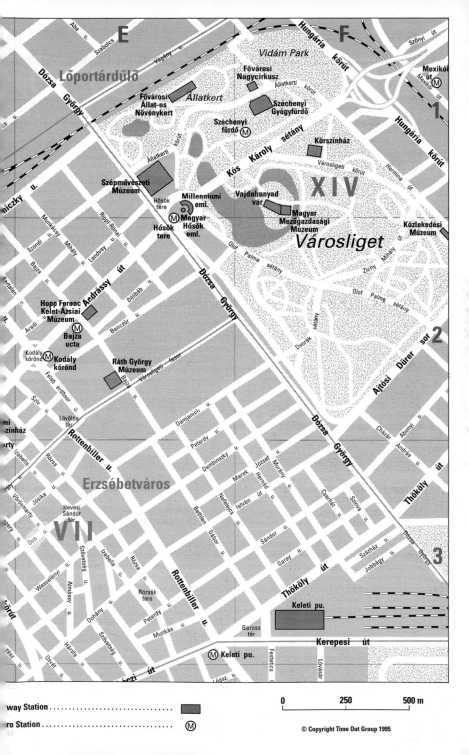

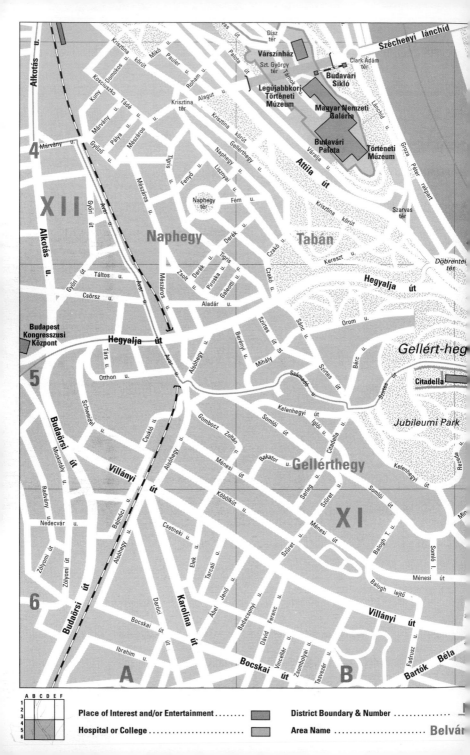

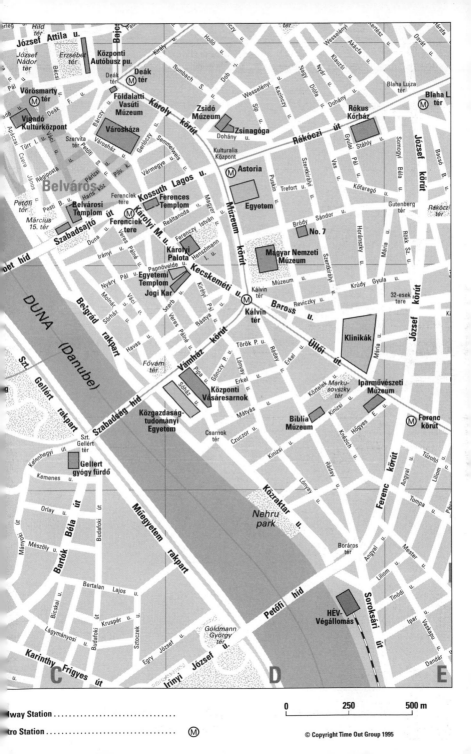

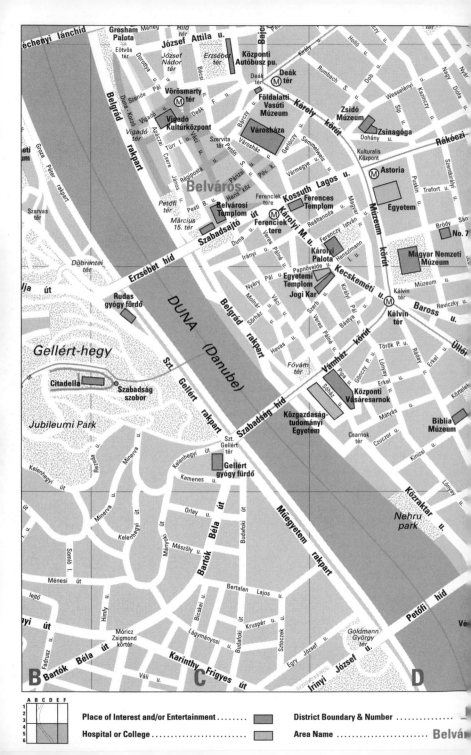

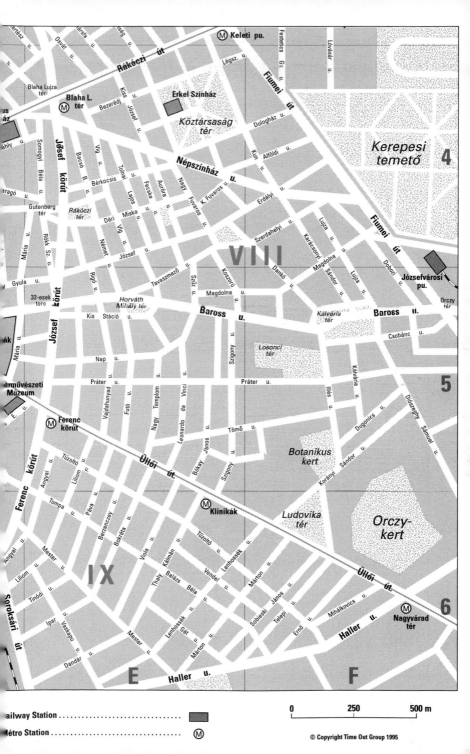

Traveling through Central & Eastern Europe?
American Express is here to help

Albania

Tirana
World Travel*
Durresi 11
Tel.: (355) (42) 27908

Bulgaria

Sofia
MegaTours.*
Levski Str. 1
Zip: 1000
Tel.: (359) (2) 872 567,
808 889

Varna
MegaTours.*
Slivnitsa Blvd. 33
Tel.: (359) (52) 232 115

Croatia

Dubrovnik
Atlas Travel Agency*
Pile 1
Zip: 50000
Tel.: (385) (50) 442 222

Opatija
Atlas Travel Agency*
C/O Hotel Kvarner
Park 1 Maj
P.O. Box 70
Zip: 51410
Tel.: (385) (51) 271 032

Poreč
Atlas Travel Agency*
Zagrebacka 17
Zip: 51440
Tel.: (385) (531) 432 273

Pula
Atlas Travel Agency*
Petra Drapsina 1
Zip: 52000
Tel.: (385) (52) 237 32

Split
Atlas Travel Agency*
Trg Preporoda 7
Zip: 58000
Tel.: (385) (21) 430 55

Zadar
Atlas Travel Agency*
Obala Kneza
Branimira 12
Zip: 57000
Tel.: (385) (23) 314 339

Zagreb
Atlas Travel Agency*
Zrinjevac 17
Zip: 41000
Tel.: (385) (1) 427 623,
427 633

Czech Republic

Brno
B.V.V. Fair Travel *
Starobrnenska 20
Zip: 60200
Tel.: (42) (5) 422 177 45

Karlovy Vary
American Express
Bureau de Change**
Mirove nam. 2
Zip: 36001
Tel.: (42) (17) 322 7551

Prague
American Express
Travel Service
Vaclavske nam. 56
Zip: 11000
Tel.: (42) (2) 2421 9992,
2422 9883

Estonia

Tallinn
Estravel*
Suur-Karja 15,
P.O. Box 3727
Zip: EE 0001
Tel.: (372) (6) 313 313,
313 318

Hungary

Budapest
American Express
Hungary Ltd.
Deak Ferenc. U. 10
P.O. Box: 698,
P.O. Box Zip: 1365
Zip: 1052
Tel.: (36) (1) 266 8680

Latvia

Riga
Latvia Tours*
Grecinieku Str. 22/24
Tel.: (371) 882 0020

Lithuania

Vilnius
Lithuanian Tours*
Seimyniskiu Str. 18
Zip: 2005
Tel.: (370) (2) 724 156

Poland

Gdansk
Orbis Travel*
22 Heweliusza Str.
Zip: 80-890
Tel.: (48) (58) 314 045

Krakow
Orbis Travel*
Cracovia Hotel
1. F. Focha Ave
Zip: 30-111
Tel.: (48) (12) 224 632,
219 880

American Express
Bureau de Change**
Rynek Gkowny 41
Zip: 31-013
Tel.: (48) (12) 229 180

Warsaw
American Express
Travel Service
Dom Bez Kantow
Krakowskie
Przedmiescie 11
P.O. Box: 159
Zip: 00-069
Tel.: (48) (2) 635 2002

American Express
Bureau de Change**
Marriot Hotel
Al. Jerozollmskie 69/75
Zip: 00-697
Tel.: (48) (2) 630 6952,
630 6953

Zakopane
Orbis Travel*
Krupowki Str. 22
P.O. Box: 64
Zip: PL 34-500
Tel.: (48) (165) 4151,
4609

Romania

Bucharest
Minerva International*
2-4 Ghe Manu Str.
Tel.: (40) (1) 312 3969

Russia

Moscow
American Express
Travel Service
21a Sadovaya-
Kudrinskaya
Zip: 103001
Tel.: (7) (95) 956 9000,
956 9004

St. Petersburg
American Express
Travel Service
Grand Hotel Europe 1/7
Ul. Mikhailovskaya Str.
Zip: 191073
Tel.: (7) (812) 329 6060

Slovak Republic

Bratislava
Tatratour*
Frantiskanske nam. 3
Zip: 81101
Tel.: (42) (7) 335 536

Košice
Tatratour*
Alzbetina 6
Zip: 04001
Tel.: (42) (95) 248 72,
213 34

Piestany
Tatratour*
Winterova 28
Zip: 92101
Tel.: (42) (838) 253 05

Poprad
Tatratour*
Nam. Sv. Egidia 9
Zip: 058 01
Tel.: (42) (92) 637 12

Žilina
Tatratour*
Marianske nam. 21
Zip: 010 01
Tel.: (42) (89) 475 29

Slovenia

Ljubljana
Atlas Ambassador*
Mestni TRG 8
Zip: 61000
Tel.: (386) (61) 222 741,
222 711

Portoroz
Atlas Express*
Obala 55
Zip: 66320
Tel.: (386) (66) 732 64

*Representative Office, **Exchange Office*

Street Index

Around Budapest

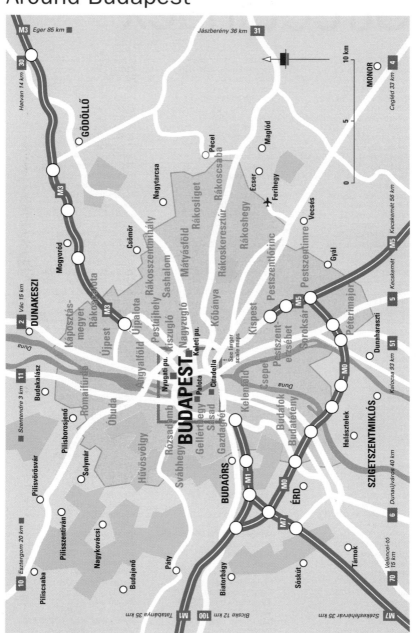

Trips Out of Town

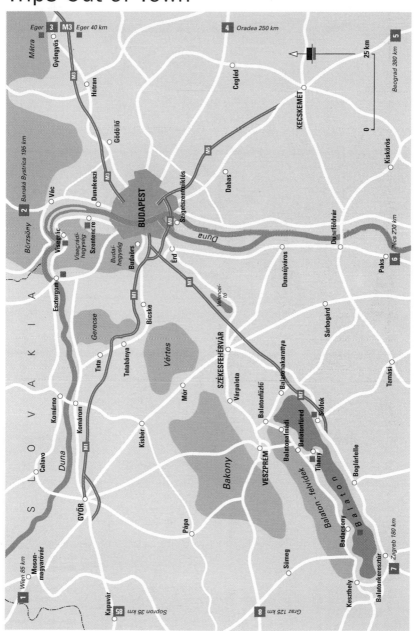

Eger 3 M3 Eger 40 km

4 Oradea 250 km

5

Mátra

Gyöngyös

Cegléd

25 km

Beograd 380 km

Hatran

KECSKEMÉT

0

Gödöllő

M3

Banská Bystrica 195 km

Vác

Dunakeszi

M5

Dabas

Kiskőrös

BUDAPEST

Szigetszentmiklós

Börzsöny

Visegrád

Szentendre

Duna

Dunaújváros

Dunaföldvár

Pécs 270 km

6

Visegrádi-hegység

Budai-hegység

Budaörs

Érd

Paks

Esztergom

Velencei-tó

Velence

M7

Gerecse

Bicske

SLOVAKIA

Tata

Tatabánya

Vértes

SZÉKESFEHÉRVÁR

Balatonkarattya

Sárbogárd

Tamási

Komárno

Komárom

Mór

Várpalota

Balatonfűző

M7

Siófok

Kisbér

Balatonalmádi

Balatonfüred

Boglárlelle

Calavo

Duna

M1

Bakony

VESZPRÉM

Tihany

Balaton

Balaton - felvidék

GYŐR

Pápa

Sümeg

Badacsony

Zagreb 180 km

7

Wien 85 km

Moson-magyaróvár

Keszthely

Balatonkeresztúr

1

85 Sopron 35 km

Graz 125 km 8

Kapuvár

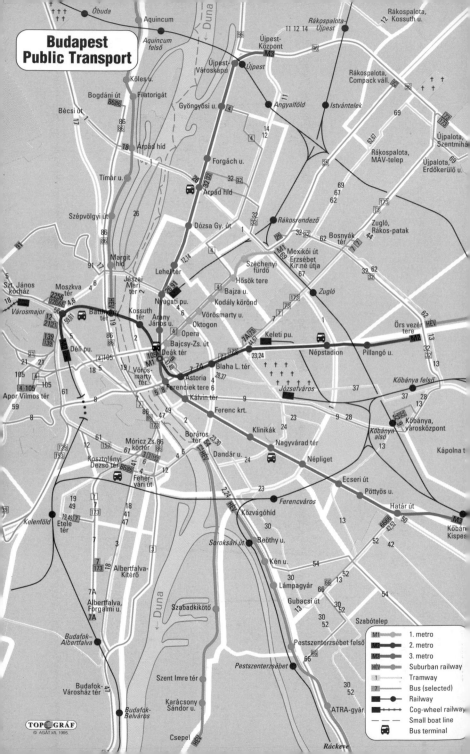